Supply Chain Management in the Big Data Era

Hing Kai Chan
University of Nottingham Ningbo, China

Nachiappan Subramanian
University of Sussex, UK

Muhammad Dan-Asabe Abdulrahman
University of Nottingham Ningbo, China

A volume in the Advances in Logistics, Operations, and Management Science (ALOMS) Book Series

IGI GLOBAL
DISSEMINATOR OF KNOWLEDGE

www.igi-global.com

Published in the United States of America by
IGI Global
Business Science Reference (an imprint of IGI Global)
701 E. Chocolate Avenue
Hershey PA 17033
Tel: 717-533-8845
Fax: 717-533-8661
E-mail: cust@igi-global.com
Web site: http://www.igi-global.com

Library of Congress Cataloging-in-Publication Data

Names: Chan, Hing Kai,1973-editor | Subramanian, Nachiappan, 1973-editor | Abdulrahman, Muhammad Dan-Asabe, 1966-editor.
Title: Supply chain management in the big data era / Hing Kai Chan; Nachiappan Subramanian; Muhammad Dan-Asabe Abdulrahman, editor.
Description: Hershey, PA : Business Science Reference, [2017] | Series: Advances in logistics, operations, and management science | Includes bibliographical references and index.
Identifiers: LCCN 2016032838| ISBN 9781522509561 (hardcover) | ISBN 9781522509578 (ebook)
Subjects: LCSH: Business logistics--Management. | Business logistics--Data processing.
Classification: LCC HD38.5 .S8875 2017 | DDC 658.50285/57--dc23 LC record available at https://lccn.loc.gov/2016032838

This book is published in the IGI Global book series Advances in Logistics, Operations, and Management Science (ALOMS) (ISSN: 2327-350X; eISSN: 2327-3518)

British Cataloguing in Publication Data
A Cataloguing in Publication record for this book is available from the British Library.

Advances in Logistics, Operations, and Management Science (ALOMS) Book Series

ISSN:2327-350X
EISSN:2327-3518

Mission

Operations research and management science continue to influence business processes, administration, and management information systems, particularly in covering the application methods for decision-making processes. New case studies and applications on management science, operations management, social sciences, and other behavioral sciences have been incorporated into business and organizations real-world objectives.

The **Advances in Logistics, Operations, and Management Science** (ALOMS) Book Series provides a collection of reference publications on the current trends, applications, theories, and practices in the management science field. Providing relevant and current research, this series and its individual publications would be useful for academics, researchers, scholars, and practitioners interested in improving decision making models and business functions.

Coverage

- Networks
- Services management
- Organizational Behavior
- Information Management
- Production management
- Marketing engineering
- Finance
- Computing and information technologies
- Operations Management
- Risk Management

The Advances in Logistics, Operations, and Management Science (ALOMS) Book Series (ISSN 2327-350X) is published by IGI Global, 701 E. Chocolate Avenue, Hershey, PA 17033-1240, USA, www.igi-global.com. This series is composed of titles available for purchase individually; each title is edited to be contextually exclusive from any other title within the series. For pricing and ordering information please visit http://www.igi-global.com/book-series/advances-logistics-operations-management-science/37170. Postmaster: Send all address changes to above address.

Titles in this Series

For a list of additional titles in this series, please visit: www.igi-global.com

Knowledge Management Initiatives and Strategies in Small and Medium Enterprises
Andrea Bencsik (Széchenyi István University, Hungary & J. Selye University, Slovakia)
Business Science Reference • copyright 2017 • 442pp • H/C (ISBN: 9781522516422) • US $200.00 (our price)

Handbook of Research on Information Management for Effective Logistics and Supply Chains
George Leal Jamil (InescTec, Portugal) António Lucas Soares (University of Porto, Portugal) and Cláudio Roberto Magalhães Pessoa (FUMEC University, Brazil)
Business Science Reference • copyright 2017 • 554pp • H/C (ISBN: 9781522509738) • US $310.00 (our price)

Optimum Decision Making in Asset Management
María Carmen Carnero (University of Castilla – La Mancha, Spain) and Vicente González-Prida (University of Seville, Spain)
Business Science Reference • copyright 2017 • 523pp • H/C (ISBN: 9781522506515) • US $215.00 (our price)

Green Supply Chain Management for Sustainable Business Practice
Mehmood Khan (Abu Dhabi University, UAE) Matloub Hussain (Abu Dhabi University, UAE) and Mian M. Ajmal (Abu Dhabi University, UAE)
Business Science Reference • copyright 2017 • 330pp • H/C (ISBN: 9781522506355) • US $185.00 (our price)

Multinational Enterprise Management Strategies in Developing Countries
Mohammad Ayub Khan (Tecnológico de Monterrey, Mexico)
Business Science Reference • copyright 2016 • 490pp • H/C (ISBN: 9781522502760) • US $200.00 (our price)

Strategic Management of Sustainable Manufacturing Operations
Rameshwar Dubey (Symbiosis International University, India) and Angappa Gunasekaran (University of Massachuesetts, Dartmouth, USA)
Business Science Reference • copyright 2016 • 419pp • H/C (ISBN: 9781522503507) • US $215.00 (our price)

Editorial Advisory Board

Table of Contents

Section 4
Social Media Data Research

Detailed Table of Contents

In this chapter, we will introduce practical issues and implementation challenges from the industry perspective. In particular, we explain three aspects based on the panel discussions from the set of representatives participated in a big data conference from three dominant industries such as e-commerce, health care and computer hardware, which are sought of big data for their growth and development. We introduce overall challenges and explain typical industry based practical issues, how they visualize the big picture for their strategic development and how industries are gearing towards converting the challenges to big opportunities through the partnership of universities. Finally, based on the content analysis we offer potential trends and future research directions.

This chapter discusses various roles of smart information in Supply Chains (SC) of digital age and tries to answer an important question - What types of collaborative arrangements facilitate smart operations to improve planning, production and timely replenishment? We have conducted longitudinal case studies with firms practicing SC collaborations and also using smart information for operations. Based on the case analysis, the companies are further classified as ‘smart planning’ and ‘traditional planning’. Research findings show the importance of aligning SC partnerships based on smart information requirements. These findings are based on case studies of Indian firms with global SC collaboration. We also discuss the role of Big Data for the companies using smart planning.

It has been observed that the less than truck load (LTL) industry is going through significant transformation. After the last few years of decline in revenue, due to weak economy, the profitability of the LTL is on the rise. A strategy based on improving freight flow and density, and tightening terminal capacity is finally producing results for many LTL's, at the same time other LTL's are investing on expanding terminal network's while making bigger gains in the revenue. The availability of big data has revolutionised the way the LTL industry operates. The data assists in planning, efficient routing, safety control, fuel conservation, driving habits, etc. Analysts believe that big data still has a bigger role to play and it will have significant impact on the LTL industry in the coming days. This chapter discusses the challenges and opportunities for LTL carriers as it arises due to the emergence of big data.

Big Data refers to complex and unstructured data that is difficult to analyse and utilize with traditional applications and analyses. Big Data comes from a variety of sources, including tracking and sensor devices which are widely used in logistics and supply chain management, and relate to Radio Frequency Identification (RFID) technology. Thus, this chapter reviews the literature on RFID adoption in supply chain/logistics management from 1995-2015. We identify current trends in the literature, drawing on the three levels of decision making, that is, strategic, tactical, and operational. We suggest that more research needs to be conducted with regards to the intangible benefits of RFID, the use of RFID big data for achieving higher performance, and to shift the focus from the 'what' and the impacts on performance to the 'how' and the ways RFID is adopted and assimilated in organizations and supply chains. Finally, the managerial implications of our review as well as the limitations and future research directions are outlined.

The crowdsourcing and Internet of Things (IoT) have played a significant role in revolutionizing the information age. In response to pressing need, we have attempted to develop a theoretical framework which can help disaster relief workers to improve their coordination using valuable information derived using comprehensive crowdsourcing framework. In this study we have used two-prong research strategies. First we have conducted extensive review of articles published in reputable journals, magazines and blogs by eminent practitioners and policy makers followed by case studies: stampede in Godavari River at Rajahmundry (2015), earthquake in Nepal (2015), flood in Uttarakhand (2013). Finally we have concluded our research findings with further research directions.

The importance of integrating and coordinating supply chain business partners have been appreciated in many industries. In the global manufacturing industry, supply chain business partners' information integration is technically a daunting task due to highly disconnected infrastructures and operations. Information, software applications, and services are loosely distributed among participant business partners with heterogeneous operating infrastructures. A secure, and flexible information exchange architecture that can interconnect distributed information and share that information across global service provision applications is, therefore, immensely advantageous. This chapter describes the main features of an ontology-based web service framework for integrating distributed business processes in a global supply chain. A Scalable Web Service Discovery Framework (SWSDF) for material procurement systems of a manufacturing supply chain is described. Description Logic (DL) is used to represent and explain SWSDF. The framework uses a hybrid knowledge-based system, which consists of Case-Based Reasoning (CBR) and Rule-Based Reasoning (RBR). SWSDF includes: (1) a collection of web service descriptions in Ontology Web Language-Based Service (OWL-S), (2) service advertisement using complex concepts, and (3) a service concept similarity assessment algorithm. Finally, a business scenario is used to demonstrate functionalities of the described system.

Section 4
Social Media Data Research

Social media has recently emerged as a key tool to manage customer relations in industry. This chapter aims to contribute a step-by-step Twitter Analytic framework for analysing the tweets in a fiscal crisis. The proposed framework includes three major sections – demographic analytic, content analytic and integrated method analytic. This chapter provides useful insights to develop this framework through the lens of the recent Volkswagen emission scandal. A sizable dataset of #volkswagescandal tweets (8,274) was extracted as the research sample. Research findings based upon this sample include the following: Consumer sentiments are overall negative toward the scandal; some clustered groups are identified; male users expressed more interest on social media in the topic than female users; the popularity of tweets was closely related with the timing of news coverage, which indicates the traditional media is still playing a critical role in public opinion formation. The limitations and practical contribution of the current study are also discussed.

The Internet has changed the face and the pace of retail offering an opportunity to sell products online. This has led to the fast growth of e-commerce sites in which retailers envision a source of competitive advantage. Before they are able to benefit from e-commerce however, they have to understand the range of factors, which impact consumers' e-commerce acceptance. Even more, to ensure sustainability of online product sale, retailers have to go a step further and understand not only consumers' intentions to purchase online but also factors driving product re-purchase. To date, a number of factors driving consumers' e-commerce purchase and re-purchase have been examined. Most recently, the concept of swift guanxi has been studied. This study extends this stream of research by analysing social media data being a result of swift guanxi in order to help retailers in their online strategies improvement.

The hospitality industry is one of the fastest-growing industries in the world. The growth of this industry has been accompanied by issues of sustainability development. Employees expect firms to have the ability to address their negative impacts on the environment and society. However, firms are generally unable to reach such expectations due to an inability to acquire feedback from employees, which leads to employee dissatisfaction. In addition, there has been a lack in the theoretical linkage between employee engagement and sustainability development. Thus, this study determines the critical factors of employee engagement based on big data (using social media and quantitative and qualitative data) and integrates such data by using decision-making tests and laboratory evaluation methods to identify these interrelationships. The findings reveal that sustainability development can be enhanced through aggressive employee engagement, which also can generate a positive influence on economic performance. A detailed discussion is also presented.

Preface

The development of this edited book is inspired by the organization of the 9th International Conference on Operations and Supply Chain Management, which was held in July 2015 and was hosted by the University of Nottingham Ningbo China. The theme of the conference is "Data-Driven Research for Supply Chain Management". The lead editor of this book is the conference co-chair, and the other editors are the organizing committee members. It is found that from the panel discussions, presentations, and paper submissions from the conference applications of big data to operations or supply chain management are premature. There is a need to consolidate recent works and to construct a clearer roadmap for future research in this area.

Data-driven research is a new research paradigm which may bring in a new discipline for supply chain management, which has witnessed the prime value of information systems and information sharing in the last few decades. With that background, information sharing will introduce a huge amount of data and its intelligence can be very useful to firms competing in the digital economy or big data era. This line of thought can also blend with supply chain service innovation. Despite promised benefits, however, the area is under-researched.

One significant driver to the data-driven research is the pace of technological development in the last two decades. Computational power has improved drastically, data collection has never been easier, and data storage seems to have reached a stage of unlimited capacity. Mobile devices such as smart phones, Internet-of-Things are ubiquitously available for data generation and collection. Consequently, a massive amount of data is available, and can be stored in various professional cloud services, for example. Obviously, these data contain fruitful information. Despite this, converting these valuable data into information remains a challenge. The main obstacle is the unorganized nature of the data. It is not surprising that such research arena remains superficial and stays at a high level. In this connection, new business models and practices are required to fully utilize the data, which in turn can create lots of opportunities for data-driven research in the operations and supply chain management domain to improve excellence.

In fact, this recent trend can be considered as an extension of traditional supply chain innovation and management, which require interdisciplinary methodologies from multiple fields including supply chain management, information systems, knowledge management, etc. This edited book provides a collection of recent and original contributions covering a variety of aspects of innovation and operations in supply chain management and decision sciences in the big data era. Not only theoretical research studies are featured in this book, but a number of practical articles are selected. This is definitely a source of good practical reference.

The book is organized into four sections: Insights from the Academia and Practitioners (Section 1), Big Data on Operations and Supply Chains (Section 2), Big Data and Emerging Technology (Section 3), and Social Media Data Research (Section 4). Section 1 contains two chapters which are the summaries of two panel discussions at the 9th International Conference on Operations and Supply Chain Management. Not only academics' views are included, but the practitioners' views on big data are discussed. Section 2 consists of four chapters that outline the impact of big data on various operations management or supply chain management issues (for example, inventory management, preventive maintenance, transportation). Section 3 reveals the relationships between big data and some emerging technologies on supply chain management. As mentioned before, technological development is a catalyst to big data research and hence it is worth studying such relationships. Three types of technologies are discussed in three chapters under this section. Finally, Section 4 presents three studies utilizing social media data to facilitate a couple of supply chain activities. Social media data are user-generated and hence a good use of them will improve customer service. The set of data is also a significant source of big data. That being said, their unstructured and qualitative characteristics are different to manipulated. Details of the chapters are summarized below.

Chapter 1, "Big Data Analytics: Academic Perspectives," provides a summary of the challenges, opportunities, and emerging research approaches on big data research in operations and supply chain management from the academics' point of view. Examples on data mining, data visualization, etc., are given. This chapter is a reflection of an academic panel discussion at the 9th International Conference on Operations and Supply Chain Management.

Chapter 2, "Big Data Analytics: Service and Manufacturing Industries Perspectives," is a sister chapter of Chapter 1. Likewise, the chapter originates from a panel discussion at the 9th International Conference on Operations and Supply Chain Management, but this panel consists of a number of industrial practitioners, who are senior management people in different types and scales of companies. Their discussion provides insights on practical issues and implementation challenges from the industry perspective.

Chapter 3, "How Smart Operations Help Better Planning and Replenishment: Empirical Study – Supply Chain Collaboration for Smart Operations," starts discussing how various data can influence smart operations. Several case studies in different industries, including frozen food, textile, petroleum, packaging, and electrical equipment manufacturer, are employed to illustrate the idea. Such smart operations are particularly useful to resource planning, supplier management, and so on.

Chapter 4, "Big Data Analytics for Predictive Maintenance Strategies," discusses how big data can facilitate predictive maintenance. Obviously predictive maintenance is an important industrial operation, which aims to reduce the risk of disruption. Consequently, supply chain activities can be carried out smoothly. Traditional approaches based heavily on statistical methods and historical data. This study utilizes big data to perform predictive maintenance in a semiconductor manufacturing environment. Fuzzy logic and artificial neural network are incorporated in the decision support system in order to extract and analyse the data. The case example provides excellent practical value to the readers.

Chapter 5, "Data-Driven Inventory Management in the Healthcare Supply Chain," employs big data techniques to improve inventory management in the healthcare supply chain. More specifically, classification and regression tree algorithm is employed to predict sales data from historical data. Data from a real-life example are used to verify that the algorithm outperforms standard static statistical methods. Again, the practical value of this chapter is equally important to the one presented in Chapter 4.

Chapter 6, "Role of Operations Strategy and Big Data: A Study of Transport Company," turns the discussion to another type of important supply chain operations, namely, transportation. This study aims to reveal how big data collected by Internet-of-Things can improve less than truck load operations. Traditionally, such operations are not always cost efficient and hence profit margin sometimes is low.

Chapter 7, "Big Data and RFID in Supply Chain and Logistics Management: A Review of the Literature and Applications for Data-Driven Research," supplements the discussion in Chapter 6 by providing a fabulous literature review in the same area. Nevertheless, the focus is not just put on less than truck load operations, but general supply chain and logistics operations. The authors suggest a number of research directions that are valuable to the researchers in this field.

Chapter 8, "Developing an Integration Framework for Crowdsourcing and Internet of Things with Applications for Disaster Response," develops a framework to bridge crowdsourcing operations and Internet-of-Things, with an application on disaster response. It is well-known that disaster is difficult to detect; so if it happens one important issue is the reaction. With the Internet-of-Things technology, information can be conveyed even under such circumstances. Qualitative interviews were conducted to support the proposed framework.

Chapter 9, "Supply Chain Coordination Based on Web Services," proposes a semantic web services, which encompasses knowledge-based system to facilitate supply chain integration and coordination. More specifically, different business scenarios are modelled using case-based reasoning system. Detailed descriptions of the system are presented in the chapter.

Chapter 10, "Exploring the Hidden Pattern from Tweets: Investigation into the Volkswagen Emissions Scandal," explores how social media data, more specifically tweets in this study, can reveal the hidden information about the famous diesel-gate incident. A mixed text-mining method provides a sentiment on the users' reaction to the incident. The results provide insights on how to manage and design supply chain network with respect to the incident.

Chapter 11, "Swift Guanix Data Analysis and Its Application to E-Commerce Retail Strategies Improvement," extracts a different type of online data, e-commerce social media data based on the communications between a fashion retailer and its consumers. The objective of the study is to apply content analysis to study whether or not swift guanix generated from such communications can improve trust for on-line purchasing. This study contributes to the development of e commerce strategy.

Chapter 12, "Applying Big Data with Fuzzy DEMATEL to Discover the Critical Factors for Employee Engagement in Developing Sustainability for the Hospitality Industry: Multi-Criteria Decision Making/Group Decision Making," applies big data for making decisions, an important area of operations and supply chain management. With the help of big data, relative importance between different selection criteria can be obtained without human judgement. Therefore, the decision is more objective.

The editors believe that the collection of chapters is relevant and beneficial to the needs of professionals, researchers, post-doctoral and graduate students working in the field of supply chain management in various functions such as purchasing, logistics, operations, and supply chain strategy, whose research interests are in big data or data-driven research.

Hing Kai Chan
The University of Nottingham – Ningbo, China

Nachiappan Subramanian
University of Sussex, UK

Muhammad Abdulrahman
The University of Nottingham – Ningbo, China

Acknowledgment

The editors would like to take this opportunity to express their gratitude to the following parties:

All contributors. Without your support and quality contributions, this book would not have been able to be published.

All reviewers. Your voluntary effort and time devoted in reviewing the articles have maintained a good selection of chapters. Your constructive comments also help safeguard the quality of the chapters.

The University of Nottingham Ningbo China and Nottingham University Business School China for their kind support to host the conference, and their generous financial support.

Finally, we are grateful to the IGI Global staff for their superb support and patience during the production of this book. Special mention goes to Courtney Tychinski, the Development Editor of this book, and Jan Travers, the Director of Intellectual Property and Contracts, as the book has encountered a couple of delays and their support in due course is very much appreciated.

Hing Kai Chan
The University of Nottingham – Ningbo, China

Nachiappan Subramanian
University of Sussex, UK

Muhammad Abdulrahman
The University of Nottingham – Ningbo, China

Section 1
Insights from the Academia and Practitioners

Chapter 1
Big Data Analytics:
Academic Perspectives

Muhammad D. Abdulrahman
The University of Nottingham – Ningbo, China

Nachiappan Subramanian
University of Sussex, UK

Hing Kai Chan
The University of Nottingham – Ningbo, China

Kun Ning
The University of Nottingham – Ningbo, China

ABSTRACT

This chapter discusses the scholarly views on big data analytics with respect to the challenges in terms of visualization and data driven research in smart cities and ports. The prominent challenges and emerging research on structuring data, data mining algorithms and visualization aspects are shared by academic experts based on their ongoing research experience. Scholars agreed that being able to analyze huge data at once is highly critical for the embracement and success of big data research and the utilization of its findings particularly for entities with highly dynamic and complex demands such as cities and ports. It was noted that developing robust ways of handling and clean qualitative social media data as well as getting well-trained and highly skilled human resources in all aspects of big data analysis and interpretation remains a major challenge.

DOI: 10.4018/978-1-5225-0956-1.ch001

INTRODUCTION

This chapter brings together the academic perspectives on Data-Driven Research for Supply Chain Management. It includes scholars' presentations from The 9th International Conference on Operations and Supply Chain Management that took place in Ningbo China from 12-15 July 2015. Prominent challenges identified in data analytics process include structuring data, visualization, data analytics and data driven research in smart cities and ports.

A unique area with significant big data utilization is smart city development. Smart city are being planned all over the world. Smart city basically means a city that provides a high quality and efficient life to its in habitants through resource optimization (Calvillo et al. 2016). A key aspect of smart city project is accurate and wide-ranging data collection. The expansion of big data and the evolution of Internet of Things (IoT) technologies have played an important role in the feasibility of smart city initiatives. Data collection requirement in smart city projects are in many areas such as security, transportation, logistics, shipping and IoT. Once collected, the data needs to be analyzed. Data analysis and accurate interpretation is highly critical for a successful use of big data application and utilization. A key aspect of big data analysis this is the data structure.

A data structure is a term which is usually used to refer to systematic forms of organizing data (Tsitchizris & Lochovsky, 1982). As a concept, a data structure is important while analysing the information and it has been used within the research and practise of the information disciplines (Beynon-Davies, 2016). The Computer Sciences Corporation (CSC) lists five tops trends that are going to affect future supply chains. These are: mobile communication, cloud computing, intelligent robots, manufacturing digitalization and deep learning. Firstly, computer science which has changed the world in terms of how we do things and communicate from the early days to now will be affected by man-made physical objects. In the near future most things, if not all, will be computerised. The second step is statistics and its applications for understanding key issues and decision makings. There is an ongoing convergence between existing technologies. Company C is sells expensive game cards to students, as part of its business portfolio. The company engages some the students in creating the graphic cuts for game players. It discovered in 2004 that someone at Stanford University found that the graphics processing unit (GPU) can be used for computations, which the company immediately turned into a business. The graphics processing unit (GPU) has now become a computational engine, used in the area of simulation, computational finance, and weather modelling. Company C is familiar with high performance computing and is a top 500. A Top500 basically means top 500 most powerful non-distributed computer systems on this planet. TOP500 supercomputers consist of thousands of control display unit (CDU) in one single system. In this case, graphics processing/processor unit (GPU) is basically used. So there is tremendous growth in terms of using the GPU as a simulation engine.

GPU is used for MapReduce which is getting wide publicity and usage in today's big data processing. A MapReduce program is a filtering and sorting programme with the associated summary of the operation such as counting the number items in a queue and yielding items frequencies, amongst others. Basically it is a framework that allows for massive data analyses. One of challenges in large data, with millions of unstructured data, is the difficulty of pooling and acquiring such data. It is now possible to analyse complex and dynamic situations based on MIT student's development. For example, during Arab's spring (revolutionary waves of demonstrations and protests which started in December 2010 in Tunisia) MIT research student had wanted to analyze the twitters of those in the Arab's Spring uprising but was frustrated because he found that the database was extremely slow. To overcome this, the student simply developed his own database that allow for the type of processing speed he wanted. The student, as expected, immediately became popular and his database company grew and attracted offers of million dollars by both Google and Facebook to buy his database programme. The student is reported to be waiting to get a billion dollars offer before selling.

Visualization (or scientific visualization) analyses data in depth to provide clear understanding and insight on data, generating image and/or graphics allowing the observation of a simulation or calculation process, that are invisible in traditionally (Jia et al, 2016). Visualization provides methods of visual interaction with simulation and calculation (Jia et al, 2016). People want to analyse large data in a very quick time. However, very large bytes of data are not easy to extract, analyze and interpret to gain insights. When you have a lot of data such as twitters and audio search, one of the things is how you are going to visualize them, to get meaningful insights. The question is will you analyse the data all at one look? It is challenging. Some people have actually explored things like official wall, where people have huge infrastructure and wall to look at how the data looks like. That allows you to have more insight into the data.

There is an example of visualization called cave. It is used in the scientific community, and in the areas like supply chains and others. This is how the starters look at data which is macro data. The whole idea and concept is that people are able to walk through billions and millions of atoms inside and try to understand the structure of that particular place. There is also large scale geographical information system (GIS) designed to capture, store, analyse, and present spatial and/or geographical data used for city planning, traffic planning, etc. People can do a walk through, that is, walking through data and perform simulation on it.

Data and statistical analyses have been used in human various human endeavours as demonstrated in the history of artificial intelligence. It provides new opportunities for competitive advantage by extracting huge value from large amounts of data (Wang et al, 2016). In particular, the very first artificial intelligence application was inspired by in 1943 based on the structure of the human brain. For example, neural-network was first introduced in 1943. It was fundamentally based on statistical measures and pure logic. While neural-network died off in the 70s and early 80s, it somehow picked up again in the late 80s and now has become very important in the labour market in the 20th century in the last few years.

All of these centre on machine learning. So what is machine learning? Learning is formulating models based on experience and optimization of different scenarios. For example, firms using and tracking data to develop transportation model. This involves data classification, regression, clustering, etc. Machine learning is promising because of huge amount of data coming availability today and the growing need to be able to analyse and predictions future directions. Many companies - Wal-Mart, Facebook, Google, Alibaba, etc. - are now collecting huge amounts data from customers and anyone using their services. Machine learning is the training of machines on how to collect and utilise these data to enable useful business analysis and predictions. There are two parts to machine learning: Infras-engine and the training aspect. The other part is on the training side of things. The two parts are very compute-intensive (i.e. the applications requiring lots of computation like meteorology and other scientific applications programmes) because the applications require lots of computers to execute the complex analysis required. A couple of models are doing considered very well, vector machines, random forests, graphical models, Gaussian mixture models, etc. By far however, the most inspiring aspect is design the network. Human brain is made up of neurons that communicate to one another through electricity and sparks. This has inspired neural network which does not work exactly the same way. So, how does a computer carries out perceptions of models? When humans visualise an image, how do our brains work? Human brain does not necessarily collect all the information at once. For example, people extract others' features such as the shape of their noses, eyes, position of mouth, angle of ears, etc. to determine who the person is. Same goes with audio. People extract the features of audio signal, and then translate these sound features to predict information being sent across. In future, machines will be able to do same and human translators will be replaced by automatic machines.

The above are traditional areas where deep learning or machine learning has been used. Together there are about ten (10) layers of large networks for neural networks just about a year ago while currently, we have about 20 layers. There are almost a billion 10-layer networks, a billion parameters that are actually optimized. This requires 30 tester flout computing power model used to do the training of about 10 million images. This will allow people to carry out image classifications, object detections and localization. A simple example of this application is that when People do a search on websites looking for a certain book, the website should be able to tell them their preferences. This is possible because the website able to mine such individuals' data. This is the example of Google search. It can tell what a picture is and potentially who is the person. Another example is video. Facial recognition will be done in real time, telling who is being visualised instantly. This can potentially help ease real time surveillance such as immigration, sports, and so on.

The above scenario is a simple case. Imagine thousands of cameras across the city, all streaming in real time data. The data can be easily analysed because the analysts have the architecture and system to analyse them in a correct form as described above. And also now we have the technology to take in all the data that we have and to learn or investigate if we have the right models for our decisions making. We can also train the machine to learn and analyse directly. This is where artificial intelligence is headed toward. For example, we make machines play many complex games or simulations, like traffic simulation, logistics, etc., and then artificial intelligence will be smart enough to find a way of optimizing the best way to play or the simulation based on a certain cost function. This is artificial intelligence 0.1 version. So what are the three drivers of deep learning? Firstly, there is the existence of more data. Deep learning is not something new. As mentioned earlier, the first version of neural network was done in 1943. It almost died out in the 80s because of lack of enough data, not enough powerful computers to do those computations. However, it has resurfaced because of three things - better models, more data and more powerful accelerators.

The GPU is an interesting item for machine learning. A lot of the competition right now for recognizing images has used GPU to do the learning. It is the first Google network built with 1000 CPU...cost about 5 million dollars, take about 100 gigawatt of power, with a similar project consisting of three GPU servers on top of it.

It is believed that over 600 developed companies in the US are currently developing artificial intelligence. Companies like in China, Alibaba, Baidu, and Tencent are doing acquisitions of some of companies engaged in either data analysis or artificial intelligence. At the moment one of the challenges company Cfaces is being able to recruit other genius because Alibaba, Baidu are in fierce competing with company C for talent in the sector.

The global demand for intelligence systems is growing, whether in manufacturing, transportation, security, factory assembly lines, etc. In the area of deep learning, for example, how can managers detect potential problem in supply chain or manufacturing before such problem happens? Managers would like to be able to detect abnormality before they occur and many other different behaviour detections. AI is not just about deep learning; it is also about computing, cognitive vision, natural language processing, affective computing, etc. Therefore the future and potential for AI can only be imagined.

VISUALIZATION ANALYSIS CASE STUDY

The data for this case study is from Company A. The data was collected by Company A itself and is on diabetes. Generally, it is difficult to collect the data of end-customers in the medical industry. Actually, between the company and their end-customers is a long supply chain channel. Based on the pattern of distributor, the supply chain became quite long. So in the front-end of the SC, they spend a lot of time to plan and to foresee the risks in the future the model used. Given the long SC and demand being continuously enlarged, bullwhip effect cannot be avoided. Therefore it is necessary to prepare some inventory to deal with the uncertainty in the market. So the visualization analyse is necessary.

Data Pre-Processing

As most of the values in the data base are in Chinese, this has to be recoded in format to make it computer identifiable and readable data. The pre-processing part requires data cleaning to take care of lots of missing values and mistakes in the data using some algorithm. The data recoding part cost more time to ensure data accuracy and reliable results making pre-processing very important. Simple regression is used and reliability test shows that the regression model is comparatively accurate. Company A provided five months data, and they use the first four months data for training to get a trained model. So in the fifth month, they have the real data and also a fitting result. It is shown that the sales are consistent every day which indicates the results are accepted.

Predictive Analytics and Data Visualization

Visualization analysis is very important in data mining. Data mining results cannot be shown to be effective without visualization. With visualization, some information from text and figures can be shown and examined. The heat map is used show a different view to explore data visualization for decision making. The colour and size in the heat map represent the density of sales, the amount in different cities for a particular product. Also in a ratio figure, it shows sales and volumes of one product at the same time, and it's the difference from the previous one.

Models and visualization analysis can help with the decision making of companies and provide some reference to the smart stock deployment and support decision making in SC. It can also assist in reactive rescheduling. Although regression model results proven to be very good, complex models such as logit can also be used to get accurate results models and visualization analysis in the future. We can also add more features like temporal –spatial features and, besides inventory, accurate information location in SC in needed. Finally, machinery intelligence can also be helpful in the future and the use of survey may also help explain the models.

DATA MINING CASE STUDY

As is mentioned, data mining and machine learning technics are very good for marketing purposes. According to Wikipedia (2016), data mining is "It is the computational process of discovering patterns in large data sets involving methods at the intersection of artificial intelligence, machine learning, statistics, and database systems". There are 7 Vs-volume, velocity, variety, veracity, variability, visualization and value. Visualization stands as the more important future and development. Visualization extracts patterns in data in a human-consumable format and machine is able to interpret the meaning of the extracted patterns. Data is basically the raw facts while figures, statistics and information serve as the connecting relationship with data. This relation is important in data driven approach. Natural data, like geographical, geological and human data, machine generated data and simulated data are more important data for academics. Static data is data recorded that doesn't change, however, dynamic data is continuous, linear data that grows linearly and we have data which explodes further down the line. For example, social media data like Weibo and Twitter, these are all exploding data.

Over the past two years, this presenter has been looking into social media data with different topics, like freejahar, PRU13, NSA, royal baby, Mccann, and MH370. Those data are quite important for understanding the society, and that is one of my research areas. For example, the two brothers in Boston marathon bombing that killed people. While the elder brother died, the younger brother became highly controversial because American teenage girls fell in love with his look. The data from communities online on these two brothers showed that US young teenager girls are supporting a terrorist. This is about rationality of data and visualization. When mapped, the interaction between the US teenage girls and with US news channel, certain patterns were found with many clusters. By applying certain technics on the data, the important people in the network are recognized. So by using various methods - sample of data mining and machine learning methods, it is possible to classify and determine the different group of people spreading information.

Right from the very beginning of the data and to the evolution of the network, the final decline and the integration of this particular teenager groups, all can be analysed. This type of data analysis is important in the future especially with marketing business, relationships, social information.

SOCIAL MEDIA ANALYSIS

The challenge of analysing social media data is that such data are qualitative in nature and they are highly constructed. They are not like inventory data; they are just something we don't know. The objectivity is highly correlated to the qualitative nature of the data. In this study narrated above, the presenter uses social media data and created conceptual analysis and relational analysis, essentially trying to extract the relationship between what to analyse within the dataset. The focus is on how to analyse the data and how to clean the data. The first thing is to try and conceptualize the dataset. After the conceptualization of the data, to identify the relationship among this concept should be done followed by the identification of the factor to focus on. For example, in the Company A case, their focus could be sales volume which represents the code or the things they would like to analyse and extract from the data. After this code, he can map those social media data to a number of concepts and then try to identify the relationship.

There is a case study from Facebook website where over 916 comments of social media data were extracted and model created. This model can be used for the development. This is a hierarchical model that can identify the relationship among different codes. But for operation SC management, they are just a number of factors, a number of criteria.

SMART PORT

With the expanding of information technology, the word "smart" becomes popular recently. This concept has been introduced to many areas, such as healthcare, ecommerce, infrastructure construction and logistics (Hall, 2000). The definition of smart is to create more "instrumented, interconnected, and intelligent systems" through information technology to address some of the world's pressing issues and achieve socio-economic growth (Wikipedia, 2016). Ports are major economic centers that play crucial role in providing goods and services. Ocean carriers are getting quite larger recently moving huge amount of goods between nations and preferred ports must be competitive in terms of cost, efficiency and security. Key issues in selecting ports are the destination and the total logistics cost. The logistics aspect centers on five rights: right goods, right place, right time, right condition and right cost. Efficient distribution network is "the last frontier of competitive advantage".

There are 678 major ports on the coastline of China with each competing and wanting to be the best. The key questions for each port, however, are: what are its unique features? What are its selling points and why should anyone us it? Rethinking the nature or the boundary of the port and its economic growth changes its role. Some ports are holistic in nature supporting not only good stransporting but also social services.

Port customers are looking for total solution. This is important as sometimes the port is not necessarily the end destination. Therefore, port users compare the connectivity to other constructs and the port ranges. If you want to stock items on the port, how or where do you stock the items? What technology do you use to stock those items? And then the optimization, and then look at the total package, what's the landing cost or total cost? So for the centric port providers, how do we combine these solutions? These factors and activity clusters, light manufacturing, warehousing, etc., are being formed and/or performed at the port itself.

Following natural disasters like earthquake and Tsunamiin Japan, some nations are establishing wind technologies at their coastlines. For example, Germany has gone for wind tech on its coastlines, and they are focused very much on Wind technology. Ports have to deal with these companies. Offshore wind farm are merging very fast. The wind structures and components have to be designed shipped. However, Germany is battling workforce problem of older and younger workers that centers on effective knowledge transfer. How do they transfer knowledge from older to younger workers? There is also a problem of how to design technology that does not need to rely on labor force. German age structure of 1950, 2010 and 2030 has people who are living longer and getting older.

The wind farm equipment needs to be developed, built, installing and possibly recycled. There are a lot of subsidies because of countries like the Netherlands, Germany, UK, Ireland; small islands sometimes can take advantage of those.

The above indicates the following scenarios: Scenario no.1 put people first. Having sufficient well-trained and skilled staff available is critically important compared with having a given level of technology. Simulation gaming which a big aspect of staff is training. The first game was developed in Nottingham in collaboration with Germany in engineering which allow people to reduce design time, development, manufacture and market launch time of products. There is also the need to compress the learning cycle to as short as possible. How can people transfer and capture knowledge, use it to develop a simulation game in order to train the future workers in very short period of time?

Scenario 2 is full force ahead – making sure information systems are developed and full integration of the systems. With shortage of skilled labor and high average age of workforce and then level of technology remains unchanged (as in the case of Germany above) is in fact is a big challenge. For academics, how do we raise the skill levels in which our institutions?

The fourth scenario can be called smart port. There are shortages of skilled labor, and then high average age of workforce. They want efficient processes, digitalization of processes and then integrated and powerful information systems. The focus becomes how to utilize and make a port which is free from pain through automation and digitalization that will warrant very little intervention skilled personnel so we can have automatic control tower?

Things have changed and life is changing. Competition is also intensifying. Sometimes work is stable, other times unstable. Initially Europe merged together, a lot of countries get together to form an economic block. And then some old democratic systems wish for rights and to operate independently. In Greece there is a dilemma. Even if the public is voting against this austerity packages which are demanded by the founding bodies. They have to sell port. Ports have been privatized. Around the world people with money wish to buy a port. A lot of people are bidding for the port. Merges and acquisitions are happening. How do we develop port-centric logistics

Figure 1. Word cloud

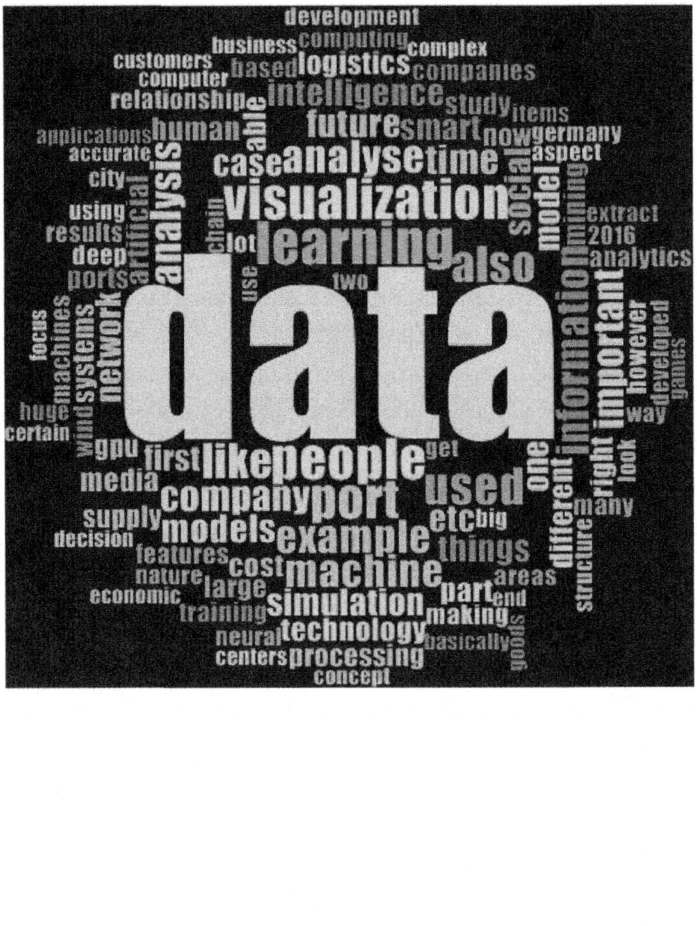

capability? And then at the bottom I put simulation games as a way of transferring knowledge and competence development. How can we apply simulation games as a way to compressing time to market and enhancing skill?

FUTURE RESEARCH DIRECTIONS

The above scholarly views on big data analytics indicate a number of future research directions. The discussions suggests a need for sustained effort at developing more robust and quick way of analyzing huge data, especially qualitative data such as twitters and audio search and to visualize and accurately interprets such data. Scholars agreed that being able to analyze huge data at once is highly critical for the embracement and success of big data. Specifically, the challenge scholars noted are in data gathering, efficient structuring and visualization for entities with highly dynamic and complex demands such as cities and ports. Other future research directions to examine and develop include:

- How intelligence systems such as AI can be used in various fields (manufacturing, transportation, security, factory assembly lines, etc.) to detect potential problem before such problem occurs?
- Developing robust ways of handling the challenge of qualitative social media data - how to clean and analyze social media data.
- Efficient port distribution network for competitive advantage.
- Human capital development in terms of well-trained and highly skilled staff in all aspects of big data analysis and interpretation.
- Developing a painless port through automation and digitalization that warrants little or no intervention of skilled personnel (with automatic control tower).

REFERENCES

Beynon-Davies, P. (2016). Instituting facts: Data structures and institutional order. *Information and Organization*, *26*(1-2), 28–44. doi:10.1016/j.infoandorg.2016.04.001

Calvillo, C. F., Sánchez-Miralles, A., & Villar, J. (2016). Energy managementandplanninginsmartcities. *Renewable and Sustainable Energy Reviews.*, *55*, 273–287.

Hall, R. E. (2000). The vision of a smart city. In *Proceedings of the 2nd international life extension technology workshop*.

Jia, C., Wang, H., & Wei, L. (2016). Research on Visualization of Multi-Dimensional Real-Time Traffic Data Stream Based on Cloud Computing. *Procedia Engineering*, *137*, 709–718. doi:10.1016/j.proeng.2016.01.308

Tsitchizris, D. C., & Lochovsky, F. H. (1982). *Data models*. Prentice-Hall.

Wang, G., Gunasekaran, A., Ngai, E. W. T., & Papadopoulos, T. (2016). Big data analytics in logistics and supply chain management: Certain investigations for research and applications. *International Journal of Production Economics*, *176*, 98–110. doi:10.1016/j.ijpe.2016.03.014

Wikipedia. (2016a). *Data mining*. Retrieved from https://en.wikipedia.org/wiki/Data_mining

Wikipedia. (2016b). *Smart planet*. Retrieved from https://en.wikipedia.org/wiki/SmartPlanet

Chapter 2
Big Data Analytics:
Service and Manufacturing Industries Perspectives

Nachiappan Subramanian
University of Sussex, UK

Muhammad D. Abdulrahman
The University of Nottingham – Ningbo, China

Hing Kai Chan
The University of Nottingham – Ningbo, China

Kun Ning
The University of Nottingham – Ningbo, China

ABSTRACT

In this chapter, we will introduce practical issues and implementation challenges from the industry perspective. In particular, we explain three aspects based on the panel discussions from the set of representatives participated in a big data conference from three dominant industries such as e-commerce, health care and computer hardware, which are sought of big data for their growth and development. We introduce overall challenges and explain typical industry based practical issues, how they visualize the big picture for their strategic development and how industries are gearing towards converting the challenges to big opportunities through the partnership of universities. Finally, based on the content analysis we offer potential trends and future research directions.

DOI: 10.4018/978-1-5225-0956-1.ch002

INTRODUCTION

This chapter is based on the perspectives of the firms that participated in the 9th International Conference on Operations and Supply Chain Management that took place in Ningbo China from 12-15 July 2015. The major topics discussed in the conference are big data, visualization, and university - industry collaboration opportunities. The participating companies whose perspectives are summarized here are from quite different industries. For example, Company A is a well-known international company in health care sector while Company B is large scale e-commerce firm. Company C is a famous foreign company that specializes in computer graphics. Company D is a small cross-border e-commerce company. These firms firstly provide their respective perspectives on big data. Secondly, the firms looked at the application of visualization. Thirdly, they looked at the possible collaboration between academics and industry.

The growth of three industries that participated in the panel such as e-commerce, computer graphics, and other service oriented firms use mobile network as a platform that are pushing their limits of existing network designs. Various channel of interactions in sectors such as public health, and economics made big data analytics as a means to achieve growth (Einav & Levin, 2014). Almost all the industries are someway or other involved in big data because of its spreading influence (Liu et al, 2016). Big data is generally considered as an information that are presented with large data volumes and complex data structures (Khoury & Ioannidis, 2014), such as social media data (such as Twitter and Weibo), mobile phone call records, commercial website data (e.g., eBay, Taobao), geographical information, search engine data, and also smart card data. The big challenge is how to extract meaningful information by the way of analysis from the huge volume and complex data is referred as visualization. Typically visualization supports us to make a good strong from the massive data based on the deeper understanding and insights on the contextual real time data. In addition visualization offers a way to gain visual interaction along with simulation (Jia et al, 2016).

HEALTHCARE PERSPECTIVE

During the proceedings of the conference, Company A suggested that the most disruptive technology in supply chain is big data analytics, based on their survey. This is closely followed by digital supply chain. A recent PWC report noted that there are different interpretations for industry 4.0 in Germany, US and China. The report noted however, that despite the differences, "Data application and integration will be the key ability of the industrial age of the Internet" as very important. Additionally, industry 4.0 will bring opportunities in five different aspects that include interconnection, integration, data, innovation, and transition. Two of these aspects, interconnection thinking and data, will be leading survival modesfo r companies in the future. These firms envisage big challenges in data operation in the age of Internet of Technologies (IoT) and called for increased discussions on challenges of using big data. Moreover recently some companies started to distribute their data in a way that paves way to visualize the data to recognize the importance and benefits. It is obvious that firms have huge data but not all are able to make use of such data by way of accurate and independent analysis. This has necessitated the need for collaboration among industries and higher institutions to effectively utilize the available data. The collaboration between universities and the industry is increasingly perceived as a motive to enhance innovation through knowledge exchange. University interaction aims mainly to encourage knowledge and technology exchange (Bekkers & Bodas Freitas, 2008; Siegel, Waldman, & Link, 2003). In the conference, the discussions were focused on how to help both university and companies to be benefited by the collaboration.

Views and Challenges of Using Big Data

Information technology related challenges such as inadequate integration of healthcare systems and poor healthcare information management are seriously hampering efforts to transform IT value to business value in the healthcare industry (Bodenheimer, 2005; Herrick et al., 2010). The consequences are unnecessary cost for both patients and healthcare service providers are increased. Thus, healthcare organizations and companies are seeking effective mechanisms that can help to consolidate organizational resources to improve organizational performance, and maybe even create new and more effective data-driven business models (Agarwal et al., 2010; Ker et al., 2014). Typically in healthcare industry, the practitioners still do not understand well how big data analytics can create value for their organizations (Sharma et al., 2014). Thus, there is an urgent need to understand the impacts of big data analytics and explore its potential benefits driven by big data analytics (Wang et al, 2015).

Company A is a large scale international healthcare company. From their perspective, collecting data is a big challenge in itself already. The company noted that while they can use technology to deal with gathered data, it's still difficult to actually get the data by individual company. This is because they are facing a long channel down the supply chain and not directly connected to the end customers. Therefore, how to get the data is already a big challenge. Gathering data from hospital is even harder because of associated ethical issues.

Big data is already used to medicine research and development, but it is still a challenge in supply chain (SC). For example, in China they have got 24,000 registered hospitals and about 900,000 hospitals in total including the community hospitals and health centers. It's difficult to get data from them, especially routine daily data in each operating units. Accurate inventory is also a problem, according to the health care firm. The firm is currently able to do some tracking with code scanning, but they can't do this for all the items. So they hope they can find a way to collect data more effectively to reduce the cost and inventory, and then to help the patients. In their effort during data collection, the firm spent 7or 8 years to design a system for data collection from their distributors as well as to track the inventory stock. This seems to be a time consuming long process for the firm. Once the system for data gathering is in place, the firm then moves into the second step which is to make decisions on how to use the data collected.

In terms of data application, there are several challenges. The medical industry is easily affected by policies and this in turn will have impact on their firms' supply chain. To overcome some these challenges, the firms have to do an enormous work to keep pace with changing regulations and policies while maintaining required service level. It is noted that if the firm can collect additional data and visualize them using purchasing strategies then it is possible to improve the resilience of the entire supply chain.

Visualization

Big data is permeating into each part of an organization and it has impacts on almost all the industries. Big data collected by healthcare industry can serve as a valuable source of evidence for related firms in the supply chain to make sensible decisions. However, good quality data is the key. This indicates that visualization has an important role it is essential to have an effective method to mine big data to make some sense (Jia et al, 2016). As is known, collecting data is already different in healthcare industry, and visualization helps a lot recently.

The healthcare firm currently has a free online tool that is accessible to all its distributors. This has enable distributors to simply upload available data to do demand forecasting, and to do some purchasing analysis. There is also an app for iPhone. For internal operations the company has an iPad app for its sales marketing team. The iPad app enables marketing team to read the inventory data of the company as well as that of its distributors. This help in total visualization of the distributors' activities as the marketing them is able to simulate key potential issues. For example, the team is able to simulate how a given distributors' activity affects the service level of the firm and then take needed proactive steps accordingly. Based on the accumulation experience over the years of using the internal inventory data analysis explained above, the company built an end to end supply chain, and with rich inventory data at hand, the company is very confident of handling any unexpected supply chain issues.

Industry: University Collaboration

Company A is actively engaged with a university for research in big data analysis and to explore potential opportunity in big data. The company acknowledges that engaging with University is both expensive and time consuming, though necessary. It was noted that if only one company works with one university, this would not result in a significant breakthrough in realizing the potential of big data. Most of the companies worldwide are encouraged to engage with multiple institutions to realize the benefits of opportunities in big data. Company A noted that there are many human factors that affect data collection and analysis but such factors will be greatly improved with extended and collective participation of other players. The company is currently transiting to consolidate their primary distributor to achieve a bigger logistic platform. This will enable the company to obtain more comprehensive data that can then be shared with its distributors. The company sees a very bright future and potently big business opportunity in this strategic move.

E-COMMERCE PERSPECTIVE

Big data brings in prospective opportunities to e-commerce as well as it introduces lot of challenges. The smartphone ownership which is increasing at a rapid pace also affects the data collection in business to customer e-commerce. Thus, collecting personal data is now inescapable for the e-commerce companies (Eastin, et al, 2016). The privacy should be taken into account while collecting and using data from consumers (Cleff, 2007).

Views and Challenges of Using Big Data

In this part, the views of two e-commerce companies, Company B and Company D are presented. Company B is a leading e-commerce company in China. The company's biggest challenge is not in the big data algorithm development or to share size of data sample itself but 'how to make sense of the data.' The question, according to company B is how do business people understand the data and utilize the data into practice to increase their efficiency? This, according to Company B is the key issue which is difficult to unravel. The company is now doing things like data forecasting and big data pricing which it considers providing them with right opportunities given accurate data. It however, still faces the problem of making business people understand and use the data.

Company D is a new and private cross-border e-commerce company. The company operates business to business (B to B) and business to customer (B to C) business models. In the B to B model, the company use enterprise resource planning (ERP) which is focused on cross-border e-commerce. It uses key functions like order management and logistics management to deal with the data, enable it to generate qualitatively and quantitatively competitive data. The firm also obtains other derivative business from these data such as distribution and financial business. For the B to C business model, data collection is quite difficult for Company D compared with Company B (see company B discussion above). Limited by the company size, Company B can only use some social platforms to get the activities and action nodes of its customers. The problem it faces is how to collect high quality and reliable data and how to manage such data effectively.

Visualization

Company Buse visualization at several levels. The first is on customer level where the company can capture the user portrait according to their purchasing records. This record is then used to classify and customize marketing for such customers. In offline, the company uses heatmap - a graphical data representation to represent the data matrix as colors - to analyze the addresses of its customers and accordingly organize its distribution stations and containers. The company also provides relevant after-service data and uses a visualization analysis which provides overall analysis of inventory. Visualization analysis is the second level while the third level is marketing. At marketing level, specifically in pricing, the company use big data to provide reference to business people. It uses econometric model with the data from online and offline to generate dynamic and pricing models. Additionally, the company carries out sales promotion analysis, which is almost a daily occurrence in China. In doing this, the company needs to establish which kind of promotion is most efficient and the kind of target based on their previous findings and experiences. This leads to inventory preparations using relevant resources as inputs.

Most of Company D's bid on data analysis is based on visualization because part of their data is real-time data. Results of data analyzed on their platform are provided to relevant customers. Hence, visualization is throughout the entire process.

Industry: University Collaboration

Firms suggested that collaboration with higher institutions should be encouraged. Specifically, Company B suggested willingness to facilitate Industry – university collaboration. The company however believed that it essential for academics to demonstrate the extent to which they understanding existing business models without which big data analysis will be useless. The company suggested that some leading companies in their area are now building their own eco-chain. For example, such firms now have own support ventures that is helpful to analyze their data. The company suggests the possibility of given academics access to these data as their third party. With respect to e-commerce, the company thinks it is possible to have Big Data Alliance followed by having a Big Data Alliance for supply chain. If they can facilitate the cooperation of brands and retailers at the data level, this will result in multi-party benefits.

Company D is slightly different from the other firms, according to its representative. Company D is growing in wild and unorganized manner because it failed to set up the key data constructs at the first day when they established. Currently Company D faces the problem of their data being separated and managed by different departments. Company D is ready to collaborate with relevant universities but noted key limitations such as students from universities not having requisite experience. According to the company, while students can analyze the data they are unfortunately unable to interpret such data accurately or make good business decision. The company recognizes that this will need time.

COMPUTER GRAPHICS PERSPECTIVES

Big data generate different challenges to computer graphics. Especially data visualization is not yet profitable from all the possibilities of computer graphics and the visualization of large-scale data is still a challenge, especially in the field of creating layout. How to visualize graph structures with millions of nodes is still an open question to be solved. Another challenge is the development of appropriate user interface metaphors when compared with level of details, lighting and shading, etc. which are already well understood to produce images of high quality (Encarnação & Fellner, 2015).

Views and Challenges of Using Big Data

Company C is a famous multinational company which develops computer graphics hardware and it is actually defined as a visualization company. The company has been working on big data for over 8 years now. Company C does not consider data collection as a big challenge. It knows what big data is all about, what it can be used for and the potential benefits associated with big data utilization. The company offers big data support to other firms by helping them to understand what they can do with big data and enabling them to visualize what their customers are doing or will potentially be doing based on the big data analysis

Visualization

Company C provides an example about deep learning in which an experience doctor can read 50*300days pictures(CT). However, these CT pictures can be computerized in the form of big data to integrate the intelligence of hundreds experts. The computer is therefore smarter, faster and more accurate compared with the limited ability of the human doctor. The question is how to get investment into such field? Company C suggests making least investment now to reap huge results in near future. It gave the example of Google brain in which Google invested $30,000,000 for 1000 servers to get the large amount of calculation done, but now firms only need 3 servers and about $30,000 to finish the same calculation. The initial huge investment by Google is considered as Google's contribution to global IT development. A major issue however, is that companies are not always having data to be analyzed and in most cases it needs few other technical analysis. It was noted that this is not suitable for small and medium enterprises to bank on huge investment and expertise requirements. Company C suggests firms to collaborate with universities to help them generate models which are really important to their businesses. A good partner will significantly results in more and faster results with less effort from participating partners.

University: Industry Collaboration

Company C already has working relationship with universities, and they believe that the universities needs data and companies need results. Basically the universities are keen in conducting data mining research with limited budget. Therefore collaboration with university to save them money while investing in education will make the ecosystem better.

FUTURE DIRECTIONS

In this part, we use a diagraph (see Figure 1) to show relationship between visualization (A) and challenges (B) based on the panel discussion of three industry representatives. We try to capture relationships between two major challenges. If challenges (B) increase, it will reduce the profit. However, visualization (A) will help to certain extent to increase the profit. We also analyzed the words frequency and word similarity using Nvivo 11. We analyzed the words like data, collect, col-

Figure 1. The findings of the relationship

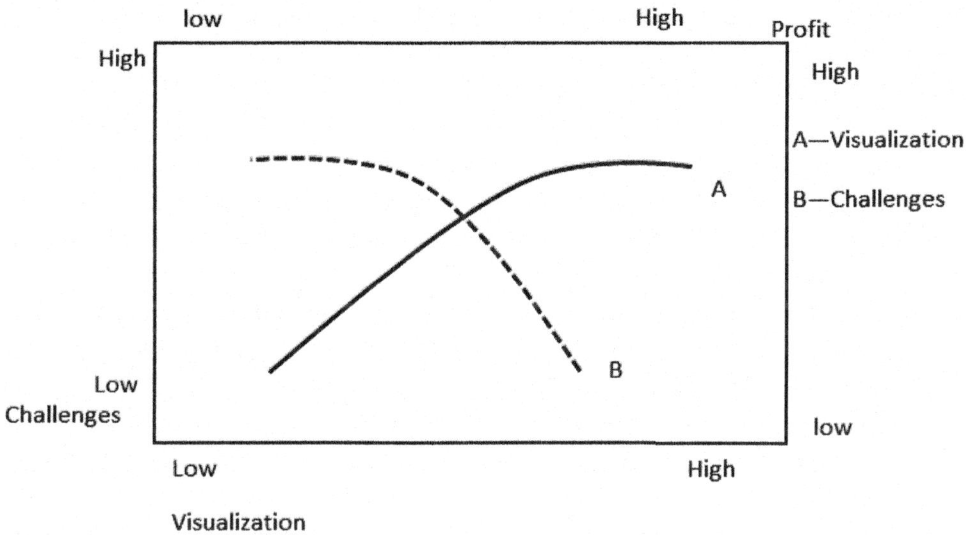

Figure 2. Word cloud

laboration, challenge, and visualization as shown in Figure 2. The results show that data is the most used word with Pearson correlation coefficient of -0.33.

Potential Research Directions

- Big data collection is a challenge and until now companies collect transaction based structured data for decision making. Even though they possess big data they can't exactly visualise because of lack of sophisticated analysis and competent data analysts.
- Other than company point of view big data collection in supply chain is a challenge. In future researchers need to explore this aspect in addition to the complicated ethical based industry.
- Creating value business models using big data is a challenge for companies
- Development of algorithm and usage of suitable techniques to visualize is not well known
- Big data has been well used to deal with operational issues at firm level but need further investigation at the strategic level.
- How to deal with human factors in data collection and to ensure quality is a serious issue?
- Dealing with privacy issues is a demanding challenge
- There is a need to develop curriculum to train students to engage them in university institution partnership.

REFERENCES

Agarwal, R., Gao, G., DesRoches, C., & Jha, A. K. (2010). Research commentary—the digital transformation of healthcare: Current status and the road ahead. *Information Systems Research*, *21*(4), 796–809. doi:10.1287/isre.1100.0327

Bekkers, R., & Bodas Freitas, I. (2008). Analysing knowledge transfer channels between universities and industry: To what degree do sectors also matter? *Research Policy*, *37*(10), 1837–1853. doi:10.1016/j.respol.2008.07.007

Bodenheimer, T. (2005). High and rising health care costs. Part 1: Seeking an explanation. *Annals of Internal Medicine*, *142*(10), 847–854. doi:10.7326/0003-4819-142-10-200505170-00010 PMID:15897535

Cleff, E. (2007). Privacy issues in mobile advertising. *International Review of Law Computers and Technology*, *21*(3), 225-236.

Eastin, M. S., Brinson, N. H., Doorey, A., & Wilcox, G. (2016). Living in a big data world: Predicting mobile commerce activity through privacy concerns. *Computers in Human Behavior, 58*, 214–220. doi:10.1016/j.chb.2015.12.050

Einav, L., & Levin, J. (2014). Economics in the age of big data. *Science, 346*(6210), 1243089. doi:10.1126/science.1243089 PMID:25378629

Encarnação, J. L., & Fellner, D. W. (2015). Computer graphics "Made in Germany" Darmstadt, the leading "Computer Graphics and Visual Computing Hub" in Europe: The way from 1975 to 2014. *Computers & Graphics, 53*, 13–27.

Herrick, D. M., Gorman, L., & Goodman, J. C. (2010). *Health Information Technology: Benefits and Problems*. Dallas, TX: National Center for Policy Analysis.

Jia, C., Wang, H., & Wei, L. (2016). Research on Visualization of Multi-Dimensional Real-Time Traffic Data Stream Based on Cloud Computing. *Procedia Engineering, 137*, 709–718. doi:10.1016/j.proeng.2016.01.308

Ker, J. I., Wang, Y., Hajli, M. N., Song, J., & Ker, C. W. (2014). Deploying lean in healthcare: Evaluating information technology effectiveness in US hospital pharmacies. *International Journal of Information Management, 34*(4), 556–560. doi:10.1016/j.ijinfomgt.2014.03.003

Khoury, M. J., & Ioannidis, J. P. A. (2014). Big data meets public health. *Science, 346*(6213), 1054–1055. doi:10.1126/science.aaa2709 PMID:25430753

Liu, J., Li, J., Li, W., & Wu, J. (2016). Rethinking big data: A review on the data quality and usage issues. *Journal of Photogrammetry and Remote Sensing, 115*, 134–142. doi:10.1016/j.isprsjprs.2015.11.006

Sharma, R., Mithas, S., & Kankanhalli, A. (2014). Transforming decision-making processes: A research agenda for understanding the impact of business analytics on organisations. *European Journal of Information Systems, 23*(4), 433–441. doi:10.1057/ejis.2014.17

Siegel, D., Waldman, D., & Link, A. (2003). Assessing the impact of organizational practices on the relative productivity of university technology transfer offices: An exploratory study. *Research Policy, 32*(1), 27–48. doi:10.1016/S0048-7333(01)00196-2

Wang, Y., Kung, L. A., & Byrd, T. A. (2015). Big data analytics: Understanding its capabilities and potential benefits for healthcare organizations. *Technological Forecasting and Social Change*. doi:10.1016/j.techfore.2015.12.019

Section 2
Big Data on Operations and Supply Chains

Chapter 3
How Smart Operations Help Better Planning and Replenishment?
Empirical Study – Supply Chain Collaboration for Smart Operations

Usha Ramanathan
Nottingham Trent University, UK

ABSTRACT

This chapter discusses various roles of smart information in Supply Chains (SC) of digital age and tries to answer an important question - What types of collaborative arrangements facilitate smart operations to improve planning, production and timely replenishment? We have conducted longitudinal case studies with firms practicing SC collaborations and also using smart information for operations. Based on the case analysis, the companies are further classified as 'smart planning' and 'traditional planning'. Research findings show the importance of aligning SC partnerships based on smart information requirements. These findings are based on case studies of Indian firms with global SC collaboration. We also discuss the role of Big Data for the companies using smart planning.

DOI: 10.4018/978-1-5225-0956-1.ch003

INTRODUCTION

In current competitive business scenario, it is widely recognized that supply chains, not individual organisations, are responsible for the success or failure of businesses. This has necessitated close relationships among supply chain (SC) members. In the past few decades, in an attempt to improve the overall performance and the efficiency of SCs, many companies have been engaged in collaboration with other SC members. Consequently, several SC management initiatives such as Vendor Managed Inventory, Efficient Consumer Response, Continuous Replenishment and Accurate Response have been proposed in the literature to improve the flow of materials as well as information (Sari, 2008; Ramanathan & Muyldermans, 2010). In this line, Collaborative Planning Forecasting and Replenishment (CPFR) is a relatively new initiative that combines the intelligence of multiple trading partners in planning and fulfilment of customers' orders by linking real time sales data and marketing best practices. In this chapter, we have used the case study approach to understand the actual level of collaboration among SC partners for information exchange. The companies (or firms) chosen for this purpose of study have global operations, maintaining SC collaborations with upstream and downstream partners. These studies are rather used to compare the supply chain collaboration (SCC) practices in information exchange and smart operations, and not intended for cross-country comparison.

In general, businesses interested in improving either cost effectiveness or overall SC performance tend to collaborate with other SC members (McIvor et al., 2003; McCarthy & Golicic, 2002; Matchette & Seikel, 2004). In this line, the businesses with similar objectives work closer to achieve the desired excellence in common SC processes such as planning, forecasting, production and replenishment (Ramanathan & Muyldermans, 2010). However, the extent and intensity of collaboration vary greatly based on individual business objectives, which in turn define the level of SC collaboration (Larsen et al., 2003, ECR Europe, 2002; Ramanathan, 2012). Precisely, the company's attitude and behaviour towards transparent information exchange in line with their business objectives decide the level of collaboration. In SC collaborative relationships, information exchange is considered an integral part of bridging all the SC members (Ramanathan & Muyldermans, 2010). While, the exchange of point-of-sales (POS) information and inventory records are widely encouraged within the SCs (Gavirneni et al., 1999; Raghunathan, 1999), the role of other real time information such as promotional plans, forecasts and production levels for planning are not much discussed in great detail in the literature. Until recently, significance of smart planning and role of social media are not explained in such a way to motivate many SC members to use and analyze big data for business enhancement.

The research study reported in this chapter explores the operations of supply chain collaboration and highlights the corresponding benefits in different firms using case studies of companies operating in 'smart planning' and 'traditional planning' environments. The main reason for considering two different types of companies is that the information exchange may or may not be important for companies operating in traditional planning (similar to make-to-stock) as the general objective of the business is selling the products in stock (both finished and work-in-progress stock). Meanwhile, in smart planning environment the production is mainly based on the real time demand or orders placed by the downstream buyers and hence there may or may not be a need for other information. In simple terms, 'smart planning' uses real time data and 'traditional planning' uses historic data. In this research, the role of information exchange among collaborating partners is analysed with a focus on its role in demand planning. Here real time data refers to the sales data, information from social media such as twitter, Facebook, on-line feedback and complaints.

The rest of the chapter is organized as follows: Section 2 explores the literature on SC information exchange and also describes the research approach of this study. Section 3 explains the research design and the role of case companies in the SCs. Section 4 discusses the cross-case analysis in detail. The role of smart information in case companies are further discussed in Section 5. Based on the importance of SC information, the role of SC collaboration is analyzed in Section 6. Finally, section 7 summarises the findings and also discusses the possible future work.

LITERATURE ON SUPPLY CHAIN INFORMATION AND RESEARCH APPROACH

Today's competitive and unpredictable business world complicates the demand planning. In many SCs, order variability increases from downstream to upstream and can result in excess inventory and huge obsolescence throughout SCs (Lee et al., 1997). To avoid such problems, information exchange and SC collaborations are encouraged in the literature. Sports Obermeyer (manufacturer of fashion skiwear) identified that the real success of a product was dependent on customers' response to the product (Fisher et al., 1994). In case of Sports Obermeyer the exchange of POS data from downstream members helped the upstream members to understand the demand patterns, which in turn assisted the future planning, production and replenishments. But any such information exchange is possible only when there is a mutual benefit for SC members on collaboration (Toktay et al., 2000).

According to CPFR, the purposes of various SC relationships are mainly of three types: production planning, information sharing and forecasting, and replenishment. Companies that collaborate for production planning may need to have cross-functional activities and clear power sharing agreements to better align their production processes (Akkermans et al., 1999; Beamon, 1999). Companies that collaborate for information sharing and forecasting may need to accept organisational changes, both internal and external to the company, to improve the performance (Barratt and Oliveira, 2001; Forme et al., 2007). This will help the SC partners in joint decision making. Companies that collaborate for timely replenishment need to maintain effective logistical performances (Simchi-Levi & Zhao, 2005; Chen & Paulraj, 2004). Most of these studies have discussed the purpose of the SC relationship, but in isolation from the effort of SC information sharing.

Lee (2002) has presented a framework that matched SC strategies with demand and supply uncertainties of both functional and innovative products. Normally, the functional products are those with stable demand patterns (Fisher, 1997). However, the demand of functional products need not be quite stable in the presence of sales promotions. In recent years, sales promotions at retail outlets have become a common practice, especially in the UK to increase normal sales. These sales promotions result in huge fluctuations in the demand pattern of the functional products in contrast to a stable demand pattern as defined in Lee (2002) and Fisher (1997). On the other hand, to execute sales promotions, active participation from all SC partners is highly critical. The SC collaboration may be a good option to improve the agility in SCs (Aviv, 2007). This is mainly because the CPFR framework encourages transparent information exchange as one of the key elements of collaboration (VICS, 2002). This particular aspect of information exchange in SC collaborations is considered further in this research to identify the role of information exchange in SC processes.

In contrast to traditional SC practices, today's SC management is more transparent to all SC operators. Healthy collaborative arrangements among SC partners have been proved to be a successful integral part of many world-class businesses such as Wal-Mart, Sara Lee, Nabisco etc (Lee, 2002). Following the successful adoption of CPFR in the US, many companies around the globe have tested the collaborative partnerships in SCs (Seifert, 2003). In this effort of collaboration, transparent information exchange among SCs hopes to reduce uncertainty and avoid excess inventory (Holweg et al., 2005; Chen et al., 2000).

Initially at the inception of CPFR, understanding of the collaboration process and the framework to collaborate have been considered the two basic requirements for a collaborative SC (Barratt & Oliveira, 2001; Ramanathan et al., 2011). In later stages, the information sharing has been recognised as one of the key elements for the success of the collaboration (Seifert, 2003). Li and Wang (2007) asserted that the benefit of information sharing is dependent on two factors: one is content and another is proper use of information. Distorted information due to behavioural issues (such as lack of trust and less-transparent business operations) and an inefficient use of available data will lead to poor business performance such as excess inventory in each level of the SCs (Nyaga et al., 2010). Hence, it will be important for the collaborating companies to decide on what information to exchange in order to reduce costs, to create more accurate demand forecasts, to make flexible production plans, and also to achieve timely replenishments (Ramanathan & Muyldermans, 2010).

Once the information is in place, data analysis is another important aspect for the companies to plan and decide. Sharing of demand information with upstream members can help reducing the manufactures' SC cost (Raghunathan, 1999) and also can reduce the inventory cost of both supplier and buyer (Gavirneni, et al., 1999, Lee, et al., 2000; Graves, 1999). Sharing demand information along with current inventory status facilitates achieving reductions in inventory cost (Chen 1998; Cachon & Fisher, 2000). Depending on the data analysis capabilities (technology and manpower) of the parties involved, the benefit of information sharing will also range from basic inventory reduction to higher profit earning. The manufacturer can reduce the variance in demand forecasts if POS data and market-data-sharing are found influential in achieving forecast accuracy. A more detailed discussion on the value of information sharing in SCs is given in Li et al. (2005). Sanders and Premus (2005) attempted to model the relationship between firms' IT capability, collaboration and performance.

Most of the above discussed literature lists the benefits of exchanging POS or inventory data but not any other real time information such as social media data. Recognizing the types of information to be shared among SC members to build-in more visibility is a big challenge in achieving collaboration (Barratt & Oliveira, 2001). Ryu et al. (2009) presented a simulation study on the evaluation of SC information (SCI) sharing. They compared the value of exchanging short term forecasts and long-term forecasts among SC players. Under high demand variability, long-term forecasts analysis performed better than short-term forecasts analysis. Accordingly, under low demand variability, short-term forecasts analysis performed better than long-term forecasts analysis. Using store level SKU data, Ali et al. (2009) found that simple time series forecasting will be appropriate for normal sales without promotions. They suggested using advanced analysis techniques for sophisticated input to improve forecast accuracy of promotional sales. See Table 1 for more literature on information sharing in SCs for various purposes.

While most of the articles supported sharing the POS data for cost reduction and forecasting, a study in Japanese manufacturing sector by Nakano (2009) claimed that internal forecasting analysis (with-in the firm), but not external collaborative forecasting (with other SC players), had significant impact on logistics and production performance. However, his structural equation model results identified a positive relationship between internal forecasting analysis and planning, and external (upstream/downstream) collaborative forecasting. Sometimes the POS data may distract decision making particularly if the product demand is highly fluctuating

Table 1. Literature on purpose of information sharing

Authors	Information	Purpose
Bourland et al. (1996)	Inventory	Minimising inventory cost
Cachon and Fisher (1997)	Historical data (no need to invest)	Decision on technology investment
Chen (1998)	Demand and inventory	Minimising total inventory cost
Gavireneni et al. (1999)	POS and Inventory	Minimising inventory cost
Cachon and Fisher (2000)	Demand and inventory	Minimising inventory cost
Lee et al.(2000); Smaros (2007)	Demand information	Minimising inventory cost ; Demand forecast
Raghunathan (2001)	Order history (no need to invest)	Decision on technology investment
Kulp et al. (2004)	Demand information (Asymmetric)	Improve supplier benefit
Byrne and Heavey (2006)	Inventory, sales, order status, sales forecast, production/ delivery schedule	Total SC cost saving
Chang et al.(2007)	POS & market data	Improve responsiveness to demand fluctuations
Ketzenberg (2009)	Demand, recovery yield, capacity utilisation	Capacity utilisation showed more value than any other information in a capacitated closed loop SC.
Ryu et al. (2009)	Demand information	Study changes in inventory level and service level
Ali et al. (2009)	SKU-store level data	Forecast promotions
Ramanathan and Muyldermans (2010); Ramanathan (2012)	Electronic point of sales data	Improve promotional sales forecasting and help managers to identify the actual demand factors

(Steckel et al., 2004). Aviv (2001; 2007), using mathematical models, proved that collaborative forecasting (CF) could improve the forecast accuracy of products with short lead times and also CF could improve the overall performance of SC by about four percentage. However, depending on other factors, such as explanatory power of the SC partners, the supply side agility, and the internal service rate, the performance improvement will differ (Aviv, 2007).

The quality of the information exchanged among the SC partners is another important factor of analysis that decides the performance. The overall SC performance has been proved higher with high quality information from SC partners (Forsuland & Jonsson, 2007; Zhao et al., 2002). But, obtaining the high quality information in the SC requires a high level of cooperation and trust among various players (Barratt and Oliveria, 2001; Fliedner, 2003). Good inter-organisational communication among various SC players is therefore necessary (Paulraj et al., 2008). This inter-organisational communication is vital especially during sales promotions to achieve good forecast accuracy because the buying behaviour of customers are influenced by various factors (Sun, 2005). Identifying the underlying demand factors using SCI can help improving the accuracy of demand forecasting, particularly for promotional sales (Ramanathan & Muyldermans, 2011; Danese & Kalchschmidt, 2011). In 21st century, companies operating in high competitive markets are using Big data, especially social media data, to understand demand fluctuations, to identify issues with product/delivery and also to analyse the customer needs.

Further in this research, case analyses of five manufacturing and processing companies unveil the operations of SC collaborations with a special focus to information exchange for demand planning and hence supports the decision making.

RESEARCH DESIGN AND CASE DESCRIPTIONS

Research Design and Case Studies

We employ a case study approach to understand the extent of collaborative arrangements of manufacturers/suppliers with downstream SC members. In this effort, companies operating in different environments such as 'smart planning' and 'traditional planning' are studied. As suggested by Yin (1994), in this research five different types of cases are considered for descriptive analysis (Table 2). However, all these multiple cases are chosen under a single unit of analysis namely SCI exchange for data analysis (Voss et al., 2002). All the five case companies practice SC

Table 2. Research plan for case studies

		Complexity of Planning	
		Easy to Plan	**Difficult to Plan**
Type of Environments	**Smart Planning**	Petroleum Company	Textile Company Electrical Company Frozen-food Company
	Traditional Planning	Packaging Company Electrical Company Frozen-food Company	Textile Company

collaboration with downstream customers. We have used a three stage approach to analyses the cases under study:

Stage 1: Understand the operations using real-time information for planning and decision making
Stage 2: Critically analyze the modifications made in the operations' planning and decision making in line with the SC information
Stage 3: Compare the changes made in planning & decision making in the presence and the absence of the SC information

We have further classified the products of the case companies based on the level of difficulty of demand planning (Ramanathan, 2012). From the case study observations, based on the demand forecasts accuracy we classify the products into two categories – 'easy to plan' and 'difficult to plan'. 'Easy to plan' represents 'planning matching with execution' (for example timely replenishment) with accuracy of 50% and above. The planning accuracy of products falling below 50% has been considered as 'difficult to plan'. From the cases studied, it has been identified that the products are following two main types of planning – 'smart planning' and 'traditional planning'. Hence, this research analyses the cases in two main dimensions, namely type of planning and complexity of planning due to demand variability (easy to plan and difficult to plan) (see Table 2).

Case Descriptions

Study 1: Frozen-Food Manufacturer

The first case involved a leading frozen food manufacturer, Frozen-food Co and some of their customers (retailers and wholesalers), located in the UK and Europe. The case company produces a variety of 'ready-made' food and sells those products through major retailers in the UK and European countries. Frozen-food Company is involved in various promotional sales and hence it maintains a healthy collaborative relationship with their customers. The demand planning complicates at the time of promotional sales. In this study, the main focus is relation between Frozen-food Company with its downstream partners and the role of SCI exchange. The company uses quarterly point of sale data and order demand information for planning delivery.

Study 2: Fashion Textile Material Manufacturer

The second case study involves a manufacturer of textile materials, Textile Company, situated in India. They export their products to many countries around the world. The company produces both customised and standard textile materials. The company collaborates with their downstream partners for information exchange and replenishment. Since 2006, the company has been involved in a formal collaborative arrangement with some of its customers in the USA (Wal-Mart and Jo-Ann stores). The company uses the latest communication technology for quick data transfer. Information technology and data transfer are of prime importance for this company to compete in the competitive market. For repeat orders with standard product specification, the company follows traditional planning. Although the company is involved in both traditional and smart planning, decision making at times of complexity seems to be under strict control of top management.

Study 3: Petroleum Company: Refiners and Distributors

The third case study was conducted in a Petroleum company who refines and distributes crude oil within India. This company owns and operates the largest refinery in the country producing crude oils of international standards. With a capacity of 335,000 Metric Tonnes per annum this refinery accounts for over 40% of the country's total oil production. The company has retail outlets all over the country. The case study was conducted at its main distribution centre. This company has just one primary supplier; while it has many customers. The case company is a main distributor for the products namely Gasoline, High Speed Diesel, Superior Kerosene Oil, Furnace Oil, Light Diesel Oil, and Aviation Turbine Fuel. The customers of the company are mostly distributors to many other private and public customers. The company has strong SC collaborations with both the upstream and the downstream partners. Real time information exchange between the company and their clients is mainly used for timely replenishments and placing orders.

Study 4: Packaging Material Manufacturer

Packaging Company is a manufacturer of packing materials, situated in India. This company was established in 1966 in India and has four manufacturing plants across the country. The products of the company include Jumbo size bags for - the petrochemical industry, the mineral industry, the dyeing industry and the pharmaceutical industry. This firm has manufacturing plants in four different locations in India. The products of Packaging Company are being used by their customers to export the goods and machinery internationally. The company manufactures to stock and also to orders. The company's communication with their customers is mainly through the recent online technology namely iMail Server. The company's recent upgrade of communication technology has removed earlier communication difficulties and has helped avoiding replenishment delays. This smart information is being used for ad-hoc planning. However, main planning of the company considers using historical data.

Study 5: Flame Proof Electrical Equipment Manufacturer

The fifth case study is about an electrical equipment manufacturing company, Electrical Company. This is a privately owned Electrical Engineering Company based in Melbourne, Australia. Since 1949, the company has been functioning as a manufacturer and supplier of Explosion Protected Lighting and Electrical equipment of high quality for domestic and international markets. Their products are used by oil companies in Australia and are exported to over 20 countries in the Asia-pacific and Middle East regions. Due to its global operations, the company has manufacturing plants and distribution centers across the world. We have conducted this study in India. This company uses two different approach of planning depending on facilities available in their client base as not many clients are having smart technology for instant information exchange.

The interviews with all five case companies have been conducted in different periods of time with top and middle managers. A list of the main contacts, the period of interviews, the number of personal and telephonic interviews is shown in Table 3. The prime focus in this research is to better understand the collaborative arrangement and information exchange with downstream partners in each of the companies, to facilitate the process of demand planning including production and replenishment. Interviews and company visits helped to understand the SCI for demand analysis and also to understand the use of SCI in planning and its further role in firm's decision making. Since quantitative sales information were made available only by some companies, in this research, we have not attempted to compare the benefit of collaboration in terms of sales.

The purpose of collaboration in the case companies is mainly to forecast and/or plan timely replenishment. Accordingly, each of the case companies differs in its information need, which is analysed further by comparing each of the cases with the other company on various attributes.

CROSS-CASE ANALYSIS

Table 4 reports the case study details of all of the five cases considered in this research. This cross case detail outlines the products of the company in the environment of 'smart planning' and 'traditional planning'. The supplier base of Petroleum Company and Frozen-food Company are local operators, while the other companies

Table 3. Details of case company interviews

Company	Main Contact	Period	No. of (Face-to-Face) Interviews	No. of Telephone Interviews	Total Hours
Frozen-food Company	Planning Manager	2012	2	-	6
	Customer Demand Analyst				
Fashion textile Company	Secretary to MD*	2007-2009; 2011;2015	6	5	12
	Planning Manager				
Petroleum Company	Distribution Manager	2007-2008;2011	3	1	6
	Logistics Manager				
Packaging Company	Managing Director	2007-2009;2012	6	3	12
	Planning Manager				
	Demand Analyst				
Electrical Company	Operations Manager	2007-2008	3	0	5
	Distribution Manager				
				Total hours of interview	**41**

*people at different positions were interviewed

have global supply base. Except Petroleum Company all of the other companies have more than 5 suppliers. Customers of Petroleum Company are operating locally within the countries. However, all of the other companies are also dealing with global customers. This necessitates intense information exchange. Some products of the case companies are considered as functional while textile products are considered as fashion driven and electrical products are considered as innovative. All the companies have more than 5 product lines with more than 15 stock keeping units (SKU).

Frozen-food Company is the newest companies of all the cases considered. Petroleum Co. is in the market for more than 50 years with mature products, while the life cycle stage of other products are either in mature or growth stage. This classification of product life cycle is given by the company based on the products. The shelf life of all of the products varies from 2 days to 2 years and more. The production and distribution lead time also varies widely from 2 days to 6 months. Except Petroleum Co. all the companies have low supply uncertainty. But demand uncertainty of promotional products is quite high while demand varies from low to medium for other products under 'smart planning' and 'traditional planning' environ-

Table 4. Case study details

	Frozen-Food Co. Study-1	Textile Co. Study-2	Petroleum Co. Study-3	Packaging Co. Study-4	EEM Co. Study-5
Planning Environment	Traditional	40% Smart 60% Traditional	Smart	Traditional	75% Smart 25% Traditional
Location of suppliers **Number of suppliers**	India 7-15	Yarn: India Machinery: Switzerland, Italy 10-30	India 1	Jute: India Paper: India Machinery: India, Japan 5-15	India, Australia 5-10
Location of customers **Number of customers** **Type of customers**	UK and Europe > 4000 Retailers	Europe, USA, UK, Dubai, Abu Dhabi, & India > 200 Wholesalers/ Retailers	India > 2000 Distributors wholesalers/ retailers	India, Japan (more than 100 Customers) >100 OEM/ Wholesalers	India, Australia, Thailand, Malaysia, Korea, Japan, Iran, Australia, Indonesia, Saudi Arabia, Qatar, India > 50 OEM/Wholesalers
Product type	Functional	Fashion driven	Functional	Functional	Innovative
Number of product lines/ product families	10	5	6	5	5
Number of SKUs	>80	>50	>15	Unlimited	Unlimited
Product life cycle length	Very long	Short	Very long	Long	Short or Medium
Product life cycle stage	Growth / Mature	Growth	Mature	Growth	Growth
Product shelf life (Short/ Medium/ Very long)	2 days - 9 months (Short)	2 - 6 months (Short)	Very long	1-2 years (Medium)	Very long
Total lead time	3 days – 2 weeks	6 weeks – 8 weeks	Real time basis (refining 24 hours)	3-4 days (excluding logistics)	One week – six months
Supply uncertainty	Low	Low	Medium	Low	Low
Demand uncertainty	Normal sales-Low Promotions-High	Normal sales-Low Promotions-High	Low	Low	MTS-Medium MTO- Low
Main reasons for demand fluctuation	Promotions	Promotions, seasons, trend	Price, new vehicles and new customers	Government policy and new product introduction of downstream partners	New projects and new regulations on safety products

continued on following page

Table 4. Continued

	Frozen-Food Co. Study-1	Textile Co. Study-2	Petroleum Co. Study-3	Packaging Co. Study-4	EEM Co. Study-5
Main reasons for collaboration with downstream members	Promotions Timely replenishment	Promotions Timely replenishment	Timely replenishment	N/A	N/A
Main reasons for collaboration with upstream members	Timely replenishment	Timely replenishment	Timely replenishment	Timely replenishment New projects information	Timely replenishment New projects information
Purpose/ information exchange	Planning Replenishment	Planning Replenishment	Replenishment	Replenishment	Replenishment
Technology used to communicate and for information exchange	Web based	Advanced communication: Blackberry for all partners and workers to check email; kiwi to contact Switzerland and Germany, Skype to communicate with UK and USA.	Advanced automated inventory status, emails, web server, SMS, phone and fax	Simple communication: Telephone, fax and emails	Simple communication: Telephone, fax and emails, web based information exchange is under development to check inventory position.
Important information exchanged - downstream	Promotion plans, inventory, price, delivery time, order, feedback	Promotional sales discount, trend, seasonal, order, replenishment plans inventory, local forecast, feedback	Inventory, replenishment plans, order, feedback	Inventory, production, order, local forecast	Inventory, production, order, local forecast, Feedback and complaints
Information used in forecasting	Historical sales promotional plans, local forecast, special days	Historical sales promotional plans, local forecast, seasons and trend	Historical sales	Historic sales	N/A
Information used in replenishment	Sales forecast and inventory status	Historical sales, discount, trend, production, logistics, Government policy	Inventory status	Inventory status	Inventory status

ment. Both demand and supply uncertainty are classified as low or medium or high based on the products.

The use of SCI for forecasting and replenishment is different for all these companies. This is mainly because the main purposes of collaboration in each of the case companies are of two types - promotional planning and timely replenishment. The companies involved in promotional sales (Frozen-food Company and Textile Company) exchange detailed information with downstream partners for planning and forecasting analysis while the others exchange limited or less detailed information with downstream partners and it is mainly for timely replenishment. To facilitate such information exchange, each of the case companies is engaged in different levels of SC collaborations with downstream SC partners. Frozen-food. and Textile Company are involved in intense SCI exchange with downstream partners especially for promotional sales. However, frozen-food Company has not invested in real-time information exchange due to financial constraints. But still it is trying to use web-based low cost technology to maximize the information exchange.

ROLE OF SMART INFORMATION

Some of the case companies studied use selective SCI for planning, forecasting and replenishment, while the others use commonly or easily available SCI for planning the daily operations. For example, the historical sales information is used by the Frozen-food Company for planning and forecasting and POS data is used for replenishment; however, the sales information is used mainly for the long-term planning in Packaging Company but not for the short term-planning.

The products of all of the cases studied can be classified under two main categories 'smart planning' and 'traditional planning'. Planning and forecasting of petroleum products is rather simple in comparison to the other companies. Hence, these products are further classified, based on the level of difficulty in demand planning, into 'easy to plan' and 'difficult to plan'. It is important to note that the short term forecasting is more important for products, such as standard packaging materials and frozen-food, than other products. This is because in a traditional environment, orders are received from customers and hence the demand is known. In this case, the demand forecast is important to avoid the bullwhip effect (Lee et al., 1997). Accurate demand forecasts can also help reducing stock-out and excess inventory. Based on the levels of difficulty in demand planning, different forecasting approaches are applied.

Currently, Frozen-food Company uses simple forecasting technique, and the company gets irregular orders from its suppliers (from European buyers). This leaves the company from not benefitting by the quantity discounts offered by logistics operators (i.e. when orders are placed as full truck loads). Planning manager of the company expressed his views as:

We understand that we could save at least 15% of our logistics cost by making use of full load or economic order quantity. Currently we place orders to our suppliers as and when we get orders from our buyers. However, in future we will try and use real time information and demand forecasts to place our orders that will help us to avail discounts on full truck load, offered by our logistics partners.

Interview with frozen-food gave a clear indication of its plan of using - the simple forecasting techniques, namely moving average to predict the demand and Economic order quantity (EOQ) models to order a full truck load in obtaining price discount. Companies would benefit from reduced inventory levels, while maintaining high service and at the same time earning the quantity discounts when it would engage in a closer collaboration for example with suppliers of frozen-food. That collaboration could involve making end customer demand visible, applying simple forecasting procedures and EOQ policies (with possibly joint replenishments for the slow-moving items) and perhaps even engaging in a VMI arrangement with suppliers.

Petroleum Company maintains a good collaborative relationship with down-stream SC partners so as to make timely replenishments. A highlighting point on forecasting from a Logistics Manager of the company is

We do not want to spend a huge amount of time and money in forecasting as our supply source is limited. Our daily sales records make us prepared for future timely replenishments.

Currently, Petroleum Company exercises VMI and inventory pooling with some retail customers. This inventory pooling facility can be extended to others to obtain full benefit of SC collaboration. Demand variability of products at Petroleum Co. is low, and hence the demand for these two products can be determined by simple fore-casting techniques, for example, moving average or exponential smoothing method.

From the cases, it is clear that the SC companies, manufacturing frozen-food products and textile products, are difficult to forecast when sales promotions are offered by retailers. To forecast these products, different demand factors need to be identified (Ramanathan and Muyldermans, 2011). More sophisticated planning and decision tools can be used to better match the demand with explanatory factors (Ramanathan, 2012). It is possible to say the products that are 'difficult to plan' can combine both traditional quantitative data and other quantitative social media data for analysis and decision making. This can help the company to improve demand planning and timely replenishment (see Table 5). Difficult to plan situation will arise in the following cases:

- **Sales Promotions:** Frozen-food and textile Company.
- **Products with Short Shelf Life or Short Life Cycle:** Textile Company for fashion driven products.
- **After Market Spare Parts:** Electric Company for maintenance revamping and overhauling.

The demand for petroleum and crude oil are mostly stable and smooth. Hence, it should be easy for Petroleum Co. to forecast the demand using standard forecasting techniques such as exponential smoothing or moving average method. However, SC collaboration with downstream partners is essential to make end customers' demand visible and also to ensure timely replenishments.

The companies operating in 'Traditional environment' such as Packaging Company and Electrical Company do not make any short-term plans using the SCI from downstream partners. SCI from downstream partners is normally used to make long term forecasts and material resource planning. From the above discussions, we can understand that the type of companies, classified based on the number of echelons, will not necessarily have a common planning requirement. The complexity of order fluctuations based on the end-demand normally helps to identify the SC collaborative arrangement for planning. Based on the current practices of SCs, we discuss the SC collaboration appropriate to each of these case companies further in the next section.

Table 5. Suggested SC collaboration

		Complexity of Planning	
		Easy to Plan	**Difficult to Plan**
Type of Environments	Smart Planning	• Use standard forecasting techniques for demand planning • Make end customer demand visible • Use VMI to ensure timely replenishment	• Use Big data to identify demand factors • Analyse data for decision making • Use SCC for transparent information exchange
	Traditional Planning	• Use SCC to know demand information	• Make end customer demand visible • Involve SC partners in planning and decision making

SUPPLY CHAIN COLLABORATION IN THE CASE COMPANIES

New Managerial Approach for Current Practices

Frozen-food Company maintains a good collaborative relationship with downstream partners, especially retailers. But, the promotional sales information is not well communicated in all cases. This is reflected in the high order variability. By establishing collaboration with up- and downstream partners, the company can improve the visibility of end customer demand. Engaging in a VMI arrangement could be highly beneficial (regular replenishment of orders in full truck loads). In order to achieve this VMI arrangement, the company needs to have reliable staff representatives working in close relationships with European retailers.

Textile Company believes that establishing the basic communication at transactional level is enough with new customers or relatively new customers (Ramanathan, 2012). Currently, Textile Company motivates existing customers for future collaboration through offering free samples. If these 'free samples' sell quickly in the local market, customers may plan the future promotion in collaboration with Textile Company. The communication between the two parties concentrates on promotional sales only. In other words, the information exchange between Textile Company and their customers is elaborate at the time of promotions but restricted at all the other times. This relationship on promotional sales can generally be extended by the company further on future business expansions. As this company is also seeking customer feedback, this qualitative information can be fed into the process of decision making.

Petroleum Company has well established collaboration and VMI with downstream partners (nearly 20 percent customers) to ensure timely replenishment. This arrangement can be extended further for the remaining customers. Electrical and Packaging Companies do not maintain well established downstream SC collaboration for a few customers with irregular orders as they do not find much value on downstream SCI. These two companies can think of establishing both downstream and upstream SC collaboration. As most of the products are manufacturing to orders, the collaboration with upstream SC partners may help the companies to have raw materials on time for production.

All the case companies studied are using POS data for demand forecasting analysis and social media data for understanding the market. Reviews, complaints and feedback are main concerns of the company managements for planning and quality improvements (long-term plans). In case of the Textile Company, social media comments are of high importance for product design development and delivery.

The suggestions made in this section (see Table 5) have been conveyed to the case companies. Later at the time of writing this chapter that was nearly after three years of conducting the case studies, we were informed by the companies that they were progressing well in the SCI and demand planning, after adopting the suggested levels of SC collaborations.

New Perspectives of SC Collaboration

This research has considered functional products, fashion products and innovative products in two different environments. However, the demand fluctuations of functional products are not the same for all cases considered in this study. Some companies have promotional sales as a regular feature of business strategy. The cases considered for this study included both functional products (frozen-food products) and fashion driven products (textile products). According to Lee (2002) functional products will have low demand variability compared to innovative (fashion apparels) products. However, the demand patterns are highly fluctuating for these two products as the sales are affected by promotions. Analysis of these cases suggested considering all possible SCI to improve forecasting and replenishment. Hence, for Textile and Frozen-food Company a high level collaboration with downstream SC partners will be beneficial. In simple terms, supply chain collaboration with information exchange for smart operations will be ideal for these two companies.

Demand for crude oil or petroleum products are easy to predict and hence planning is not complicated. In this case information from downstream SC partners is required to ensure timely replenishment. Information exchange includes aggregated demand and inventory status. Based on stock levels, the replenishment can be made on time. Hence, vendor managed inventory (VMI) is suggested for these types of companies. Demand planning of products of Packaging Co. and EEM Co. do not benefit much by information from downstream SC partners. Hence, transactional level of collaboration is found beneficial by these two companies. In summary, it is possible to conclude that the environments where planning is difficult, require a high level of collaboration with downstream SC partners (e.g. CPFR), the environments where planning is easy require a medium level of collaboration with downstream SC partners. The companies with smart planning can achieve timely delivery with the help of SC collaboration and inventory can be managed by vendors. Here, it is also ideal to use the social media data to make any adjustment on original plans of delivery based on current real-time difficulties. Recent conversation with Textile Company in 2015 revealed that the company has started using social media data, especially Facebook and twitter, in their planning and delivery operations to improve operational performance of the company.

While the previous literature identified that different levels and degrees of collaboration were possible (Larsen et al, 2003; Danese, 2007; Ramanathan, 2012), this current research related SCI with type of planning and its level of complexity to decide on the appropriate level of SC collaboration. Our research has answered a main research question on types of collaborative arrangements and forecasting approaches in SCs. This can be considered as one of the key contributions to the literature.

CONCLUSION AND FUTURE RESEARCH

All the cases analysed were of two types: Planning with traditional approach and planning with smart information. In the traditional planning environment, SCI from downstream partners helped short-term forecasting and replenishments. In the smart planning environment, SCI from downstream partners was used for both long-term and short-term forecasting and planning. It has been largely agreed that the use of Vendor Managed Inventory will be sufficiently supporting the replenishment when planning is easy with smart information. The demand planning is complicated for some companies even in the presence of smart information due to its complex nature of operations. Those companies can involve in high level 'futuristic' SC collaboration with transparent information exchange (Ramanathan, 2012). Adapting web-based collaborative tool, such as CPFR, is one of the options to have high level of SCC with real-time data. In the cases we considered some products with traditional planning approach were easy to plan while the others were difficult to plan. Easy to plan products, following traditional approach of planning, can be controlled by planning with the help of knowing demand information. However, 'difficult to plan' environment following traditional planning approach will warrant support from downstream SC partners in order to obtain detailed demand information. In this case, higher level of information exchange (such as Big data) and data analysis can be used in planning and decision making.

Significant results have emerged from this research. The results strongly support SC collaboration in traditional planning environments with promotional sales. It is also evident that the exchange of detailed sales information from downstream to upstream SC members might improve the accuracy of demand forecasts. Information exchange is also required to ensure timely replenishment. Lucrative benefits of collaboration encourage many SC members to initiate the process of collaboration. This is reflected in recent SCs having information exchange as one of the core processes in a formal or less formal collaboration (Chang *et al.*, 2007). Some companies use the demand forecast information in other SC processes to operational performance (Danese and Kalchschmidt, 2011). It is widely agreed by academics and practitioners (Fisher, 1997; Lee, 2002) that in order to achieve good SC performance, it is essential to have collaboration among SC members. This research has identified the need for SC collaboration in all cases. But high level of data requirement is identified for companies operating in a high competition and volatile market. In these cases information from SC members may not be sufficient to sustain the market and hence the concept of Big Data of combining qualitative and quantitative sales data will support planning operations and replenishment. It is also important to consider future investments on Big Data carefully for data use and information sharing in relation to the profitability.

The data analysis and further consultation of companies, namely Packaging Co. and EEM Co., helped to point out that the short term planning is not so important because the company receives orders from customers, hence demand is known. But material requirements planning is vital to ensure compliance with due dates and also to make sure the company get raw materials from its suppliers on time. A close relationship with upstream SC members may help them to have smooth production process with shorter lead times and also to ensure timely replenishment. Supply side collaboration with smart operations may assist companies in

- Resource planning.
- Supplier selection based on lead time/quality/reliability.
- Real-time information exchange including sales data and social media data.
- Delivery plans.

Future research on supply side (upstream) collaboration can potentially guide the managers to decide on what information needs to be exchanged with upstream SC partners. Such information exchange can guide them to decide on whether to make or buy raw materials required for production. For example, Packaging Co. is currently producing its raw material (fabric). But in case of urgent orders, to reduce lead time the company buy fabric from other suppliers. SC collaboration with upstream partners may be particularly interesting in certain environments with a complex supply base and stringent capacity constraints (necessitating frequent make or buy decisions).

This research was based on case companies producing functional, fashion driven and innovative products. To make the findings of these cases more general, a larger number of cases need to be analyzed, considering other environments. Cases similar to Saturn's after-market spare parts and Sports Obermeyer can be considered (Cohen et al., 2000; Fisher et al., 1994). Future research can also include companies with difficulty in planning and forecasting in the presence of Big Data. This will help to draw a general conclusion on the information need in different SCs in different manufacturing environments.

REFERENCES

Akkermans, H., Bogerd, P., & Vos, B. (1999). Virtuous and vicious cycles on the road towards international supply chain management. *International Journal of Operations & Production Management*, *19*(5/6), 565–581. doi:10.1108/01443579910260883

Ali, Ö. G., Sayın, S., Woensel, T., & Fransoo, J. (2009). SKU demand forecasting in the presence of promotions. *Expert Systems with Applications*, *36*(10), 12340–12348. doi:10.1016/j.eswa.2009.04.052

Aviv, Y. (2001). The effect of collaborative forecasting on supply chain performance. *Management Science*, *47*(10), 1326–1343. doi:10.1287/mnsc.47.10.1326.10260

Aviv, Y. (2007). On the benefits of collaborative forecasting partnerships between retailers and manufacturers. *Management Science*, *53*(5), 777–794. doi:10.1287/mnsc.1060.0654

Barratt, M., & Oliveira, A. (2001). Exploring the experiences of collaborative planning initiatives. *International Journal of Physical Distribution & Logistics Management*, *31*(4), 266–289. doi:10.1108/09600030110394932

Beamon, B. M. (1999). Measuring supply chain performance. *International Journal of Operations & Production Management*, *19*(3/4), 275–292. doi:10.1108/01443579910249714

Bourland, K. E., Powell, S. G., & Pyke, D. F. (1996). Exploiting timely demand information to reduce inventories. *European Journal of Operational Research*, *92*(2), 239–253. doi:10.1016/0377-2217(95)00136-0

Byrne, P. J., & Heavey, C. (2006). The impact of information sharing and forecasting in capacitated industrial supply chains: A case study. *International Journal of Production Economics*, *103*(1), 420–437. doi:10.1016/j.ijpe.2005.10.007

Cachon, G. P., & Fisher, M. (1997). Campbell soups continuous product replenishment program: Evaluation and enhanced decision rules. *Production and Operations Management*, *6*, 266–275. doi:10.1111/j.1937-5956.1997.tb00430.x

Cachon, G. P., & Fisher, M. (2000). Supply chain inventory management and the value of shared information. *Management Science*, *46*(8), 1032–1048. doi:10.1287/mnsc.46.8.1032.12029

Chang, T., Fu, H., Lee, W., Lin, Y., & Hsueh, H. (2007). A study of an augmented CPFR model for the 3C retail industry. *Supply chain management. International Journal (Toronto, Ont.)*, *12*, 200–209.

Chen, F. (1998). Echelon reorder points, installation re-order points, and the value of centralized demand information. *Management Science*, *44*(12), 221–234. doi:10.1287/mnsc.44.12.S221

Chen, F., Drezner, Z., Ryan, J. K., & Simchi-Levi, D. (2000). Quantifying the Bullwhip effect in a simple supply chain: The impact of forecasting, lead times and information. *Management Science*, *46*(3), 436–443. doi:10.1287/mnsc.46.3.436.12069

Chen, I. J., & Paulraj, A. (2004). Towards a theory of supply chain management: The constructs and measurements. *Journal of Operations Management*, *22*(2), 119–150. doi:10.1016/j.jom.2003.12.007

Cohen, M. A., Cull, C., Lee, H. L., & Willen, D. (2000). Saturn's supply-Chain Innovation: High Value in After-Sales Service. *Sloan Management Review*, *41*(4), 93–101.

Danese, P. (2007). Designing CPFR collaborations: Insights from seven case studies. *International Journal of Operations & Production Management*, *27*(2), 181–204. doi:10.1108/01443570710720612

Danese, P., & Kalchschmidt, M. (2011). The role of the forecasting process in improving forecast accuracy and operational performance. *International Journal of Production Economics*, *131*(1), 204–214. doi:10.1016/j.ijpe.2010.09.006

Europe, E. C. R. (2002). European CPFR Insights. ECR European facilitated by Accenture, Brussels.

Fisher, M. L. (1997). What is the right supply chain for your product? *Harvard Business Review*, *75*(2), 105–116.

Fisher, M. L., Hammond, J. H., Obermeyer, W. R., & Raman, A. (1994, May-June). Making supply meet demand in an uncertain world. *Harvard Business Review*, 83–93.

Fliedner, G. (2003). CPFR: An emerging supply chain tool. *Industrial Management + Data Systems, 103*(1/2), 14-21.

Forme, F. G. L., Genoulaz, V. B., & Campagne, J. P. (2007). A framework to analyse collaborative performance. *Computers in Industry*, *58*(7), 687–697. doi:10.1016/j.compind.2007.05.007

Gavirneni, S., Kapuscinski, R., & Tayur, S. (1999). Value of information in capacitated supply chains. *Management Science*, *45*(1), 16–24. doi:10.1287/mnsc.45.1.16

Graves, S.C. (1999). A single-item inventory model for a non-stationary demand process. *Manufacturing and Service operations Management, 1*(2), 50-61.

Holweg, M., Disney, S., Holmström, J., & Småros, J. (2005). Supply Chain Collaboration: Making Sense of the Strategy Continuum. *European Management Journal, 23*(2), 170–181. doi:10.1016/j.emj.2005.02.008

Ireland, R. K., & Crum, C. (2005). *Supply chain collaboration: How to implement CPFR and other best collaborative practices. J.* Ross Publishing Inc.

Ketzenberg, M. (2009). The value of information in a capacitated closed loop supply chain. *European Journal of Operational Research, 198*(2), 491–503. doi:10.1016/j.ejor.2008.09.028

Kulp, S. C., Lee, H. L., & Ofek, E. (2004). Manufacturer Benefits from Information Integration with Retail Customers. *Management Science, 50*(4), 431–444. doi:10.1287/mnsc.1030.0182

Larsen, T. S., Thenoe, C., & Andresen, C. (2003). Supply chain collaboration: Theoretical perspectives and empirical evidence. *International Journal of Physical Distribution & Logistics Management, 33*(6), 531–549. doi:10.1108/09600030310492788

Lee, H. L. (2002). Aligning Supply Chain Strategies with Product Uncertainties. *California Management Review, 44*(3), 105–119. doi:10.2307/41166135

Lee, H. L., Padmanabhan, V., & Whang, S. (1997). The Bullwhip Effect in Supply Chains. *Sloan Management Review, 38*(3), 93–102.

Lee, H. L., So, K. C., & Tang, C. S. (2000). The value of information sharing in a two-level supply chain. *Management Science, 46*(5), 626–643. doi:10.1287/mnsc.46.5.626.12047

Li, G., Yan, H., Wang, S., & Xia, Y. (2005). Comparative analysis on value of information sharing in supply chains. *Supply Chain Management. International Journal (Toronto, Ont.), 10*(1), 34–46.

Li, X., & Wang, Q. (2007). Coordination mechanisms of supply chain systems. *European Journal of Operational Research, 179*(1), 1–16. doi:10.1016/j.ejor.2006.06.023

Matchette, J., & Seikel, A. (2004). How to win friends and influence supply chain partners. *Logistics Today, 45*(12), 40–42.

McCarthy, T. M., & Golicic, S. L. (2002). Implementing collaborative forecasting to improve supply chain performance. *International Journal of Physical Distribution & Logistics Management, 32*(6), 431–454. doi:10.1108/09600030210437960

McIvor, R., Humphreys, P., & McCurry, L. (2003). Electronic commerce: Supporting collaboration in the supply chain? *Journal of Materials Processing Technology*, *139*(1-3), 147–152. doi:10.1016/S0924-0136(03)00196-1

Nakano, M. (2009). Collaborative forecasting and planning in supply chains. *International Journal of Physical Distribution & Logistics Management*, *39*(2), 84–105. doi:10.1108/09600030910942377

Nyaga, G. N., Whipple, J. M., & Lynch, D. F. (2010). Examining supply chain relationships: Do buyer and supplier perspectives on collaborative relationships differ? *Journal of Operations Management*, *28*(2), 101–114. doi:10.1016/j.jom.2009.07.005

Paulraj, A., Lado, A. A., & Chen, I. J. (2008). Inter-organizational communication as a relational competency: Antecedents and performance outcomes in collaborative buyer-supplier relationships. *Journal of Operations Management*, *26*(1), 45–64. doi:10.1016/j.jom.2007.04.001

Raghunathan, S. (1999). Interorganizational collaborative forecasting and replenishment systems and supply chain implications. *Decision Sciences*, *30*(4), 1053–1071. doi:10.1111/j.1540-5915.1999.tb00918.x

Raghunathan, S. (2001). Information sharing in a supply chain: A note on its value when demand is non-stationary. *Management Science*, *47*(4), 605–610. doi:10.1287/mnsc.47.4.605.9833

Ramanathan, U. (2012). Supply chain collaboration for improved forecast accuracy of promotional sales. *International Journal of Operations & Production Management*, *32*(6), 676–695. doi:10.1108/01443571211230925

Ramanathan, U., Gunasekaran, A., & Subramanian, N. (2011). Supply chain collaboration performance metrics: A conceptual framework. *Benchmarking: An International Journal*, *18*(6), 856–872. doi:10.1108/14635771111180734

Ramanathan, U., & Muyldermans, L. (2010). Identifying demand factors for promotional planning and forecasting: A case of a soft drink company in the UK. *International Journal of Production Economics*, *128*(2), 538–545. doi:10.1016/j.ijpe.2010.07.007

Ryu, S.-J., Tsukishima, T., & Onari, H. (2009). A study on evaluation of demand information sharing methods in supply chain. *International Journal of Production Economics*, *120*(1), 162–175. doi:10.1016/j.ijpe.2008.07.030

Sanders, N. R., & Premus, R. (2005). Modelling the relationship between firm IT capability collaboration and performance. *Journal of Business Logistics*, *26*(1), 1–23. doi:10.1002/j.2158-1592.2005.tb00192.x

Sari, K. (2008). On the benefits of CPFR and VMI: A comparative simulation study. *International Journal of Production Economics*, *113*(2), 575–586. doi:10.1016/j.ijpe.2007.10.021

Seifert, D. (2003). *Collaborative Planning Forecasting and Replenishment: How to create a supply chain advantage*. Saranac Lake, NY: AMACOM.

Simchi-Levi, D., & Zhao, Y. (2005). Safety Stock Positioning in Supply Chains with Stochastic Lead Times. *Manufacturing & Service Operations Management*, *7*(4), 295–318. doi:10.1287/msom.1050.0087

Smaros, J. (2007). Forecasting collaboration in the European grocery sector: Observations from a case study. *Journal of Operations Management*, *25*(3), 702–716. doi:10.1016/j.jom.2006.06.005

Steckel, J. H., Gupta, S., & Banerji, A. (2004). Supply chain decision making: Will shorter cycle times and shared point of sale information necessarily help? *Management Science*, *50*(4), 458–464. doi:10.1287/mnsc.1030.0169

Toktay, L. B., Wein, L. M., & Zenios, S. A. (2000). Inventory management of remanufacturable products. *Management Science*, *46*(11), 1412–1426. doi:10.1287/mnsc.46.11.1412.12082

VICS. (2002). *CPFR guidelines Voluntary Inter-industry Commerce Standards*. Available at: www.cpfr.org

Voss, C., Tsikriktsis, N., & Frohlich, M. (2002). Case research in Operations Management. *International Journal of Operations & Production Management*, *22*(2), 195–219. doi:10.1108/01443570210414329

Yin, R. K. (1994). *Case study research Design and Methods Applied Social Research Methods Series* (2nd ed.; Vol. 5). London: Sage Publications.

Zhao, X., Xie, J., & Leung, J. (2002). The impact of forecasting model selection on the value of information sharing in a supply chain. *International Journal of Production Economics*, *142*, 321–344.

Chapter 4
Big Data Analytics for Predictive Maintenance Strategies

C. K. M. Lee
The Hong Kong Polytechnic University, China

Yi Cao
The Hong Kong Polytechnic University, China

Kam Hung Ng
The Hong Kong Polytechnic University, China

ABSTRACT

Maintenance aims to reduce and eliminate the number of failures occurred during production as any breakdown of machine or equipment may lead to disruption for the supply chain. Maintenance policy is set to provide the guidance for selecting the most cost-effective maintenance approach and system to achieve operational safety. For example, predictive maintenance is most recommended for crucial components whose failure will cause severe function loss and safety risk. Recent utilization of big data and related techniques in predictive maintenance greatly improves the transparency for system health condition and boosts the speed and accuracy in the maintenance decision making. In this chapter, a Maintenance Policies Management framework under Big Data Platform is designed and the process of maintenance decision support system is simulated for a sensor-monitored semiconductor manufacturing plant. Artificial Intelligence is applied to classify the likely failure patterns and estimate the machine condition for the faulty component.

DOI: 10.4018/978-1-5225-0956-1.ch004

INTRODUCTION

Maintenance can be defined as all actions which are necessary to retain or restore a system and a unit to a state, which is necessary to fulfill its intended function. The main objective of maintenance is to preserve the capability and the functionality of the system while controlling the cost induced by maintenance activities and the potential production loss. Correspondingly, failures can be defined as any change or anomaly in the system causing an unsatisfactory level of performance. Although only certain failures will cause severe risk in productivity and safety, most failures lead to disruptive, inconvenient, and expensive breakdowns and loss of quality. Maintenance plans are designed to reduce or eliminate the number of failures and the costs related to them.

There are two broadly accepted methodologies aiming at continuously enhancing maintenance excellence, with different focuses. As a human factor management oriented policy, total productive maintenance (TPM) involves all employees, especially the operators, in the maintenance program in order to achieve optimality in overall effectiveness and zero breakdowns. Through the operators' participation in maintenance, such as through inspections, cleaning, lubricating and adjusting, early detection of hidden defects, before service breakdown. TPM aims to diminish and eliminate six significant losses of equipment effectiveness – i.e. breakdowns, setup and adjustment, idling and stoppages, reduced speed, defects in process, and reduced yield (Jardine & Tsang, 2013).

Reliability-centered maintenance (RCM) is another approach to strengthening the system's reliability, availability and efficiency which focuses on design and technology. RCM program is based on systematic assessment of maintenance needs after a complete understanding of the system function and the types of failure causing function losses.

Types of Maintenance

Maintenance activities can be categorized into three types:

1. Reactive or corrective maintenance,
2. Preventive maintenance (PvM), and
3. Predictive maintenance (PdM).

The following terms are also respectively used for the above three categories interchangeably as:

1. Breakdown maintenance or unplanned maintenance,

2. Planned maintenance, and
3. Condition based maintenance (CBM) or prognostic and health management (PHM).

Reactive or corrective maintenance follows the run-to-failure methodology, which is the repair and/or replacement work after an equipment outage has occurred. This primitive maintenance approach, which has been applied in industry for decades, and is still considered the best maintenance policy for non-critical components with short repairing time in the system. However, in most cases, an equipment failure can lead to unexpected production delay and lower the production efficacy rate, or more seriously, cause severe damage to other components and/or injury to people. One goal of a proactive maintenance plan is to reduce the overall requirement for reactive maintenance and to apply PvM and/or PdM strategies on any feasible occasion.

Preventive maintenance is performed based on a certain periodic interval to prevent and correct problems before breakdown without considering the actual health condition of a system. Basic preventive maintenance, including inspections, lubrication, cleaning and adjustment is the first step to be undertaken. After that, rectification or replacement can be undertaken only for components identified with defects and/or considerable risk of failure. Generally, most PvM actions can be implemented by operators with basic training.

Predictive maintenance is a trend-oriented policy that begins with identifying the states of each component within the equipment. PdM greatly relies on engineering techniques and statistical tools to process the data and analyze the health condition in order to predict possible equipment failure (Lee, Ardakani, Yang, & Bagheri, 2015). The prediction of the equipment condition is based on the finding that most types of failures, which occur after a certain degradation process from a normal state to abnormalities, do not happen instantaneously (Fu et al., 2004). Through degradation monitoring and failure prediction, PdM reduces the uncertainty of maintenance activities and enables identifying and solving problems before potential damage. Condition-based maintenance, the alternative term for PdM, imposes more emphasis on real-time inspections using RFID devices and wireless sense networks (WSNs). The three key steps of CBM are monitoring and processing, diagnosis and prognosis, and maintenance decision making.

BIG DATA ACHITECTURE

Big Data is not only a matter of volume increased of the collected data, but also includes the evolution of data peculiarities, namely data variety and data velocity. The intrinsic pattern of comprehensive data becomes the major driver for companies to investigate the use of big data analytics. The features of big data are broadly recognized as "4Vs" – i.e. volume, velocity, variety and value (Xin & Ling, 2013).

- **Data Volume:** Data volume is the primary attribute of data. Due to the dramatically boost in data volume and the rising demand of data storage, database management has been modified as petabyte-scale data management. The storage needs can be easily satisfied by increasing data warehouse capacities but at the same time, the data transfer and processing will become too slow to be operated and handled by a single computer. Therefore, a super-computer or high capacity server is required for operation. On the other hand, the cost is also a major concern for implementing with advanced computing equipment. The data growth in the supply chain and logistics system becomes too large and too complex in the traditional data warehouse and system architecture. In addition, big data analytics makes good use of multiple modes during the computation. This Big Data Analytics method can handle large volume data.
- **Data Velocity:** With the use of automatic data retrieval systems (e.g. sensor network, wireless network and electronic data interchange through the Intranet and Internet), the speed of data transaction is rapidly increased. Moreover, this allows companies to collect instant information and accelerate the speed of data production and streaming. The data transfer and transformation are more intensive nowadays. If the company chooses to extract real time information from several automatic data retrieval systems, the speed of data processing from big data must be as expeditious as possible to meet the requirement of quick response.
- **Data Variety:** The analytics process of data mining has been expanded from structured data to unstructured data, typically the images, videos, audio and text, etc. The systematic relationship is longer limited by numerical results, but also prohibits pattern finding in unstructured data. This motivates companies to investigate semi-structured and unstructured data for their decision making process. The major purpose of big data analytics is to resolve the problem of incompatible data formats and non-aligned data structures of unstructured data with data mining techniques.
- **Data Value:** Big data analytics creates value for data mining in order to find the intrinsic and multidimensional attributes from the enormous amounts of data. To a certain extent, a big data-driving model can perform as a support vector machine to establish supervised learning, which allows the model to adapt and evolve from time to time. Value creation is a significant process contributing to organizations' continuous improvement and demand prediction. We need to understand that big data analytics is not only in statistical analytics, but also in more complicated and tailor-made analytics. In general,

big data analytics come into existence for resolving data storage problems as well as providing valuable insights for organizations.

The acquisition and processing of big data largely improves the transparency along the supply chains providing accurate and timely information for managerial decision making. Companies and organizations operate on the huge amounts of data by classifying trends and identifying patterns to produce invaluable knowledge.

Meanwhile the flood of big data with high speed and many variations has challenged the limited storage and conventional data mining methods. Challenges are also from processing and analyzing the large amount of unstructured data which are the major components in the big data acquired. Technologies have been advancing towards better performance in the big data context regarding integrated platforms, predictive analytics, and visualization (Lee, Kao, & Yang, 2014). Big data and predictive analysis are strongly interconnected. Without proper analytics, big data is just a deluge of data, while without big data, predictive analytics, the strength of statistics, modeling, and data mining tools for analyzing current and historical conditions will be undermined.

BIG DATA ANALYTICS

The descriptive tasks of big data analytics identify the common characteristics of data with the purpose of deriving patterns and relationships existed in the data. The descriptive functions of big data mining include classification analysis, clustering analysis, association analysis, and logistic regression.

- **Classification Analysis:** Classification is a typical learning models used in big data analytics, which aims to build a model for making prediction on data feature from the predefined set of classes according to certain criteria. A rule-base classification is used to extract IF-THEN rules to classify as different categories. The examples include neural network, decision trees and support vector machine.
- **Clustering Analysis:** Clustering analysis is defined as the process of grouping data into separate cluster of similar objects, which helps to segment and acquire the data features. Data can be divided into different subgroups according to the characteristics. The practitioners may formulate appropriate strategies for different clusters. The common example of clustering technique are K-means algorithm, self-organizing map, hill climbing algorithm and density-based spatial clustering.

- **Association analysis:** Association model helps the practitioners to recognize groups of items that occur synchronously. Association algorithm is developed for searching frequent sets of items with minimum specified confidence level. The criteria support and confidence level helps to identify the most important relationships among the related items.
- **Regression Analysis:** Regression represents the logical relationship of the historical data. The focus in regression analysis is to measure the dependent variable given one or several independent variables, which support the conditional estimation of expected outcome using the regression function. Linear regression, non-linear regression and exponential regression are the common statistical method to measure the best fit for a set of data.

MAINTENANCE STRATEGIES

The Big Data platform has the ability to handle huge amounts of data in manufacturing or production logistics databases along with the development of computerized maintenance management systems (CMMS), which assist decisions making so as to formulate maintenance strategies.

Maintenance procedures will be undertaken when a machine failure has occurred in the CrM strategy. Manufacturers are required to keep components inventories for maintenance, repair and operations (MRO) in order to prevent disruption of the overall production by failure of machine parts or equipment. Compared to the CrM strategy, maintenance performance in the PvM strategy follows a fixed time, interval basis or condition based schedules to avoid fatal machine failure. The design of PvM is a protective, process-oriented approach in which machine failure and downtime cost could be reduced by taking proper prevention and prevention to smoothen the production. Decisions on maintenance schedules is based on a machine's physical properties or asset condition. Extra resources are spent on non-value-added activities to estimate and measure the condition rules for PvM (Exton & Labib, 2002). However, PvM attempts to provide an empirical basis for the development of a framework design of manufacturing flexibility at machine idle periods and during maintenance activities. The assumption behind a PvM policy is that the machine failure follows the bathtub curve in Figure 1. Scheduled maintenance happen in the wear-out phase in order to reduce the failure rate (Sikorska, Hodkiewicz, & Ma, 2011). However, the most conspicuous deficiency in PvM is still the apparent random failure within the useful life period. The impact of failure in a critical machine is a tremendous risk to the downtime costs and, it in turn becomes bottleneck in production logistics operations.

Figure 1. Classical Bathtub Curve
(Klutke, Kiessler, & Wortman, 2003)

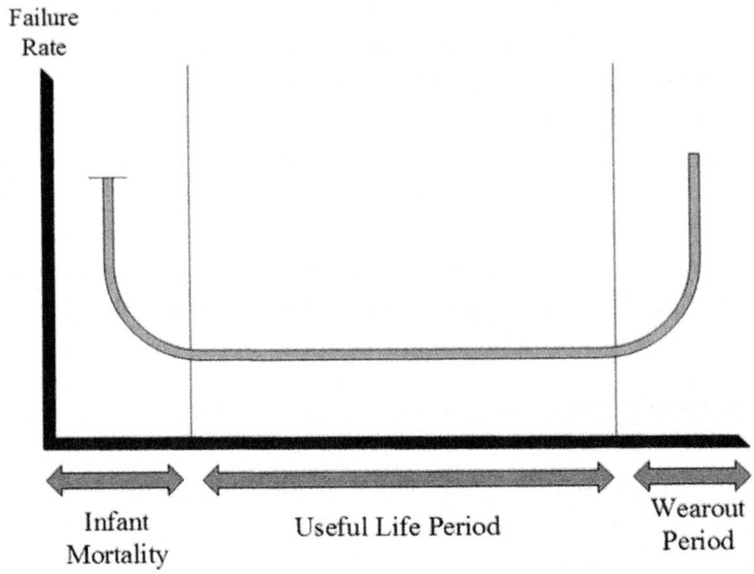

To remedy random machine failure in maintenance management, PdM has been well developed carrying out observation of the machine degradation process and symptoms from normal to flawed situations (Wu, Gebraeel, Lawley, & Yih, 2007). PdM is a sensor-based content-awareness philosophy based on the foundation of "Internet of Things". The intelligent maintenance prediction support system monitors the machine status by utilizing real time sensory data (Kaiser & Gebraeel, 2009). Advance maintenance in PdM policy is able to provide insights for maintenance scheduling in advance in order to eliminate unanticipated machine breakdowns, and minimize maintenance costs as well as downtime, before the occurrence of random machine failure (Garcia, Sanz-Bobi, & del Pico, 2006).

The important factors associated with PdM in Maintenance Policy Management (MPM) emphases criticality, availability of sensory data, reliability, timeliness, relevance and knowledge-oriented strategy.

- **Criticality in Failures:** PdM strategy has been heavily concentrated in real time machine condition monitoring through diagnostics and prognostics for reimbursement of foreseeable machine downtime cost. In reliability study, the critical assets must have a higher rank in priority formulate PdM strategy to predict the most likely time for the next machine breakdown and random error, as this will have the greatest impact on the production operations This changes the maintenance objective from avoiding breakdown to accepting downtime and taking maintenance action ahead of the schedule.

- **Availability of Sensory Data:** PdM policy is highly dependent on extract-transform-load (ETL) operational data in close condition-based monitoring. The current operational status and abnormal performance could be assessed by equipping sensors to identify failure modules or machines. Lack of sensory data may result in unpromising maintenance prediction.
- **Reliability:** Maintaining critical machine performance and leveraging the overall cost to sustain production are the major targets of PdM policy. The system must provide the correct measures and reliable performance in prediction to address feasible and foreseeable machine failure, and build confidence in operation.
- **Timeliness:** The prediction for maintenance modules must have a high level of confidence level before the undesired event occurs, and the data size and data transmission speed administered in a timely manner. The time series of the maintenance schedule and delivery of MRO should be taken into consideration the maintenance management in order to facilitate the production, with zero tolerance of equipment failure.
- **Relevance:** The MPM system needs to be developed based on the opinions of experts. The collected sensory information must be recorded and analyzed on a real time basis. In order to improve data quality, extraction of relevant data for maintenance decision making is crucial in regard to engineering aspects. Inappropriate integration of a sensor and machine may cause poor estimation and inaccuracy prediction of the current machine performance.
- **Knowledge-Objective Oriented Strategy:** The concept of the PdM strategy involves a belief that the implicit knowledge from collaboration of sensory information did contribute to the maintenance in advanced. The knowledge transfer system facilitates the disclosure of implicit information to maximize production efficiency and minimizes the adverse impact of idling time under maintenance and unawareness of potential failure. The decision of PdM policy could be assessed by the involvement of Big Data Mining Techniques to detect and defeat anomalies at an early stage.

PREDICTIVE MAINTENENACE IN BIG DATA FRAMEWORK

The ideology of a PdM is to create transparency of the machine condition and in the utilization of available information for maintenance decision making. In Figure 2, the framework of a big data platform in PdM is designed for closer integration of data acquisition and the maintenance decision support system (MDSS), which highlights the dataflow process in diagnostics and prognostics modeling for PdM. Case examples are provided in the following section to describe the framework of MPM for a semiconductor machine under Big Data Platform, and operations of MDSS. The operating data from vibration, heat and pressure sensors, which provide sensory information stored in the Big Database, are embedded on the semiconductor machine to evaluate the machine condition. The diagnostics and prognostics process may involve real time data and historical data for data mining procedures. The advantage of Big Data Architecture are capable to manage huge units of data and perform ETL in a timely manner by using appropriate data processing algorithms, such as Map-Reduce technique. The Big Data platform can build an intelligent agent

Figure 2. Predictive maintenance model in big data platform

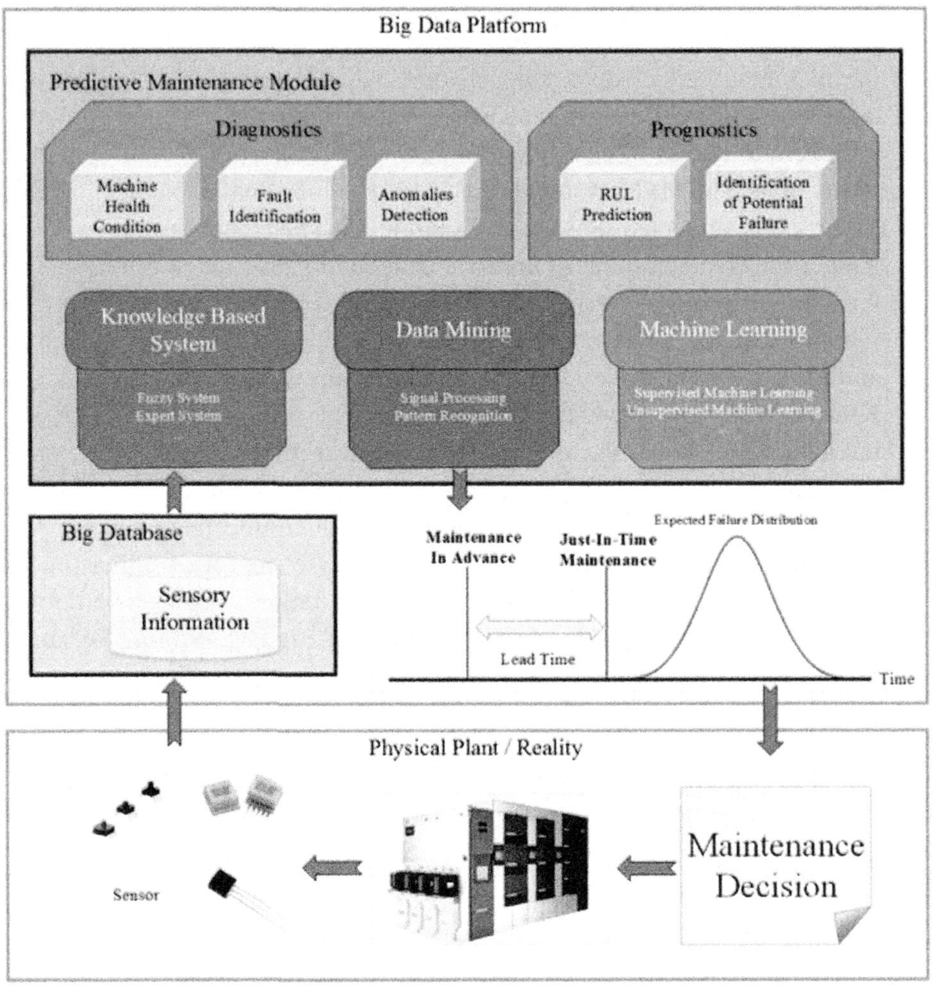

to connect the PdM module and the sensor knowledge from the actual machine. The PdM module consists of two major systems: a diagnostics system and a prognostics system. PdM analysis is a powerful tool to identify machine/components failure, and provide surprisingly accurate future breakdown using time-series data by well-developed analytic processes. The predictive maintenance module closely supervises the machine condition and constantly aids the analytics process of diagnosis and prognosis. The results from Artificial Intelligence (AI) will then be further processed and evaluated by the MDSS. Certain operational guidance and estimation of failure events, such as foreseeable situations, time to breakdown and estimated downtime, are recommended for maintenance decision making. With the implementation of the big data platform, more precise sensory data acquisition and accurate maintenance decisions could be made from the suggested algorithms in order to manage critical machines, with the objectives of maintenance in advanced or just-in-time (JIT) maintenance for supply chain management.

It is practical for a decision makers to select appropriate analytic processes and recognize the functionalities of algorithms for maintenance planning. Therefore, a comprehensive discussion of algorithm design is presented herein. The common practices of AI techniques can be classified as Knowledge Based System (KBS), Data Mining (DM) and Machine Learning (ML) (Faiz & Edirisinghe, 2009).

- **Knowledge Based System:** These types of analytics process require logical deduction and cognitive reasoning to resolve complex problems and support decision making. KBS attempts to extract rules for algorithm contexts by human intelligence and expert opinion, which are of practical significance. The practical necessity of KBS is increased due to the advancement of sensor-based PdM. KBS encourages a more flexible way to increase quality in problem solving and in extracting relevant data into knowledge for decision making, i.e., machine failure identification, classification in maintenance policies. A variation of sensory information causes data-booming in the analytics process. The rule-based and inference engine expert system have the ability to simulate a human expert in reducing the complexity in MPM and in discovering hidden machine failures.
- **Data Mining:** The goal of the DM process is to create a constructive model of patterns recognition and feature analysis, which is able to classify data into groups, detect irregular features and measure the dependencies of data. Moving toward a total productive manufacturing system, DM is an instrument that is able to mine all kinds of manufacturing knowledge, such as job shop scheduling, manufacturing process, quality control, yield improvement, and even predictive maintenance strategy. In the data mining technique, the accuracy of the information discovered increases along with the increase in

gathered data from the sensors and the historical maintenance data, which is able to foresee failure from pattern behavior of the operating machine data and the increased reliability of MDSS.

- **Machine Learning:** ML is another dimension of the analytics process. The mechanism of KBS and DM are either to discover knowledge and insight beforehand for the working process of the algorithm, which is concerned information and knowledge extraction from massive data. However, ML deals with automatic reasoning and artificial cognitive resolution by an intelligence agent. ML works as an online measurement of a health detection system to reveal machine degradation and anomalies from the models. Self-learning and reinforcement in ML, together with normal degradation allow the forecasting of random machine failure effectively and efficiently in order to plan for the best before failure occurs.

THE RELATIONSHIP BETWEEN DIAGNOSTICS AND PROGNOSTICS

In most cases, there is a measureable process of degradation before a machine fails. Figure 3 illustrates the degradation process of a system, sub-system, or component into failure. Through functioning life, the system may continuously degrade to a condition with an observable drop in its performance level and initial faults may occur during the degradation progress. The incipient defects continuously proliferates and the severity gradually increases which causes the system to fail to perform its required function and fails. In order to predict and prevent failures in advanced, diagnostics and prognostics techniques are studied and employed to evaluate the current health conditions and forecast future performance.

Figure 3. Fault to failure progression

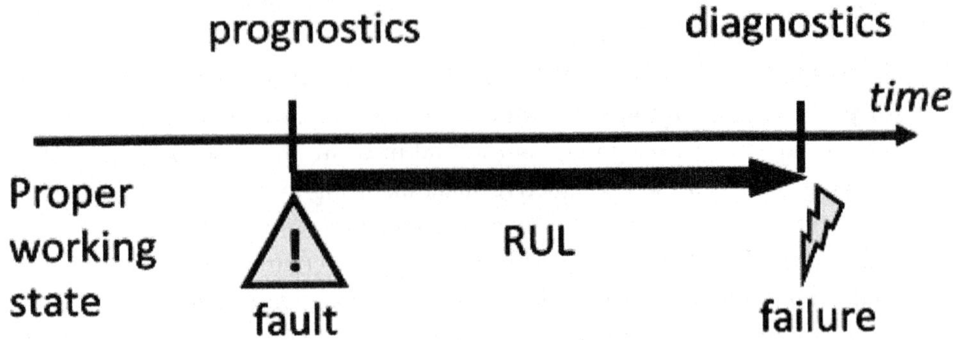

Figure 4 indicates the inputs and outputs of the machine diagnostics and prognostics process. The diagnostics process determines how the system has degraded and investigates the cause or nature of such a degraded condition. Faults are detected, isolated and identified to create a diagnostic record, and the faults possibilities are computed to find the potential failure pattern. The diagnostic operations follow an analysing approach from effect to cause. On the other hand, prognostics considers time as a vital factor and focuses on predicting the future condition of the system or component and in calculating accurately the remaining useful life before the failure. The prediction is conducted from cause to effect. The analysing and computing process is based on current system conditions and future operational requirements. Although similar information and knowledge bases are shared, the difference between the two concepts now becomes obvious. Diagnostics is to investigate and determine a failure mode within a system; while prognostics is to compute a rather accurate result of the remaining useful life before final failure.

The following sections present a diagnostics and prognostics system in Big Data Analytics with a case example. The system flowchart is shown in Figure 5. Fault identification is one of the diagnostics modules. The classification of machine failure is critical to smoothen the production, as not all the failures require emergency maintenance. The result from the diagnostic model is able to assist in the development of prognostics model. The reliability of the prediction could be increasingly improved from a known machine failure.

Figure 4. Inputs and outputs with the diagnostic–prognostic process structure

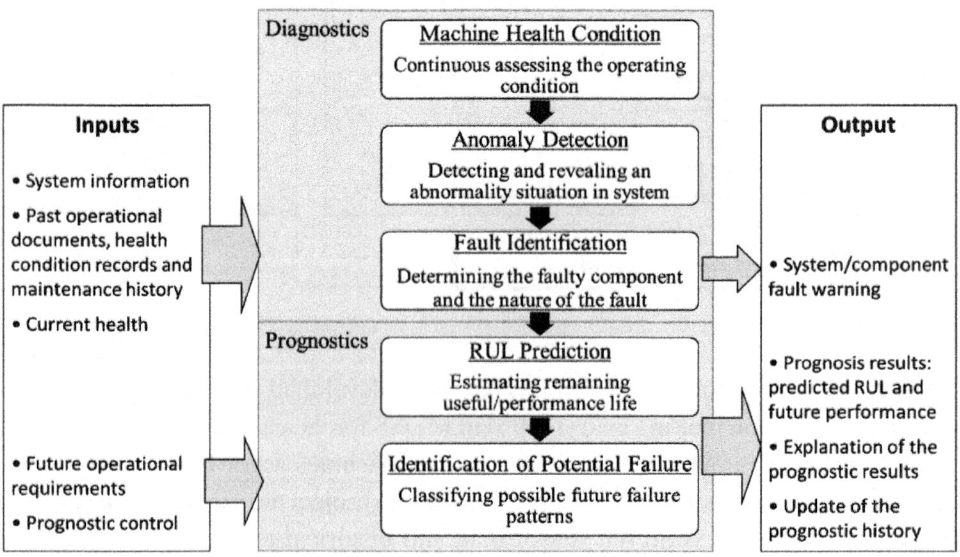

Figure 5. Flowchart of the proposed MDSS for case company

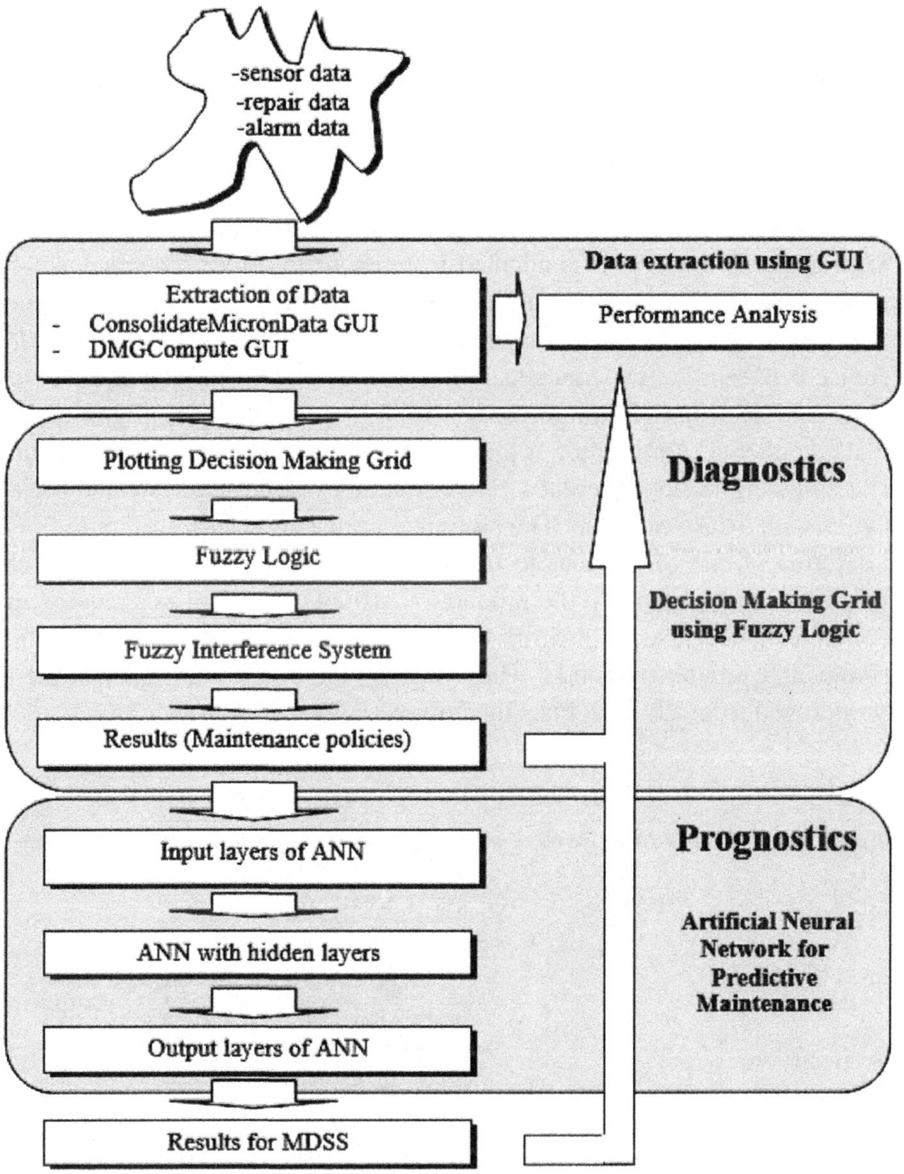

The machine failure identification has been developed and incorporated with the current decision making grid (DMG) in MDSS for the case company. The DMG model works like a map which categorizes the machines according to a set of pre-defined parameters/criterions. The criteria for this project are the downtime and the frequency of failures from the sensor data and historical record (Exton & Labib,

Figure 6. Decision Making Grid by the case company

Frequency	Downtime		
	Low	Medium	High
Low	OTF	**FTM1**	CBM
Medium	**FTM1**	**FTM2**	**FTM3**
High	SLU	**FTM3**	DOM

2002). Other criteria, such as cost, availability of MRO and the bottleneck problem, can also be included by expanding it from merely a 2 dimensional analysis to a 3 or more dimensional analysis model. Higher dimensional models can produce a more comprehensive and accurate analysis. The DMG then proposes the different types of maintenance policies based on the state in the grid which then determine the appropriate maintenance actions for the MDSS. These maintenance policies subsequently lead to be the formation of the following strategies; Operate to failure (OTF), fixed time maintenance (FTM), skill level upgrade (SLU), condition based monitoring (CBM) and design out machine/component (DOM), as shown in Figure 6.

- **Operate to Failure:** There are too many low downtime and low downtime frequency components which made it impossible or too expensive for applying scheduled PdM maintenance. These components/machines are allowed to operate to failure as they are deemed as having minimal impact on the system. Ideally, if operators of the machine are also maintenance technicians, which agrees with the TPM policy, OTF 'faults' can be further reduced without the need for reporting and waiting for the technician to bring the machine back to normal operating state. A CrM approach is suggested for OTF situation.
- **Fixed Time Maintenance:** PvM is also called Fixed Time Maintenance. A more flexible PvM can be chosen which is determined either by availability, machine not in use, or by the severity of the faults. Faults with higher downtime and frequency faults are allowed to have shorter fixed time maintenance,

whereas faults with lower downtime and frequency can extend the duration of their fixed time maintenance.

- **Skill Level Upgrade:** This strategy falls on the high frequency and low downtime grid. Faults that fall under this strategy are faults caused by human errors, such as the accidental pressing of the wrong switch/button. For this grid, the human factor oriented policy will be emphasized, either through the human/operator or through the machine. From the human perspective, operators can undergo skill level upgrading so that they can ratify the problem personally without any assistance from a maintenance technician. Whereas from the machine side, human errors can be reduced by designing more human oriented machine systems.
- **Condition Based Monitoring:** This strategy falls in the low frequency and high downtime grid. This matches RCM policy where studies and measurement need to be done to determine the underlying reliability condition of the machines. Sensors are usually be applied to feed monitoring data for machine learning in a PdM approach.
- **Design Out Machine/Component:** This strategy falls on the high frequency and high downtime grid. Machines/components that are prescribed in this grid region are usually unable to manage the current production level or are subjected to substantial wear and tear after prolonged usage. Either the need to upgrade to a better machine/components or a replacement of a new machine has to be undertaken.

FUZZY LOGIC FOR DIAGNOSTICS MACHINE FAILURE

Fuzzy logic is an approximate reasoning model to estimate the possible outcome based on a set of rules. This method has been proven to be a prominent control system that have been implemented in different engineering application, hardware monitoring and conditional-based assessment. The process of Fuzzy Logic is a simple, rule-based by using IF-THEN statements that imitate the decision making of humans to classify the type of responsive performance by defining the intermediate possibilities. Uncertainty in maintenance management, such as non-linear, imprecise and incomplete knowledge representation can be resolved by the adoption of fuzzy logic. As a consequence, conclusions are derived with certainty factor from a predefined fuzzy sets.

The research focus of predictive maintenance is to discover and recognize critical random failure, involving low frequency and high downtime of maintenance. The guidance from diagnostics in MDSS presents satisfactory knowledge rules to suggest maintenance action afterwards. Fuzzy Logic in KBS is merely a suitable algorithm for machine faliure identification in an imprecise enironment. The linkage between machine failure and classification of maintenance policies are frequently vague and subject to various sensory information. In practice, however, a need to refine the DGM model is required due to two scenarios. The first scenario is when data is located close to each another but at different sides of the policy boundary, leading to applying different strategies, despite being closely similar with one another. The next scenario is when two data points are located at both ends of the boundary within the same grid, leading to applying the same strategies, despite being far apart, as shown in Figure 7. Therefore, the concept of Fuzzy Logic can be applied to reshape the rigid boundaries,and make it more logical for the system.

A Fuzzy Logic design for semiconductor equipment is provided with two factors: downtime records and frequency records as in Figure 8. All membership functions (MF) are selected as trapezium shape, with two numerical inputs and one numerical output involved, as shown in Figure 9. Defuzzification is a method of extracting a crisp value from a fuzzy set as a representative value. In general there are five methods, for defuzzifying a fuzzy set A in a universe of discourse Z. These methods are the Centroid of Area (COA) or Center of Gravity, Mean of Maximum (MOM), Bisector of Area (BOA), Smallest of Maximum (SOM) and Largest of Maximum (LOM). COA is selected as the defuzzification strategy for the model. A fuzzy if-then rule is applied on the interface, as shown in Figure 10. When all rules and membership functions are settled, the Fuzzy Logic Rule Viewer and Fuzzy Logic Surface Viewer can be examined in Figure 11. With the help of fuzzy logic, the

Figure 7. Decision making grid formaintenance policies

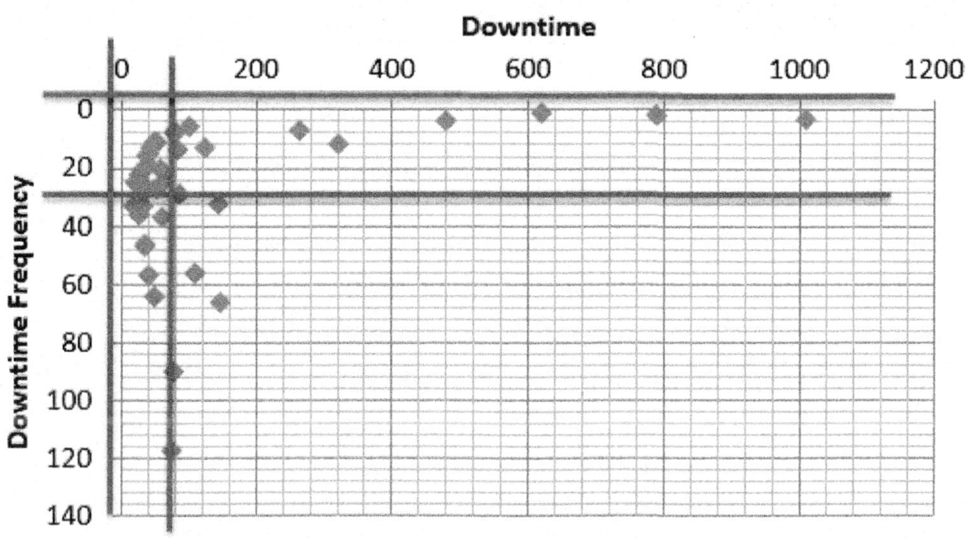

known machine failure problem associated with breakdown time and frequency can be reviewed for the current machine. Figure 12 shows the result of machine fault identification from semiconductor A and B

Figure 8. Fuzzy logic: fuzzy inference system editor

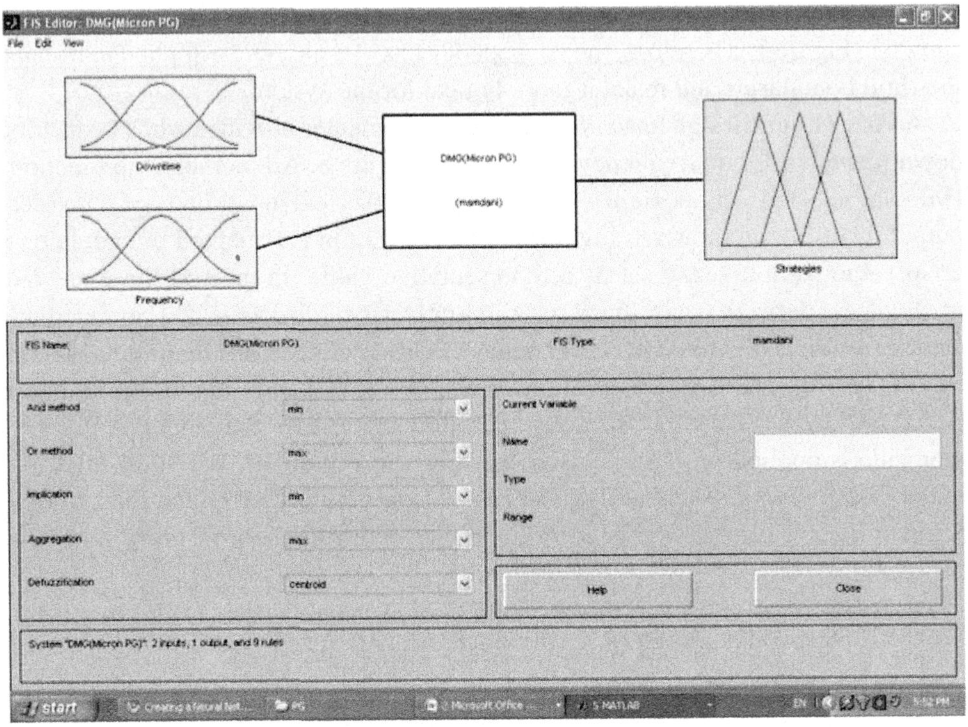

Figure 9. Fuzzy logic membership input function editor: downtime and frequency

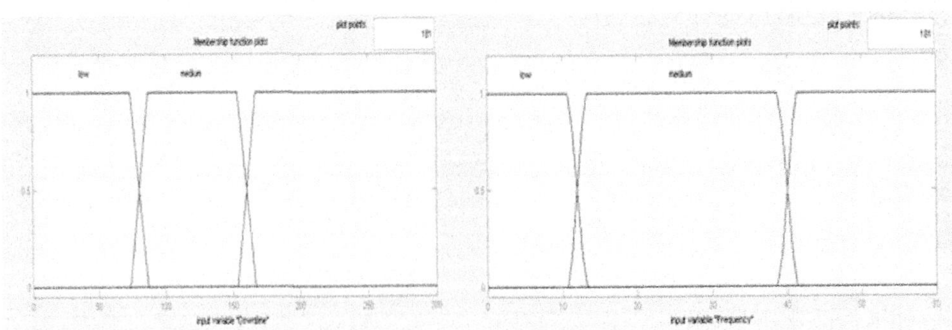

Figure 10. Fuzzy logic MF rules and output: maintenance policies

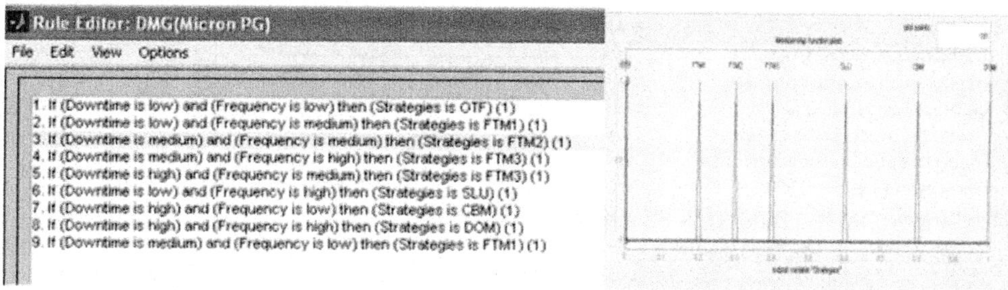

Figure 11. Fuzzy logic surface viewer

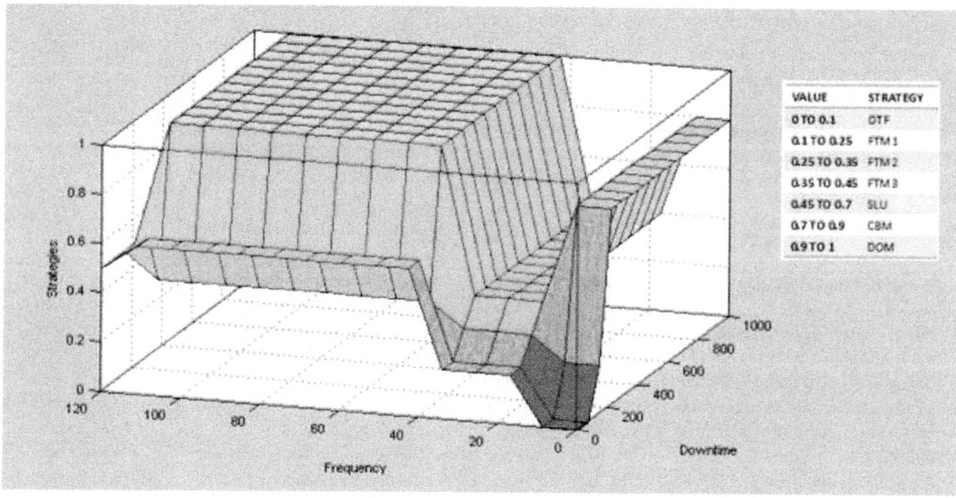

ARTIFICIAL NEURAL NETWORK FOR PROGNOSTICS MACHINE FAILURE

Prognostics is a model that is able to predict machine failure compared with normal behavior on a real time basis. Maintenance in advanced is better adopted to the necessity of repairs for an in-service machine in order to mitigate the disruption of the overall production. A health condition assessment is required to check the machine status frequently. Machine failure can be caused by normal degradation and random failure. Basic KBS and DM are incapable of distinguishing random failure and normal degradation, since machine degradation follows time progression rather than by rules. Therefore, an adoptive approach of machine learning to prognosticate the next random failure is required. The Artificial Neural Network

Figure 12. Maintenance policies for seminconductor machine A and B

Machine A	Value	STRATEGY
"'ALIGNMENT SENSOR SERCH ERRO'	0.4	FTM3
"'(2215)BG TAPE PEELING ERROR(PH133'	0.5183	SLU
"'VACUUM SORCE PRESSURE DRO'	0.5537	SLU
"'(2807)LABEL VACUUM ERROR(PSW256'	0.4	FTM3
"'(1B8C)APPLY STAGE VACUUM ERRO'	0.3	FTM2
"'SPIN St CYCLE TIME OVE'	0.8	CBM
"'FRONTSIDE OCR READ FAI'	0.6	SLU
"'(2260)PEEL TABLE LOCK ERROR(PSW087'	0.8	CBM
"'GR2 St WAFER THIN LIMI'	0.3	FTM2
"'(1B6B)H4 St PAD CLAMP ERRO'	0.6	SLU
"'(2309)UNLOAD WORK DETECT ERR.(PH157'	0.2	FTM1
"'(2420)OCR READ ERRO'	0.8	CBM
"'GR1 St WAFER THIN LIMI'	0.8	CBM
"'SLURRY SUPPLY UNIT ERRO'	0.6	SLU
"'PORT2 BCR READ FAI'	0.3	FTM2
"'(1700)W_TABLE LOW END DETECT ERROR'	0.8	CBM
"'H1 St PAD WAFER NOT CLAMPE'	0.6	SLU
"'BROKEN WAFE'	0.2	FTM1
"'(3026)FRAME CASS .NOT PLACEMENT(PH220'	0.2	FTM1
"'Bubbles trapped between wafer and DC tap'	0.3	FTM2
"'(2805)LABEL IS ON PRINTER SEC.(PH255'	0.2	FTM1
"'(2822)LABEL PRINT ERRO'	0.2	FTM1
'(4100)CASS'	0.2	FTM1
"'(1B84)S2F41 TIMEOU'	0.2	FTM1
"'(1B7D)RM CYCLE TIMEOU'	0.2	FTM1
"'CHILLER WATER FLOWLES'	0.2	FTM1
"'(151)300mm FRAME DETECT ERROR(LS044'	0.2	FTM1
"'POS St ALIGNMENT CYCLE TIME OVE'	0.2	FTM1
"'(150)200mm FRAME DETECT ERROR(LS043'	0.1002	FTM1
"'(2803)LABEL CHUCK HEAD LOW DET.ERR(L253'	0.2	FTM1
"'PORT-2 pdo cannot reach positon d'	0.0734	OTF
"'Backside stai'	0.8	CBM
"'GR1 St WAFER THICK LIMI'	0.2	FTM1
"'(3109)FRAME STOCKER COVER OPEN(CSW001'	0.1	FTM1

Machine A	Value	STRATEGY
"'(4061)AUTO CAN NOT STAR'	0.2	FTM1
"'H2 St T-AXIS MOTOR SERVO ALAR'	0.2	FTM1
"'(1811)CUTTING ERROR(PH064'	0.2	FTM1
'True Stall'	0	OTF
"'BACKSIDE OCR READ FAI'	0.2	FTM1
"'(1B6E)H4 St PAD WAFER NOT CLAMPE'	0.2	FTM1
Machine B	**Value**	**STRATEGY**
'Storage unit front cover overload'	1	DOM
'Disconnected communication with DGP8760'	0.8	CBM
'Ring frame reading error'	0.6	SLU
'BROKEN WAFER'	0.4	FTM3
'Pick-up tape tip detection error'	0.6	SLU
'Wafer ID control PC communication timeou'	0.8	CBM
'Peeling heater head temperature too low'	0.8	CBM
'Printer error'	0.6	SLU
'Positioning TBL: WID GRANT'	0.8	CBM
'Arm-2 Z-axis movement time up error. Pls'	0.2	FTM1
'Alignment unit communication timeout'	0.2	FTM1
'No ring frame in frame stocker'	0.2	FTM1
'No workpiece on frame transfer arm'	0.6	SLU
'Spinner detects ionizer abnormal signa'	0.2	FTM1
'Wafer ID reading error'	0.6	SLU
'TAPE MISMOUNT OR OFFSET ON FRAME'	0.6	SLU
'Sensor is abnormal when robot is in acti'	0	OTF
'Exhaust capacity of the machine decrease'	0	OTF
'No workpiece on workpiece storage guide'	0.2	FTM1
'No change in sensors when atomizing nozz'	0.8	CBM
'AVG THICKNESS OUT-OF-CONTROL (OOC)'	0.2	FTM1
'True Stall'	0	OTF
'Host comm: Received terminal message. P'	0.2	FTM1
'Error recovery completed'	0.8	CBM
'T3 Time-out in Host Communication.'	0.2	FTM1
'Remote command timeout'	0.2	FTM1
'Barcode: ID of cassette B cant be read.'	0.8	CBM

(ANN) model is a supervised learning method to estimate the Remaining Useful Lifetime (RUL) of a machine from degraded failure, or to differentiate anomalies from normal machine behavior. ANN can be used as a time series or forecasting of unanticipated machine failure with online sensory data, which is able to learn patterns from the training data set to distinguish the normal machine behavior and any anomalies. The prediction in machine failure involves Big Data management with the purpose of strengthening the data quality. Continuous data collection from different sensors installed in the machine supports the quality of prediction.

Figure 13 illustrates the mechanism of the ANN model. The basic ANN algorithm estimates the feasible outputs for prediction maintenance from observation data or sensory information in order to understand the machine condition. ANN provides assurance in resolving prediction and performance assessment with suffi-

Figure 13. Artificial neural network

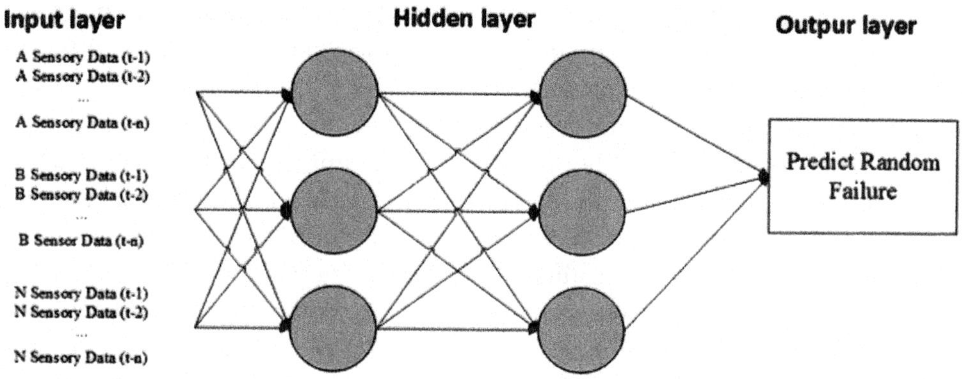

cient continuous input data. Vibration, heat and temperature sensors are established for the evaluation of the semiconductor machine. ANN is a simple artificial neuron processing system, which included input nodes, number of hidden layers, weighted factors of adjacent layers and output nodes. The hidden layers function as connectors between the input nodes and output nodes to transform and extract features of the input space. The prediction accuracy of ANN is dependent on the training process. The training process allows adjustment the synaptic weighting of input and develops the overall network by the construction of hidden layer. Before the actual running of the prediction, correct data and wrong data must be available in the training of supervised learning algorithm to ascertain its reliability in prediction. As a rule of thumb, 60% of the dataset is needed for training and the remaining dataset is for running test. Big Databases are able to collect huge amounts of historical and online data to enhance the accuracy of an ANN model through trial and error.

The predictive tasks in MDSS are presented in the following three main functions:

- **Health Condition Assessment:** The main goal is to monitor the machine performance and machine components degradation. In MPM, considerable maintenance actions could be resolved by component replacement. The sensor network can effectively enhance MRO order processing and improve flexibility in maintenance scheduling for the component substitution. The machine downtime caused by component damage could be reduced to meet the aim of agile production recovery.
- **Anomalies Detection Assessment:** Anomalies detection is an approach in root cause analysis. Machine anomalies may take place when the machine are not working normally. The cause of consistency anomalies is not straight-

forward to detect. ML algorithms are capable of measuring the machine performance from the current and normal conditions for identifying anomalies. The features of abnormality in machine performance are provided for further inspection by the repair technicians.

- **Remaining Useful Lifetime Assessment:** The major challenge in asset management is to optimize the machine lifetime utilization. Different machine usage may conclude variability of depreciation. In addition, longer lead time in machine replacement causes an uncertainty in the production and supply chain performance. The estimation of remaining useful lifetime by sensory information can effectively leverage the machine lifetime utilization and prediction for the machine replacement and performing a just-in-time machine replacement policy.
- **Scheduling Optimization for Maintenance in Advance:** Prediction of foreseeable machine failure is used to assess the machine expected performance in the future and optimize the maintenance schedules with less adverse effect on production disruption. Unanticipated machine failure may give a longer downtime and cease the manufacturing process. The prediction from the ANN model emphasizes proactive maintenance and provides the right time to conduct inspection. ANN captures the possible reasons, like the timeline of the machine failure event, reasons, duration and relevance information of the machines by triggered sensory information. With systematic maintenance in advanced, unplanned machine stopping can be eliminated.

MANAGERIAL IMPLICATIONS AND RECOMMENDATIONS

The entire Big Data framework requires human intelligence and expert opinion in the design stage. It is difficult for the manufacturer to manage and, control big data and select relevant information for MDSS. The availability of sensors and technological advancement enable explorative research of Big Data Analytics, and allows organizations to expand their capability to enhance the data transparency of machine status for manufacturers. The speedy data flow and collection of abundant data through WSNs enhance the potential of analytical performance. The adoption of Big Data in MDSS state a significant step in machine health condition diagnosis. The proposed approach helps to mitigate machine failure during production and uncover the hidden patterns through Big Data Analytics. However, management faces three major challenges of transformation traditional maintenance to advanced MDSS.

Various industries noticed that the size of data has been exponentially increasing and accelerating due to the comprehensive use of sensor network. The transition from conventional database to non-relational database is not only upgrading the storage capacity, but also requiring an infrastructure and expertise to process, and handle structured and unstructured data. Handling and understanding on the petabytes or even exabyte of data has become a challenge for IT teams. More advanced capability in data warehouses and network connection expedites real time data processing.

Due to the complexity of data type, the current processing techniques could not meet the demand of Big Data Infrastructure. Due to the enormous data booming via WSNs, a cohesive platform for processing structure and unstructured data becomes an essential element for any enterprises. The major purpose of Big Data Infrastructure is to resolve the problem of incompatible data formats and non-aligned data structures. The impact on inconsistency of unstructured data requires pre-processing of data input to enhance the performance of Big Data Mining.

Investigating the unstructured data in manufacturing not only create the value for the production engineer but also support MDSS with more vigorous and sophisticated Big Data Analytics. Several research paper mentioned that analyzing the unstructured data is the first priority in decision-making and prediction (Li, Bagheri, Goote, Hasan, & Hazard, 2013; Muhtaroglu, Demir, Obali, & Girgin, 2013; Wielki, 2013). However, not all the unstructured data can be beneficial to knowledge development and decision-making process. The relevant machine data must be fit for purpose of maintenance policy selection. Proper domain experts in place are critical to interpret the sensory information for predictive maintenance during the design stage of Big Data Analytics. Furthermore, enhancing data quality by the adoption of suitable sensors in the machine is also an importance for the company. Big Data offers tremendous insight to the diagnostics and prognostics of the machine status. Nonetheless, the information reliability from predictive maintenance is only available with appropriate sensors selection and adoption. In today's Big Data Analytics, research focus has been shifted from Volume of data to quality data.

Regarding the complexity of Big Data Analytics in MDSS, collaboration of industrial expertise and scholars must be involved to have sufficient breadth and depth of domain knowledge to design an appropriate Big Data Analytics for maintenance strategies. The proactive approach to predict machine failure provides a high level reliability for excellence in maintenance management. Further benefit can be summarized as reducing the frequency of corrective maintenance, increasing machine performance and enhancing overall production reliability.

FUTURE RESEARCH DIRECTIONS

Future research is oriented to the utilization of manufacturing information in the Cyber Physical System (CPS). Big Data Analytics are able to achieve better transparency of production, which provides knowledge insight to practitioners. With the technological advancement in Internet of Things and the utilization of sophisticated prediction tools, specialized automotive networks in a manufacturing company could be developed for real time monitoring and control at the strategical level. Incorporating the manufacturing computational intelligence into the machine health monitoring allow the manufacturers to enhance the overall system reliability and production efficiency, especially in reducing the machine downtime. Predictive maintenance is not only about health assessment but also detect the abnormality of the machine before it breaks down. To have a step forward from predictive maintenance, production plant should realize the importance of just-in-time maintenance strategy for the whole production process. Implementation of CPS synthesizes data from WSNs to enable the remaining life prediction so as to improve the asset utilization. Risk assessment and impact evaluation of machine failure will also allow production engineers to estimate the production system reliability. This motive turns the predictive manufacturing system into a "self-aware-and-self-adjustment" system, with intelligent machines and sensors in Big Data era.

CONCLUSION

In this book chapter, the predictive maintenance model and Big Data Analytics in managerial aspects are presented. The feature extraction through Big Data Analytics can be beneficial to managing the machine condition and in predicting machine failure. The MDSS in Big Data is able to suggest maintenance strategies and provide insight for management to tackle maintenance issues. The proactive strategies in maintenance can be achieved by embedded sensors and real time based machine monitoring systems. Besides, the prediction from Big Data Analytics and suggested analytics processes are well-designed to reduce the maintenance turnaround time and substantially enhance the production system availability. MRO and maintenance resources can be planned in advanced to facilitate the process during the machine downtime. Moreover, it provides flexibility to design maintenance schedules to mitigate the risk of unplanned stoppings. The overall maintenance efficiency can be much improved by the implementation of predictive maintenance under a Big Data platform.

ACKNOWLEDGMENT

The research is supported by The Hong Kong Polytechnic University. The authors would like to thank the case company for providing the data. Our gratitude is also extended to the Research Committee and the Department of Industrial and Systems

Engineering of the Hong Kong Polytechnic University for support in this project (RUE9) and (RU8H).

REFERENCES

Exton, T., & Labib, A. (2002). Spare parts decision analysis–The missing link in CMMSs (Part II). *Journal of Maintenance & Asset Management*, *17*(1), 14–21.

Faiz, R., & Edirisinghe, E. A. (2009). Decision making for predictive maintenance in asset information management. *Interdisciplinary Journal of Information, Knowledge, and Management*, *4*, 23–36.

Fu, C., Ye, L., Liu, Y., Yu, R., Iung, B., Cheng, Y., & Zeng, Y. (2004). Predictive maintenance in intelligent-control-maintenance-management system for hydroelectric generating unit. *Energy Conversion. IEEE Transactions on*, *19*(1), 179–186.

Garcia, M. C., Sanz-Bobi, M. A., & del Pico, J. (2006). SIMAP: Intelligent System for Predictive Maintenance: Application to the health condition monitoring of a windturbine gearbox. *Computers in Industry*, *57*(6), 552–568. doi:10.1016/j.compind.2006.02.011

Jardine, A. K., & Tsang, A. H. (2013). *Maintenance, replacement, and reliability: theory and applications*. CRC Press.

Kaiser, K. A., & Gebraeel, N. Z. (2009). Predictive maintenance management using sensor-based degradation models. *Systems, Man and Cybernetics, Part A: Systems and Humans. IEEE Transactions on*, *39*(4), 840–849.

Klutke, G.-A., Kiessler, P. C., & Wortman, M. (2003). A critical look at the bathtub curve. *IEEE Transactions on Reliability*, *52*(1), 125–129. doi:10.1109/TR.2002.804492

Lee, J., Ardakani, H. D., Yang, S., & Bagheri, B. (2015). Industrial big data analytics and cyber-physical systems for future maintenance & service innovation. *Procedia CIRP*, *38*, 3–7. doi:10.1016/j.procir.2015.08.026

Lee, J., Kao, H.-A., & Yang, S. (2014). Service innovation and smart analytics for industry 4.0 and big data environment. *Procedia CIRP*, *16*, 3–8. doi:10.1016/j.procir.2014.02.001

Li, L., Bagheri, S., Goote, H., Hasan, A., & Hazard, G. (2013). *Risk adjustment of patient expenditures: A big data analytics approach*. Paper presented at the Big Data, 2013 IEEE International Conference on. doi:10.1109/BigData.2013.6691790

Muhtaroglu, F., Demir, S., Obali, M., & Girgin, C. (2013). *Business model canvas perspective on big data applications.* Paper presented at the Big Data, 2013 IEEE International Conference on. doi:10.1109/BigData.2013.6691684

Sikorska, J., Hodkiewicz, M., & Ma, L. (2011). Prognostic modelling options for remaining useful life estimation by industry. *Mechanical Systems and Signal Processing*, *25*(5), 1803–1836. doi:10.1016/j.ymssp.2010.11.018

Wielki, J. (2013). *Implementation of the big data concept in organizations-possibilities, impediments and challenges.* Paper presented at the Computer Science and Information Systems (FedCSIS), 2013 Federated Conference on.

Wu, S.-j., Gebraeel, N., Lawley, M. A., & Yih, Y. (2007). A neural network integrated decision support system for condition-based optimal predictive maintenance policy. *Systems, Man and Cybernetics, Part A: Systems and Humans. IEEE Transactions on*, *37*(2), 226–236.

Xin, N. Y., & Ling, L. Y. (2013). *How we could realize big data value.* Paper presented at the Instrumentation and Measurement, Sensor Network and Automation (IMSNA), 2013 2nd International Symposium on.

Chapter 5
Data-Driven Inventory Management in the Healthcare Supply Chain

Shuojiang Xu
University of Nottingham, UK

Kim Hua Tan
University of Nottingham, UK

ABSTRACT

From 21st century, enterprises combine supply chain management with big data to improve their products and services level. In China healthcare industry, supply chain decisions are made based on experience, due to the environment complexities, such as changing policies and license delay. A flexible and dynamic big data driven analysis approach for supply chain decisions is urgently required. This report demonstrates a case study on CRT forecasting model of inventory data to predict the market demand based on pervious transaction data. First a basic statistic approach has been applied to represent the superficial patterns and suggest some decisions. After that a CRT model has been built based on the several independent variables. And there is also a comparison between CRT and CHAID models to choose a better one to further build an improved model. Finally some limitations and future work have been proposed.

DOI: 10.4018/978-1-5225-0956-1.ch005

INTRODUCTION

In Chinese healthcare industry, business is highly impacted by changing policies and volatile economy, available information for supply chain management in the ecosystem is in an unstructured manner, which has potential risk to support high growth. Due to environment complexity and dynamics in emerging market, current supply chain processes to capture market intelligence is more or less rely on individual's interpretation, supply chain decision requires data outside the company is facing challenges, the consequence is service and cost implication to end to end supply chain. To facilitate the supply chain decision-making process, inventory management, distribution network, etc. are all important parameters in successful supply chain management. Demand forecasting on inventory is an important part to support the supply chain decision making. This chapter is going to forecast the market demand based on the pervious transaction data.

Demand forecasting is commonly used in many filed to support the rescheduling and decision making. Decision tree, naïve Bayesian, regression, K-means and other algorithms are applied to achieve the goal. And machine learning algorithms are adopted, such as random forest and artificial neural networks, to improve the forecasting accuracy. The forecasting technologies are universally used in energy demand prediction (Srinivasan, 2008), power demand prediction (AI-Anbuky, Bataineh, & AI-Aqtash, 1995), water demand prediction(Msiza1, Nelwamondo, & Marwala, 2008) and etc. All these researches were based on basic regression theory and applied different machine learning techniques.

There are some works have been done by other researchers to improve the forecasting accuracy. In 2007, an improvement had been done by Luis Aburto and Richard Weber, they developed a hybrid intelligent system combining auto-regressive Integrated Moving Average (ARIMA) models and neural networks for demand forecasting, which leads to fewer sales failures and lower inventory level (Aburto & Weber, 2007). Another comparative experiment had been done, in 2008, to test that whether neural networks, recurrent neural networks and support vector machines are better than traditional naïve forecasting, trend, moving average and linear regression. The results show that recurrent neural networks and support vector machines are the best in these three methods, but their performance is not significantly better than the regression model (Carbonneau, Laframboise, & Vahidov, 2008). In January 2016, Kausar. S Attar proposed a methodology to use the Artificial Bee Colony (ABC) algorithm to optimize the Support Vector Regression (SVR) parameters (Attar, 2016). According to Saima Aman and other researchers' opinion, comparing with larger group, the smaller group is harder to predict, therefore better models are required (Aman et al., 2015).

This chapter is going to conquer the methodological weakness appearing in the most of the papers cited above. Linear regression algorithm is commonly used in the researches mentioned above, but there are several limitations (D'ALISA et al., 2006): a) the linear regression cannot deal with ordinal data, such as the hospital level; b) potential correlation between apparent independent variables may weaken the variance explanation of the dependent variable; c) the interaction between two or more variables may be more predictive for the model than a unitary change in each individual variable. But it is not easy to explore the meaningful interaction from many candidate variables; d) the linear regression or multiple-linear regression cannot handle the multiple types of data. The regression algorithm is suitable for the dataset only with scale data.

In the chapter, the classification and regression tree (CRT) algorithm has been employed to structure the predictive model. This algorithm overcame the above disadvantages. CRT algorithm has been used to model the variables from the inventory dataset to possibly predict how many products the customer will require. The algorithm can more confidently show the association between the dependent variable (quantity of products) and the independent variables, such as outbound order data, customer province, and seller level, comparing with the ordinary regression algorithm.

BACKGROUND

Supply Chain Management

The supply chain is the trace of a good or service from the firm to the user, including raw material purchase, good manufacture, distribution and consumption. In the past, people discussed the Supply Chain Management (SCM) with complicated terminology which leads to limited comprehension of the concept and its efficacy for practical application (Ross, 1998). Mentzer and et al, stated one, comprehensive definition of the SCM, which is the systemic, strategic coordination of the traditional business functions and the tactics across these business functions within a particular company and across businesses within the supply chain, for the purposes of improving the long-term performance of the individual companies and the supply chain as a whole (Mentzer et al., 2001).

The aim of supply chain management is to combine suppliers, manufacturers, warehouses and stores to produce and distribute the right number of products to the appropriate location in the accurate time. By applying the supply chain management, the firms can reduce the total supply chain cost and satisfy customers' requirements (Radhakrishnan, Prasad, & Gopalan, 2009). The supply chains have significantly expanded into international locations in the last decades of the twentieth century, such as vehicle, computer and apparel industries (Dornier, Ernst, Fender, & Kouvelis, 1998; Taylor, 1997). Supply chain manage is no longer the business activity in the single country, it now becomes to a global business model. This expansion brings challenges and opportunities to scholars and researchers in supply chain management. Plentiful cosmopolitan supply chain models have been made to solve business problems, such as variability and uncertainty in currency exchange rates, economic and political instability, and changes in the regulatory environment (Dornier et al., 1998). The business environment and problems are in an unstable manner and rapidly changing every day. There are some emerging issues due to the environment uncertainty for the supply chain. The first is that the global companies are more and more outsourcing their factories all over the world. The second is that many firms handle the sourcing problems with a myopic point of view. They only concern immediate interests from enterprise-level in the supply chain. The third issue is that the product quality delivered to the customer can influence the supply chain performance, such as mission and strategy (Keeney, 1994).

Inventory Management

Supply chain is the arrangement of firms obtaining raw materials, product manufacturing, distribution and consumption. All the raw materials, goods in process and end products throughout the supply chain, known as the set of items, are stored as the inventory. Excess inventories and shortage of inventories are the main reasons that cause the supply chain cost. Clear and sufficient inventory management can significantly improve the quality of the ultimate service and then decrease the supply chain cost (Radhakrishnan et al., 2009). Therefore inventory management is considerable important for the supply chain management, especially the inventory prediction. If the firm can predict the customers' behavior and demand, then the advanced supply chain management can be applied to prepare the inventories, such as raw material purchase and distribution. Another hottest topic is inventory optimization in the inventory system. The system determines the quantity of each item should be kept, the timing to replenish low items and the quantity of items to fill the vacancy (Levi, Pal, Roundy, & Shmoys, 2007).

Data Science

Data driven research is becoming more and more popular nowadays. It is necessary to apply a field of technology to support this kind of research. Then the data science comes into researchers' sight. Waller and Fawcett state (Waller & Fawcett, 2013), "Generally, data science is the application of quantitative and qualitative methods to solve relevant problems and predict outcomes." The existence of data science is over thirty years. In 1974, the word, data science, had been used in Peter Naur's contemporary data processing methods survey. The International Federation of Classification Societies (IFCS) conference firstly included the data science as a part of the conference title which is "Data Science, classification, and related methods" (Press, 2013). With the development of data science, it is no longer a single discipline within the science field. It has integrated science and business, research and practice. Professor Jeff Stanton of Syracuse University was quoted by Dumbill et al.: "From a teaching perspective, as a faculty member I can teach someone how to do a t-test in 10 min, and I can teach them how to write a Python program in half an hour, but what I cannot teach them very easily is the domain knowledge. In other words, in a given area, if you are from healthcare, what you need to know in order to be effective at analysis is very different than if you are in retail. That underlying domain knowledge, to be able to have a student come up to speed on that is very hard. (Dumbill, Liddy, Stanton, Mueller, & Farnham, 2013)" The idea is that it is necessary for data scientists to know both data science and business knowledge. Waller and Fawcett suggest several disciplines to the data science in the supply chain management field, such as statistics, forecasting, optimization, applied probability, analytical mathematical modeling, finance, economics, marketing and accounting (Waller & Fawcett, 2013). There are two parts of the disciplines, the first part is related to quantitative disciplines and the second part is about business.

MAIN FOCUS OF THE CHAPTER

The dataset, used in this chapter, was transformed from industrial partner's real transaction dataset. Due to the confidential protocol, the real dataset cannot be published in this chapter. All monetary information has been converted into percentage based on a default value. This dataset is the sales record of one inventory supporting the whole China market. There are 22239 sales records in the raw dataset. In the transformed dataset, all the variables and data structure are same as the real transaction dataset, except the value of the data. The Table 1 shows the name and type of the variables.

Data Preparation

The raw dataset is usually defective. When the recorder is filling out record, it can cause the problem data in the record, thus affect the integrity of the dataset. Before any data analysis and mining, the cleaning process is necessary to be implemented

Table 1. Name and type of the variables from dataset

Name	Type
Outbound order date	Scale
Invoice date	Scale
Natural year	Scale
Customer province	Nominal
Customer city	Nominal
Seller level	Nominal
Customer level	Nominal
Customer class	Nominal
Bill type	Nominal
Product code	Nominal
Hierarchy code	Nominal
Selling price	Scale
Quantity	Scale
Total bill	Scale

Table 2. Problem types and solutions in data preparation process

Problem Type	Example	Solution
Incomplete	• Missing value • Unknown value	• Ignore the sample • Fill in use a global constant • Fill in use mean or median • Fill in use the most probable value
Noise	Outliers	• Binning (by bin means or boundaries) • Regression • Cluster

to remove or fill out the problem data. Table 2 states some common problems and the potential solution to each problem.

1. In the dataset, there are 40 records from year 2014, but the chapter is aiming to build a model for year 2015. Therefore this part has been removed from the dataset.
2. There are two types of bill in the dataset, outbound sales bill and return record. Outbound sales bill records the products shipped out from the inventory. Return record is used to note the products returned to the inventory. This chapter is

focusing on the outbound sales bill, therefore the return records has been removed, the number of return records in this part is 1159.

3. By checking the quantity of the order, there are 855 records with negative value. The reason may be that the recorder mistakenly fills out the bill. The negative value has been manually changed to positive.
4. For the categorical variable, seller level, the missing value has been filled with a global variable which is 'unknown'.
5. For the variable, 'customer class', there are only 2 records with missing value of customer class. Then the 2 records have been removed from the dataset.
6. For the 'customer province' variable, there are 28 records with missing province and also with the missing city. The total bill of these records is very small comparing with the total sales bill.
7. Invoice date, natural year, customer city, customer level, product code, hierarchy code and selling price are same as the raw data.
8. Because the statistical analysis and predictive analysis are all done by the software, SPSS, it is necessary to recode the raw data to the data that SPSS is able to understand. The Table 3 gives an example about how to recode the data. The recode process is usually applied to the nominal data or ordinal data. The scale data can be understood by the SPSS automatically.

Statistics

Descriptive analysis of the transformed dataset has been employed to describe and investigate all the variables. A summary statistics is used to describe the profile of each variable in the dataset. And different types of graphs, such as bar graph and histogram graph, have been used to describe the individual variable or the distribution of one variable on another variable. Then the correlations between outbound order date, customer province, customer city, seller level, customer level, customer

Table 3. Coding sheet

Variable	Coding Instruction
Customer class	• C1→1 • C2→2
Hierarchy code	• H1→1 • H2→2 • H3→3 • H4→4
Product code	• P1→1 • P2→2 • P3→3

class, product code, hierarchy code, selling price, quantity and total bill has been calculated to find the inter connection between these variables, it also can be called as factor analysis. Then the dimensionality reduction can be applied to simplify the dataset by using the factor analysis. The CRT algorithm has been used to develop a predictive model of the quantity of the products for a sales bill.

CRT Modeling

CRT is a type of decision tree, which combines the advantages of classification decision tree and regression algorithm. It creates different types of tree based on different types of dependent variable. When the dependent variable is nominal, the CRT is classification tree. By contrast, CRT is regression tree when the dependent variable is scale.

The algorithm recursively partitions dependent variable into two groups referencing the cut-off value. The variable, province, can be split based on a cut-off value of the variable, quantity. At the beginning of the tree, the inseparable values of the independent variable are the root of the tree. Then the root can be split into two subgroups and these groups are called as ‘parent’ branches which can be divided into two more subgroups. This process will carried on until the subgroup cannot be split into any two more groups. Each ‘terminal’ branch is the output of the CRT system.

Each branch represents the interaction between the parent independent variable and sub-group independent variable. In the process of tree making, each split is going to maximize the variance explanation of the dependent variable. There is no distributional assumption in the CRT algorithm and scale variable will be treated as the ordinal variable. The CRT algorithm has been widely applied in many filed mixed with some machine learning algorithm. In this chapter, the CRT has been applied in SPSS 22.

SOLUTIONS AND RECOMMENDATIONS

Statistics

Figure 1 provides the summary sales bill of this inventory from the beginning of January to the end of May. It can be seen that the sales bill is periodic and the period is around 7 days. According to the calendar of 2015, on every Monday, the sales bill will rapidly increase and reach the peak on Thursday and then go down to the valley on Sunday. Obviously, there is a significant increment from 23rd March to 2nd April. According to the dataset, the reason is, there are much more purchases of products (P13) from different provinces from 23rd March to 2nd April. This may

Figure 1. Summary sales bill January to May

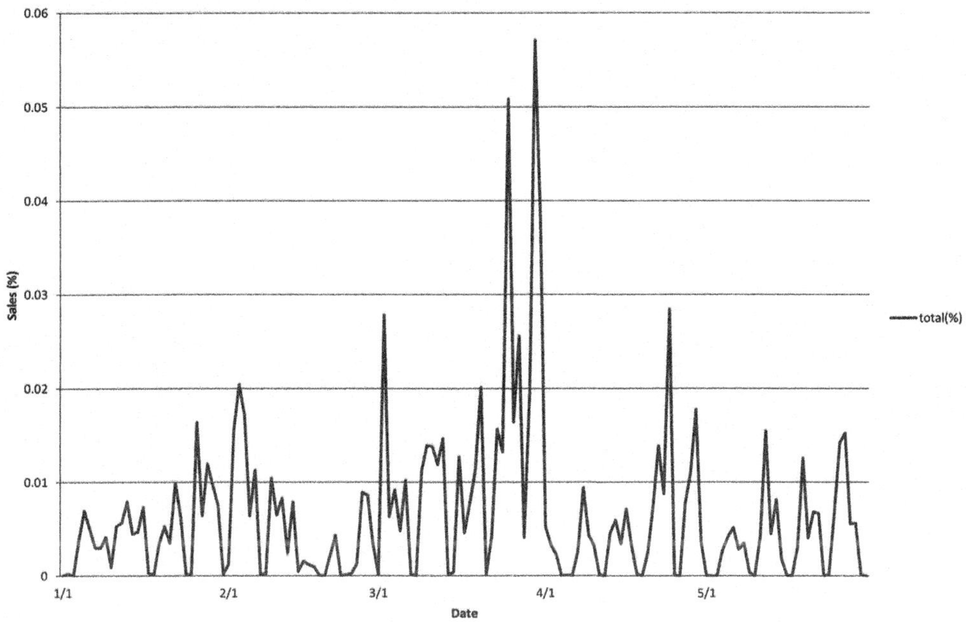

be something need to be identified in the future. This is exactly the challenge for the company. If this incident can be predicted, the company can be better off with enough time to prepare the fluctuation.

The summary statistics has been provided in Table 4. For the customer class, 59.80% of sales bill comes from C1 customers and the rest of bill comes from C2 customers. There is only 19.6% difference between two types of customer classes. Therefore there is no tendency to which side.

Hierarchy Code is a series code which links to several products. It's similar to assortment or category. Within one hierarchy code, there can be several kinds of products, generally these products will have things in common but also have special characteristics, such as the shampoo with different perfume. For hierarchy code, H1 and H2 contribute 99.32% of the total sales bill, which almost take the entire sales bill. Therefore the company should pay more attention to the products within these two hierarchy code. And the H3 and H4 are not very popular to the company, but there are also some potential opportunities, if the company can locate the problem leading to the low demand, it is possible to change the characteristics of the product to meet the customers' requirement and then increase the income.

For product code, P1, P13, P26, P6 and P27 are the most important products for this company, these types of products contribute 92.01% of total sales bill and other products just take 7.99% of total sales bill. Considering the hierarchy code,

Table 4. Summary statistics of the dataset

Category	Level	Percentage
Total sales bill	-	100.00%
Customer class	C1	59.80%
	C2	40.20%
Hierarchy code	H1	63.80%
	H2	35.52%
	H3	0.68%
	H4	0.00%
Product code	P1	30.71%
	P13	23.61%
	P26	19.56%
	P6	11.13%
	P27	6.99%
	other	7.99%
Province	32	21.78%
	31	10.42%
	11	8.36%
	33	7.80%
	44	7.18%
	51	6.13%
	21	5.17%
	50	4.55%

it can be found that, P1, P6 and P26 comes from hierarchy code H1, and P13 and P27 are under the H2. It suggests the company to pay more attention to these 5 types of products

For province, the province with code 32 contributes 21.78% of the total sales bill, which is the largest province. Other provinces, such as 31, 11, 33 and 44 also have large contributions to the total sales bill. Therefore, the company should pay more attention to these provinces.

CRT Modeling

To generate a forecasting decision tree, outbound order date, customer province, seller level, customer level, customer class, hierarchy code, product code and selling price are used as independent variables and the quantity is the dependent variable. Because the inputs include scale and nominal variables and the output is scale variable, the decision tree will be regression tree by CRT algorithm. The records from January to April have been used as the training dataset and the records of May have been used as the validation dataset. The percentages of these two types of dataset are 80% and 20%.

According to the structure of the tree, the province is coming to the first variable which has the most significant impact on the output. According to the evaluation criterion of the tree, 30 provinces have been divided into 2 groups. Then each group will be calculated again, based on the new variable. The structure is shown in Table 5.

Then the generated tree has been applied to the validation dataset, records of May. After the validation, the total sales bill of each in May has been calculated and compared with the actual records. CRT is not the only method can be applied into this chapter. CHAID is also available to this dataset. Then the same processes have been applied using CHAID algorithm. The aim is to find which approach is better. Figure 2 shows the actual and forecasting sales bill in May. Figure 3 demonstrates the differences between the actual and forecasting sable bill.

Table 5. The summary of the CRT modeling

Specifications	Growing Method	CRT
	Dependent Variable	quantity
	Independent Variables	Outbound, sellerlevel, customerlevel, customerclas, province, HierarchyCode, Product, price
	Validation	None
	Maximum Tree Depth	5
	Minimum Cases in Parent Node	100
	Minimum Cases in Child Node	50
Results	Independent Variables Included	Province, outbound, price, customerclass, HierarchyCode, sellerlevel, customerlevel, Product
	Number of Nodes	45
	Number of Terminal Nodes	23
	Depth	5

Figure 2. Actual and forecasting sales bill in May

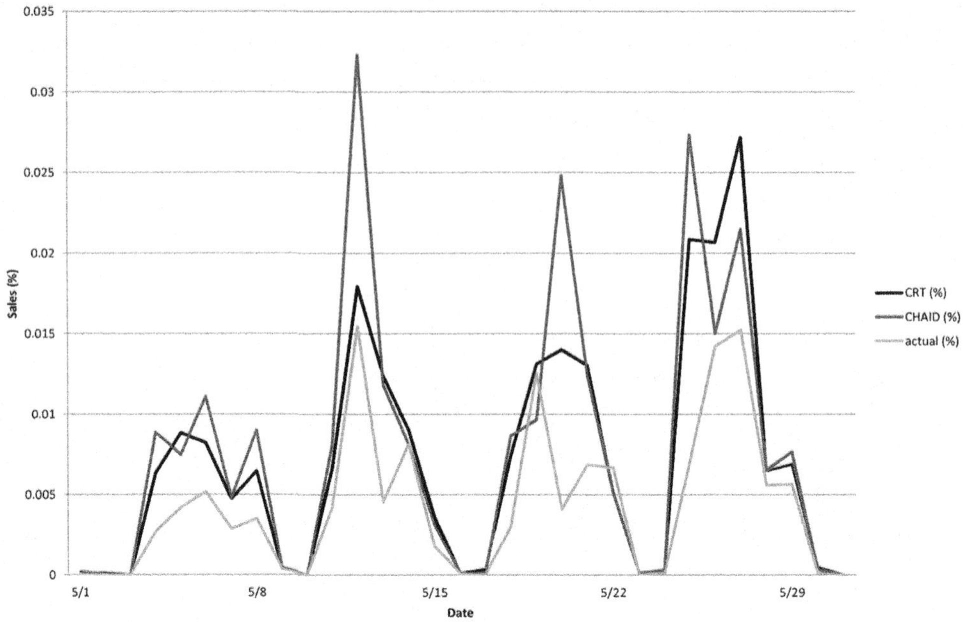

Figure 3. Differences between the actual and forecasting bill

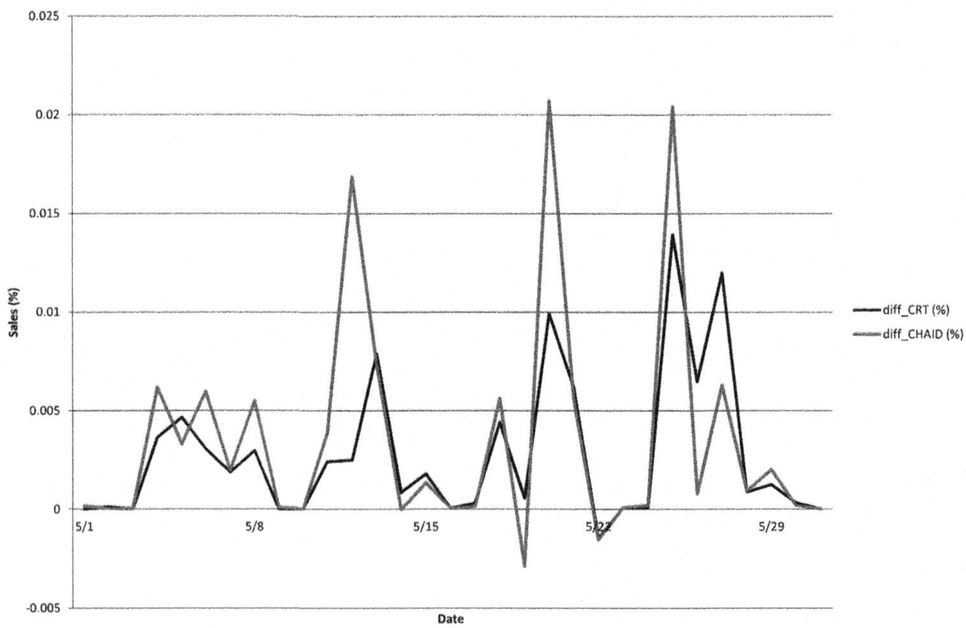

The performance of CRT prediction is better than CHAID, as the former is closer to the actual sales bill in May. The Figure 2 and 3 also prove the result. The reason is that when CHAID is facing to the scale variable, it will chop the continuous data into several smaller parts with a single value in each part. This mechanism will lead to the bigger difference between the forecasting results and the actual data, because all different values have been forced to the same value. In contrast, the CRT will deal the scale variable as the continuous data, and the decision tree will become a regression tree.

DISCUSSION

Statistics

In the statistics part, the summary sales bill of this inventory from the beginning of January to the end of May has been shown in Figure 1. And the Table 4 shows the summary statistics. The statistics method clearly indicates the key products and the key provinces. It also shows the significant increment from 23rd March to 2nd April, there should be some matters triggering this phenomenon. Because this dataset has been transformed from the real data, it is hard to tell what matters trigger the phenomenon, which is the limitation of the transformed data. If it is possible, the real dataset is very powerful to indicate the important triggers for the big data.

CRT Modeling

The CRT modeling is different from the traditional regression methods. It is possible for CRT modeling to capture the delicate interactions across the several independent variables, such as customer level, seller level, and province.

The modeling part also tests the differences between two types of decision tress. It shows the CRT modeling is better than CHAID modeling in this chapter. From Figure 2, it can be seen that in most of the time, the prediction error of CRT is smaller than CHAID, from 1st May to 26th May. However, the error of CRT is larger than CHAID from 26th May to the end of May. From the overall statistical data, the error of CRT is larger than the actual bill. By contrast, the error of CHAID is higher than CRT, which means the CRT is better than CHAID.

Even though the CRT is better than CHAID, it still can be seen that these two modeling have comparable error with the actual bill. For CRT, the error is 65% comparing with the actual bill. 65% error is too large for a company. The large error may be caused by the unusual transactions from 23rd March to 2nd April. The next step of the research is to remove the unusual transactions and build a new regression tree using CRT modeling. Also the pruning technique will applied to improve the performance of the CRT modeling.

Some limitations of the chapter have been proposed. First, the number of records is not larger enough to support a stable tree to forecast the market demand. Second, all records come from one inventory supporting the China market which might be litter representative of the whole China market. Therefore, the records from different inventories are necessary to improve the performance of the modeling. Third, in this chapter, only 13 variables are used to describe the records. More detailed variable are needed to enrich the dataset. The Table 6 states the potential variables which may be captured in the future.

Because currently, managers make inventory management decisions based on experience. It is necessary to build a data driven supply chain management in the Chinese healthcare industry. This chapter is aiming to transfer the unstructured information, such as changing policies, market demand and government behaviors into structured market demand product intelligence. And then these kinds of information will support the supply chain managers to make decisions or reschedule the plan to increase the revenue and also decrease the cost.

To achieve the goal, in the future, the knowledge about finance, economics, marketing and accounting in supply chain management will be learned and the skill about different estimation and sampling methods, qualitative and quantitative forecasting methods and optimization methods are necessary for the chapter.

Table 6. Potential variables captured in the future

Type	Variable
When	• Quarter • Day of the week • Workday/weekend • Holiday, vacation
Where	• Country • Orientation
Who	Hospital level: 3A, 3B, 3C; 2A, 2B, 2C; 1A, 1B, 1C
Why/What	• Size of product • Color of product
How	• Mode of transport • Time of transport • Cost of transport

FUTURE RESEARCH DIRECTIONS

This chapter is a case study on healthcare inventory data, which shows the whole processes of data mining. The study is limited by the volume of the datasets. There are some future research directions to further develop the data analysis approach. The first direction is about data collection, the existing modeling methods are based on historical data which means the analysis is lagging from the dynamic market. To timely capture the market intelligence, a real-time data collection system is required for the data mining process. Second direction is the pruning criterion of the decision tree. The existing pruning algorithms are based on the accuracy of the forecasting model. However the criterion can be change to other factors. Third direction is to analyze how to deploy the patterns explored from the data. There are many patterns which are explored by many data scientists, however, few researches have been done on how to use these patterns and did not explore the interrelationships among these patterns.

CONCLUSION

This chapter is a case study on inventory dataset in the healthcare supply chain. A data cleaning method was used to pre-process the problem data in the dataset. And then a summary statistic has been applied to describe the dataset. And then, a CRT modeling has been applied to forecasting the demand based on the pervious transaction data and made a comparison with another decision model which is CHAID and got the result that the CRT is better than CHAID in this case. The CRT is different from the traditional linear regression. CRT is able to deal with the ordinal data and categorical data. This research gives a potential way to make a demand forecasting model by using the CRT algorithm. Readers can find that it is possible to use the CRT to build a demand forecasting model.

REFERENCES

Aburto, L., & Weber, R. (2007). Improved supply chain management based on hybrid demand forecasts. *Applied Soft Computing*, *7*(7), 136–144. doi:10.1016/j.asoc.2005.06.001

Al-Anbuky, A., Bataineh, S., & Al-Aqtash, S. (1995). Power demand prediction using fuzzy logic (Vol. 3). Elsevier.

Aman, S., Frincu, M., Chelmis, C., Noor, M., Simmhan, Y., & Prasanna, V. K. (2015). *Prediction Models for Dynamic Demand Response*. Paper presented at the 2015 IEEE International Conference on Smart Grid Communications (SmartGridComm): Data Management, Grid Analytics, and Dynamic Pricing.

Attar, K. S. (2016). *Proposed Methodology of Intelligent System Using Support Vector Regression for Demand Forecasting*. Academic Press.

Carbonneau, R., Laframboise, K., & Vahidov, R. (2008). Application of machine learning techniques for supply chain demand forecasting. *European Journal of Operational Research, 184*(3), 1140–1154. doi:10.1016/j.ejor.2006.12.004

D'alisa, S., Miscio, G., Baudo, S., Simone, A., Tesio, L., & Mauro, A. (2006). Depression is the main determinant of quality of life in multiple sclerosis: A classification-regression (CART) study. *Disability and Rehabilitation, 28*(5).

Dornier, P. P., Ernst, R., Fender, M., & Kouvelis, P. (1998). *Global Operations and Logistics: Text and Cases*. Academic Press.

Dumbill, E., Liddy, E., Stanton, J., Mueller, K., & Farnham, S. (2013). *Educating the Next Generation of Data Scientists*. Academic Press.

Keeney, R. L. (1994). *Creativity in decision making with value-focused thinking*. Sloan Management Review.

Levi, R., Pal, M., Roundy, R. O., & Shmoys, D. B. (2007). Approximation algorithms for stochastic inventory control models. Mathematics of Operation Research, 32.

Mentzer, J. T., DeWitt, W., Keebler, J. S., Min, S., Nix, N. W., Smith, C. D., & Zacharia, Z. G. (2001). *Defining supply chain management*. Academic Press.

Msiza, I. S., Nelwamondo, F. V., & Marwala, T. (2008). Water Demand Prediction using Artificial Neural Networks and Support Vector Regression. *Journal of Computers, 3*(11).

Press, G. (2013). *A very short history of data science*. Academic Press.

Radhakrishnan, P., Prasad, V. M., & Gopalan, M. R. (2009). *Genetic Algorithm Based Inventory Optimization Analysis in Supply Chain Management*. Academic Press.

Ross, D. F. (1998). *Competing Through Supply Chain Management*. Academic Press.

Sanders, N. R. (2014). *Big Data Driven Supply Chain Management: A Framework for Implementing Analytics and Turning Information into Intelligence*. Academic Press.

Srinivasan, D. (2008). Energy demand prediction using GMDH networks. Elsevier.

Taylor, D. (1997). *Global Cases in Logistics and Supply Chain Management*. International Thompson Business Press.

Waller, M. A., & Fawcett, S. E. (2013). *Data science, predictive analytics, and big data: A revolution that will transform supply chain design and management*. Academic Press.

KEY TERMS AND DEFINITIONS

CHAID: An abbreviation of Chi-squared Automatic Interaction Detection and an algorithm of decision tree technique.

CRT: An abbreviation of Classification and Regression Tree and a mixed algorithm of decision tree technique and regression technique.

Data Mining: A multi-disciplinary process to discover patterns hidden in data.

Demand Prediction: A process to predict future market demand.

Inventory: A detailed list of all the items in stock.

Statistics: A discipline to collect and interpret quantitative data.

Supply Chain: A trace of products or service from supplier to customer.

Chapter 6
Role of Operations Strategy and Big Data:
A Study of Transport Company

Arvind Upadhyay
University of Brighton, UK

Mahmood Ali
University of Business and Technology Jeddah, Saudi Arabia

Vikas Kumar
University of the West of England, UK

John Loonam
Dublin City University Business School, Ireland

ABSTRACT

It has been observed that the less than truck load (LTL) industry is going through significant transformation. After the last few years of decline in revenue, due to weak economy, the profitability of the LTL is on the rise. A strategy based on improving freight flow and density, and tightening terminal capacity is finally producing results for many LTL's, at the same time other LTL's are investing on expanding terminal network's while making bigger gains in the revenue. The availability of big data has revolutionised the way the LTL industry operates. The data assists in planning, efficient routing, safety control, fuel conservation, driving habits, etc. Analysts believe that big data still has a bigger role to play and it will have significant impact on the LTL industry in the coming days. This chapter discusses the challenges and opportunities for LTL carriers as it arises due to the emergence of big data.

DOI: 10.4018/978-1-5225-0956-1.ch006

INTRODUCTION

This chapter presents a discussion on LTL and impact IT in general and big data in particular is making in LTL sector. This chapter starts off with discussing operations strategy for LTL load and then role of IT in LTL is discussed, which if followed by overview of impact of big data on LTL and issues associated with incorporating big data into daily operations and decision making. This chapter covers few problems linked with typical large scale logistics LTL carrier (Zhang, 2010) and suggesting the possible approaches to handle these problems.

This part addresses the following topics:

- OR Tools
- Strategic Issues
- Integration
- Practicalities
- LTL and big data

In the operation research (OR) Tools, authors discussed some of the famous models prevalent in the market. Math behind the models has not been discussed but authors have tried to understand the logic behind the models and their applicability in the context of a large LTL service provider. In strategic issues, authors discuss the need and requirements of a large LTL service provider from the strategic, tactical and operational point of view. We also introduce the concept of positioning for the large LTL service provider so that the company can understand where it wants to go in the future and adapt the strategy for that goal. Integration discusses how the models can be integrated in the company. Authors discuss the investment, infrastructure and culture integration for the implementation of new system / model. Practicalities summarise and deal with some investment and emerging issues for a large LTL company. Role of big data in LTL is the main focus in last part, which also covers some issues linked with big data in LTL.

BACKGROUND

A load plan specifies how the freight is routed through a line haul terminal network operated by a less than truck load (LTL) carrier. A typical LTL shipment usually travels from an original (O) terminal to a destination (D) terminal, and pass thorough usually one or two intermediate break bulk terminals en-route. The main problems are large line haul problem, daily P&D operation (vehicle routing problem), balance problem. Currently, the given Omega corp (a hypothetical company) in case is using constraint programming as well as classical math programming based approach to solve vehicle routing problem. For the large line-haul problem, company uses MIP based approached and simulator. For balance problem, company uses revenue management model. For solving the LTL load plan, there were many methods suggested by scholars. Powell-Sheffi (1989) proposed a heuristics approach using add-drop local search method. This method is quite simple and easy to implement in small level organization but in medium and large scale organizations, the calculation and math gets more complicated, hence difficult to implement. Powell- Koskosidis (1992) uses a gradient-based local search method and the lagrangian heuristic approach with a relaxation of minimum service level constraints. It provides a good quick solution with tight lower bound. However, the solution is not very precise since for the precise solution it takes longer execution times. Powell (2001) introduced a new approach to solve the load plan designing problem for LTL. The strength of his approach lies in the fact that it explicitly recognizes the structure of most LTL networks and uses it to improve the efficiency of the algorithms as well as to sequence the research. The most important modelling assumption in his research is handling of level of service, which is each load planning link is a certain minimum frequency which must be maintained if direct service is offered.

OPERATIONS STRATEGY ISSUES IN LTL

Strategic Issues

Recently, a significant work has been carried out on the problem of configuring hub-and spoke networks for trucking companies that operates less-than-truck load services. This problem consists of determining the number of consolidation terminals (hubs), their locations and the assignment of the spokes to the hubs, aiming to minimize the total cost, which is composed of fixed and variable cost. Cunha and Silva (2007) devised a heuristic based on genetic algorithms for the companies that operate LTL service in Brazil. Their genetic algorithm incorporates an efficient local improvement procedure that is applied to each generated individual of the population. This approach differs from the similar formulation found in literature in the sense that it allows variable scale reduction factors for the transportation cost according to the total amount of freight between hub terminals, as occurs to LTL. Another important difference is its non-linear objective function that allows economies of scale for the transportation costs that may vary according to the total amount of freight between hub terminals. This can be easily incorporated in the case study company because this company also moves freight using hubs and spokes correspond to service centres. They have 300 service centres in US and Canada and

90 hubs. For using this genetic algorithm, they can divide the whole area in some local centre (by joining the service centres) and then incorporating the efficient local improvement procedure that is applied to each generated individual local centres.

Jarrah et al (2009) presented a novel and comprehensive model for designing LTL service networks. They categorize their problem as being a capacitated multi- commodity fixed-charge network design (CMND) problem. In the objective functions, costs are: (Loaded Trailer transportation cost, which considers the cost of loaded trailer moves between terminals), (Handling cost for the freight), (Empty re-positioning cost). The complete network design model is then minimize the objective function subject to the constraints (the number of trailers moved over a link *l* and departing on day *d* should be greater than or equal to the sum of all freight on flow trees that use link *l*, on day *d*, divided by the capacity counts the number of trailers that move on link *l* on day *d*). Their formulation captures the basic network design constraints; the load planning requirement that all freight at a location irrespective of the freight's origin, loads to the same next terminal. Their model is specifically for medium and large scale LTL companies (up to 1.3 million binary variables and 1.3 million constraints in their case). They used a set of efficient IP sub problems and a coordinating master problem. Using slope-scaling and load-planning tree generation, they were able to generate high quality solution which resulted in saving of millions of dollars for the target company. Their LTL network design model has the three main components; e.g. weekday freight fluctuations, service level by Origin to Destination (O-D) and Pickup / delivery cut-off times and break-bulk handling times. In the given case study, Omega corp operates like airline or FedEx and use a hub and spoke network correspond to service centre. Therefore, it is easy to integrate in the Omega corp system due to the similarity in the operation. The operation from one service centre to another service centre is their main key operation and they should keep it in house because this will help them in controlling their main operation. The cross dock operation and moving from one trailer to another trailer can be outsourced and given to sub service provider. They also mention in the case study that the company driver don't do long haul driving across the country hence it is good idea for them to outsource this activity to sub service provider. It will help the company to concentrate on their core competence (which is efficiently moving the freight from one service centre to another service centre and outsource the secondary activity (long haul across the country).

Hence in developing operations research technology strategy for a typical large logistics LTL company all these factors should be kept in mind. There is always a trade-off between high quality precision service and the investment. The Omega corp is a large size company, but the priority of the company defines the future strategy for the company. Designing operational research technology strategy for a typical large logistics LTL company is based upon positioning of the company.

Where the company wants to position itself? Which market segment and who will be their prospective customers? Hence before designing operations research technology strategy, company should think about its positioning. Positioning is a strategic tool initially developed for consumer marketing but now it's equally applicable in Industrial organizations also. According to Kotler (2000) positioning is seen as an act of deigning the company's offering or image to occupy a distinct place in the target market's mind whereas industrial marketers see it as the firm's unique way of delivering value to customers. It is possible to distinguish between resource based strategy and competence based strategy for positioning the Omega corp's products and services. The classical positioning model by Johnston and Clark (2001) can be used by the company to position them. And the company can position in the area mentioned in the below figure. As in case of logistics carrier, there are a mix of tangible and intangible products and services, hence the company should focus in the centre of service and market focused. In case of Omega corp, sometimes they have to customize their operation according to the requirements of their customers hence they can work on the competence model by Hertz and Alfredsson (2003). This model is quite similar to the classical positioning model as discussed above but it also tackles the issue of general problem solving ability of a company.

Juga et al (2008) pointed out the strategic positioning of logistics service providers and they indicate the main strategic positions are efficient bulk transport capability, responsiveness as strategic advantage, logistics competencies with the local root and organising for global coordination and local responsiveness. Most of these are applicable for the medium and large scale logistic service providers.

Integration

Roy (2001) discusses the strategy for logistics service providers at different level. He defines that there are different types of strategic problem at different level as shown in table 1.

He also pointed out that in large scale LTL logistics companies, the freights are picked-up during the day, and the relevant information is registered in the on- board computers and forwarded to the terminal where it is fed to the CIS. For all such operations, real-time information technology is needed, which is readily available in market at a higher price. Hence most of the companies don't buy this real-time technology and have to wait until the pick-up trucks arrive at the terminal at the end of the day in order to find out what was actually picked up during the day. In case of Omega corp, it's not mentioned that they already have real-time information technology or not. Usually companies also use their own in-house developed information system for transferring the information in real-time. The question here is not only getting real-time information in LTL operation but also to optimise the

Table 1. Typical planning problem at different levels

Planning Level	Pick-up and Delivery	Terminal Activities	Long Distance
Strategic	• Outsourcing • Fleet selection	• Terminal location • Terminal Design	• Fleet mix • Outsourcing
Tactical	• P&D Zone design • Door assignment	• Load Planning • Work scheduling	• Seasonal • transportation plan
Operational	• Delivery routes • Truck Loading	Daily adjustments to plan and schedule	• Vehicle routing • Week-end dispatch
Real-time	• Pick-up assignment • Door assignments	Hourly adjustments to plan and schedule	Real time dispatch

(Source: Roy, 2001)

process; e.g. assigning the pick-up trucks, scheduling the work freight and revising the load plan. Due to the emergence of new computer technology, same models can be now used for solving the problems in operational environment also.

In Omega corp, routing of delivery trucks is an operational problem and it is very commonly found in other similar organizations. These can be solved by using the advanced quasi real-time technology system. Gregory et al (1999) discuss the relationship between strategy, structure and logistics in the context of a changing environment. They devised a framework which suggests that the performance will be higher when the firm's strategy and structure are in alignment with the logistics system. The Omega corp can help the sub service provider in designing their own network. By doing this, the sub service provider will work perfectly aligned with Omega corp. In the extension of the Omega corp's LTL network design, they can impart the same model for sub service provider and can enhance their capability to smoothly running their business. By helping their sub service provider in providing the network design support, the Omega corp can also share the investment (in infrastructure and technology) with the sub service provider. Hence it will be win-win situation for both of them and they both can gain (for the Omega corp, it's the sharing of investment with their sub service provider and for sub service provider, it's the knowledge and competence in the network design which they will get from Omega corp at a much lesser cost).

This model seems to be quite suitable for the company in the case due to its large scale. The major hindrance is that IP problems are quite large and takes lot of time to run. In their case, it took two hours to run, so they used it for weekly load planning. But if they have to change the load plan in middle of week, then this can be a problem. Another issue is infrastructure and investment for such model. The company needs a pool of operation research analysts who are full time dedicated for such project. The analysts not only need the knowledge of operations research but also need to know the knowledge of lower level computer language (C / C++) with calls to the Xpress MIP library. If the operation research analysts are strong, then they can customize the model according to their requirement and can make changes in the variables and constraints. The company also need high performance IT system with machines with multiple processors. Usually such projects creates lots of resistance from the inside employees and that's why for such projects to implement, the company should dedicate a project sponsor / champion who is fully responsible for such project. The operational execution cost of a given load plan is estimated by a three phase approach. Firstly, loading and matching pups to determine the timed path for each commodity and combined loaded trailers on a direct into dispatches. Secondly determining the dispatch windows and thirdly constructing driver tours. Integer programming is used for the dynamic load planning approach and uses a path based optimization model on the time space network.

Practicalities

Omega corp also uses the revenue management to understand the relationship between price and demand. During the last couple of years of recession, logistics service companies suffered because shippers had the upper hand in both truck load (TL) and LTL. Now the economy has shown some signs of improvements, the logistics service companies are working on new pricing strategies. Revenue management is one of the most famous for differential pricing strategies. According to FedEx freight president Bill Logue, 'FedEx has been closely examining its LTL network and the LTL market in an effort to determine how to get back to double digit margin and for that they plan to combine its FedEx freight and FedEx national LTL operations, effective January 30, 2011'. This suggests that FedEx is consolidating its two separate businesses and working on new formula for the different pricing. It's easy to theoretically define the models for load plan but it becomes difficult when we actually implement in system. As authors discussed earlier, the integration problem and investment becomes the major problems but the infrastructure also plays a vital time. For the large LTL logistics company, the precision of the load plan solution and the quality is very important and there is always a trade- off between investment and execution time / precision quality. Hence the main issue is how much to adapt new model / OR tools in the company' system and what should be the time line. The better option is to include the sub service provider (as authors discussed earlier also), so that the company can share the investment and also it can enhance its whole network for the quick precise delivery of service. At the beginning, Omega corp should go step by step, implementing new system only for its service centre operation and then for movement of freight (line- haul) problem. Followed by pickup and delivery operation, revenue management and further on. Next, Omega corp can go to assist their sub-service providers to implement the same system, so that they can align their operation with the Omega corp. In the following section, this paper examines advances in field of IT in LTL. The first section discusses the state of LTL in the age of current information technology. This is followed by a discussion on impact of big data on LTL.

LTL IN THE AGE OF INFORMATION TECHNOLOGY

Developments in IT field have profound impact on the freight transportation. Different transportation modes are maximizing the application of information technology in their daily operations and decision making. They are increasingly becoming efficient by using communication technologies and different IT applications and software for routing and scheduling, vehicle monitoring and maintenance and record keeping. Golob and Regan (2001) find that intermodal freight transportation, particularly maritime and air cargo is being transformed by IT. Tracking and tracing technologies for containers and packages are gaining widespread use, and web-based information clearing houses are providing key information to improve the efficiency of modal transfers. Crainic et al. (2009) propose that LTL motor carriers will attain substantial benefits from the use of information technology and decision technologies. Similarly, emergence of internet-based community of interests and electronic auction mechanisms will directly and significantly affect the operations and performances of freight carriers including LTL. The loads that could be obtained by accessing these markets would reduce the need to move empty vehicles to balance the operations. Such markets complement the more traditional auctions of distribution routes of major industrial or retail firms (Ledyard et al., 2002). In a study conducted George Mason University in association with a logistic technology company, 74billions data points logged from GPS tracking devices installed in 552,000 vehicles, researchers are examining whether data on the movement of goods-carrying trucks can be correlated to provide a timely view of the direction of consumer spending, business investment and other economic fundamentals (Chao, 2015). Lai et al. (2004) study the effect role IT technology adoption in third party logistics. They find that significant competitive advantage can be achieved in the area cost reduction, providing innovative and customized services, and improved service quality. Whilst, Jiang et al (2005) find lack of research in the area of data mining and the use of data in transportation industry.

LTL AND BIG DATA

Big data is a term used to define large or complex data set resulting from the exponential growth of data, structured or unstructured. According to McKinsey, big data refers to dataset whose size are beyond the ability of typical database software tools to capture, store, manage and analyse. The data originate from several different heterogeneous, for example, there are now countless digital sensors worldwide in industrial equipment, automobiles, electrical meters and shipping crates. They can measure and communicate location, movement, vibration, temperature, humidity, even chemical changes in the air (NY Times, 2012). According to IDC report, the data is growing at 50 percent a year, or more than doubling every two years. Bain (2013) explains big data as the mining and processing petabytes worth of information to gain insight into customer behaviour, supply chain efficiency and other essential factors of business performance. According to Transparent Market Research (2013) report, the global market for big data was estimated at US$6.3 billion in 2012 and is expected to increase to US$48.3 billion by year 2018 (a CAGR of 40.5%). Although there is a limited scientific research on how big data will impact the logistics sector (Waller & Fawcett, 2013), still many applications and technologies are practiced in the industry. Such as in transportation industry the application of Telematics technology has contributed significantly towards collection of big data. Telematics refers to the use of wireless and information storing devices to capture and transmit data in real time back to organisation. This access to data in real time play essential role in improving the operational efficiency, lowering overheads and in gaining the competitive position in LTL. Using the data, LTL can improve driver safety, increases assets utilisation and lower cost of operations. According to Szakonyi (2014) analysis of big data could suggest several strategies for efficient drayage operation since this could be the most volatile link in the supply chain. Port of Oakland successfully analysed the number of trucks needed after the implementation of rule which banned pre-2007 model trucks. By collecting data they were able to identify number of trucks which will be needed and numbers of trucks which will not meet the regulations and, potential resulting lesser movement of containers.

Some other benefits which could be derived from big data analysis include:

1. **Diver Identification:** Identifying individual driver which capturing real service time and generating driver's activity report.
2. **Driver Safety Monitoring:** Monitoring driving habits of driver which on the road and also identifying unsafe driving habits.
3. **Fuel Consumption:** Monitoring and collect the fuel usage data. This could be used to identify and minimise unproductive idle time.
4. **Diagnostics:** Vehicle diagnostics and performance monitoring.

Big data offers significant support to LTL against the challenges presented by US Government's new Compliance Safety Accountability (CSA) initiative which is termed as most significant and comprehensive safety program in deregulation era (Logistic management, 2011). This initiative involves several layer of safety evaluation adding data from roadside inspections. It rates carriers on seven behaviour analysis and safety categories including unsafe drivers, fatigued driving hours of service, vehicle maintenance, driver fitness, cargo security, crash incident rate and controlled substances (FMCSA, 2015). The CSA will have significant impact on LTL performance and productivity. This will requires significant amount to data to be collected throughout the LTL operation for analysis and safety improvement purposes. The big data collected at individual company level or at all LTL sector level, could provide LTL with significant understanding and knowledge to comply with SAC initiative. This is turn will improve the safety of LTL operations. The continuously updated data can keep a latest check on driver's performance and update LTL management when a driver s most likely to be audited by government safety agency due any safety or road violations. For example, Schneider national trucking builds a system of sensors on its truck, trailers and intermodal containers to monitor locations, driving behaviour and fuel levels to avoid losing productivity and safety audit. Besides, safer operations, big data in LTL could contribute towards assessing the economic driving condition. Bousonville at el. (2015) suggest that areas such as fuel consumption per distance, break usage, uniform speed profile, accelerator pedal movement, number of stops and others, could be significant determinants of evaluating the economics driving habits of the driver. The data could be collected using telematics on-board devices which can monitor and record the patterns and later could be used to further analysis. This could assist LTL in identifying the truck which is not being operated efficiently and the drivers which are not efficient and wasting resources and not following the regulations. Such, in one of the instances, data indicated to LTL that some if its trucks were being unnecessarily idled after night-time loading therefore costing carrier higher fuel bill. In addition, data could also assist in determining which truck is not being utilized to their potential. Another potential use of big data in LTL could be to recruit, keep and train the drivers. It is critical since according to a study industry could face shortfall of as many 400,000 drivers in the coming years. In addition, experts estimate that is cost as much as US$ 10,000 to attract and train new drivers (Logistic management, 2011). To overcome drivers' shortage issues, Cassidy (2014) find that organisations are using big data to recruit and train driver while recording and monitoring their performance through on-board devices. The data is used to understand driver's needs, planning driver's day, route planning for customer's appointments and training requirements, if any. This helps originations in observing every aspect of driver's daily life which could lead to improved driver retention.

When it comes to decision making by shippers in regards to freight rate, big data agility contributes towards enhanced decision making shippers. It enables them to access, view, and compare the current and historical data, thus enabling them to achieve quicker and easier rate management. The access to historical data enables instant comparison between the rates thus giving LTL ability to respond to the competition by updating rates in shortest time period. Another benefit of big data according to Vallancourt (215) is that it integrates shippers with carriers rate base, which enables shipper to view, in LTL, which lane a carrier operate most efficiently and at the lowest cost. The carrier then can select to haul the freight that satisfy their needs with no risk selecting the medium which is not efficient (Vallancourt, 2015). In LTL's relationship with its business partners, big data provides transparency to remove any bias or unfair treatment. Big data could enables decision making which is more focused and objective thus providing LTL peace of mind that they would receive the quantity of freight and rate as they expected which in turn assist them in future planning. The access to data also enable LTL's shipper to receive *sustainable* rates while providing an opportunity for collaboration between shipper and LTL on service requirement which could lead to efficient working relationship. Another major big data impact area is supply chain and its logistic partners. The data collected from across the supply chain and LTLs, could create a platform to formulate a joint strategy for shared transportation activity between the supply chain partners for mutual benefits. Further, data can be shared with the carriers to remove any misunderstandings between the supply chain partners including LTLs, therefore every partner in supply chain is informed and work effectively. Integrating big data in LTL could be a game changer, however, there are certain issues which need careful consideration and are discussed in the following section.

Issues

Issue 1: According to McKinsey report (2011), company's "data drive mind-set" is the key indicator of big data value to companies. Therefore LTL which are not data driven and more reply on subjective intuition most likely will stay away from big data. This specific mind-set could become a barrier to entry or to appropriate implementation.

Issue 2: The LTL's lack of expertise with big data collection and analysis could require them to either hire services of external consultants or acquire new in-house expertise and training.

Issue 3: Big data raises the concerns about the privacy issue since the information could be shared. However, Anderson and Rainie (2012) find that enthusiasts see great potential for using big data, whilst privacy advocates are worried as more and more data is collected.

Issue 4: Analysing the big data and generating conclusion could be complicated process. The huge data set and its fine-grained measurement, statisticians and computer scientists note, there is increased risk of "false discoveries." The trouble with seeking a meaningful needle in massive haystacks of data, says Trevor Hastie, a statistics professor at Stanford, is that "many bits of straw look like needles" (NY Times, 2012).

Issue 5: Time required to collect and analyse data could be a cumbersome process. According to Tom Benusa of Transport America, data from multiple sources could be huge and it must be in usable standard format. This process often could be one or two years before data is assimilated in the process and reap the benefits.

Issue 6: Data grouping could be another issue in the light of current trends of data aggregation. When analysing data it should be noted that a set of data connected do not make it useful unless there is an existing relationship among the variables and, in-depth and rigorous grouping process is carried out before making any prediction.

CONCLUSION

This chapter focuses on issues associated with Less Than Truck (LTL) Load and the role of IT in big data era. There are various operations research and strategic tools strategies which are used by LTL carriers to cope with changing business environment. There are lots of benefits due to availability of big data, e.g. driver identification, driver safety monitoring, monitoring fuel consumption and vehicle performance monitoring. However all the benefits of big data are possible only when the LTL industry has proper big data driven mind-set and adequate infrastructure. As analysing big data is also a challenging issue for small LTL carriers hence they have limited benefits from big data. In future, big data is going to play a vital role in LTL industry due to the advancement in technology and Information Technology.

REFERENCES

Anderson, J., & Rainie, L. (2012). *The future of big data, pew research*. Retrieved November 14, 2015, from http://www.pewinternet.org/2012/07/20/the-future-of-big-data/

Bain. (2013). *Big data: The organization challenge*. Retrieved November 7, 2015, from www.bain.com

Bousonville, T., Ebert, C. & Rath, J. (2015). *A comparison of reward systems for truck drivers based on telematics data and driving behavior assessments*. Technical reports on Logistics of the Saarland Business School.

Cassidy, W. (2014). *Tech savvy truckers search big data for drivers.* Retrieved November 4, 2015, from http://www.joc.com/trucking-logistics/labor/tech-savvy-truckers-search-big-data-drivers_20140523.html

Chao, L. (2015). *Riding on that truck: Big data on economy.* Retrieved November 6, 2015, from http://www.wsj.com/articles/riding-on-that-truck-big-data-on-the-economy-1430954699

Crainic, T., Gendreau, M., & Potvin, J. (2009). Intelligent freight transportation systems: Assessment and the contribution of operations research. *Transportation Research Part C, Emerging Technologies*, *17*(6), 541–557. doi:10.1016/j.trc.2008.07.002

Cunha, B., & Silva, M. (2007). A genetic algorithm for the problem of configuring a hub-and-spoke network for a LTL trucking company in Brazil. *European Journal of Operational Research*, *179*(3), 747–758. doi:10.1016/j.ejor.2005.03.057

Federal Motor Carriers Safety Administration (FMCSA). (2015). *Motor Carriers Safety Administration*. Retrieved November 11, 2015, from https://www.fmcsa.dot.gov/registration/commercial-drivers-license/compliance

Golob, T., & Regan, A. (2001). Trucking industry adoption of information technology: A multivariate discrete choice model. *Transportation Research*, *10*(Part C), 205–228.

Gregory, S. (1999). Logistics, strategy and structure: A conceptual framework. *International Journal of Physical Distribution & Logistics Management*, *29*(Iss: 4), 224–239. doi:10.1108/09600039910273948

Hertz, S., & Alfredsson, M. (2003). Strategic development of third party logistics providers. *Industrial Marketing Management*, *32*(2), 139–149. doi:10.1016/S0019-8501(02)00228-6

Jarrah, A. (2009). *Large-Scale, Less-than-Truckload Service Network*. Informs.

Jinag, W., Vaidya, J., Balaporia, Z., Clifton, C., & Banich, B. (2005). Knowledge Discovery from Transportation Network Data. In *IEEE Computer Society Proceedings of the 21st International Conference on Data Engineering*. Tokyo, Japan: IEEE.

Johnston, R., & Clark, G. (2001). *Service Operations Management*. Harlow, UK: Prentice-Hall.

Jugga, J. (2008). Strategic positioning of logistics service providers. *International Journal of Logistics: Research and Applications*, *11*(6), 443–455. doi:10.1080/13675560802373472

Kotler, P. (2000). *Marketing Management*. Upper Saddle River, NJ: Prentice-Hall.

Lai, F., Li, D., Wang, Q., & Zhao, X. (2004). The Information Technology Capability Of Third Party Logistics Providers: A resource based view and empirical evidence from China. *Journal of Supply Chain Management*, *44*(3), 22–38. doi:10.1111/j.1745-493X.2008.00064.x

Larson, P. D. (1998). Carrier reduction: Impact of logistics performance and interaction with EDI. *Transportation Journal*, *38*, 40–47.

Ledyard, J. O., Olson, M., Porter, D., Swanson, J. A., & Torma, D. P. (2002). The first use of a combined value auction for transportation services. *Transportation Journal*, *32*(5), 4–12.

Logistic Management Report. (2011). *LTL Special Report: Rising out of the doldrums*. Retrieved November 9, 2015, from http://www.logisticsmgmt.com/article/ltl_special_report_rising_out_of_the_doldrums/special_reports

Lohr, S. (2012). *The age of big data*. Retrieved November 4, 2015, from http://www.nytimes.com/2012/02/12/sunday-review/big-datas-impact-in-the-world.html?_r=1&scp=1&sq=Big%20Data&st=cse

McKinsey Report. (2011). *Big data: The next frontier for innovation, competition, and productivity*. Retrieved November 5, 2015, from http://www.mckinsey.com/insights/business_technology/big_data_the_next_frontier_for_innovation

Powell, B., & Koskosidis, A. (1992). Shipment routing algorithms with tree constraints. *Transportation Science*, *26*(3), 230–245. doi:10.1287/trsc.26.3.230

Powell, B., & Sheffi, Y. (1989). Design and implementation of an interactive optimization system for network design in the motor carrier industry. *Operations Research*, *37*(1), 12–29. doi:10.1287/opre.37.1.12

Powell, W. (2001). *A local improvement heuristic for the design of less-than-truckload motor carrier networks*. Princeton University.

Roy, J. (2001). Recent Trends in Logistics and the need for real-time Decision Tools in the Trucking Industry. *Proceedings of the 34th Hawaii International Conference on System Sciences*.

Szakonyi, M. (2014). Big data to rescue. *The Journal of Commerce*, 64-65.

Waller, J., & Fawcett, B. (2013). Data science, predictive analytics, and big data: A revolution that will transform supply chain design and management. *Journal of Business Logistics*, *34*(2), 77–84. doi:10.1111/jbl.12010

Zhang, Y. (2010). *Advances in LTL Load Plan design*. (Doctorate Thesis). Georgia Institute of Technology.

Section 3
Big Data and Emerging Technology

Chapter 7
Big Data and RFID in Supply Chain and Logistics Management:
A Review of the Literature and Applications for Data Driven Research

Thanos Papadopoulos
University of Kent, UK

Angappa Gunasekaran
University of Massachusetts – Dartmouth, USA

Rameshwar Dubey
Symbiosis Institute of Operations Management, India

Maria Balta
Brunel University, UK

ABSTRACT

Big Data refers to complex and unstructured data that is difficult to analyse and utilize with traditional applications and analyses. Big Data comes from a variety of sources, including tracking and sensor devices which are widely used in logistics and supply chain management, and relate to Radio Frequency Identification (RFID) technology. Thus, this chapter reviews the literature on RFID adoption in supply chain/logistics management from 1995-2015. We identify current trends in the lit-

DOI: 10.4018/978-1-5225-0956-1.ch007

erature, drawing on the three levels of decision making, that is, strategic, tactical, and operational. We suggest that more research needs to be conducted with regards to the intangible benefits of RFID, the use of RFID big data for achieving higher performance, and to shift the focus from the 'what' and the impacts on performance to the 'how' and the ways RFID is adopted and assimilated in organizations and supply chains. Finally, the managerial implications of our review as well as the limitations and future research directions are outlined.

INTRODUCTION

Over the last years, there has been an increased interest in big data (e.g. Riggins & Fosso-Wamba, 2015; Fosso-Wamba et al., 2015; Zhong et al., 2015; Wang et al. 2016). Companies have invested in creating and acquiring the necessary capabilities in order to obtain value from big data and attain competitive advantage (ibid). Big data may come from different sources, such as mobile devices, Internet of Things, and tracking and sensor devices which are widely used in logistics and supply chain management, including radio frequency identification (RFID), which is the focus of this chapter. In particular, this chapter reviews the literature on IT and in particular RFID in Supply Chains to identify current data-driven research and suggest future research avenues. In particular, the chapter presents a critical analysis of the articles published in the last 20 years (1995-2015) through a systematic literature review. The relationship between RFID and big data has been highlighted in the literature. RFID tagging is generating huge operational and strategic data across diverse industries' value chains in terms of volume, velocity, variety, value, and veracity (Wamba et al., 2015). DeRoos (2013) had predicted that the number of RFID tags will increase from 1.3 billion in 2005 to about 30 billion in 2013.

Ferrer et al. (2010) have argued for the further study of RFID for the following reasons:

1. Although the idea of RFID is not new, organizations have started to investigate the potential of RFID and the generation of Big Data that follows its use, and therefore managers are under pressure to grasp the application and benefits of RFID and related Big Data for organizational and supply chain performance,
2. Experts suggest that the RFID brings superior supply chain and logistics performance (Wyld, 2005; Ferrer et al., 2010),
3. The rapid evolution of RFID technology creates uncertainty and speculation with regards to the benefits that RFID may bring to organizations and supply chains,

4. Managers are still struggling with the investment justification of RFID as well as with selecting the appropriate configuration that will deal with operational needs and enhance operational performance.

The majority of current studies in RFID are quantitative in nature and may draw on particular frameworks including for instance, diffusion of innovations, technology acceptance model, the unified theory of acceptance and use of technology. Furthermore, there are studies that look into the behavioural aspect of technology for supply chain and logistics management (SCLM). There is a need, however, to systematically review this role of IT for SCLM. To address this gap, this chapter:

1. Provides a systematic review of the literature related to the role of IT through RFID in SCLM; and
2. To classify the literature, it uses the well-known framework by Gunasekaran et al. (2004) that is based on the role of IT in each of the decision making levels, that is, strategic, tactical, and operational.

Our results illustrate on one hand the growing importance of IT and RFID applications for, *inter alia*, supply chain integration and efficiency. On the other hand the majority of the papers are either outlining the benefits of RFID for supply chains, or they are conceptual. Our contribution lies in not only comprehensively reviewing the literature on Big Data through focusing on RFID in supply chains through a 20-year period, but also to provide endorsements for the future study of RFID big data and performance within organizations and supply chains.

The chapter is structured as follows. In the next section the framework and methodology for our review on the use of IT and RFID in supply chains is presented. It follows our review by classifying the relevant articles into levels of decision making. Our chapter ends with a discussion of the theoretical contributions, the managerial implications of this review, as well as limitations and future research directions.

FRAMEWORK AND METHODOLOGY USED FOR THE REVIEW OF THE LITERATURE ON THE USE OF IT AND RFID IN SUPPLY CHAINS

Framework for the Classification of the Literature

We classify the literature on IT and RFID in supply chains using the well-known framework of Anthony (1965). Anthony has proposed the ‘strategic’, ‘tactical’, and ‘operational’ levels, which are related to the traditional levels of top management, middle management, and operational management. In our review, we use this framework to classify and relate IT and RFID use with particular levels of decision making and levels of use.

This framework has been used in Gunasekaran et al. (2004) in their review of the literature on supply chain performance. Their literature review was based on the levels of decision making, that is, strategic, tactical, and operational that relate to the level of management authority and responsibility for performance. Furthermore, it has been used in studies of IT/IS evaluation in organizations (e.g. Irani & Love, 2002), as well as justifying investments in IT (Gunasekaran et al. 2001), and in reviewing the literature on IT/IS justification (Gunasekaran et al., 2006).

Methodology for the Review of the Literature

The authors have identified and classified the relevant as well as updated literature review according to the guidelines of Rowley and Slack (2004). Specific criteria have been applied for conducting systematic literature review. First step, relevant databases such as Emerald, Science Direct, Taylor and Francis, Wiley Online Library have been selected as they host subject related journals: Journal of Operations Management, International Journal of Operations and Production Management, Production and Operations Management, International Journal of Production Economics, Production Planning and Control, and Supply Chain Management: An International Journal.

More specifically, we performed Boolean keywords and subject term searches of all scholarly journals published in the aforementioned databases between 1995 and 2015 inclusive. Our initial search terms consisted of RFID, technology and supply chain management; the following keywords were used separately and in combination (using "and/"or") RFID, technology, information technology, technology adoption and supply chain. The selected keywords were found in the title, abstract and the main body of the literature review. This yielded 247 articles. Second step, the authors have adopted a specific framework which assisted them to classify the literature on RFID within technology and supply chain management literature by focusing on different definitions, constructs and trying to explore research avenues opportunities. Third step, involves the exclusion of duplicate or irrelevant articles. The irrelevant articles were determined by skimming each abstract and eliminating those that were clearly not about RFID within the area of supply chain management and technology adoption. All relevant articles identified have been reviewed for RFID and their practical implications. Managerial implications, limitations, and future research directions have been identified. All authors have collaborated and interacted on all the aspects of the systematic literature review by reading the title, abstract and full text and acted as reviewers in the process. In a few cases of disagreement whether initial selected articles should be included and classified, further discussions took place until agreement was reached. The final sample contained 27 articles which the authors have studied and analysed in depth and the results of the analysis are provided in the following sections.

REVIEW OF THE LITERATURE ON IT AND RFID IN SUPPLY CHAINS

In this section we review the literature on IT and RFID in supply chains. The results of the literature review are shown in Table 1, where it is extrapolated the number of papers per journal.

In the next sections, we present the papers identified per level of decision making, that is, strategic, tactical, and operational. The articles are extrapolated in Table 2 and discussed in the next subsections.

IT and RFID at the Strategic Level of Decision Making

The strategic level is concerned with the "design, implementation, management, and strategic direction of functions, operations, or processes that are highly critical and risky" (Gunasekaran et al., 2015: p. 156). Decisions at this level belong to the top level and include financial plans, competitiveness, and decisions such as sourcing (Gunasekaran & Patel, 2001).

At the strategic level, the majority of papers are view RFID as an investment and discuss the relationship of RFID on supply chain and organizational performance. For instance, Miragliotta et al. (2009) have proposed an analytical model to assess the

Table 1. Journal name and number of articles identified per journal

Journal Name	Number of Articles Identified
Journal of Operations Management	4
Production and Operations Management	5
International journal of production and operations management	4
International journal of production economics	5
Production Planning and control	7
Supply chain management: an international journal	2
Total:	27

Table 2. Relevant articles per levels of decision making

Levels of RFID Decision Making	Articles
Strategic	Gunasekaran and Ngai (2004); Dehning et al. (2007); Lee and Ozer (2007); Whitaker et al. (2007); Lin and Ho (2009); Miragliotta et al. (2009); Autry et al. (2010); Lee and Lee (2010); Smart et al. (2010); Sarac et al. (2010); Reyes et al. (2012); Quetti et al. (2012); Zelbst et al. (2012); Pfal and Moxham (2014); Chong et al. (2015); Fan et al. (2015); Wamba and Ngai (2015); Wamba et al. (2016)
Tactical	Gunasekaran and Ngai (2004); Barratt and Oke (2007); Dehning et al. (2007); Whitaker et al. (2007); Visich et al. (2009); Smart et al. (2010); Sarac et al. (2010);
Operational	Gunasekaran and Ngai (2004); Camdereli and Swaminathan (2007); Chow et al. (2007); Delen et al. (2007); Dehning et al. (2007); Heese (2007); Lin and Ho (2009); Visich et al. (2009); Zelbst et al. (2009); Smart et al. (2010); Sarac et al. (2010); Laosirihongthong et al. (2013); Pero and Rossi (2014); Crumbly and Carter (2015); Wamba and Ngai (2015);

costs and benefits of RFID in the fast moving consumer goods supply chain, based on an assessment of RFID applications as well as on an in-depth literature review. Their model could help managers and decision makers on taking important 'go' or 'no-go' decisions with regards to the adoption of RFID. In a later study, Pfal and Moxham (2014) have discussed the achievement of sustainable competitive advantage with the use of particular technologies, inter alia, RFID. They underlined the value of RFID for rendering the supply chain visible and as a strategic capability within retail supply networks, and adopted the resource-based view of the firm (Barney 1991; Grant 1991; Peteraf 1993) to explore RFID as a resource with the characteristics of being valuable, rare, imperfectly mobile, not imitable and non-substitutable. Wamba and Ngai (2015), however, are not focusing on the manufacturing, but in the healthcare sector. They investigate issues related to the implementation of RFID projects, underlining their strategic nature. Their issues are mostly technological (data management, security, and privacy), as well as organizational and financial. Chong et al. (2015) continued the debate by Miragliotta et al. (2009) and proposed a model that predicts the RFID adoption from the perspectives of the users. In particular, they have used the unified theory of acceptance and use of technology (UTAUT), integrating it with individual differences (neuroticism, conscientiousness, openness to experience, agreeableness and extraversion) and demo- graphic characteristics (i.e. age and gender) to predict the adoption of RFID in the healthcare supply chain. Their results illustrated the applicability of UTAUT and individual characteristics in predicting the adoption of RFID. Finally, Wamba et al. (2016) have proposed and tested a conceptual model that investigates the technological, organisational, environmental and managerial characteristics of small and mid-sized enterprises (SMEs) in the intention of the SMEs to adopt RFID, using 453 SME managers from the USA, the UK, Australia and India. They found that the intention to adopt RFID stems from the projected benefits related to the achievement of relative advantage and compatibility, the firms' size as well as to the country where the RFID is to be adopted. However, the complexity of RFID, the competitive environment, manager characteristics (e.g. age, education and gender) and industry sector do not play an important role.

The majority of studies at this level underline the importance of RFID for transparency and visibility in the supply chain, and relate its adoption to the achievement of competitive advantage. Furthermore, the studies are, in their majority, treating RFID as a 'thing' that is ready to be implemented or adopted, but do not investigate the social and organizational impacts of RFID adoption. The use of technology adoption models is also popular, and these models do not investigate how RFID is being adopted. In this vein, there are limited, if any, studies that follow a case study approach and try to provide answers to 'how' RFID is adopted, instead of proposing conceptual models that relate RFID to performance and measuring or projecting its future impact.

IT and RFID at the Tactical Level of Decision Making

The tactical level is concerned with decisions related to resource allocation and benchmarking performance against particular targets to be met in order to achieve results that are determined at the strategic level (Gunasekaran & Patel, 2001).

RFID contributes to the achievement of the particular targets as set by the organizational and supply chain strategy. Barratt and Oke (2007) have discussed supply chain visibility as an outcome of RFID adoption and use, from an RBV perspective, and its link to the strategic level through the provision of sustainable competitive advantage, whereas Visich et al. (2009) look into the implementation of RFID and its effect on managerial processes, using the 'automation'/ 'information'/'transformation' framework based on the impact of IT on organizations and supply chains. In particular, they suggest that the implementation of RFID does not bring transformational or informational benefits with regards to operational or managerial processes. On the contrary, automational effects on operational processes are identified through inventory control and efficiency improvements (which relate to the managerial decision making level, that is, the tactical level). Informational effects for managerial processes are also observed, including "improved decision quality, production control and the effectiveness of retail sales and promotions coordination" (p. 1290). Smart et al. (2010) investigated the different adoption costs related to RFID by interviewing middle managers and participants in the RFID adoption process in supply network settings, and by looking into public information on RFID development, and offer a classification of different costs using six categories of generic process innovation costs (development, switching, cost of capital, implementation, initiation, and relational). They also extend this categorization by adding a seventh category, that is, ethical costs, which are associated with privacy and health issues. Finally, Sarac et al. (2010), in their review of the impact of RFID technologies on supply chain management, highlight the benefits related to the tactical level of decision making, and in particular the increase in the efficiency and speed of processes, as well as the improvement of information accuracy.

Literature on RFID at the tactical level discusses the various benefits from adopting RFID for managerial control as well as performance targets (e.g. sustainable competitive advantage) determined at the strategic level. The majority of studies, as in the case of the strategic level, relate to the impact of RFID on performance using particular metrics and benchmarks, as well as to the different costs incurred, supply chain visibility and transparency. There are limited recent studies on the use of RFID at the tactical level, and less, if any, that explore the adoption process of RFID using qualitative methods (e.g. interviewing appropriate stakeholders). Furthermore, the majority of studies provide a linear relationship between adoption of RFID and particular organizational and supply chain outcomes, and do not focus on the social and organizational impacts, looking thereby into the softer side of RFID adoption.

IT and RFID at the Operational Level of Decision Making

At the operational level, the RFID adoption benefits low-level workers and managers. Operational objectives and day-to-day performance are measured against these the use of RFID to achieve tactical objectives (Gunasekaran & Patel, 2001).

Heese (2007) has studied the use of RFID in order to deal with inventory inaccuracy and the impact of the latter on supply chain performance; Heese also looked into the impact of parties' incentives to adopt RFID in cases of decentralized supply chains. Their study was complemented by Camdereli and Swaminathan (2007), who investigated the operational problem of misplaced inventory subject to uncertain demand through RFID. They look into the incentives of players who are to invest in this technology and analyzed those scenarios where adoption costs are spread between the players and whether it is either the retailer or manufacturer who pay for the variable costs of adoption. In a later study, Laosirihongthong et al. (2013) have looked into the adoption of RFID in Thailand, and identified and prioritized enabling factors based on different objectives that determine the implementation of RFID. Cost has been identified as a major drawback of its implementation, while the achievement of superior operational performance is not only based on 'hard' measures, but also on softer factors that are mostly intangible in nature, which relate to the implementation process. However, the study of Pero and Rossi (2014) did not focus on soft factors, but on the infrastructure and technological considerations for RFID in order to increase visibility in Engineer-To-Order (ETO) supply chains and to overcome processing problems. Finally, Crumbly and Carter (2015) have discussed the importance of RFID adoption for reducing product recalls. Using qualitative research and the 6Ts framework (traceability, transparency, testability, time, trust, and training) they have illustrated the benefits in mitigating risk within the manufacturing and warehouse facilities.

The articles here are discussing the benefits of RFID for supply chains and logistics and adoption issues. They are using, in their majority, management science or quantitative methods and aim at exploring the impact of RFID on efficiency as well as on mitigating risk, in both developed and developing countries. However, apart from a limited number of studies, if any, literature referring to the operational level (as in other levels) does not focus on social and organizational (softer) sides of adoption, and provides utopian view of RFID. There are limited studies that look into the adoption process from a longitudinal point of view, paying attention to the underlying politics and power issues between stakeholders that influence the adoption process and the acquisition of benefits; the latter are usually tangible and do not refer to softer and intangible benefits, e.g. less worker stress.

DISCUSSION

Theoretical Contributions

The literature review presented in this chapter gave an overview of the RFID adoption and benefits for the strategic, tactical, and operational level of decision making (Anthony, 1965; Gunasekaran et al., 2001; Gunasekaran et al., 2004; 2006). The literature review provided is unique in that it focuses on articles in high-impact journals and classifies literature with regards to the benefits and assistance RFID provides. Furthermore, our literature review highlights the following gaps to be addressed:

1. Literature on all decision-making levels (strategic, tactical, and operational) has not considered explicitly the social and organizational impacts (softer impacts) of RFID adoption. On the contrary, literature refers to either tangible benefits, or infrastructure related to RFID (as in the case of Pero and Rossi (2014)).
2. The majority of benefits discussed are tangible and financial in nature, related to performance –usually supply chain performance and organizational performance, both financial in nature. There is no reference to sustainable performance or social performance as an outcome of the use of RFID.
3. The majority of studies seem to embrace quantitative methodologies (Camdereli and Swaminathan, 2007; Heese, 2007; Laosirihongthong et al., 2013) and quan-

titative models of adoption, i.e. UTAUT (Miragliotta et al., 2009). Therefore, the literature is lacking studies that are qualitative in nature and aim at answering questions on 'how' instead of 'what'. More studies are therefore needed that are longitudinal in nature and can provide an in-depth view of the different stakeholder views related to the RFID adoption and its impact on performance.

4. There are no studies that relate data from RFID, big data and supply chain performance. Given the attention of the literature of supply chain and logistics management on big data (Wamba et al., 2015; Gunasekaran et al., 2016), more studies need to be conducted that relate the impact of RFID big data on supply chain performance.
5. Few, if any, scholars refer to developing countries. The majority of studies discuss the benefits, adoption, and impact of RFID for the 3 levels of decision making, but there limited studies on their impact on developing countries. Such studies are useful, given that the majority of multinational companies have suppliers in developing countries and there is a need for technologies such as RFID that could provide better visibility and transparency of the products and parts produced and transported from developing countries to all over the world. Big Data produced by RFID may be the key to those businesses in developing countries to gain competitive advantage.

Managerial Implications

The literature review demonstrates the diversity of IT and RFID use for the strategic, tactical and operational levels. Given that the focus of managers is on gaining access and making sense of Big Data stemming from RFID applications, managers need to acknowledge how they can use IT (and RFID) for the benefit of each one of the levels, but also the challenges related to the application of IT and RFID for each one of the levels. The characteristics of the organization and in particular the criticality of the task to be improved by the introduction of IT and also whether the organization belongs to service or manufacturing supply chain, the organizational goals and objectives, the type of business, the nature of the market, and the technological competence of the organization (Gunasekaran & Kobu, 2007).

Our classification and review can inform IT and supply chain managers about the different uses and adoption of RFID, and provide useful lessons regarding its further adaptation, exploration and exploitation by managers in their strategic, tactical, and operational levels. Such a classification allows mangers to consider the different benefits that would accrue from the use of RFID within and across these levels. Relevant metrics should, therefore, be introduced or investigated upon in order to evaluate the use of RFID/IT for each one of these levels, based on the organizational context. Such metrics should also consider a wide stakeholder participation that would help link the technologies between strategic, tactical and organizational levels.

SUMMARY, LIMITATIONS, AND FUTURE RESEARCH DIRECTIONS

This chapter focused on RFID technology as one of the sources of Big Data concerning logistics and supply chain management. We reviewed the literature on RFID in supply chain management and logistics based upon the level of decision making and contribution of IT across 3 different levels, that is, strategic, tactical, and operational. Our review of the literature and the 27 articles suggested that the majority of scholars are concerned with issues of adoption as well as the projected benefits and costs of RFID investments, and others with providing tools and frameworks for RFID investment justification. Our review has also highlighted particular research gaps including the use of Big Data. Understanding the use and adoption of RFID will be the first step in understanding the nature of Big Data stemming from RFID technologies, and this data can be a source of competitive advantage and higher performance from a logistics and supply chain management perspective.

Our paper has a number of limitations:

1. We conducted our search using particular databases and following the ABS journal ranking. Our results are therefore influenced by these choices and it may be that the choice of other databases would provide other results. However, both databases and the ABS ranking are recognized as providing a comprehensive list.
2. We selected those articles in a 20 year period, however the number of articles was not high. The reason is that RFID adoption has started much later than 1995. Although we included the ABS4 and ABS3 journals according to the ABS journal ranking list, our list is not exhaustive but considers the majority of works within this research area.
3. We selected keywords that lie at the heart of our research (Ngai et al., 2008; Chen et al., 2014; Gunasekaran et al., 2015). The decision to use these keywords belongs to all authors. Other keywords may have led to different results, but would have also been another type of research or research topic, against our research aim.
4. We classified the literature using the well-known framing of Anthony (1965), which has been used in other reviews in the past. Other frameworks also exist, but our selection is based on the relevant literature.

Notwithstanding the aforementioned limitations, we suggest future research directions on the role of IT and RFID in supply chains and logistics:

1. We provided a theoretical classification of the relevant articles based on the framework by Anthony (1965) that has been used in the past in both supply chain and IT/IS literature. Our framework could be further validated by practitioners in order to propose additional ways through which RFID could help improve supply chains and logistics.
2. Our proposed classification may be further developed by interviewing IT and supply chain managers in order to understand the practical challenges involved with using/adopting IT and RFID for supply chains and logistics. The use of interviewees from different sectors could help acknowledge the differences in priorities and decision making within and across the sectors.
3. We have not looked into the use of IT for supply chains that cut across developed and developing countries. Embracing IT and subsequently RFID would be challenging. Therefore, future research could investigate such use and give us more in-depth insights on the future of RFID for supply chains and logistics.
4. More research needs to be conducted on the RFID big data and other sources of big data in order to further understand the impact of RFID on supply chains, logistics, and performance.

REFERENCES

Anthony, R. N. (1965). *Planning and Control Systems: A Framework for Analysis*. Boston: Harvard University.

Autry, C. W., Grawe, S. J., Daugherty, P. J., & Richey, R. G. (2010). The Effects of Technological Turbulence and Breadth on Supply Chain Technology Acceptance and Adoption. *Journal of Operations Management*, *28*(6), 522–536. doi:10.1016/j.jom.2010.03.001

Barney, J. B. (1991). Firm resources and sustained competitive advantage. *Journal of Management*, *17*(1), 99–120. doi:10.1177/014920639101700108

Barratt, M. A., & Oke, A. (2007). Antecedents of Supply Chain Visibility: A Resource-based Theory Perspective. *Journal of Operations Management*, *25*(6), 1217–1233. doi:10.1016/j.jom.2007.01.003

Camdereli, A. Z., & Swaminathan, J. M. (2010). Misplaced inventory and radio-frequency identification (RFID) technology: Information and coordination. *Production and Operations Management*, *19*(1), 1–18. doi:10.1111/j.1937-5956.2009.01057.x

Chen, L., Olhanger, J., & Tang, O. (2014). Manufacturing facility location and sustainability: A literature review and research agenda. *International Journal of Production Economics*, *149*, 154–163. doi:10.1016/j.ijpe.2013.05.013

Crumbly, J., & Carter, L. (2015). The impact of information technology on product recalls: Exploring the role of the six "Ts" of supply chain management. *Production Planning and Control*, *26*(12), 958–968. doi:10.1080/09537287.2015.1009521

De Roos, D. (2013). *Big data in practice: requirements, Plan.* Infrastruct. Retrieved from: http://www.thinkconference.ca/wp-content/uploads/2013/04/Dirk-deRoos-Big-Data-In-Practice_2013-April-25.pdf

Ferrer, M., Santa, R., Hyland, P. W., & Bretherton, P. (2010). Relational factors that explain supply chain relationships. *Asia Pacific Journal of Marketing and Logistics*, *22*(3), 419–440. doi:10.1108/13555851011062304

Fosso Wamba, S., Akter, S., Edwards, A., Chopin, G., & Gnanzou, D. (2015). How 'big data' can make big impact: Findings from a systematic review and a longitudinal case study. *International Journal of Production Economics*, *165*, 234–246. doi:10.1016/j.ijpe.2014.12.031

Fosso Wamba, S., Gunasekaran, A., Bhattacharya, M., & Dubey, R. (2016). *Determinants of RFID adoption intention by SMEs: an empirical investigation*. Production Planning & Control, Published Online.

Fosso Wamba, S., & Ngai, E. W. T. (2015). Importance of issues related to RFID-enabled healthcare transformation projects: Results from a Delphi study. *Production Planning and Control*, *26*(1), 19–33. doi:10.1080/09537287.2013.840015

Grant, R. M. (1991). The Resource-Based Theory of Competitive Advantage: Implications for Strategy Formulation. *California Management Review*, *33*(3), 114–135. doi:10.2307/41166664

Gunasekaran, A., Irani, Z., Choy, K.-L., Filippi, L., & Papadopoulos, T. (2015). Performance Measures and Metrics in Outsourcing Decisions: A Review for Research and Applications. *International Journal of Production Economics*, *161*, 153–166. doi:10.1016/j.ijpe.2014.12.021

Gunasekaran, A., & Kobu, B. (2007). Performance measures and metrics in logistics and supply chain management: A review of recent literature (1995–2004) for research and applications. *International Journal of Production Research*, *45*(12), 2819–2840. doi:10.1080/00207540600806513

Gunasekaran, A., & Ngai, E. W. T. (2004). Information systems in supply chain integration and management. *European Journal of Operational Research, 159*(2), 269–295. doi:10.1016/j.ejor.2003.08.016

Gunasekaran, A., Ngai, E. W. T., & McGaughey, R. E. (2006). Information technology and systems justification: A review for research and applications. *European Journal of Operational Research, 173*(3), 957–983. doi:10.1016/j.ejor.2005.06.002

Gunasekaran, A., Patel, C., & McGaughey, R. (2004). A framework for supply chain management performance measurement. *International Journal of Production Economics, 87*(3), 333–347. doi:10.1016/j.ijpe.2003.08.003

Gunasekaran, A., Patel, C., & Tirtiroglu, E. (2001). Performance measure and metrics in a supply chain environment. *International Journal of Operations & Production Management, 21*(1/2), 71–87. doi:10.1108/01443570110358468

Heese, S. (2007). Inventory record inaccuracy, double marginalisation and RFID adoption. *Production and Operations Management, 16*(5), 542–553. doi:10.1111/j.1937-5956.2007.tb00279.x

Irani, Z., & Love, P. E. (2002). Developing a frame of reference for ex ante IT/IS investment evaluation. *European Journal of Information Systems, 11*(1), 74–82. doi:10.1057/palgrave.ejis.3000411

Laosirihongthong, T., Adebanjo, D., & Choon Tan, K. (2013). Green supply chain management practices and performance. *Industrial Management & Data Systems, 113*(8), 1088–1109. doi:10.1108/IMDS-04-2013-0164

Lee, H., & Özer, Ö. (2007). Unlocking the Value of RFID. *Production and Operations Management, 16*(1), 40–64. doi:10.1111/j.1937-5956.2007.tb00165.x

Lee, I., & Lee, B. C. (2010). An investment evaluation of supply chain RFID technologies: A normative modelling approach. *International Journal of Production Economics, 125*(2), 313–323. doi:10.1016/j.ijpe.2010.02.006

Lin, C. Y., & Ho, Y. H. (2009). RFID technology adoption and supply chain performance: An empirical study in China's logistics industry. *Supply Chain Management: An International Journal, 14*(5), 369–378. doi:10.1108/13598540910980288

Miragliotta, G., Perego, A., & Tumino, A. (2009). A quantitative model for the introduction of RFId in the fast moving consumer goods supply chain: Are there any profits? *International Journal of Operations & Production Management, 29*(10), 1049–1082. doi:10.1108/01443570910993483

Ngai, E. W. T., Moon, K., Riggins, F., & Yi, C. (2008). RFID research: An academic literature review (1995-2005) and future research directions. *International Journal of Production Economics, 112*(2), 510–520. doi:10.1016/j.ijpe.2007.05.004

Pero, M., & Rossi, T. (2014). RFID technology for increasing visibility in ETO supply chains: A case study. *Production Planning and Control, 25*(11), 892–901. doi:10.1080/09537287.2013.774257

Peteraf, M. A. (1993). The Cornerstones of Competitive Advantage: A Resource-Based View. *Strategic Management Journal, 14*(3), 179–191. doi:10.1002/smj.4250140303

Pfahl, L., & Moxham, C. (2014). Achieving sustained competitive advantage by integrating ECR, RFID and visibility in retail supply chains: A conceptual framework. *Production Planning and Control, 25*(7), 548–571. doi:10.1080/09537287.2012.729100

Quetti, C., Pigni, F., & Clerici, A. (2012). Factors Affecting RFid Adoption in a Vertical Supply Chain: The Case of the Silk Industry in Italy. *Production Planning and Control, 23*(4), 315–331. doi:10.1080/09537287.2011.627661

Reyes, P. M., Li, S., & Visich, J. K. (2012). Accessing antecedents and outcomes of RFID implementation in health care. *International Journal of Production Economics, 136*(1), 137–150. doi:10.1016/j.ijpe.2011.09.024

Riggins, F. J., & Fosso Wamba, S. (2015). *Research Directions on the Adoption, Usage and Impact of the Internet of Things through the Use of Big Data Analytics*. The 48 Hawaii International Conferences on System Sciences (HICSS), Kauai, HI.

Rowley, J., & Slack, F. (2004). Conducting a literature. *Management Research News, 27*(6), 31–39. doi:10.1108/01409170410784185

Sarac, A., Absi, N., & Dauzere-Peres, S. (2010). A literature review on the impact of RFID technologies on supply chain management. *International Journal of Production Economics, 128*(1), 77–95. doi:10.1016/j.ijpe.2010.07.039

Smart, A., Bunduchi, R., & Gerst, M. (2010). The costs of adoption of RFID technologies in supply networks. *International Journal of Operations & Production Management, 30*(4), 423–447. doi:10.1108/01443571011029994

Visich, J. K., Li, S., Khumawala, B. M., & Reyes, P. M. (2009). Empirical evidence of RFID impacts on supply chain performance. *International Journal of Operations & Production Management, 29*(12), 1290–1315. doi:10.1108/01443570911006009

Wang, G., Gunasekaran, A., Ngai, E. W. T., & Papadopoulos, T. (2016). Big Data analytics in logistics and supply chain management: Certain investigations for research and applications. *International Journal of Production Economics, 176*, 98–110. doi:10.1016/j.ijpe.2016.03.014

Whitaker, J., Mithas, S., & Krishman, M. S. (2007). A Field of RFID deployment and return expectations. *Production and Operations Management, 16*(5), 599–612. doi:10.1111/j.1937-5956.2007.tb00283.x

Wyld, D. C. (2005). *RFID: The Right Frequency for Government*. Washington, DC: IBM Center for the Business of Government.

Yee-Loong Chong, A., Liu, M. J., Luo, J., & Keng-Boon, O. (2015). Predicting RFID adoption in healthcare supply chain from the perspectives of users. *International Journal of Production Economics, 159*(0), 66–75. doi:10.1016/j.ijpe.2014.09.034

Zelbst, P. J., Green, K. W., Sower, V. E., & Reyes, P. M. (2012). Impact of RFID on manufacturing effectiveness and efficiency. *International Journal of Operations & Production Management, 32*(3-4), 329–350. doi:10.1108/01443571211212600

Zhong, R. Y., Huang, G. Q., Lan, S., Dai, Q. Y., Chen, X., & Zhang, T. (2015). A big data approach for logistics trajectory discovery from RFID-enabled production data. *International Journal of Production Economics, 165*, 260–272. doi:10.1016/j.ijpe.2015.02.014

Chapter 8
Developing an Integration Framework for Crowdsourcing and Internet of Things with Applications for Disaster Response

Rameshwar Dubey
Symbiosis International University, India

ABSTRACT

The crowdsourcing and Internet of Things (IoT) have played a significant role in revolutionizing the information age. In response to pressing need, we have attempted to develop a theoretical framework which can help disaster relief workers to improve their coordination using valuable information derived using comprehensive crowdsourcing framework. In this study we have used two-prong research strategies. First we have conducted extensive review of articles published in reputable journals, magazines and blogs by eminent practitioners and policy makers followed by case studies: stampede in Godavari River at Rajahmundry (2015), earthquake in Nepal (2015), flood in Uttarakhand (2013). Finally we have concluded our research findings with further research directions.

DOI: 10.4018/978-1-5225-0956-1.ch008

INTRODUCTION

With the advent of computers (in1970's), World Wide Web (www) (in 1990's) and internet of things (IoT) (present), the global society has moved to the "information age". The information age offers huge information created due to convergence of internet of things and crowdsourcing which can offers huge opportunities in terms of predictive analytics and forecasting events which are highly unpredictable in nature. The proliferation of semiconductor devices and their applications coupled with the ease and speed of online dissemination enables people to both witness and documents the accidental or unexpected and has permanently changed the way we understand and respond to events around us (Tierney, 2014). The Internet of Things (IoT) and Machine-to-Machine (M2M) communications connect millions of devices to generate data which is voluminous, high variety and high velocity. Johnson (2014) in one of his blogs has argued that to achieve high level of interconnectivity, the enterprises that depend on those machines need them to work reliably, securely, and cost-effectively – without human intervention. Thus in such case crowdsourcing could offer most efficient and reliable solutions. The word crowdsourcing has become quite popular lexicon in business dictionary. However the word crowdsourcing has been extensively used in various contexts in these days. There are multiple explanations to offer shape to the emerging context. However the common understanding related to crowd sourcing is deriving data from crowd who are quite active in digital space to get broader picture. Afuah and Tuci (2012) have attempted to provide an explanation related to crowdsourcing as a tool for solving complex firm related problems rather than relying on its own internal resources or contract to external partners like suppliers. Franzoni and Sauermann (2014) have further attempted to investigate the role of growing crowd science in open collaborative projects. Bloodgood (2013) in response to Afuah and Tuci (2012) work further suggested the need for capturing the value from crowdsourcing. Luttgens et al. (2014) have further attempted to identify the success factors behinds implementation of crowdsourcing and the barriers of the crowdsourcing initiatives. Chiu et al. (2014) have further to decision support systems literature by proposing a framework in which they have argued the role of crowdsourcing at various phases of decision making process.

Gao et al. (2011) have argued that how crowdsourcing applications based on social media applications such as Twitter and Ushahidi provide a powerful capability for collecting information from disaster scenes and visualizing data for relief decision making. Narvaez (2012) has argued that crowdsourcing can be effective in disaster preparedness if properly supported by better usage of technology. Sievers (2015) has further argued for embracing crowdsourcing as a strategy to address emergency planning by state and local governments. As we have noted that there is a rich body of literature on crowdsourcing and its application in disaster relief activities, research on crowdsourcing and IoT integration is scant. Santos et al. (2013) have argued that how IoT support responses to urban disasters. Tierney (2014) has further argued in the favour of crowdsourcing using social media platform to impact the disaster response. However, it is less understood from review of existing literature that how crowdsourcing can further support IoT to generate more reliable data which improve the efforts of disaster relief workers (i.e. disaster response). Hence in an attempt to answer our research objective, we posit some specific research questions as:

RQ1: What are the enablers of crowdsourcing which can guide disaster response?
RQ2: What are the enablers of IoT?
RQ3: How can crowdsourcing and IoT can be integrated?

The rest of the paper is organized as follows. The second section of the paper is devoted to classification of literature based on guiding research questions. The third section is devoted to research methodology. The fourth section is devoted to case analyses. The fifth section is devoted to discussions based on case analyses and theoretical framework. Finally we conclude our research and identified further research opportunities to advance the current research to next orbit.

RELATED RESEARCH

Crowdsourcing

Estelles-Arolas and Gonzalez-Ladron-de-Guevara (2012) have attempted to define crowdsourcing based on extensive literature review. They have attempted to establish some commonalities among existing definitions on crowdsourcing. The common characteristics which shape crowdsourcing definition are the crowd, the task at hand, the recompense obtained, the crowdsourcer or initiator of the crowdsourcing activity, what is obtained by them following the crowdsourcing process, the type of process and the call to participate. However we have also reviewed some of the important articles which have contributed to the crowdsourcing literature (see Howe, 2006 & 2008; Alonso et al. 2008; Brabham, 2008; Vukovics & Bartolini, 2010; Behrend et al. 2011; Armstrong et al. 2012; Franzoni & Sauermann, 2014). Tarrell et al. (2013) have attempted to provide a brief snapshot on the evolution of crowdsourcing based on 135 articles drawn from information sciences journals and other conference proceedings. Charalabidis et al. (2014) in their studies have attempted to develop a passive crowdsourcing framework for government agencies, exploiting the extensive political content continuously created in numerous Web 2.0 social media (e.g. political blogs and microblogs, news sharing sites and online forums) by citizens without government stimulation, to understand better their needs, issues, opinions, proposals and arguments concerning a particular domain of government activity or public policy based on Greece, Austria and UK users.

Crowdsourcing in Emergency

On the basis of preceding section discussions based on review of academic literature we can argue that crowdsourcing is a model that uses crowd knowledge and expertise to decisions which is quick and cheaper than any other sources of information. Rogstadius et al. (2013) have argued that use of SMS texting is one of the most robust forms of communication during disasters. During massive catastrophe (e.g. a 9.0 earthquake), electric wire cables get uprooted resulting into power failure hence most of the sensors which are supported by power may stop functioning but people continue to have reduced but useable access to SMS texting through their mobile devices. For example, though voice communication was lost on landlines and cellular lines in the recent earthquakes at various locations (e.g. Nepal, Christchurch, Japan, Haiti), SMS texting continued to be operational, making Twitter, with its SMS framework and GPS coordinates, a valuable disaster tool. Tierney (2014) has argued that in emergency situation, crowdsourcing describes a method of information collection that utilizes data received from volunteers to enable stakeholders to participate in disaster response through online forums, such as wikis and crisis mapping. In recent years the volunteers have exchanged views and opinion using social networking platform like Twitter which is one of the social networking service has played significant role in guiding response towards disasters. Tierney (2014) argued that information generated using social networking platform is automatically geotagged with longitude and latitude coordinates that is, in turn, processed onto a centralized map for public inspection and verification, serving as a source of information for relief operations. The social media has played significant role in recent days. Twitter feeds assisted in coordinating help, shelter, and food for the distressed. Mobile food truck drivers scrambled into operation, micro-blogging their locations while distributing provisions to the cold and famished (Tierney, 2014). As microbloggers uploaded geotagged information, hybrid alliances formed between online platforms and offline places. An interactive crisis map of Manhattan with links to Facebook, Twitter, text, or email connected those in trouble with local evacuation centers and emergency shelters with real-time updates from the Red Cross, FEMA, and other municipal agencies. Narvaez (2012) has further argued that if information gathered using social networking platform is properly organized, then it is believed that crowdsourcing can offer better supports in terms of ground actions. Kawasaki et al. (2013) have further investigated the impacts of geospatial technological developments on disaster response. Houston et al. (2015) in their recent published work have made an attempt to study social media and its usage in disaster planning and preparedness.

From preceding discussions we can argue that crowdsourcing is people-driven programs, like information related to disaster affected places, traffic related information from thousands of commuters, and weathers related information, crowd behaviour at religious places or any large events.

Internet of Things (IoT)

Internet of Things (IoT) has attracted significant attentions from practitioners and academia. Xia et al. (2012) argued that IoT refers to the networked interconnection of everyday objects, which are often equipped with ubiquitous intelligence. Hence, IoT will increase the ubiquity of the Internet by integrating every object for interaction via embedded systems, which leads to a highly distributed network of devices communicating with human beings as well as other devices. The Internet of Things (IoT) connect millions of diverse machines over networks, the goal is to make the combination of those machines greater than the sum of each type and to provide people with greater information and insight as the ecosystem expands (Johnson, 2014). Da Xu et al. (2014) argued that to achieve high level of interconnectivity, businesses that depend on those machines need them to work reliably, securely, and cost-effectively – without human intervention. Johnson (2014) argues that in such case crowdsourcing can be high beneficial. Johnson (2014) further argues that crowdsourcing is often associated with crowd but however, once machines and sensors become connected, they can directly collaborate through data to provide a more comprehensive crowd-sourced view of a vast number of scenarios. Jian et al. (2015) further argues based on their research that various types of micro-sensors in smart communication devices can measure a significant amount of potentially useful information. Jian and colleagues further argues that mobile crowd sensing (MCS) between users with smart mobile devices is a new trend of development in IoT. With the powerful sensing capability of smart device and user mobility, various services could be provided by building a trusted chain between service requesters and suppliers (Yang et al. 2013). However, the research related to integration of crowdsourcing with IoT in context to emergency response is still underdeveloped.

METHODS

The preceding discussions surrounding literature may have provided some directions related to evolution of crowdsourcing practices and its perceived usefulness in emergency situation. However, the literature is incomplete and it is clear that crowdsourcing, IoT and its impact on disaster response need to be investigated to provide a clear understanding regarding what are the enablers of crowdsourcing, IoT and how the integration of independent source of data can help to improve disaster response. In the present study we have used case study approach as suggested by Eisenhardt (1989) in case of new topic or emerging research areas like of ours. Pagell and Wu (2009) attempted to build comprehensive theory surrounding sustainable supply chains using case studies of ten exemplars organizations. Ketokivi and Choi (2014) have further noted that in recent years the case study approach has been mis-used due to lack of guiding framework. Hence in our present research we have adopted Ketokivi and Choi (2014) "case research decision tree". We first examined our research question using duality criterion (i.e. Can the empirical context and data ultimately lead to more general theoretical insight?). Hence, we felt "yes" thus we finally decided to use case study approach.

Sample

To answer our three fundamentals questions:

RQ1: What are enablers of crowdsourcing which can assist disaster response?
RQ2: What are the enablers of IoT?

To answer this fundamental research question we have identified three recent disasters occurred in India. First, we selected Nepal earthquake (2015), stampede in Godavari River at Rajahmundry (2015) and flood in Uttarakhand (2015). The data were collected between 2014 January to 2015 July. There are varied opinions regarding selection of number of cases in multiple case research studies. However in our research we reviewed Eisenhardt (1989) and Pagell and Wu (2009) suggests seven cases as the maximum that a person can mentally process. Yin (1994) and others are more circumspect in regards to hard numbers and instead suggest that data should be collected until saturation. In operations and supply chain management research there are numerous examples of multiple case study research using from three to eleven cases (e.g. Pagell, 2004; Wu & Choi, 2005; Matos & Hall, 2007; Pagell & Wu, 2009). We used three cases as we felt that we have enough data to process in one study.

We followed theoretical sampling approach (see, Eisenhardt, 1989; pagell & Wu, 2009) across different events occurred at three different places because social media has played significant role in guiding disaster relief team unlike a decade ago when SMS, Twitter and other social networking space were not popular.

Interview Protocol

As suggested by Eisenhardt (1989) and Pagell and Wu (2009) we have used semistructured interview protocol for two reasons. We had designed the sample to include disasters of different nature; hence the semistructured protocol has offered us immense flexibility to gather data related to crowdsourcing and use of IoT in disaster relief activities. Second, there was some theoretical underpinning for items included in the protocol as suggested by Kounelis et al. (2014), Afuah and Tuci (2012) and Brabham (2008).

Data Collection

Our research design was based on the recommendations of Eisenhardt (1989), Yin (1994) and Pagell and Wu (2009). The initial protocol called for interviews with senior members of disaster relief team who played significant role in each of these three events. We requested to interview:

- A senior member from Border Road Organisation (A body under Ministry of Defence).
- A senior member from a NGO.
- A senior member from local state government.
- A spoke person from the local team who were the first to reach to disaster affected place.

Our collection included multiple researchers, a taped and transcribed record of the conversations, multiple respondents, an opportunity to visit some of the locations at Nepal and Rajahmundry. We have used Triangulation approach to validate data. Triangulation involves combining observations from multiple researchers, data from multiple sources (in this study interview, and observational from the tours) to reduce biases and improve reliability and validity (Eisenhardt 1989; Yin 1994; Pagell & Wu, 2009).

Coding and Analysis

Miles and Huberman (1994) have argued that only following Triangulation of data may not be sufficient enough to prevent biases. In such cases the coding and final model building should happen after the data is completely collected. Hence we strictly followed the instructions as suggested by (Miles & Huberman, 1994; Pagell

& Wu, 2009). We have finally performed coding using multiple iterative processes. Coding was done to identify the enablers of crowdsourcing and IoT in disaster relief process. We have identified some of the enablers through literature review but we have also included some others enablers which were unique but not captured by the literature. We used within case analysis and cross case analysis as suggested by Pagell and Wu (2009). The enablers were presented in Table 1 and Table 2 as:

Table 1. Enablers of crowdsourcing previously identified in literature

Enablers	Previously Linked to Crowdsourcing	Uttarakhand Flood (2013)	Nepal Earthquake (2015)	Stampede at Rajahmundry (2015)
Facebook	Yes	Yes	Yes	Yes
Smartphone	Yes	Yes	Yes	Yes
Twitter	Yes	Yes	Yes	Yes
Role of volunteers	Yes	Yes	Yes	Yes
Leadership	Yes	Yes	Yes	Yes
Training and Development	No	Yes	Yes	No
Incentives to volunteers	Yes	No	No	No
Social media data analytics	Yes	No	No	No

Table 2. Enablers of Internet of Things (IoT)

Enablers	Previously Linked to IoT	Uttarakhand Flood (2013)	Nepal Earthquake (2015)	Stampede at Rajahmundry (2015)
Governance	Yes	No	No	No
Top management belief	No	No	No	No
Top management participation	No	Yes	Yes	Yes
Building trust among IoT and human	Yes	No	No	No
Reduction of behavioural Uncertainty	No	No	No	No
Collaboration	Yes	Yes	Yes	Yes
Security of information	Yes	Yes	Yes	Yes

CONCLUSION

Our analysis suggests that the enablers of crowdsourcing which enhances the response of disaster relief teams are equal parts of the enablers which are reported in prior literature and some new enablers. Our findings are summarized in the Figure 1.

Figure 1. CS-IoT model

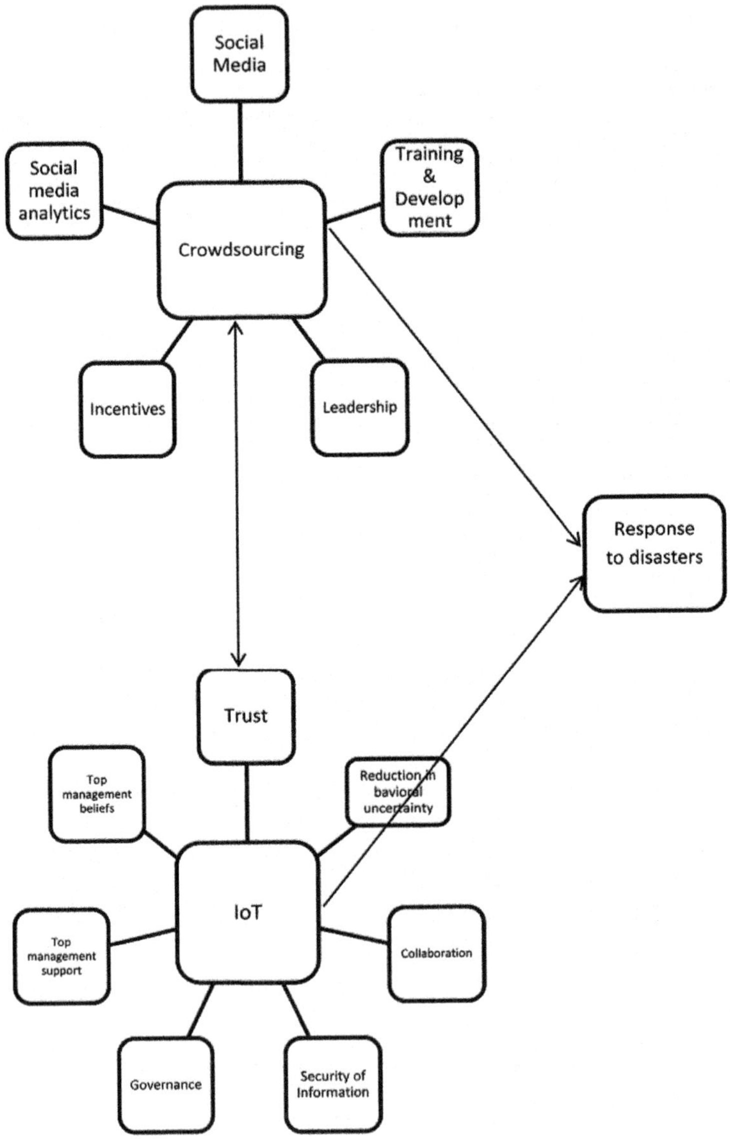

The model (CS-IoT) is based on analysis using three case studies which we have included in our research based on Ketokivi and Choi (2014) guidelines for case analysis. Literature indicates that social media, social media analytics and incentives to the volunteer have significant influence on the data collected using crowdsourcing. However our case analysis further conform the literature and further identifies that training and development and leadership styles have significant influence on the volume, variety, velocity, veracity and value of the data. Our analysis further suggests that IoT can be exploited in most beneficial way if trust between IoT and human can be established. It has been identified that collaboration among humanitarian supply chain network partners have strong influence on IoT performance which is not well argued in existing literature. Our analysis further suggests that reduction in behavioural uncertainty among the partners will further help to build effective coordination. Hence our analysis using three case studies helps to explore some interesting insights which current literature failed to reflect. The present study can be largely benefitted if the integrated framework (CS-IoT) can be empirically tested using longitudinal data.

REFERENCES

Afuah, A., & Tucci, C. L. (2012). Crowdsourcing as a solution to distant search. *Academy of Management Review*, *37*(3), 355–375. doi:10.5465/amr.2010.0146

Alonso, O., Rose, D. E., & Stewart, B. (2008, November). Crowdsourcing for relevance evaluation. In *ACM SigIR Forum* (Vol. 42, No. 2, pp. 9-15). ACM. doi:10.1145/1480506.1480508

Armstrong, A. W., Cheeney, S., Wu, J., Harskamp, C. T., & Schupp, C. W. (2012). Harnessing the Power of Crowds. *American Journal of Clinical Dermatology*, *13*(6), 405–416. doi:10.2165/11634040-000000000-00000 PMID:23039257

Behrend, T. S., Sharek, D. J., Meade, A. W., & Wiebe, E. N. (2011). The viability of crowdsourcing for survey research. *Behavior Research Methods*, *43*(3), 800–813. doi:10.3758/s13428-011-0081-0 PMID:21437749

Bloodgood, J. (2013). Crowdsourcing: Useful for problem solving, but what about value capture? *Academy of Management Review*, *38*(3), 455–457. doi:10.5465/amr.2012.0318

Brabham, D. C. (2008). Crowdsourcing as a model for problem solving an introduction and cases. *Convergence (London)*, *14*(1), 75–90. doi:10.1177/1354856507084420

Charalabidis, Y. N., Loukis, E., Androutsopoulou, A., Karkaletsis, V., & Triantafillou, A. (2014). Passive crowdsourcing in government using social media. *Transforming Government: People. Process and Policy*, *8*(2), 283–308.

Chiu, C. M., Liang, T. P., & Turban, E. (2014). What can crowdsourcing do for decision support? *Decision Support Systems*, *65*, 40–49. doi:10.1016/j.dss.2014.05.010

Da Xu, L., He, W., & Li, S. (2014). Internet of Things in industries: A survey. *Industrial Informatics. IEEE Transactions on*, *10*(4), 2233–2243.

Eisenhardt, K. M. (1989). Building theories from case study research. *Academy of Management Review*, *14*(4), 532–550.

Estellés-Arolas, E., & González-Ladrón-de-Guevara, F. (2012). Towards an integrated crowdsourcing definition. *Journal of Information Science*, *38*(2), 189–200. doi:10.1177/0165551512437638

Franzoni, C., & Sauermann, H. (2014). Crowd science: The organization of scientific research in open collaborative projects. *Research Policy*, *43*(1), 1–20. doi:10.1016/j.respol.2013.07.005

Gao, H., Barbier, G., & Goolsby, R. (2011). Harnessing the crowdsourcing power of social media for disaster relief. *IEEE Intelligent Systems*, *26*(3), 10–14. doi:10.1109/MIS.2011.52

Houston, J. B., Hawthorne, J., Perreault, M. F., Park, E. H., Goldstein Hode, M., Halliwell, M. R., & Griffith, S. A. et al. (2015). Social media and disasters: A functional framework for social media use in disaster planning, response, and research. *Disasters*, *39*(1), 1–22. doi:10.1111/disa.12092 PMID:25243593

Howe, J. (2006). The rise of crowdsourcing. *Wired Magazine, 14*(6), 1-4.

Howe, J. (2008). *Crowdsourcing: How the power of the crowd is driving the future of business*. Random House.

Jian, A., Xiaolin, G., Jianwei, Y., Yu, S., & Xin, H. (2015, April). Mobile Crowd Sensing for Internet of Things: A Credible Crowdsourcing Model in Mobile-Sense Service. In *Multimedia Big Data (BigMM), 2015 IEEE International Conference on* (pp. 92-99). IEEE. doi:10.1109/BigMM.2015.62

Johnson. (2014). *How crowdsourcing is Helping Connect Internet of Things*. Retrieved from http://asmarterplanet.com/blog/2014/11/aeris-internet-of-things.html

Kawasaki, A., Berman, M. L., & Guan, W. (2013). The growing role of web-based geospatial technology in disaster response and support. *Disasters*, *37*(2), 201–221. doi:10.1111/j.1467-7717.2012.01302.x PMID:23278379

Ketokivi, M., & Choi, T. (2014). Renaissance of case research as a scientific method. *Journal of Operations Management*, *32*(5), 232–240. doi:10.1016/j.jom.2014.03.004

Kounelis, I., Baldini, G., Neisse, R., Steri, G., Tallacchini, M., & Guimaraes Pereira, A. (2014). Building Trust in the Human? Internet of Things Relationship. *Technology and Society Magazine, IEEE*, *33*(4), 73–80. doi:10.1109/MTS.2014.2364020

Lüttgens, D., Pollok, P., Antons, D., & Piller, F. (2014). Wisdom of the crowd and capabilities of a few: Internal success factors of crowdsourcing for innovation. *Journal of Business Economics*, *84*(3), 339–374. doi:10.1007/s11573-014-0723-7

Matos, S., & Hall, J. (2007). Integrating sustainable development in the supply chain: The case of life cycle assessment in oil and gas and agricultural biotechnology. *Journal of Operations Management*, *25*(6), 1083–1102. doi:10.1016/j.jom.2007.01.013

Middleton, S. E., Middleton, L., & Modafferi, S. (2014). Real-time crisis mapping of natural disasters using social media. *IEEE Intelligent Systems*, *29*(2), 9–17. doi:10.1109/MIS.2013.126

Miles, M. B., & Huberman, A. M. (1994). *Qualitative data analysis: An expanded sourcebook*. Thousand Oaks, CA: Sage Publications.

Narvaez, R. W. M. (2012). *Crowdsourcing for disaster preparedness: Realities and opportunities*. (Master's thesis). Graduate Institute of International and Development Studies, Geneva, Switzerland.

Neisse, R., Steri, G., Fovino, I. N., & Baldini, G. (2015). SecKit: A Model-based Security Toolkit for the Internet of Things. *Computers & Security*, *54*, 60–76. doi:10.1016/j.cose.2015.06.002

Pagell, M. (2004). Understanding the factors that enable and inhibit the integration of operations, purchasing and logistics. *Journal of Operations Management*, *22*(5), 459–487. doi:10.1016/j.jom.2004.05.008

Pagell, M., & Wu, Z. (2009). Building a more complete theory of sustainable supply chain management using case studies of 10 exemplars. *Journal of Supply Chain Management, 45*(2), 37-56.

Rogstadius, J., Vukovic, M., Teixeira, C. A., Kostakos, V., Karapanos, E., & Laredo, J. A. (2013). CrisisTracker: Crowdsourced social media curation for disaster awareness. *IBM Journal of Research and Development*, *57*(5), 4–1. doi:10.1147/JRD.2013.2260692

Santos, R., Orozco, J., Ochoa, S. F., & Meseguer, R. (2013). The Internet of things to support urban incident responses. In Ubiquitous Computing and Ambient Intelligence. Context-Awareness and Context-Driven Interaction (pp. 286-293). Springer International Publishing. doi:10.1007/978-3-319-03176-7_37

Sievers, J. A. (2015). Embracing Crowdsourcing A Strategy for State and Local Governments Approaching "Whole Community" Emergency Planning. *State & Local Government Review*, *47*(1), 57–67. doi:10.1177/0160323X15575184

Tarrell, A., Tahmasbi, N., Kocsis, D., Tripathi, A., Pedersen, J., Xiong, J., & de Vreede, G. J. et al. (2013). Crowdsourcing: A snapshot of published research.*Proceedings of the Nineteenth Americas Conference on Information Systems*.

Tierney, T. F. (2014). Crowdsourcing Disaster Response: Mobilizing Social Media for Urban Resilience. *The European Business Review*. Retrieved from http://www.europeanbusinessreview.com/?p=4911

Vukovic, M., & Bartolini, C. (2010). Towards a research agenda for enterprise crowdsourcing. In *Leveraging applications of formal methods, verification, and validation* (pp. 425–434). Springer Berlin Heidelberg. doi:10.1007/978-3-642-16558-0_36

Wu, Z., & Choi, T. Y. (2005). Supplier–supplier relationships in the buyer–supplier triad: Building theories from eight case studies. *Journal of Operations Management*, *24*(1), 27–52. doi:10.1016/j.jom.2005.02.001

Yang, L., Yang, S. H., & Plotnick, L. (2013). How the internet of things technology enhances emergency response operations. *Technological Forecasting and Social Change*, *80*(9), 1854–1867. doi:10.1016/j.techfore.2012.07.011

Yin, R. (1994). *Case study research: Design and methods. CA*. Thousand Oaks, CA: Sage Publications.

Chapter 9
Supply Chain Coordination Based on Web Service

Kamalendu Pal
City, University of London, UK

ABSTRACT

The importance of integrating and coordinating supply chain business partners have been appreciated in many industries. In the global manufacturing industry, supply chain business partners' information integration is technically a daunting task due to highly disconnected infrastructures and operations. Information, software applications, and services are loosely distributed among participant business partners with heterogeneous operating infrastructures. A secure, and flexible information exchange architecture that can interconnect distributed information and share that information across global service provision applications is, therefore, immensely advantageous. This chapter describes the main features of an ontology-based web service framework for integrating distributed business processes in a global supply chain. A Scalable Web Service Discovery Framework (SWSDF) for material procurement systems of a manufacturing supply chain is described. Description Logic (DL) is used to represent and explain SWSDF. The framework uses a hybrid knowledge-based system, which consists of Case-Based Reasoning (CBR) and Rule-Based Reasoning (RBR). SWSDF includes: (1) a collection of web service descriptions in Ontology Web Language-Based Service (OWL-S), (2) service advertisement using complex concepts, and (3) a service concept similarity assessment algorithm. Finally, a business scenario is used to demonstrate functionalities of the described system.

DOI: 10.4018/978-1-5225-0956-1.ch009

INTRODUCTION

All business today appreciates the value and consequence of building an effective supply chain as part of organizational proliferation and profitability. A supply chain is a network of facilities and distribution options that performs the functions of material procurement, transformation of these materials into intermediate and finished products, and distribution of these finished products to customers (Ganeshan & Harrison, 1995). Supply Chain Management (SCM) aims at improving the allocation, management and control of logistical resources. With its origins in manufacturing, SCM relies on business operations for achieving competitive advantage (Vrijhoef & Koskela, 1999). The first signs of SCM were perceptible in Toyota Motor Manufacturing's Just-In-Time (JIT) procurement system (Shingo, 1988). Particularly, JIT was used to control supplies to the factory just in the right quantities, to the right location, and at the right time, in order to optimize system-wide costs and customer affordability. The main goal was to reduce inventory level drastically, and to regulate the suppliers' interaction with the production line more effectively. It consisted of two distinct flows through the supply chain organizations: material and information. The scope of the supply chain begins with the source of supply and ends at the point of consumption. It extends much further than simply a concern with the physical movement of material. Equal emphasis is given to supplier management, purchasing, material management, manufacturing management, facilities planning, customer service, information flow, transport and physical distribution.

Supply chain management tries to bring suppliers and customers together in one concurrent business process. Its main objective is to synchronize the needs of the customer with the flow of raw material from purchasers. This balances Constraint Satisfaction Problem (CSP) with reasonable customer service, minimum inventory holding cost and optimal unit cost. In this complex CSP environment, the design and operation of an effective supply chain is of fundamental importance.

It is worth noting that the purchasing process does not finish when the customer places an order using an existing sales channel. Customers queries, before or after order placement, are inevitable. At the same time, the seller might want to contact customers with purchase confirmation and shipping information. Customer service encompasses all points of contact between the seller and the customer and is an important output of SCM. It results from the accumulated value of all business processes along the supply chain. These business processes are responsible for offering an acceptable level of customer service. Moreover, these business processes are also interdependent; if one business function fails to provide the expected level of customer service, the chain is disrupted, and the scheduled workload in other areas is destabilized. Customer satisfaction is the casualty.

To provide better quality of customer service at no additional cost or workload, all business processes along the supply chain have to be balanced. This requires trade-offs throughout the supply chain. It is essential to think in terms of a single interconnected chain rather than narrow functional business processes when considering effective trade-offs. Seamless integration along the supply chain is challenged when there is a conflict between a company's functional behaviours and objectives, as is often the case. For example, suppliers typically want manufacturers to purchasing in bulk quantities, in stable volumes, and with flexible delivery dates. However, although most manufactures desire long production shifts, they need to be flexible to their customers' requirements and fluctuating market demands. Thus the suppliers' objectives are in direct conflict with manufacturers' wish for flexibility. Indeed, since manufacturing decisions are typically made without accurate information about customer demand, the ability of manufacturers to match supply and demand depends largely on their ability to change supply volume as information about demand arrives. In the same way, the manufacturers' goal of making bulk production batches typically conflicts with the objectives of both distribution and warehouse facilities layout to reduce materials inventory. To make the situation worse, this latter goal of reducing inventory typically implies an extra cost in transportation and distribution.

System fluctuations over time are also critical criteria that need to be considered. Even when the requisition is accurately known because of prior contractual agreements, say strategic decisions need to take demand and cost variations due to changes in market trends, market and sales logistics, competitive movement and the like. These time-varying demand and cost criteria make it more complex to figure out the most appropriate supply chain strategy – the one that optimizes system-wide management costs and complies with customer needs. Global optimization indicates that it is not only essential to optimize across supply chain resource provisions, but also across business activities connected with the supply chain. In addition, SCM is capturing, storing, and analyzing data that has high volume, greater velocity, and comes from a variety of sources (e.g. machines, radio frequency identification tags, geographical positioning system data, text files, etc.). These data sources are putting very high demand on SCM for a strong data infrastructure, the right analytical tools to manipulate it, and people skilled in the use of analytics. Hence, it is essential to find out which business activities and plans optimize both chains concurrently. In this way, companies recognize the strategic importance of well-managed supply chains. For example, companies such as Dell, Toyota, and Wal-Mart have based their corporate strategy around achieving supply chain superiority over their competitors (Copacino & Anderson, 2003). These multi-national corporations have gained competitive advantages by effectively managing the complex web of supply chain business process interactions that extend across continents and across enterprises in product procurement, manufacturing and distribution.

Accomplishing supply chain superiority in today's globalized world is a hard challenge for many global companies. Effective SCM can be a competitive advantage that needs synergistic relationships between distributed corporate partners with the aim of maximizing customer experience; and providing a profit for each supply chain partners (Fugate et al, 2006; Kalakota & Whinston, 1997). The design of collaborative business process is vital for successful SCM and enabled by information and communication technologies (ICT) (Li, 2002). The main objectives of supply chain management can be categorized as follows:

- Lowering material holding cost by using appropriate Material Requirement Planning (MRP), which needs to reflect JIT inventory management in production line;
- Reducing overall production costs by streamlining the product flow within the production process and enhancing information flow between corporate business partners; and
- Improving customer satisfaction by offering quick delivery and flexibility through the seamless cooperation with distributors, warehouse operators, and other customer centric services.

Success in an increasingly competitive marketplace of global supply chain relies heavily on the quality of data, information, and knowledge which enterprises use in day-to-day business operations. Particularly, manufacturing supply chains use purchasing, distribution, material management (or inventory management), picking and packing of items, production control information in assembly lines, and at the end-user service. Integrated business information systems are the life-blood of manufacturing chains. For example, any manufacturer's profitability depends heavily on the effective inventory management systems, which helps to reduce stock-holding cost and at the same time streamlines assembly line production processes. Inventory replenishment based on classical forecast methods, where safety stock is determined on the basis of past sales and procurement data are no longer adequate to handle globalized manufacturing processes. Right information at the right time makes manufacturing chain operations much more effective. Therefore, today's globalized manufacturing business relies heavily on advanced Information and Communication Technologies (ICT), such as electronic data interchange (Lambert & Cooper, 2000); multi-agent technologies (Pal & Karakostas, 2014; Woodridge & Jennings, 19995); and in particular web service-based computing applications (Zhang et al, 2009; Cai et al, 2010).

Web service-based business applications have developed a new paradigm of communication revolution in heterogeneous data source connectivity applications (e.g. global supply chains). However, the increasing use of web services has raised new research challenges. These challenges have attracted considerable research efforts on enhancing service description semantics and service composition algorithms (Matskin et al, 2007). In the research related to semantic enhancement of web services, different approaches have been used with the aim to provide appropriate business system architectures and specific languages which would permit easy information systems integration of distributed business applications. In particular, one attractive theme is emerging from the service community research that shows how to enhance Business Process Execution Language (BPEL) by enhancing semantics to the workflow-based service composition approach (Laliwala et al, 2006). However, most of this research matches the static behaviour of web services with functional and non-functional properties. While for the candidate web service these properties are likely to be semantically similar, it is the execution values for such functional and non-functional properties that provide valuable guidelines for selecting appropriate web services.

Hence, the problem requires a methodical approach, which has specific knowledge for capturing the web service execution experiences and appropriate reasoning mechanisms based on the enhanced service descriptions. Semantic web services empower web services with semantics. Moreover, the popularity of semantic web service-based computing (Berners-Lee et al, 2001) has attracted particular attention to the area of service modeling. For example, one of the main research projects includes the US-based initiative – Ontology Web Language Service (OWL-S) (Martin et al, 2004). European projects include DIP (Data, Information, and Process Integration with Semantic Web Services), SUPER (is security-focused research project using social media in emergency management), and SOA4All (a project that provides a comprehensive global service delivery platform) (Roman et al, 2015). In these and other projects, researchers have proposed several frameworks for semantic web services, especially WSDL-S (Web Service Description Language – Semantics) (McIlraith et al, 2003; Martin et al, 2004); and WSMO (Web Service Modeling Ontology) (Romana et al, 2005).

Despite these efforts, web service discovery is still a complex task and is difficult to implement manually. Hence, Semi-automated or fully dynamic web service discovery presents a real research challenge. To address the problem, this chapter describes the functionalities of a hybrid knowledge-based service matchmaking framework, SWSDF, which uses Structured Case-Base Reasoning (S-CBR) and Rule-Based Reasoning (RBR). The remainder of the chapter is organized as follows. Section 2 outlines the overview and motivations of this chapter. It includes a brief introduction of semantic enrichment of web service using ontology; semantic web service frameworks; and ontology-based service description of a business scenario. In addition, it also provides a formal web service description for the business case using Description Logic (DL). Section 3 describes the overview of S-CBR and its relevance for semantic web services research. Section 4 presents briefly the system architecture of SWSDF and its service similarity assessment algorithm. This includes a material management business scenario and the service concept similarity assessment algorithm; including its evaluation procedure. Section 5 presents a review of relevant research approaches for web service discovery. Section 6 ends with concluding remarks.

OVERVIEW AND MOTIVATION

Web services have become the popular choice for the implementation of service delivery systems, which are distributed and interoperable. These services are built by a set of core technologies that provide these functionalities for communication, description, and discovery of services. The standards that cater these functionalities are Simple Object Access Protocol (SOAP), Web Services Description Language (WSDL), and Universal Description, Discovery, and Integration (UDDI) (OASIS, 2004). These XML-based standards use common Internet Protocols for the exchange of service requests and responses. (Extensible Markup Language, XML, is a common platform-independent data format across the enterprise) Figure 1A shows the relationship of these technologies as a standards stack for web services; and Figure 1B describes briefly service publishing, service requesting and service finding mechanisms using a simple diagrammatic representation.

When a service provider creates a new service, it describes the service using standard WSDL, which defines a service in terms of the messages to be exchanged between services and how they can be found by specifying the location of the service with an appropriate Universal Resource Locater (URL). To make the service avail-

Figure 1. Diagrammatic representation of web service technologies: a) Web service standards stack; b) Web service relationships diagram

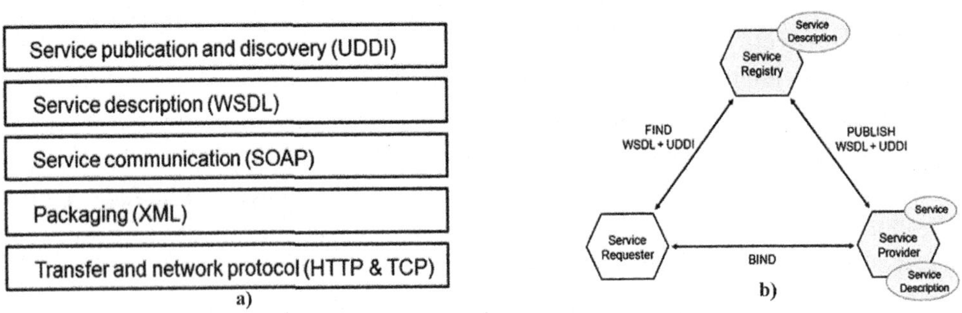

able to consumers, the provider registers the service in a UDDI registry by supplying the details of the service provider, the category of the service, and technical details on how to bind to the service. The UDDI registry will then maintain pointers to the WSDL description and to the service. When a consumer wants to use a service, it queries the UDDI registry to find the service that matches its needs and obtains the WSDL description of that service, as well as the access point of the service. The consumer uses the WSDL description to construct a SOAP message to be transported over HTTP (Hyper Text Transmission Protocol) with which to communicate with the service.

Web services are loosely coupled software components that are published, located and invoked across a network-computing infrastructure. Software-based web services are the building blocks for Service Oriented Computing (SOC), and they can be composed to provide a coarse-grained functionality and to automate business processes. In addition, technological improvements are providing more advanced communication facilities (e.g. online vendor managed inventory replenishment, payment using mobile hand-held devices). Business service facilities are providing more flexibility to its end-users and at the same time managing these business processes are becoming more complex. In SCM, many applications can be built by calling different web services available on the web or corporate intranets. These applications are highly dependent on discovering of correct web services. In particular, the description of web service consists of the technical parameters, constraints and policies that define the terms to invoke the web service. A web service definition needs four important things – *name, description, input* and *output*. Name provides business service name and it is used as a unique identifier; description represents the brief outline of the service; the input consists of number of parameters; and the output is also represented by a set of service parameters. SOAP based protocol provides the mechanism to exchange structured information in a decentralized and distributed information system.

In this way, web services aim to use the Web as a worldwide infrastructure for distributed computation purposes in order to carry out seamless integration of business processes. However, as the set of available web services increases, it becomes crucial to have automated service discovery mechanisms to help in finding services that match a requester's requirement. Finding appropriate web services depends on the facilities available for service providers to describe the capabilities of their services and for service requesters to describe their needs in an unambiguous form that is ideally machine-readable. In order to achieve this objective, ordinary web service description need to be enriched using domain ontology (or semantic markup). The next section introduces the concept of ontology and semantic annotation mechanisms of web services.

Semantic Enrichment of Web Service Using Ontology

The word ontology has its origin in philosophy, and it relates the philosophical study of the nature of existence. In information management, the term ontology has a particular meaning: "An ontology is an explicit specification of a conceptualization" (Gruber, 1993). Studer et al. (Studer et al., 1998) advocated that this specification is also formal, i.e. an ontology is an *explicit* and formal specification of conceptualizing an environment (Antoniou & Harmelen, 2008) for a particular area of interest in a human understandable, and machine-readable format, which consists of objects, concepts, relationships, axioms, individuals and assertions (Guarino & Giaretta, 1995).

Ontologies are often considered as bare building blocks for heterogeneous software system integration. The use of ontologies in computing has gained popularity in recent decades for two specific reasons: they facilitate interoperability, and they enhance computer-based reasoning practice. Particularly in computer science and information science, knowledge reuse is facilitated by the use of explicit ontology, as opposed to implicit ontology (i.e. knowledge encoded into software systems). Hence, suitable ontology languages are required to realize explicit ontologies with respect to three important aspects:

- **Conceptualization:** The language should choose an appropriate reference model, such as Unified Modelling Language (UML) based class model (OMG, 2009), and provide corresponding ontology constructs to represent factual knowledge. For example, defining the classes and related relationships in a particular area of interest, and asserting relations among classes.
- **Vocabulary:** In addition to factual knowledge, the language needs to have vocabulary (i.e. assigning symbols to concepts) and grammar rules in order to represent the vocabulary explicitly.
- **Axiomatization:** In order to capture the semantics for inference, rules and constraints are required in addition to factual knowledge. One can use these rules to produce new facts from existing knowledge.

Information sharing among supply chain business partners using information systems is an important enabler for SCM. Many research works are devoted to answering the question of 'what information to share'. Li and co-researchers (Li et al, 2006) offer four types of data to be shared across the supply chain, namely, *order*, *demand, inventory,* and *shipment*. Lambert and his fellow researcher (Lambert & Cooper, 2000) suggest supply chain issues that need to be managed, such as customer service management, inventory management, and so on. In addition, they emphasize the importance of focusing on business processes, rather than individual functions. Consequently, information about these issues needs to be shared in order to achieve efficiency and effectiveness in the supply chain. In this way, information sharing activities require that human and/or machine agents agree on common and explicit ontologies (or business related taxonomies) so as to exchange information and derive knowledge to achieve collaborative objectives of business operations. In order to share knowledge across different communities, three requirements need to be considered when developing explicit ontologies: *extensibility* – reuse existing concepts and develop ontologies in an incremental way; *visibility* – publishing information and knowledge on the Web based on common ontological grounds between information publishers and consumers; and *inferenceability* – enable logical inference on facts through axiomatization.

The semantic web inherits the power of interoperability and it can function as a distributed collaborative knowledge-base for a particular application domain. Moreover, to encode the ontology in information systems different knowledge representation techniques (e.g. graph-based, logic-based representation and other formal representation mechanisms) are used. A part of supply chain inventory management ontologies is shown in Figure 2.

In this diagrammatic representation, a procurement officer is a managerial role aimed on sourcing, procurement, and supply management for an enterprise. Corporate procurement can take place globally due to the economic benefits of the described supply chain. In this process, product costing, transportation facilities, country specific risk associated for a procurement process are all part of the procurement manager's decision-making activities. The top-level basic concepts (i.e. relevant entities or classes) are *country*, *profile*, *description*, *material*, and so on. The concept *profile* is further specialized as *costing* and *resource*. In the same way,

Figure 2. A partial state of the world represented by supply chain inventory management ontology

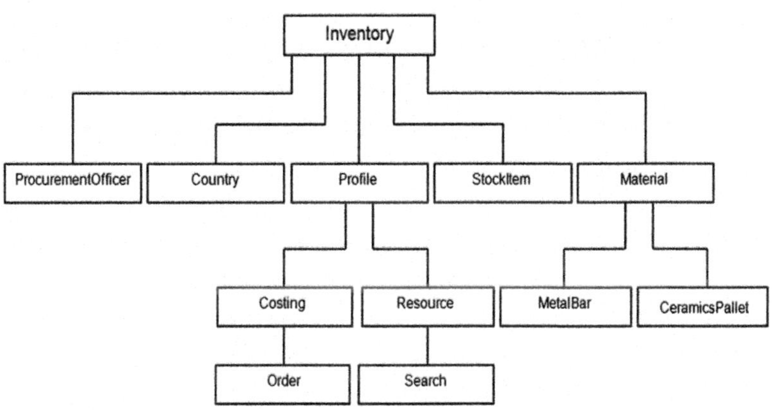

concept *material* is specialized as *metatl bar*, and *ceramics pallet*. A supply chain business process may be atomic, composed of only one logistical service, or it may be a composite process, containing a series of services that together form a workflow.

These ontologies are presented in OWL (Ontology Web Language) description format; and they can form as the basis for the semantic representation of supply chain related services. The details of logical formalism and consistency checking mechanisms are beyond the scope of this chapter. However, a part of the inventory management ontology formalism is described in Table 1, using description logics (Baader & Nutt, 2003); and some of its core concepts are adopted from the service modeling approach, which has been used for the semantic service description in SWSDF. The objective of the ontology-based semantic similarity algorithm, discussed in the later part of this chapter, is to support the discovery of relevant web services.

A Formal Definition of Web Service Ontology

The semantic web service ontology can be described as follows:

$$\theta_{service} \quad \{\alpha_{fp,} \quad \beta_{nfp.} \quad \gamma_{ip,} \quad \delta_{o} \quad \}$$

where

$\theta_{service}$ symbolizes semantic web service in a prescribed representation;

α_{fp} expresses functional characteristic attributes of service (it comprises of syntax attributes, static semantics which includes messages and operation semantics, service mediator and dynamic semantics;

β_{nfp} corresponds to non-functional attributes of service (it includes *unique service identification, service name, service type, quality of service, economic properties,* and so on)*;*

γ_{ip} stands for a collection of interface attributes (consisting of input interfaces sets, output interfaces sets, pre-condition interfaces sets, post-condition interfaces sets, and so on) for a semantic web service; and

δ_0 denotes ontology of service.

An ontology (δ_0) comprises of six constituent parts and it can be defined as follows:

$$\delta_o \quad \{ \ C, \quad A,^C \quad R, \quad A,^R \quad H, \quad X \ \}$$

Table 1. Web Service Description Examples using Description Logic Syntax

Domain Ontology Axioms
$Order \sqsubseteq Costing \sqcap \exists StockItem.\top \sqcap \exists account.\top \sqcap \exists material.\top \sqcap \exists to.\top$, $Search \sqsubseteq Resource \sqcap \exists StockItem. \sqcap \exists StockItem.\top$, $Costing \sqsubseteq Profile$, $Resource \sqsubseteq Profile$, $MetalBar \sqsubseteq Material$, $CeramicsPallet \sqsubseteq Material, sa : Country, uk : Country$,
Complex Concept
[1] $adv1 \equiv Order \sqcap stockitem.StockItem \sqcap \forall material.MetalBar \sqcap \forall account.ProcurementOfficer \sqcap \exists to.\{sa\}$
[2] $adv2 \equiv Order \sqcap stockitem.StockItem \sqcap \forall material.CeramicsPallet \sqcap \forall account.ProcurementOfficer \sqcap \exists to.\{sa\}$
[3] $adv3 \equiv Order \sqcap \forall stockitem.StockItem \sqcap \forall material.CeramicPallets \sqcap \forall account.ProcurementOfficer \sqcap \exists to.\{uk\}$
[4] $adv4 \equiv Search \sqcap \forall stockitem.StockItem \sqcap \forall material.MetalBar$
OWL-S Service Profile Instances
[1] $adv1 : Order, < adv1, StockItem >: hasInput, < adv1, ProcurementOfficer > : hasInput, < adv1, MetalBar > : hasOutput, < adv1, sa > : to$
[2] $adv2 : Order, < adv2, StockItem >: hasInput, < adv2, ProcurementOfficer > : hasInput, < adv2, CeramicPallet > : hasOutput, < adv2, sa > : to$
[3] $adv3 : Order, < adv3, StockItem >: hasInput, < adv3, ProcurementOfficer > : hasInput, < adv3, CeramicPallet > : hasOutput, < adv3, uk > : to$
[4] $adv4 : Search, < adv4, StockItem >: hasInput, < adv4, Metal >: hasOutput$

where

C symbolizes a set of concepts;
A^c expresses a collection of attribute sets, one of each concept;
R R represents a set of relationships;
A^R denotes a collection of attribute sets, one for each relationship;
H corresponds to a concept hierarchy; and
X stands for a set of axioms.

In this formalism, every concept C_i in C stands for a collection of similar object types, and can be described by the same collection of characteristic properties denoted by $A^C \quad (C_i)$. Each relationship $r_i \quad (c_{p,} \quad c_q)$ in R denotes a binary association between concepts c_p and $c_{q,}$ and the instances of such a relationship are pairs of $(c_{p,} \quad c_q)$ concept objects. The characteristic properties of r_i can be symbolized by $A^R \quad (r_i)$. In this representation formalism, H is a concept hierarchy derived from C and it is a set of parent-child (or superclass – subclass) relationships between concepts in C . Each axiom in X is a constraint on the concepts and relationships attribute values or a constraint on the relationships between concept objects. Each constraint can be expressed in a logic programming rule format. Contextual information that establishes relationships between the data and the real world aspects it applies to forms rich metadata. In this way, academic research has investigated approaches of semantic annotations in web services (Cardoso & Sheth, 2003; Patil et al., 2004) and offers different semantic web service frameworks.

Semantic Web Service Frameworks

The new breed of web semantic annotated web service is ushering the realization process of having data on the Web defined and linked in such a way that it can be used by matching not just for display purposes, but for automation, integration, and reuse of data across various applications. In this section, three main approaches, to bring semantics to web services, are discussed: WSDL-S, OWL-S, and WSMO.

- **WSDL-S:** Initially this approach was originated by a research group at the University of Georgia, USA. In this approach, the expressivity of web service description (WSDL specification) is augmented with semantics by employing ontological concepts; and it is termed as WSDL-S (WSDL-S, 2005). The idea of establishing mappings between service, task, or activity descriptions and ontological concepts was first proposed by Cardoso and Sheth (Cardoso

& Sheth, 2003). In this approach, one can specifically define the semantics of a web service for an area of interest. With the help of ontologies, the semantics or the meaning of service data and functionality can be described. In this way, integration can be accomplished in an automated way and with a higher degree of success. The WSDL elements that can be marked up with metadata are operations, messages, preconditions and effects, since all the elements are specifically described in a WSDL description.

  ◦ **Operations:** Each WSDL description may have a number of operations with different functionalities. In order to add semantics, the operations must be mapped to ontological concepts to describe their functionality.
  ◦ **Message:** Message parts, which are input and output parameters of operations, are defined in WSDL using the XML Schema. Ontologies – which are more expressive than the XML Schema – can be used to annotate WSDL message parts.
  ◦ **Preconditions and Effects:** Each WSDL operation may have a number of preconditions and effects. The preconditions are usually logical conditions, which must be evaluated to be true in order to execute a specific operation. Effects are changes in the world that occur after the execution of an operation.

- **OWL-S:** OWL-S (formally DAML-S) is emerging as a description language that semantically describes web services using OWL ontologies. OWL-S consists of three parts expressed with OWL ontologies: the service profile, the service model, and the service grounding. The profile is used to describe "what a service does", with advertisement and discovery as its objective. The service model describes "how a service works", to enable invocation, enactment, composition, monitoring and recovery. Finally, the grounding maps the constructs of the process model onto detailed specifications of message formats and protocols. In this approach, the ontology itself defines the top-level concept "Service" and three OWL-S sub-ontologies known as the "Service Profile" (SP), "Service Model" (SM), and "Service Grounding" (SG), as shown in Figure 3.
- **Service Profile (SP):** Every instance of the service class *presents* zero or more service profiles. A service profile expresses the purposes of advertising and serves as a template for service requests, thus enabling service discovery and matchmaking in a better way. The profile consists of non-functional properties - such as references to existing categorization schemes or ontologies, service provider information, and the quality rating of the service. In addition, the specification of functionality of the service is the most important information in the service profile.

Figure 3. OWL-S conceptual model

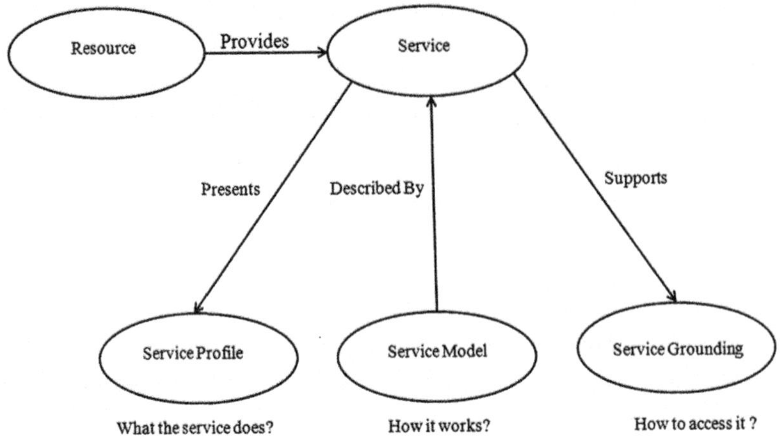

- **Service Model (SM):** A service capability needs to be described by a service model which tells "how a service works". The essential purpose of a service model is to enable invocation, enactment, composition, monitoring, and recovery. The service model views the interactions of the service as a process. A process is not necessarily a program to be executed, but rather, a specification of ways in which a client may interact with a service.
- **Service Grounding (SG):** The grounding of a given OWL-S service description provides a pragmatic binding between the logic-based and XMLS-based service definitions for the purpose of facilitating service execution. In order to map to the web service world, an OWL service can support a grounding which maps the constructs of the process model to detailed specifications of message formats, protocols, and so on. Unlike OWL-S, WSDL cannot be used to express pre-conditions or effects of executing services. Any atomic or composite OWL-S service with a grounding in WSDL is executable either by direct invocation of the (service) program that is referenced in the WSDL file, or by a BPEL engine, which processes the WSDL groundings of semantic web services.
- **WSMO:** The third approach, Web Service Modelling Ontology (WSMO), provides ontological specifications for the description of semantic web services. WSMO has been developed by the Digital Enterprise Research Institute (DERI), a European research organization that targets the integration of the semantic web with web services. The WSMO approach is based on the Web Service Modeling Framework (WSMF) (Fensel & Bussler, 2002), a framework that provides the appropriate conceptual model for developing and describing web services and their composition.

Web service modelling ontology discovery framework (WSMO-DF) is based on the WSMO framework (Roman et al, 2005) for web service discovery. In WSMO-DF, a web service is a computational entity which is able, by invocation, to achieve a goal. A *service,* in contrast, is the actual value provided by this invocation, to achieve a goal. Therefore, there are abstract web service and concrete service descriptions. The former describes web services in terms of its abstract functionality, whereas the latter contains more detailed information about the service. For example, a metal trading merchant offers an abstract service for supplying different types of metals, and requesters provide concrete descriptions of their requirements, e.g. number of pallets of a particular metal, its dimensions, quality specification, date of requirement to a particular manufacturing plant, and so on.

Web Service Description of a Business Scenario

In an inventory management system, different materials need to be procured for manufacturing supply chain management purposes. Material attribute ontology design can be viewed from higher perspectives, such as semantic meanings or logical reasoning. However, in this chapter, the main focus is on one pragmatic perspective: as a definition of concepts (or taxonomies) in the domain and associated relations. To illustrate the functionalities of domain ontologies, a simple business scenario has been used to demonstrate the activities.

- **Business Scenario:** Table 1 presents four web services advertisements using the complex concepts and the OWL-S service profile approach. The advertisement one (i.e. adv1) is classified in the Order class and requires a description and an account as inputs in order to return a *metal bar* that can be sent to South Africa (SA). In a similar way, the advertisement two (i.e. adv2) is classified in the Order class and requires a description and an account in order to return a *ceramics pallet* that can be sent to South Africa. The advertisement three (i.e. adv3) is also classified in the Order class and requires a *stock item* and an account in order to return a *ceramics pallet* that can be sent to UK. Finally, the advertisement four (i.e. adv4) is classified in the Search class and returns a *metal bar* based on the *stock item*. The above characteristic properties are expressed in the complex concept model by defining appropriate classes that describe services as a whole, whereas in the OWL-S service profile model each advertisement is expressed as an instance of the appropriate Profile subclass.

The scheme, as shown in Table 1, provides skeletons of instances for web services in material management of a global supply chain. In SWSDF, object-oriented structural matching techniques have been used in the domain of Structural Case-Based Reasoning (Bergmann & Schaaf, 2003), with Description Logic (DL) based reasoning over Profile instances. Structural CBR (S-CBR) and ontology based semantic web service management are widely used by the research community.

Semantic Web Services and Case Based Reasoning

Semantic web service initiatives define information systems infrastructure, which enrich the human-readable data on the Web with machine-readable annotations thereby allowing the Web to evolve into the world's biggest information repository which can be accessible from anywhere, at anytime. In order to achieve these objectives, one main issue would be the *markup* of web services to make them computer-interpretable. Within this markup and semantically enhanced service descriptions, powerful tools should be facilitated across the *web service lifecycle* (Papazoglou, 2012). In particular, web services lifecycle includes automatic web service discovery to find either a web service that offers a particular service, or a web service to be used that is sufficiently similar to the current service request; and automatic web service composition and interoperation that involves the run-time service selection, composition, and interoperation of appropriate web services to complete some business activity, given a high-level abstraction of service description.

At the same time, another research community has been working on similarity based *retrieval* and *adaptation* of past solutions to match new problems: two main aspects in the working semantic web service lifecycle. Case-Based Reasoning (CBR) is thriving in the applied computing community and is propagating the idea of finding a solution to a problem based on past experience of similar problems. CBR systems are a particular type of analogical reasoning system (Liang & Konsynski, 1993). It has diverse applications in many fields, such as classification systems for credit card transactions (Reategui & Campbell, 1994) and decision support systems for business acquisitions (Pal & Palmer, 1999). Attempting to imitate human reasoning, this technique solves new problems by using or adopting solutions of previously-solved old problems. A CBR system consists of a case base, which is the set of all previously solved cases that are known to the system. The case base can be thought of as a specific kind of knowledge that contains only *cases* and their *solutions*. There are four main stages in the CBR life cycle and they are:

- **Case Representation:** A case is a contextualized piece of knowledge representing an experience. Since a problem is solved by recalling a past experience suitable for solving the new problem at hand, the case search and matching processes need to be both effective and reasonably time efficient. Moreover, since the experience from a problem just solved has to be retained in some way, these need to apply to the method of integrating a new case into the case collection, too. In this way, CBR is heavily dependent on the structure and content of its collection of cases.

- **Case Storage and Indexing:** Cases are assigned indices that express information about their content, then stored in a case library. This is an important aspect for the design of CBR systems because it reflects the conceptual view of what is represented in the case. The indexing problem is central and a much focused problem in CBR.
- **Case Retrieval:** An important step in the CBR cycle is the retrieval of previous cases that can be used to solve the target problem. Whenever a new problem needs to be solved, the case library index is searched for cases which can be a potential solution. The first phase of this search is case retrieval with the aim of finding the cases which are contextually similar to the new problem. The case retrieval task starts with a problem description, and ends when a suitable matching previous case has been found. Its subtasks are referred to as Identify Features, Search, and Select best possible cases from the system's repository.
- **Case Matchmaking and Use:** Matchmaking performs comparison between the similar cases and the new request to verify if the possible solution is the one applied to prior cases. The past solutions may be reused, directly or through adaptation, in the current situation.

CBR systems typically apply retrieval and matching algorithms to a case base of past problem-solution pairs. Many successful research and industry results are paving the way of CBR in software development and deployment practice. In recent years, *ontologies and descriptive logics* (DLs) have become systems of interest for the CBR community. Many multinational organizations (e.g. IBM, British Airways, Volkswagen, NASA, and so on) are using CBR techniques for their knowledge intensive business operations (Watson, 1997). Moreover, some real-world CBR applications are taking advantage of the Descriptive Logics (DLs) reasoning mechanisms for the processes involved in the CBR cycle. However, among the different approaches considered, all focus on the fact that the formal semantics and the capabilities of the DLs maintain terminological taxonomy. These are interesting properties to measure similarity and to manage a case base.

In SWSDF, efforts of the semantic web services lifecycle management and CBR cycle are trying to find synergies between both of them. Given a certain requirement describing the user goals, automatic web service discovery typically uses a dedicated inference mechanism in order to answer queries conforming to the logic formalism and the terms defined in the ontology.

PROPOSED SYSTEM FRAMEWORK

This section briefly presents the overall architecture of the SWSDF system and illustrates the interplay of the different components. The computational framework of SWSDF is shown in Figure 4. It uses a relational similarity assessment measure between implicitly stated concepts. The proposed framework accepts the service consumer request which consists of the requirements of a new service (e.g. input, output, precondition, and so on). Next, the user requirement information is parsed for further processing; and finally semantically ranked web services are presented to the consumer. The dynamics of SWSDF are as follows:

- Initially, the service repository is populated with semantically enriched web service descriptions for specific application areas within a supply chain.
- The service requester inputs the service requirements using SWSDF's interface.
- The service matchmaking module takes the retrieved cases and the annotation of the problem description from the semantic description generator module (within the system framework), runs them through a matchmaking algorithm and forwards the closest match web service to the requester.

Figure 4. Diagrammatic representation of the SWSDF

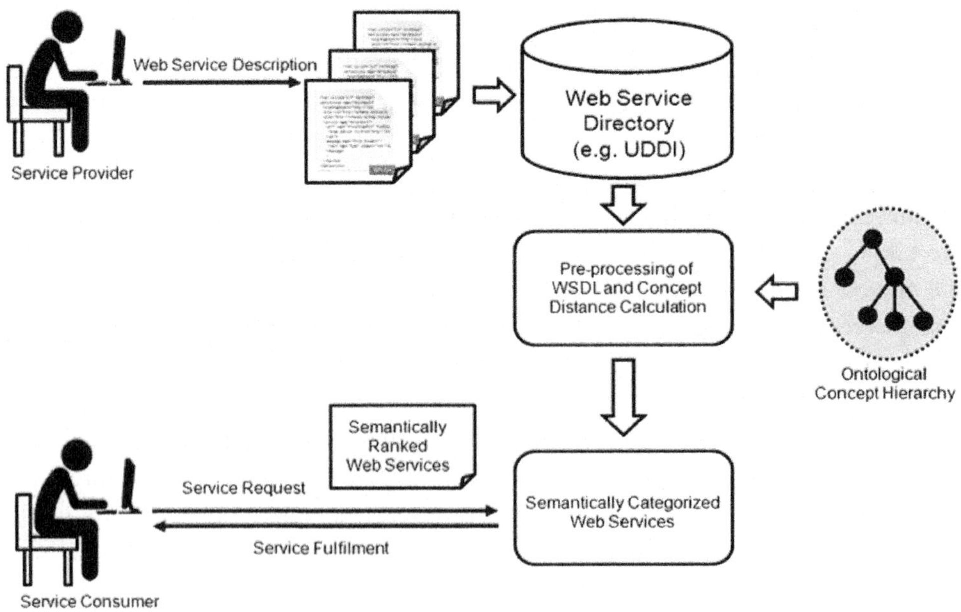

The ontologically enhanced web service descriptions are manually encoded in the SWSDF service repository. In the processing of ontological concept matching, when dealing with similarity between concepts, it not only considers inheritance (i.e. the relationship between supper-class and subclass) relations, but also considers the distance relationship between concepts. In SWSDF, on the basis of the comprehensive consideration of the inheritance relations and semantic distance between concepts, a concept similarity matching method based on semantic distance has been used. The SWSDF uses structural case-based reasoning (S-CBR) for services and the relevant ontological concepts storage purpose; and it uses a rule-based reasoning (RBR) for service similarity assessment. The algorithm, as shown in Figure 5, is used to discover semantic web services advertised within SWSDF.

Model of Concept Similarity for SWSDF

This section describes the method for measuring the degree of similarity of two OWL concepts. This measure will then be used in the next section for determining the degree of functional similarity of two services.

Figure 5. The hierarchical concept relationships

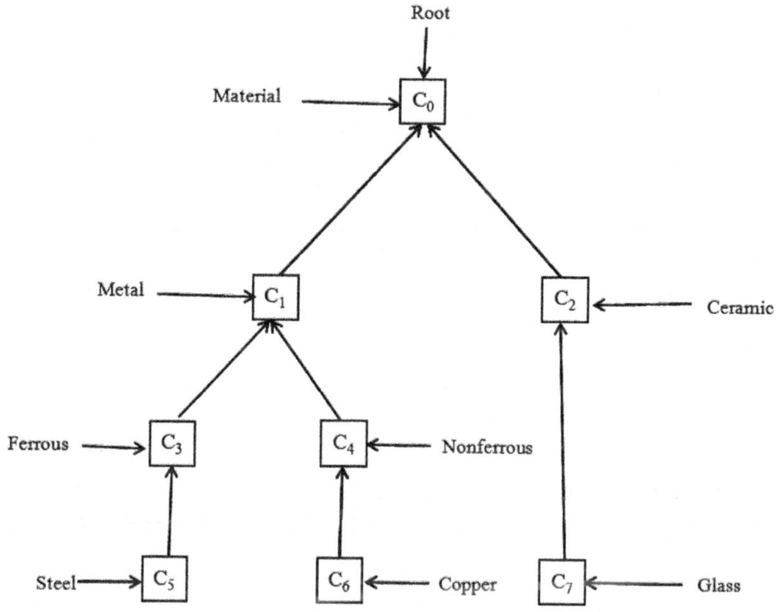

Definition 1 (*Concept Similarity*): A similarity $\sigma : C \ x \ C \ \rightarrow \ [0, \ 1]$ is a function from a pair of concepts to a real number between zero and one expressing the degree of similarity between two concepts such that:

(1) $\forall x \ \in \ C, \ \ \sigma(x, x) \ = \ 1$
(2) $\forall x, y \ \in \ C, \ \ \sigma(x, y) \ = \ \sigma(y, x)$
(3) $\forall x, y, z \ : \ if \ \ SimDis\tan ce(x, y) \ >$
$SimDis\tan ce(x, z), \ \ then \ \ \sigma(x, y) \ < \ \sigma(x, z)$

The above properties provide the range of semantic similarity function $\sigma(x \ , \ x)$. For exactly similar concepts the similarity is $\sigma(x \ , \ x) = 1$; and when two concepts have nothing in common, their similarity is $\sigma(x \ , \ y) = 0$. In this way, the output of similarity function should be in closed interval $[0,1]$ and it is a reflexive relation. In SWSDF, the following semantic similarity function has been used for computation purposes:

$$f_{similarity} \ = \ p^{SimDis\tan ce \ + \ 1}$$

In the above similarity function, the value of $p(0 \ < \ p \ \leq \ 1)$ and *SimDistance* decide the impact degree of semantic distance to semantic similarity. In SWSDF, the similarity between two ontological concepts C_i and C_j can be expressed by a number S_{ij} which can be expressed by the semantic distance among any two concepts. Given two concepts C_i and C_j, the SWSDF calculates the distance as weight allocation function as follows:

$$\omega[sub(C_i \ \ and \ \ C_j)] \ = \ 1 \ + \ \frac{1}{k^{depth \ \ (C_j)}}$$

where depth (C_i) represents the depth of concept (C_j) from the root concept to node C_j in ontology hierarchy, and k is a predefined factor larger than 1 showing the rate at which the weight values decrease along the ontology hierarchy.

Algorithm 1 has got two important properties: (1) the semantic differences between higher concepts are more in comparison to lower level concepts, and (2) the

Algorithm 1. Algorithm for semantic distance computation

```
Similarity of two concepts (C1, C2)
INPUT: Two Concepts C1 and C2
OUTPUT: Similarity Distance :: SimDistance (C1 , C2)

BEGIN
        IF C1 and C2 are same concept THEN
                    SimDistance (C1 , C2)= 0
            ELSE
             IF there exists any indirect path relations between (C1 and C2) THEN
                    SimDistance (C1 , C2) = Weight [sub (C1 , C2)]
                    ELSE
                            SimDistance (C1 , C2) = Σ_{c ∈ SPath(C1, C2)} (weight[sub(C1, C2)]
    ELSE
        SimDistance (C1 , C2) = min{SimDistance (C1 , C0)}+ min {SimDistance(C2 , C0)}
END
```

distance between sibling concepts is greater than the distance between parent and child concepts. In particular, the depth of topmost concept is considered be zero, and the lower level other concepts are related to their path length to root concept node.

Algorithm 1 takes two concepts as input and computes a semantic similarity as output.

Experimental Evaluation

The part of the type hierarchy in the matchmaker ontology and all instances used in this example are shown in Figure 5. In the experimental comparison, semantic similarity among Copper, Glass, Metal, Steel and Material are considered.

In Table 2, (a) tabulates the results of synonymy similarity (Giunchiglia et al, 2004), (b) tabulates the results of Jian and Conrath similarity (Jiang & Conrath, 1997) results, (c) tabulates the results of path similarity (Varelas et al, 2005), and (d) tabulates the results of algorithm used in SWSDF – concept similarity measure based on semantic distance.

As shown in Table 2, the synonymy similarity measure can only find similarity between the same concepts, and Jian and Conrath' similarity measure is better than the synonymy similarity measure. The path similarity measure and SWSDF's used

Table 2. The results of various similarity measures

	c_1	c_2	c_3	c_4	c_5
c_1	1.00	0.00	0.00	0.00	0.00
c_2	0.00	1.00	0.00	0.00	0.00
c_3	0.00	0.00	1.00	0.00	0.00
c_4	0.00	0.00	0.00	1.00	0.00
c_5	0.00	0.00	0.00	0.00	1.00

(a) Synonymy similarity

	c_1	c_2	c_3	c_4	c_5
c_1	1.00	0.60	0.41	0.97	0.52
c_2	0.42	1.00	0.81	0.60	0.36
c_3	0.97	0.81	1.00	0.68	0.44
c_4	0.60	0.60	0.68	1.00	0.53
c_5	0.52	0.36	0.44	0.53	1.00

(b) Jian and Conrath similarity

	c_1	c_2	c_3	c_4	c_5
c_1	1.00	0.25	0.50	0.20	0.20
c_2	0.25	1.00	0.50	0.33	0.16
c_3	0.50	0.50	1.00	0.25	0.16
c_4	0.20	0.33	0.25	1.00	0.20
c_5	0.20	0.16	0.16	0.20	1.00

(c) Path similarity

	c_1	c_2	c_3	c_4	c_5
c_1	1.0	0.48	0.65	0.51	0.38
c_2	0.48	1.0	0.65	0.51	0.38
c_3	0.65	0.65	1.0	0.71	0.48
c_4	0.51	0.51	0.71	1.0	0.59
c_5	0.38	0.38	0.48	0.59	1.0

(d) The proposed method

method are better than the above two methods. The path similarity measure can find the semantic similarity between concepts, but the similarity score is low. The SWSDF's similarity method can also get the semantic similarity between concepts, and the similarity score is high.

RELATED RESEARCH WORK

The semantic web approaches to web services give business communities the ability to describe the semantics of web services and their capabilities in a formal and machine-processable manner. A majority of the current approaches (e.g. OWL-S, WSDL-S, and WSMO) enhancing web services using semantic tagged descriptions. However, these approaches have several limitations. First, it is impractical to expect all new services to have semantic tagged descriptions. Second, descriptions of the vast majority of existing web services are specified using WSDL and do not have associated semantics. Also, from the service requestor's perspective, the requestor may not be aware of all the knowledge that constitutes the domain. Specifically, the service requestor may not be aware of all the terms related to the service request. As a result, many services relevant to the request may not be considered in the service discovery process. Akkiraju and his research group (Akkiraju et al, 2005), conjectured an attempt to design a system which can create semantic web services is by mapping concepts in a web service description (WSDL specification) to ontological concepts. This approach is known as WSDL-S. The idea of establishing mappings between service, task, or activity description and its enrichment using domain specific ontological concepts was first introduced by Cardoso (Cardoso & Sheth, 2003). Martin has also concentrated on enhancement of service descriptions, in work with other researchers on OWL-S (Martin et al, 2007), which is an important attempt to use lightweight web service description based on inputs, outputs and non-functional properties, in order to find an initial set of candidate web services for a request. Fensel has also concentrated on service enrichment and modelling, in work with Bussler on the system WSMF (Fensel & Bussler, 2002), a framework that provides the appropriate conceptual model for developing and describing web services and their composition.

Web service modelling ontology discovery framework (WSMO-DF), also contributed to semantic enrichment of web services, and is based on the WSMO framework (Roman et al, 2005) for web service discovery. In the semantic web service paradigm, discovery is performed over semantic descriptions of web services. WSMO-DF and OWL-S SP (service profile) are two frameworks that are generally used for service description purposes.

While these are a few main styles of service enrichment in semantic web service descriptions, they are by no means the only research conducted in the recent past. Later work by Pengwei and his colleagues on their semantic enhancement web service research (Wang et al, 2008) has used WSMO-DF for rich web service representation purposes. In contrast to Pengwei and his research partners (Weang et al, 2008) work, SWSDF follows the Service Profile (SP) model and uses structural ontology information.

In IRS-III (Domingue et al, 2008), an extended approach of the WSMO conceptual model is used, where OCML (Options Configuration Modeling Language) has provided internal description of service and an appropriate OCML reasoner. In contrast to SWSDF, IRS-III follows an enhanced WSMO model and a frame-based rule language for representing domain ontologies.

Li and his colleagues advocated the use of a mechanism based on the Rough sets theory to discover grid services (Li et al, 2008). The implemented software system, known as ROSSE, builds on the Rough sets theory to dynamically reduce uncertain properties when matching grid services. The evaluation results have shown that ROSSE significantly improves the precision and recall of services compared with keyword-based service matching techniques and OWL-S matching. The novelty of ROSSE is in its capability to deal with uncertain properties, that is, properties that are explicitly used by one advertisement but do not appear in another service of the same category. In SWSDF, only the common properties of an advertisement have been used.

Li and Horrocks have distinguished a number of things in a service matchmaking research porotype (Li & Horrocks, 2003), which uses a DL reasoner to match service advertisements and requests based on ontology enhanced service descriptions. In this particular project, web service descriptions are defined as Complex Concepts (CCs) in OWL and the matchmaking mechanism examines the subsumption relationships. FC-MATCH research project (Bianchini et al, 2006) uses a similar type of approach, performing text similarity matching using WordNet. In some research (Grimm et al., 2006), a software framework has been used to annotate web services using DLs. Similar to SWSDF, it follows the abstract web service model.

In the DAML-S/UDDI matchmaker (Sycara et al, 2003), OWL-S SP advertisements and requests refers to DAML concepts and the matching process that performs inferences on the subsumption hierarchy. It uses a different definition of web service filters from SWSDF and it does not consider profile taxonomies, roles or group filtering.

LARKS (Sycara et al, 2002) uses both syntactic and semantic matching. It uses five matchmaking filters, namely context matching, profile comparison, similarity matching, signature matching and constant matching. LARKS uses its own capability description and DL language in contrast to the SWSDF approach.

OWLS-MX (Klusch et al, 2008) utilizes both logic-based reasoning and content-based IR techniques for web services in OWL-S. It cannot handle profile taxonomies and it follows the static SP paradigm, unable to use dynamic ontology roles. iMatcher2 (Kiefer & Bernstein, 2008) follows the OWLS-MX approach, also applying learning algorithms in order to predict similarities. Like OWLS-MX, it uses a DL reasoner in order to unfold the annotation concepts, creating a vector on which the IR techniques are applied. iMatcher2 does not follow a standard matchmaking algorithm, which is defined through an iSPARQL strategy. WSMO-MX (Kaufer & Klusch, 2006) is a hybrid approach based on rich WSMO service descriptions.

In the DAML-S/UDDI matchmaker (Sycara et al, 2003), OWL-S SP advertisements and requests refers to DAML concepts and the matching process performs inferences on the subsumption hierarchy. It uses a different definition of web service filters from SWSDF and it does not consider profile taxonomies, roles or group filtering.

LARKS (Sycara et al, 2002) use both syntactic and semantic matching. It uses five matchmaking filters, namely context matching, profile comparison, similarity matching, signature matching and constant matching. LARKS uses its own capability description and DL language in contrast to the SWSDF approach.

In a hybrid semantic web service matchmaker for OWL-S services, known as OWLS-MX (Klusch et al, 2008), researchers have used both logic-based reasoning and content-based information retrieval techniques. Experimental evaluation results show strong justification in favor of the proposition that the performance of logic-based matchmaking can be considerably improved by incorporating non-logic based information retrieval techniques into the matchmaking algorithms. However, OWLS-MX cannot handle profile taxonomies and it follows the static SP paradigm, unable to use dynamic ontology roles. iMatcher2 (Kiefer & Bernstein, 2008) follows the OWLS-MX approach, applying also learning algorithms in order to predict similarities. Like OWLS-MX, it uses a DL reasoner in order to unfold the annotation concepts, creating a vector on which the IR techniques are applied. iMatcher2 does not follow a standard matchmaking algorithm, which is defined through an iSPARQL strategy. WSMO-MX (Kaufer & Klusch, 2006) is a hybrid approach based on rich WSMO service descriptions.

There are plenty of other approaches that are based on inputs/outputs, for example (Cardoso, 2006) (Pathak et al, 2005) (Skoutas et al, 2007). These approaches retrieve directly the input/output annotations and any taxonomical knowledge from special properties, such as service categorization. Moreover, they do not consider roles, using static annotation concepts, and do not apply further filtering on results (group filtering). METEROR-S (Verma et al, 2005) follows the WSDL-S approach, where WSDL constructs point to ontology concepts.

Thakker, Osman and Al-Dabass have reported their research in which the web service execution experiences are modeled as cases that represent the web service properties in a specific area described using OWL semantic description (Osman et al, 2006a) (Osman et al, 2006b). In this research, the service repository administrator performs the storing of service descriptions using ontology enhanced semantics for case representation. This representation is used to semantically annotate the users' queries looking for adequate services as well as the web service execution experiences in the given area. The proposed system uses frame structures to model its cases. These structures are not generalized and depend heavily on the application domain so that the constituent elements of these structures more precisely 'slots' differ from one application to another.

Lamjmi and co-researchers have proposed the WeSCo_CBR approach based mainly on ontologies and case-based reasoning meant for the web service composition (Lajmi et al, 2006a) (Lajmi et al, 2006b). They have created an ontology that describes various features of a web service using OWL representation formalism in order to bring a semi-automatic guidance for the user. In order to facilitate the processing, they proceed by transforming the user's query into an ontological formulation combining a set of ontology concepts. For each received new query, the reuse process consists on retrieving similar prior stored cases and eventually evaluating and storing the new case. In WeSCo_CBR, a case comprises the following three elements: a problem, a solution and an evaluation. The discovery of web service meeting the client's needs is accomplished by using similarity measures designed in accordance with the formalization of the problem. The most relevant case is usually determined according to its similarity with the new problem case.

In order to improve the web service discovery, Wan and Cao (Wang & Cao, 2007) have introduced an additional case-based reasoning component called CBR/OWL-S Matching Engine (Wang & Cao, 2007). In order to find out the desired web service, this matching engine uses ontologies for semantic similarity measure.

The SWSDF work has been motivated by object-oriented structural matching techniques that are used in the domain of Structural Case-Based Reasoning (SCBR) (Bergman & Schaaf, 2003), with the use of a DL reasoner to handle semantic web service descriptions and to apply an extended matchmaking algorithm. In addition, the method of allocating the weight value to concept node has been used for similarity assessment purposes.

CONCLUSION

This chapter reviews some of the business and technology challenges that companies are facing today in supply chain information sharing between business partners, and describes how a number of these difficulties could be overcome with the use of semantic web service. However, in order for semantic web service to be adopted within a global supply chain network there must be tools, which will help to automate heterogeneous data sources existing in this networked enterprise. In this chapter, a supply chain information sharing architecture between business partners is described using the semantic web service framework. The architecture is based on a hybrid knowledge-based service matchmaking framework, which uses Structural Case-Based Reasoning (S-CBR) and Rule-Based Reasoning (RBR). It uses ontology enhanced web service descriptions; object-oriented S-CBR knowledge representation, description logic (DL) for service formalization, and an algorithm to measure ontological concept similarity based on semantic distance. This algorithm considers not only the inheritance relation between concepts, but also the level of concepts in the ontology hierarchy. An experimental evaluation of the proposed algorithm is presented. In this architecture, ontological concepts play an important role in the development of the semantic web as a means for defining shared terms in web resources in SCM automation. Today, business partners within global supply chains are generating huge amounts of raw-data; and they are collecting some of this data for business intelligence purposes. This data is commonly referred to as 'big data' – because of its *volume*, the *velocity* with which it arrives in global supply chain environments, and the *variety* of forms it takes. Big data is ushering in a new era of corporate business intelligence promise; but one of main bottlenecks is how to capture this raw-data and analyze it to generate meaningful information. In the future, this research will extend the current concept-based ontological reasoning framework and investigate additional mapping techniques in order to express service descriptions in a much more enhanced form. This will allow a richer service discovery for globalized supply chain world. Particularly, one of the challenging tasks is how to handle *big data* in global supply chain environments, and how to use these untapped corporate *cyber-physical* resources to come up with better service provisions for its stakeholders. Cyber-physical systems enable new types of interconnected information service provisions by connecting networked systems with services of the automated system infrastructure. This in turn enables interaction with extended capabilities of physical business world through computation, communication and control. This infrastructure is going to be the source of next generation big data driven global supply chain information systems power house.

ACKNOWLEDGMENT

The author sincerely thanks Professor John A. Campbell, at University College London, for his constructive suggestions.

REFERENCES

Akkiraju, R., Farrell, J., Miller, J., Nagarajan, M., Schmidt, M., Sheth, A., & Verma, K. (2005). *Web Service Semantics - WSDL-S, A joint UGA-IBM Technical Note, version 1.0*. Retrieved from http://lsdis.cs.uga.edu/projects/METEOR-S/WSDL-S

Antoniou, G., & Harmelen, F. V. (2008). *A Semantic Web Primer*. Cambridge, MA: The MIT Press.

Baader, F., & Nutt, W. (2003). Basic Description Logics, The description logic handbook. Cambridge University Press.

Bergmann, R., & Schaaf, M. (2003). Structural Case-Based Reasoning and Ontology-Based Knowledge Management: A Perfect Match? *Journal of Universal Computer Science, UCS*, *9*(7), 608–626.

Berners-Lee, T., Hendler, J., & Lassila, O. (2001). The Semantic Web. *Scientific American*, *284*(May), 34–43. doi:10.1038/scientificamerican0501-34 PMID:11323639

Bianchini, D., Antonellis, V. A., Melchiori, M., & Salvi, D. (2006). Semantic Enriched Service Discovery. In *International Conference in Data Engineering Workshop*.

Cai, M. Zhang, W. Y., Zhang, K. & Li, S. T. (2010). SWMRD: A Semantic Web-based manufacturing resource discovery system for cross-enterprise collaboration. *International Journal of Production Research, 48*(120), 3445-3460.

Cardoso, J. (2006). Discovering Semantic Web Services with and without a Common Ontology Commitment. In *IEEE Service Computing Workshop*, (pp. 183-190). IEEE.

Cardoso, J., & Sheth, A. (2003). Semantic e-Workflow Composition. *Journal of Intelligent Information Systems*, *21*(3), 191–225. doi:10.1023/A:1025542915514

Copacino, W., & Anderson, D. (2003). Connecting with the Bottom Line: A Global Study of Supply Chain Leadership and its Contribution to the High Performance Business. *Accenture, 1*.

Domingue, J., Cabral, L., Galizia, S., Tanasescu, V., Gugliotta, A., Norton, B., & Pedrinaci, C. (2008). IRS-III: A Broker-based Approach to Semantic Web Service. *Journal of Web Semantics*, *6*(2), 109–132. doi:10.1016/j.websem.2008.01.001

Fensel, D., & Bussler, C. (2002). The Web Service Modeling Framework WSMF. *Electronic Commerce Research and Applications*, *1*(2), 113–137. doi:10.1016/S1567-4223(02)00015-7

Fugate, B., Sahin, F., & Mentzer, J. T. (2006). Supply Chain Management Coordination Mechanisms. *Journal of Business Logistics*, *27*(2), 129–161. doi:10.1002/j.2158-1592.2006.tb00220.x

Ganeshan, R., & Harrison, T. P. (1995). *An introduction to supply chain management*. Supply Chain Management, Version 1. Available from http://silmaril.smeal.psu.edu/misc/supply_chain_intro.html

Giunchiglia, F., Shvaiko, P., & Yatskevich, M. (2004). S-Match: an algorithm and an implementation of semantic matching. In Proceedings of 1st European Semantic Web Symposium (ESWS) (LNCS), (*vol. 3053*, pp. 61-75). Springer. doi:10.1007/978-3-540-25956-5_5

Grimm, S., Monk, B., & Preist, C. (2006). Matching Semantic Service Descriptions with Local Closed-World Reasoning. In *European Semantic Web Conference*, (pp. 575-589). doi:10.1007/11762256_42

Gruber, T. R. (1993). *A Translation Approach to Portable Ontology Specifications*. Technical Report KSL 92-71. Stanford University, Computer Science Department, Knowledge Systems Laboratory.

Guarino, N., & Giaretta, P. (1995). *Ontologies and Knowledge Base: Towards a Terminological Classification Toward Very Large Knowledge Base: Knowledge Building and Knowledge Sharing*. Amsterdam: IOS Press.

Jiang, J. J., & Conrath, D. W. (1997). Semantic Similarity Based on Corpus Statistics and Lexical Taxonomy. In *Proceedings of International Conference Research on Computational Linguistics*.

Kalakota, R., & Whiston, A. (1997). *Electronic commerce: A manager's guide*. Reading, MA: Addison Wesley.

Kaufer, F., & Klusch, M. (2006). WSMO-MX: A Logic Programming Based Hybrid Service Matchmaker. In *European Conference on Web Services*, (pp. 161-170). doi:10.1109/ECOWS.2006.39

Kiefer, C., & Bernstein, A. (2008). The Creation and Evaluation of iSPARQL Strategies for Matchmaking. In *European Semantic Web Conference*, (pp. 463-477). doi:10.1007/978-3-540-68234-9_35

Klusch, M., Fries, B., & Sycara, K. (2008). OWLS-MX: A Hybrid Semantic Web Service Matchmaker for OWL-S Services. *Journal of Web Semantics*.

Lajmi, S., Ghedira, C., & Ghedira, K. (2006). How to apply CBR method in web service composition. *Second International Conference on Signal-Image Technology and Internet Based Systems* (SITI'2006). Hammamet, Tunisia: Springer Verlag.

Lajmi, S., Ghedira, C., Ghedira, K., & Benslimane, D. (2006b). Web_CBR: How to compose web service via case based reasoning. *IEEE International Symposium on Service-Oriented Applications, Integration and Collaboration held with the IEEE International Conference on eBusiness Engineering (ICEBE 2006)*. Shanghai, China: IEEE.

Laliwala, Z., Khosla, R., Majumdar, P., & Chaudhary, S. (2006). Semantic and Rule Based Event-Driven Dynamic Web Service Composition for Automation of Business Processes. In *Proceedings of the IEEE Service Computing Workshop* (SCW06). IEEE.

Lambert, D. M., & Cooper, M. C. (2000). Issues in Supply Chain Management. *Industrial Marketing Management*, *29*(1), 65–83. doi:10.1016/S0019-8501(99)00113-3

Li, J., Sikora, R., Shaw, M. J., & Woo Tan, G. A. (2006). Strategic analysis of inter-organizational information sharing. *Decision Support Systems*, *42*(1), 251–266. doi:10.1016/j.dss.2004.12.003

Li, L., & Horrocks, I. (2003). A Software Framework for Matchmaking Based on Semantic Web Technology. In *International Conference in World Wide Web*, (pp. 331-339). doi:10.1145/775152.775199

Li, M., Yu, B., Rana, O. F., & Wang, Z. (2008). Grid Service Discovery with Rough Sets. *IEEE Transactions on Knowledge and Data Engineering*, *20*(6), 851–862. doi:10.1109/TKDE.2007.190744

Li, S. H. (2002). *An Integrated Model for Supply Chain Management Practice, Performance and Competitive Advantage*. (PhD Dissertation). University of Toledo, Toledo, OH.

Liang, T., & Konsynski, B. R. (1993). Modeling by analogy: Use of analogical reasoning in model management systems. *Decision Support Systems*, *9*(1), 113–125. doi:10.1016/0167-9236(93)90026-Y

Martin, D., Burstein, M., Mcdermott, D., Mcilraith, S., Paolucci, M., Sycara, K., & Srinivasan, N. et al. (2007). Bringing Semantics to Web Services with OWL-S. *World Wide Web (Bussum)*, *10*(3), 243–277. doi:10.1007/s11280-007-0033-x

Martin, D., Paolucci, M., McIlraith, S., Burstein, M., McDermott, D., McGunness, D., & Sycara, K. et al. (2004). Bringing Semantics to Web Services: The OWL-S Approach. *Proceeding of First International Workshop Semantic Web Services and Web Process Composition*.

Matskin, M., Maigre, R., & Tyugu, E. (2007). Computational logical semantics for business process language. In *Proceedings of second international conference on Internet and Web applications and services* (ICIW 2007). IEEE Computer Society.

McIlraith, S., & Martin, D. (2003). Bringing Semantics to Web Services. *IEEE Intelligent Systems*, *18*(1), 90–93. doi:10.1109/MIS.2003.1179199

OASIS. (2004). *Introduction to UDDI: Important Features and Functional Concepts*. Organization for the Advancement of Structured Information Standards.

OMG. (2009). *Business Process Model and Notation*. Retrieved from http://www.omg.org/spec/BPMN/1.2/(2009)

Osman, T., Thakker, D., & Al-Dabass, D. (2006a). Semantic-Driven Matching of Web services using Case-Based Reasoning. In *Fourth IEEE International Conference on Web Services* (ICWS 2006). IEEE.

Osman, T., Thakker, D., & Al-Dabass, D. (2006b). S-CBR: Semantic Case Based Reasoner for Web services discovery and matchmaking. In *20th European Conference on Modeling and Simulation (ECMS2006).*

Pal, K., & Karakostas, B. (2014). A Multi Agent-based Service Framework for supply Chain Management. *Procedia Computer Science*, *32*, 53–60.

Pal, K., & Palmer, O. (2000). A decision-support systems for business acquisition. *Decision Support Systems*, *27*(4), 411–429. doi:10.1016/S0167-9236(99)00083-4

Papazoglou, M. (2012). *Web Services and SOA: Principles and Technology*. Pearson.

Pathak, J., Koul, N., Caragea, D., & Honavar, V. G. (2005). A Framework for Semantic Web Services Discovery. In *ACM International Workshop on Web Information and Data Management*, (pp. 45-50). doi:10.1145/1097047.1097057

Patil, A., Oundhaka, S., Sheth, A., & Verma, K. (2004). METEOR-S Web service Annotation Framework. In *Proceedings of the Thirteenth International World Wide Web Conference*, (pp. 553-562).

Reategui, E. B., & Campbell, J. A. (1995). A Classification System for Credit Card Transactions, In *Advances in Case-Based Reasoning:Second European Workshop* (EWCBR-94). Springer. doi:10.1007/3-540-60364-6_43

Roman, D., Keller, U., Lausen, H., de Bruijn, J., Lara, R., Stollberg, M., & Fensel, D. et al. (2005). Web service modeling ontology. *Applied Ontology*, *1*(1), 77–106.

Roman, D., Kopecky, J., Vitvar, T., Domingue, J., & Fensel, D. (2015). WSMO-Lite and hRESTS: Lightweight semantic annotations for Web services and RESTful APIs. *Web Semantics: Science, Services, and Agents on the World Wide Web*, *31*, 39–58. doi:10.1016/j.websem.2014.11.006

Shingo, S. (1988). *Non-Stock Production*. Cambridge, MA: Productivity Press.

Skoutas, D., Simitsis, A., & Sellis, T. (2007). A Ranking Mechanism for Semantic Web Service Discovery. In *IEEE Congress on Services*, (pp. 41-48).

Studer, R., Benjamins, V. R., & Fensel, D. (1998). Knowledge engineering: Principles and methods. *Data & Knowledge Engineering*, *25*(1-2), 161–197. doi:10.1016/S0169-023X(97)00056-6

Sycara, K., Widoff, S., Klusch, M., & Lu, J. (2002). LARKS: Dynamic Matching Among Heterogeneous Software Agents in Cyberspace. *Autonomous Agents and Multi-Agent Systems*, *5*(2), 173–203. doi:10.1023/A:1014897210525

Sycara, K. P., Paolucci, M., Ankolekar, A., & Srinivasan, N. (2003). Automated Discovery, Interaction and Computation of Semanticmweb Services. *Journal of Web Semantics*, *1*(1), 27–46. doi:10.1016/j.websem.2003.07.002

Varelas, G., Voutsakis, E., Raftopoulou, P., Petrakis, E. G. M., & Milios, E. (2005). Semantic Similarity methods in WordNet and their application to information retrieval on the Web. *Proceedings of the 7th annual ACM international workshop on web information and data management*. Bremen, Germany: ACM. doi:10.1145/1097047.1097051

Verma, K., Sivashanmugam, K., Sheth, A., Patil, A., Oundhakar, S., & Miller, J. (2005). METEOR-S WSDI: A Scalable P2P Infrastructure of Registries for Semantic Publication and Discovery of Web Services. *Information Technology Management*, *6*(1), 17–39. doi:10.1007/s10799-004-7773-4

Vrijhoef, R., & Koskela, L. (1999). Role of supply chain management in construction. *Proceedings of the Seventh Annual Conference of the International Group for Lean Construction*.

Wang, L., & Cao, J. (2007). Web Services Semantic Searching enhanced by Case Based Reasoning. *18th International Workshop on Database and Expert Systems Applications*.

Wang, P., Jin, Z., Liu, L., & Cai, G. (2008). Building Toward Capability Specifications of Web Services Based on an Environment Ontology. *IEEE Transactions on Knowledge and Data Engineering*, *20*(4), 547–561. doi:10.1109/TKDE.2007.190719

Watson, I. (1997). *Applying Case-Based Reasoning: Techniques for Enterprise Systems*. Morgan Kaufman.

Wooldridge, M., & Jennings, N. (1995). Intelligent Agents: Theory and Practice. *The Knowledge Engineering Review*, *10*(2), 115–152. doi:10.1017/S0269888900008122

WSDL-S. (2005). Retrieved from: http://www.w3.org/Submission/WSDL-S/

Zhang, W. Y., Cai, M., Qiu, J., & Yin, J. W. (2009). Managing distributed manufacturing knowledge through multi-perspective modelling for Semantic Web applications. *International Journal of Production Research*, *47*(23), 6525–6542. doi:10.1080/00207540802311114

KEY TERMS AND DEFINITIONS

Case-Based Reasoning: Case-based reasoning (CBR) is one of the useful mechanisms for both modeling human reasoning and building intelligent software application systems. The basic principle of case-based reasoning systems is that of solving problems by adapting the solution of similar problems solved in the past. A CBR system consists of a *case base*, which is the set of all cases that are known to the system. The case base can be thought of as a specific kind of knowledge base that contains only cases. When a new case is presented to the system, it checks the case base for similar cases that are most relevant to the case in hand, in a *selection process*. If a similar case is found, then the system retrieves that particular case and attempts to modify it (if necessary) to produce a potential solution for the new case. The process is known as *adaption*.

Description Logic: Knowledge-based software system relies on its stored knowledge and decision-making mechanisms. At the time of knowledge-based system design and development stages, software engineers use different knowledge representation techniques; and one of the techniques is symbolic logic-based representation. Different symbolic logic representation is used for knowledge presentation purpose. Description Logics (DLs) are a family of knowledge representation languages that can be used to represent the knowledge of an application domain in a structured way.

Ontology: Information sharing among supply chain business partners using information system is an important enabler for supply chain management. There are different types of data to be shared across supply chain, namely – order, demand, inventory, shipment, and customer service. Consequently, information about these issues needs to be shared in order to achieve efficiency and effectiveness in supply chain management. In this way, information-sharing activities require that human and/or machine agents agree on common and explicit business related concepts (the shared conceptualizations among hardware/software agents, customers, and service providers) are known as explicit ontologies; and these help to exchange data and derived knowledge out of the data to achieve collaborative goals of business operations.

Rule-Based Reasoning: In conventional rule-based reasoning, both common sense knowledge and domain specific domain expertise are represented in the forms of plausible rules (e.g. IF <*precondition*(s)> THEN <*conclusion*(s)>). For example, an instance of a particular rule: IF {(*Sam has a driving license*) AND (*Sam is drunk*) AND (*Sam is driving a logistic distribution track*) AND (*Sam is stopped by police*)} THEN {(*Sam's driving license will be revoked by the transport authority*)}. Moreover, rule-based reasoning requires an exact match on the precondition(s) to predict the conclusion(s). This is very restrictive, as real-world situations are often fuzzy and do not match exactly with rule preconditions. Thus, there are some extensions to the basic approach that can accommodate partial degrees of matching in rule preconditions.

Semantic Web Service: The advantages of integrating and coordinating supply chain business partners' information service applications, which are loosely distributed among participants with a wide range of hardware and software capabilities, are immensely important issue from operation of global supply chain. Web service is an information technology-based solution for system interoperability; and in this technology business services are described in a standard web service description language (WSDL). Establishing the compatibility of services is an important prerequisite to service provision in web service operation. Web service has embraced the concepts of enriching distributed information systems with machine-understandable semantic metadata (known as ontology); and these new breed of web services are known as semantic web service. In this way, semantic web service provides a common framework for web-based services, which allows data to be shared and reuse across application, enterprise, and extended community boundaries.

Supply Chain Coordination: A supply chain consists of a network of key business processes and facilities, involving end users and suppliers that provide products, services and information. In this chain management, improving the efficiency of the overall chain is an important factor; and it needs at least four important strategic issues to be considered: supply chain network design, capacity planning, risk assessment and management, and performances monitoring and measurement. Moreover, the details break down of these issues need to consider in the level of individual business processes and sub-processes; and the combined performance of this chain. The coordination these huge business processes and their performances are of immense importance.

Section 4
Social Media Data Research

Chapter 10
Exploring the Hidden Pattern from Tweets:
Investigation into Volkswagen Emissions Scandal

Ying Kei Tse
University of York, UK

Minhao Zhang
University of York, UK

Bob Doherty
University of York, UK

Susan R. Moore
University of York, UK

Tom Keefe
University of York, UK

ABSTRACT

Social media has recently emerged as a key tool to manage customer relations in industry. This chapter aims to contribute a step-by-step Twitter Analytic framework for analysing the tweets in a fiscal crisis. The proposed framework includes three major sections – demographic analytic, content analytic and integrated method analytic. This chapter provides useful insights to develop this framework through the lens of the recent Volkswagen emission scandal. A sizable dataset of #volkswagescandal tweets (8,274) was extracted as the research sample. Research findings based upon this sample include the following: Consumer sentiments are overall negative toward

DOI: 10.4018/978-1-5225-0956-1.ch010

the scandal; some clustered groups are identified; male users expressed more interest on social media in the topic than female users; the popularity of tweets was closely related with the timing of news coverage, which indicates the traditional media is still playing a critical role in public opinion formation. The limitations and practical contribution of the current study are also discussed.

INTRODUCTION

The Volkswagen (VW) scandal broke when the United States Environment Protection Agency (USEPA) declared that over 482,000 cars in the US had been fitted with a so-called "defeat device" to guarantee the passing of Government conditions emission tests (Hotten, 2015). The "defeat device" allows a diesel car to turn on the "safety mode" to pass emission tests. Under the "safety mode", the engine of the car will run below normal power and performance (Hotten, 2015) so as to guarantee low emissions but once customers drove the car on the road, the car will automatically switch out of "safety mode" into "road mode", thus improving the performance of the car, but increasing emissions. This means that a VW car with "road mode" enabled produces significantly more air pollution than would be suggested by calculations based upon "safety mode" emissions[1]. On 23 September 2015, VW admitted that there are around 11 million diesel cars worldwide that have the relevant "defeat device" fitted (Winston, 2015).

The VW emission scandal is a new form of automobile reputational crisis, which is not related to automobile quality or safety issues (such as the Aston Martin recall in 2014). Instead, it is characterized as a form of deliberate fraud and/or criminal intent, rather than stemming from negligence or corporate wrongdoing (Hartman, 2015). According to Hartman (2015), the VW scandal has therefore "*set the bar at a whole new level*". The consequences of the VW emission scandal are threefold. Firstly, the VW scandal might raise industrial concerns regarding related diesel car supply chains. VW also supplies diesel engines to both Audi and Porsche (as subsidiary firms) and therefore these firms may also be suspected to have sold cars containing the affected engines (Rucker and Gardner, 2015; Saarinen, 2015).

Secondly, the emission fraud threatens the health of millions in Europe, because of the high levels of nitrogen oxide pollutants. The World Health Organization (WHO) estimates there are around 7 million premature deaths are associated with air pollution (Winston, 2015). Therefore, the emission scandal might make the public more concerned about the issues of air pollution and the need for sustainable development. Thirdly, the VW incident potentially increases the public mistrust of the diesel car industry as a whole, as VW plays a central role in this market sector

(Bach, 2015). In fact, it could even be argued that the scandal is risking the reputation of the entire automobile industry as a whole, and its efforts in using technology to achieve environmental sustainability (Winston, 2015; Bach, 2015). Currently, sustainability is of growing importance in business strategy and firm credibility (Elkington, 1994). In short, VW's reporting of sustainability performance data to enhance 'green' positioning and the nature of the VW scandal demonstrates highly unethical conduct (Szekely, 2015) and could harm VW's brand reputation and result in financial losses to the company (such as the government's fines and sales loss), as well as harm public health, and have knock-on reputational effects for the whole of the car industry.

For the automobile industry stakeholders (not only the company, but also the industry and governments), rebuilding public confidence is key to recovering from the emissions scandal. In the immediate post-crisis phase, communicating with consumers should be a priority in order to rebuild public trust. In this case, understanding the demands and attitudes of consumers is an essential step in designing an effective communication strategy. Due to the importance of consumer opinion, exploring data from social media could provide important insights to aid those designing such communication strategies.

Social media is an emerging tool that can be used to assess and manage relationships with customers (Agnihotri et al., 2012). According to Blackshaw and Nazzaro (2004), social media is a variety of information sources that are created, initiated, circulated and applied by consumers' intent on educating each other about products, brands, services, personalities, and issues. There are various social media platforms, such as Twitter, Facebook, LinkedIn and Instagram, where companies can keep in touch with their customers and also promote products. Accordingly, the adoption of social media could contribute to a company's long-term profitability (Hoffman & Fodor, 2010; Kaplan & Haenlein, 2010). Moreover, customer ideas and feedback generated from social media could assist company innovation as well (Piller et al., 2012). In recent years, a wide range of academic studies have investigated and explored the application of social media. For example, through analysing tweets, Bollen et al. (2011) attempt to predict changes in the stock market. Also, Veil et al. (2011a) regard social media as a particular channel for risk communication with the public. In the field of marketing research, Ngai et al. (2015) stress that social media has become a critical component in current business strategy setting. However, dealing with a company's reputational risks when faced with a crisis is still largely uncovered by academic social media research (Tse et al., 2016).

To fill this gap in academic social media research and to contribute to insights of the VW scandal for practitioners, this study aims to propose a comprehensive analytic framework for analysing the massive social media data set based on the Text Mining (TM) techniques, combined with demographic and integrated analytics to complete the rounded picture. As a tool for data mining, there are many examples of application of TM in social media, ranging from identifying customers' satisfaction levels (Liau and Tan, 2014), predicting stock market changes (Nguyen et al., 2015; Wong et al., 2008), and monitoring political preferences of the public (Ceron et al., 2014). According to Feldman and Sanger (2007), TM refers to a research method that overcomes the challenges of analysing loaded, unstructured texts by adopting different, but complimentary, approaches, including machine learning, natural language processing (NLP), information retrieval, and knowledge management. In this study, our analytic framework combines two TM techniques, which are sentiment analysis (SA) and clustering analysis (CA) in order to reveal the strength of feeling about the scandal within the sample of consumer tweets tested.

Within TM studies, sentiment analysis (SA) is widely adopted (Ghiassi et al., 2013; Kontopoulos et al., 2013; Liau & Tan, 2014; Mostafa, 2013; Paltoglou & Thelwall, 2012). SA refers to the automatic analysis approach of classifying the sentiment scores from large numbers of texts, which includes three categories – positive, neutral and negative. This technique is helpful to determine opinions of consumers towards their products or service promptly. For example, Zhang et al. (2012) apply the sentence-based SA to identify product weaknesses through exploring the sentiment from online customer reviews. Customers' attitudes towards particular product features could also be extracted by the SA approach (Zhang et al., 2012). According to Jansen et al. (2009), tweeting or microblogging is regarded as 'electronic word of mouth' (WOM), which can play a critical role in customer's buying decisions. This is because consumers tend to believe the information transfer in their social network (i.e. family or friends) rather than those from outside sources (such as online reviews) (Duan et al., 2008; Jansen et al., 2009). When managing a crisis, such as the VW emissions scandal, timely SA can help companies understand customers' opinions from their social network activity. This can be a critical first step to rebuilding corporate reputation, minimising brand damage and toxicity and regaining public trust (Tse et al., 2016).

This chapter provides a Tweets Analysis framework, which combines three types of research approach – demographic analytics, text analytics and integrated analytics. The scope of the observation period (i.e. tweets data collection time frame) is from September 22, 2015, to October 1, 2015, which is the first week after the VW emission scandal broke. A total of 8,274 tweets and associated metadata form the data sample of this chapter, which was collected using the hashtag #volkswagenscandal. The application of the proposed framework strives to examine the following research questions:

1. What is consumers' sentiment toward Volkswagen in the emission scandal?

2. What are the most common concerns and interests of consumers regarding the emission scandal?
3. How can the analysis framework provide practitioners with better decision making in PR crisis management in the future?

The next section reviews the relevant literature regarding social media, then the tweets analysis framework detail is presented. This is followed with the results of the application of the analysis framework, the findings of which are discussed and practical implications outlined for industry. Finally, alongside conclusions, limitations of this study are addressed, together with suggestions for future research.

BACKGROUND: SOCIAL MEDIA REASEARCH

With the growing tide of big data, the topic of social media has attracted extensive research from different disciplines, such as sociology (Jin et al., 2014; Veil et al., 2011b), marketing (de Vries et al., 2012; Hoffman and Fodor, 2010; Michaelidou et al., 2011), supply chain management (Chae, 2015; O'Leary, 2011), educational research (Tess, 2013), political and government research (Bertot et al., 2010; Loader and Mercea, 2011; Shirky, 2011), and financial prediction (Bollen et al., 2011; Zhang et al., 2011).

Social media has been regarded as a supplement to the traditional communication approaches, such as telephone or mail (Mcafee, 2006). With the increasing public demand for social media, individuals are currently responsible for the generation of larger quantities of publicly accessible, shared information than ever before (Oeary, 2011). According to Malita (2011), social media is defined as a set of "tools that facilitate the socialisation of content and encourage collaboration, interaction, and communication through discussion, feedback, voting, comments, and sharing of information from all interested parties". Currently, Facebook, Twitter and Linkedin are the most frequently used social media by businesses (eCoonsultancy, 2010). All of these platforms are regarded as social network sites (SNS), which is a common form of social media. According to Ellison (2007), there are three characteristics of this kind of social media, in which users:

1. Construct a public or semi-public profile within a bounded system.
2. Articulate a list of other users with whom they share a connection.
3. View and traverse their list of connections and those made by others within the system.

Due to the strengths of instant response and direct communication, practitioners and professionals have extensively studied customer relationship management and explored consumer attitudes in social media (Hajli, 2014; Jin & Phua, 2014; Liau & Tan, 2014; Pentina et al., 2013; Tsai & Men, 2013). The opinions expressed by customers in their social networks play a significant role in influencing public opinion and behaviour (Mostafa, 2013). Although previous researchers have widely analysed data from social media in various contexts, the fields of commercial crisis management and supply chain risk management are still under-researched, although Tse et al (2016) provide a good example of this type of analysis, through an analysis of the horse meat adulteration scandal in the UK in 2013.

In this chapter, we only focus on one particular social media platform - Twitter. According to ALEXA (2015), Twitter is the ninth most visited website in the world, so provides an excellent place for us to explore the opinions from customers. Moreover, the growth of Twitter is much faster than its other two major competitors – Facebook and Google+ (Bennett, 2013). Recently, the number of monthly active users of Twitters has achieved 320 million (Twitter, n.d.). The information from microblogging (i.e. Tweeting) has become a valuable resource to extract the opinion and the sentiment from customers (Zhang et al., 2012). Twitter provides a friendly environment for the client to read and create the posts quickly, as it requires users to control the length of a post in a concise manner (Jansen et al., 2009). A tweet post is a message of 140 characters, which includes three categories: original tweets, replies, and retweets. Additionally, compared with other social media platforms, the data from Twitter is more "open" (Chae, 2015). Specifically, researchers can access Twitter data through Twitter's Application Programming Interface (API) (Twitter, 2013), providing a considerable sample of data for in-depth research (Chae, 2015). However, it is not possible for us to extract valuable information from a significant amount of tweet data without the help of text mining (TM) techniques (Liau & Tan, 2014).

TWEETS ANALYSIS FRAMEWORK

According to Chae (2015), collecting tweet data (which includes both the text of the tweet and accompanying metadata [2]) begins with identifying the topic of interest using a keyword(s) or hashtag(s), and requires the use of Application Programming Interface (APIs). There are two possible data collection methods adopted, which are individual API collection and the use of data providers (such as GNIP, DataSift). Both of these data collection methods have their advantages and disadvantages. For the individual API collection, it is totally free and more flexible. However, this method can only collect 1% of publicly available Twitter data (Chae, 2015). On the other hand, through the help of commercial data providers, 100% of tweets can be accessible to the researchers. At the same time, it is a very costly option (Chae, 2015). With a variety of information in every tweet, a comprehensive framework is needed to be developed in order to peel the "onion" of the tweet. In this chapter, three main sections are covered: Demographic analytics, content analytics and integrated analytics.

Demographic Analytics

In the first step of the framework, the metadata of the tweets is scrutinised. The demographic analytics include two subsections: the tweet statistics (i.e. descriptive analysis) and the user information analysis. First, the descriptive analysis focuses on the basic statistics of the tweet data, such as the number of tweets, distribution of different types of tweets, and the number of hashtags etc. (Chae, 2015). The user information analysis focuses on a more advanced basis, for instance, the gender distribution and the geographic information of the tweet source.

Generating the simplistic but essential data (such as the basic statistics of the tweets – number of tweets, retweets, word counts, the number of hashtags and URL information) should be the purpose of this descriptive Tweet analysis (Bruns and Stieglitz, 2013; Chae, 2015), because the descriptive statistics of the tweets provide the basis for many other metrics (Chae, 2015). For instance, we can identify the most influential account/people through counting the "numbers of retweets". Moreover, a number of tweets include a URL (such as news and business report, etc.), which would be a valuable resource for examining the popular topics, and their source, used in the online discussion. According to Waller et al. (2011), "Analyses may focus on the types of resources that are referenced in URLs". On the other hand, customer information like gender and geographic information could offer the gateway for our subsequent analysis – content analysis. Although the gender information is not available in Twitter, we can predict the gender through analysing the username. Accurate prediction of a demographic attribute like gender from social media could be valuable for marketing, personalisation and legal investigation (Burger et al., 2011).

Content Analytics (or Text Mining)

Compared with the Demographic Analytics, which focuses mostly upon the data accompanying the tweet, the Content Analytics portion of the analysis focus entirely on the text of the tweets. Initially, the social media text data is "unstructured" or "raw", and is not suitable to directly be used for analysis. Hence, in the first step of the content analysis, data preparation is necessary. In this chapter, a structured text pre-processing is applied as the tool to manage the "raw texts", usingtechniques like tokenization and stemming (Delen et al., 2012; Liau & Tan, 2014).

After this, the structured text is used for the word frequency analysis to identify hot topics in the sample. Hot topics identified from the term frequency analysis then guide the way to the clustering analysis. Clustering is an important tool to automatically organise and explore information (such as unanticipated trends or correlations) from text-based data (Agnihotri et al., 2012; Liau & Tan, 2014). According to Jansen et al. (2011), clustering analysis enables companies to identify different groups of customers by extracting their similarities quickly. To explore the individual information, we also need to conduct sentiment analysis (SA), which is also known as opinion mining (Feldman, 2013). Positive and negative opinion words normally have a sentiment score of "+1" to "-1" respectively (Liau & Tan, 2014). Likewise, the tweet with sentiment score 0 represents the neutral expression. Through examining the polarity, which ranges from negative to positive, sentiment can be interpreted and understood through analysis (Chae, 2015).

Integrated Analytics

The aim of this final stage of the analysis is to combine the Demographic Analytics and Content Analytics stages. For instance, through combining the results from sentiment analysis and clustering, some interesting findings could be obtained. In this case, the general sentiment level of a particular theme could be identified. Moreover, another possible combination would be demographic information and clustering analysis. This analysis could answer the question of "what is the sentiment difference between US and UK customers?". Furthermore, the integrated analytics could also explore the particular topics with a focus upon gender, answering questions such as "is there a gender difference to opinions concerning the VW emission scandal?"

DATA ANALYSIS

The ideal method of collecting the insights from the tweets related to the VW scandal would be collecting the whole Twitter sample including the directly related tweets (i.e. tweets that explicitly mention the scandal) and indirectly related tweets (i.e. tweets that concern the scandal but do not explicitly mention it) (Chae, 2015). It is not realistic or practical to collect the entire dataset, due to the vast amount of information and the cost of obtaining it. Therefore, this chapter applies a sampling process to collect the directly related tweets data. In the pilot research, several search terms and Hashtags were tested, such as "VW" "Volkswagen" "Emission Scandal". Through reviewing the results of the key terms, the hashtag "#VolkswagenScandal" is the most relevant search term to identify our dataset. The data collection period is between 22 September and 1 October 2015, which is just ten days after the scandal exposed. In this chapter, the tweets dataset includes 8,274 tweets with the hashtag #VolkswagenScandal and their metadata. The data used in this study was collected through the NVIVO add-on software - NCapture.

Demographic Analytics

Several statistical techniques were used to conduct the descriptive analysis (Bruns and Stieglitz, 2013; Chae, 2015), such as the tweet statistics and URL analysis. Regarding the user information analysis, identifying geographic data and gender information are the focus. Python software was utilised to try to identify the gender of Twitter users.

- **Tweets Statistics:** Regarding the dataset, we first apply the basic statistical analysis for the tweets by categorising the types of tweets and hashtags. Among 8,274 original tweets, retweets, and @Volkswagen group account for 4083 (49.35%), 3365 (40.67%), 826 (9.98%). To analyse the Hashtags statistics, we applied the software called QDAminer. This chapter identifies 1434 unique Hashtags in the tweets dataset. 3506 tweets include more than two hashtags in a single tweet. According to Chae (2015), this indicates that a large amount of tweets are intersecting multiple areas of interest. For example, tweets contain two or more hashtags: #Volkswagescandal, #reputational risk and #emissions. The URL information regarded as an indirect reference from the users. In the dataset, the URLs are vital: 59.26% (4902) of the total tweets (8,274) include at least one URL. Most of these URLs are related to news websites reporting on the VW emission scandal.
- **Users' Meta-Analysis:** In the whole dataset there are 3689 unique users involved. In this case, each user posts 2.4288 tweets: 1.1068 original tweets, 0.9121 retweets, and 0.9121 @Volkswagen group. The result implies that the tweets are not particularly focused and that many users share their individual opinions. The top four significant (i.e. visibility) accounts are heat_io (243 retweets received[3]), 247Fame (198 retweets received), Greenpeace (133 retweets received) and jen2seely (94 retweets received). To identify the gender from the username, we applied the US Census Bureau library[4] to estimate the gender through Python 2.7. However, due to a large amount of public accounts that have no gender information and non-English names, there are 2286 tweets that can be identified as hailing from people of a specific gender. Among these tweets, 1628 tweets (71.21%) were posted by male users and 658 tweets (28.79%) posted by female users.

Table 1. The most visible users

Account	Types of Accounts	Retweets Received	Number of Followers
heat_io	News Media	243	5051
247Fame	News Media	198	1027
Greenpeace	Independent Organisation	133	1461511
J***seely	Individual	94	491

Content Analytics

The aim of the content analytics stage of the analysis is to scrutinise the actual text content of the tweets. Before conducting the step-by-step analysis, the process of data preparation needs to be applied to transform the "unstructured text" into "structured data". After this, three types of text mining approaches were conducted, including 1) word count analysis, 2) clustering analysis and 3) sentiment analysis. The word count analysis is based on the keywords frequency analysis and the hashtag frequency analysis. Also, using multidimensional scaling methods, several topic groups were clustered. Regarding the sentiment analysis, the lexicon-based method was adopted to capture the sentiment score from the customers.

- **Data Preparation:** To transform the unstructured text to analysable data, it is necessary to first conduct the data pre-processing. Tokenization is the first step of this process, which can be defined as the process of identifying the meaningful words through breaking up the text into discrete words (Liau and Tan, 2014). Additionally, the stopping words were removed in the second stage. For example, personal pronouns, demonstrative pronouns and prepositions were eliminated. As Twitter is a kind of informal blogging, the problem of misspelling is common. In this case, the spelling of each word within the tweets was carefully checked. Then, the stemming approach was applied to further process the text by deducting the prefixes and suffixes to normalised words (Delen et al., 2012). For instance, the words "points", "pointing" and "pointed" were all transformed to "point". To import all the data into our text analysis software – QDA Miner, all the lower case words were changed to upper cases words. At the end of the data pre-processing, the word frequency analysis can be used to reflect the quality of the data preparation. For example, those meaningless words with high frequency, which were not considered as stopping words or stemming, such as HTTP; HTTPS and RT, were excluded. Moreover, the phrases or words with duplicated meaning were transferred into a single word, for instance, "HAHA", "HAHAHA" as "lol".

- **Word Count Analysis:** The most popular key terms in tweets were emission (found in 1217[5]), CEO (620), Car (1019), German (481), Test (256), Hell (250), Software (224), Crisis (162), Cheating (295), Pollution (274), Trust (118). The themes toward the keywords in tweets were generally focused on the aspect of customer trust, and on the resignation of the VW group CEO. Moreover, 1,435 unique hashtags were found in the tweets and they appear 17,757 times. The most popular hashtags include #Volkswagenscandal, #Volkswagen, #VW, #VWGATE, #DISELGATE, #TDI, #CARTOON, #DASPROBLEM, #AUDI, #CORPGOV, #CLMATECHANGE, #ICYMI, #BMW, #HUDDERSFIELD, #MECCA, #TESLA, #FIFA, #GREEN, #SAYINGTRUTH, #FOSSILFUELS, among others. Similar to the prior research of Chae (2015), two hashtags were most common in the tweets.There were average 2.15 hashtags per tweet. In this case, it is important to investigate associations among the hashtags. In the next section, we will adopt the clustering analysis to observe the association among the hashtags and key terms.
- **Clustering Analysis:** To check the relevant hashtags of the research focus, the proximity plot was used to overview the association. As shown in Figure 1, on a single axis, the distance from a particular object to all other objects represents the strength of the association (Mostafa, 2013). Hashtags such as #DIESELGATE, #EMISSIONS, #CARMAGEDDON, #AIRPOLLUTION,

Figure 1. Proximity plot of hashtags

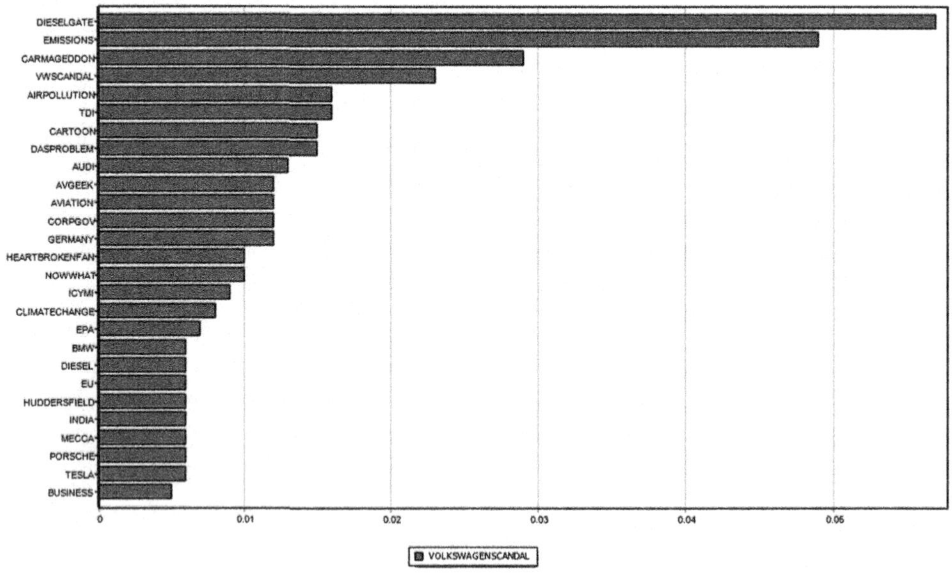

#TDI, #CARTOON, #DASPROBLEM, #AUDI are most associated with the research focus - #VolkswagenScandal. Interesting, two other brands of the automobile manufacturers also appeared in the proximity analysis, which are BMW and AUDI.

The multidimensional scaling (MDS) method allows the holistic analysis of the co-occurrence of keywords within a dataset. Co-occurrence is defined as happening every time two words appear in the same case (WordStat, 2014). Figures 2 and 3 illustrate the co-occurrence concept map based on the MDS method. The concept maps are graphic representations of the proximity values computed on all included keywords using MDS. In this case, the Jaccard's coefficient[6] was the index used to measure the co-occurrence. As shown in Figure 3, the triangle represents the high frequency terms (the size of triangle is representative of to the word's frequency) in the dataset and the distance between the concepts indicates the strength of correlation.

Below are some clustered concepts identified:

1. **Responsibility Group:** "RESPONSIBLITY" (68) [7] "SOCIAL" (65) "DANAGEROUS" (57): *Corporate Social Responsibility has become a racket - and a dangerous one* #Volkswagenscandal
2. **Recall Group:** "RECALL" (142) "FIX" (103) "WORKING" (111): #VolkswagenScandal: *No recall but Volkswagen says it's working on a fix*
3. **Spread over Risk Group:** "AUDI" (187) "SKODA" (41) "AFFECTED" (121): *Damn! The scandal spreads to Porsche and Audi #Volkswagenscanal*

Figure 2. 2D maps of clustering analysis

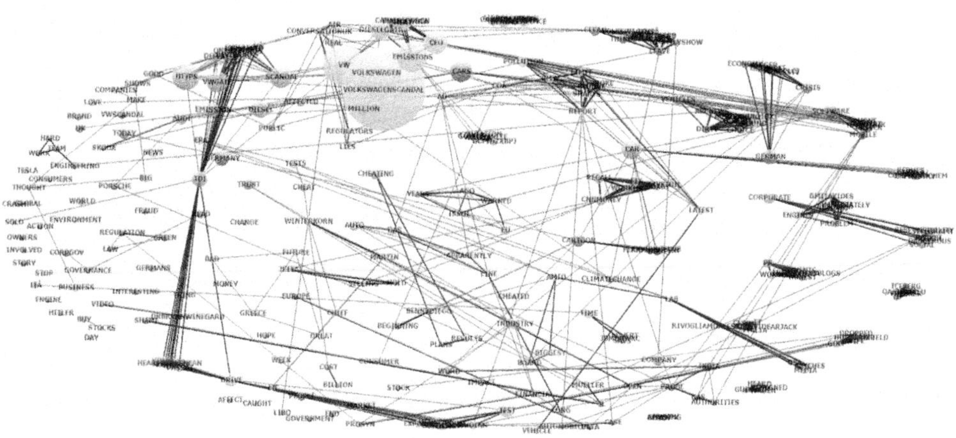

Figure 3. 3D maps of clustering analysis

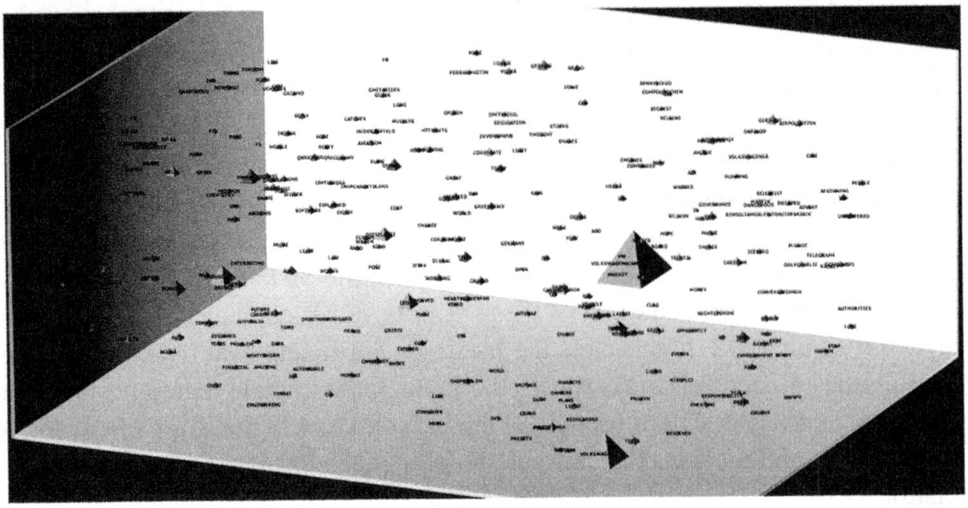

4. **Focal Group:** "VOLKSWAGEN" (2891) "DIESELGATE" (465) "EMISSIONS" (1040) "CEO" (631): *Think it's great @Volkswagen tried to screw Big #government on auto emissions. CEO should get raise. Might buy one now. #VolkswagenScandal*
5. **Air Pollution Group:** "AIRPOLLUTION"; "DEATHS"; "VIOLATIONS" *How many extra deaths from #airpollution from Volkswagen violations? #Volkswagenscanal*

- **Sentiment Analysis:** Although we can explore the key tweets or hot topics through MDS, it is difficult to systematically understand the meaning behind the tweets. Therefore, the sentiment analysis can assist the researcher to identify the opinions of the customers. Here we adopted the lexicon-based approach to annotate the tweets for determining customer's polarity through a particular dictionary of the words. We applied the dictionary of Hu and Liu (2004), due to its successful adoption in a series of research projects (Miner et al., 2012; Mostafa, 2013; Tse et al., 2016). 2006 positive words and 4783 negative words are in this library. Typically, the average sentiment score for the entire dataset is -0.21347. To clarify how the software rates the sentiment scores of individual tweets, we picked some examples from our tweets (Table 2).

Table 2. Examples of tweets with sentiment analysis

Example	Sentiment
One more brand highlighted for wrong reasons. #Curious on how it controls the damage caused. #VolkswagenScandal	-3 (negative)
Dishonesty cn get u outta mess today bt in the future it'll haunt & cost u dearly. #volkswagenscandal	-3 (negative)
#VolkswagenScandal is sickening. pple who bought BS car aren't only effected but those who have to breathe the dirty air too.#dicks	-3 (negative)

Integrated Analytics

- **Gender Group Analytics:** Compared with the male group, the topics of female users are more focused. As shown in Figures 4 and 5, the clustered topics in the male group are more than the clustered topics in the female group. Compared with the male users, female users are more likely to focus on topics such as "Cheating" and "Trust". The total aggregate female sentiment score was -0.09285, which compared to the male sentiment score of -0.1763299. Towards the VW emission scandal, the attitudes of male customers are worse than the female clients. Also, using the scale of necessary Tweets statistics, the tweeting behaviour differences were also investigated. For the identified female users, 19.6% of posts were retweets, 76.1% of posts were original tweets, and 4.3% mentioned (@Volkswagen) the involved company in their tweets. On the other hand, regarding the male users, 27.9% of posts were retweets, 53% of posts were original tweets, and 19.1% mentioned the Volkswagen group.
- **Time Series Analysis***:* Other than the gender group discussion, this chapter also breaks down the entire dataset to separate dates and times to investigate the changes in customer opinions following the development of the scandal. The time series analysis includes two sections, which are the geographic popularity changes and the sentiment changes along the time frame. First, this study breaks down the entire dataset into a 8 day - period (in a half day manner, AM/PM, see table 3 and 4) to investigate the changes in tweets frequency. The popularity of the tweets related to the VW emission scandal was the top on 24th of September afternoon. The average sentiment of the tweets is negative along the observation period. The worst sentiment score appears on the first few days after the scandal broke. Second, this analysis illustrates three days that have highest tweets frequency on the Google map

Figure 4. Clustering analysis of male users

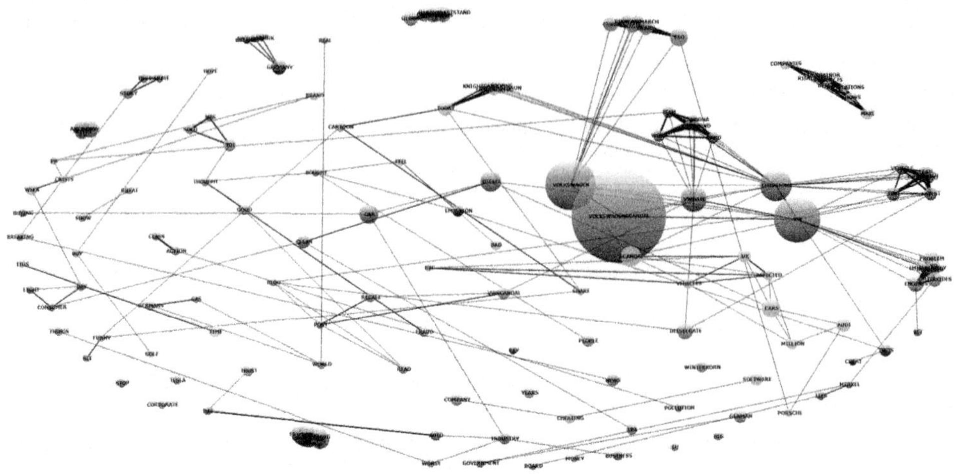

Figure 5. Clustering analysis of female

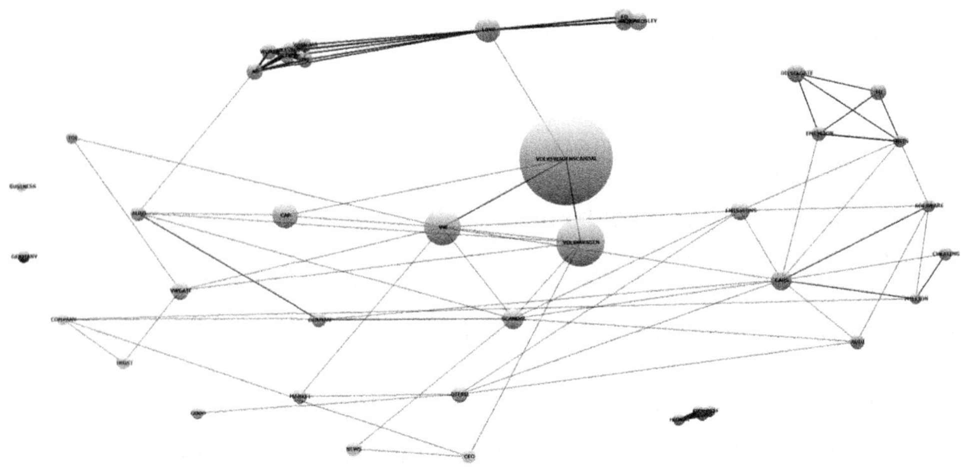

Table 3. Time series Tweets frequency

Date	24-Sep	25-Sep	26-Sep	27-Sep	28-Sep	29-Sep	30-Sep	01-Oct
AM	233	756	356	217	247	244	209	196
PM	1768	1117	624	387	642	503	655	59
Total	**2001**	**1873**	**980**	**604**	**889**	**747**	**864**	**255**

Table 4. Time series sentiment changes

Date	24-Sep	25-Sep	26-Sep	27-Sep	28-Sep	29-Sep	30-Sep	01-Oct
AM	-0.412	-0.306	-0.053	-0.046	-0.235	-0.291	-0.167	-0.281
PM	-0.183	-0.219	0.207	-0.271	-0.298	-0.207	-0.473	-0.254
Total	**-0.210**	**-0.254**	**0.112**	**-0.190**	**-0.280**	**-0.234**	**-0.399**	**-0.275**

(i.e. 24 Sep, 25 Sep and 26 Sep). As shown in Figure 6, the UK and US are the centres of discussing the emissions scandal on Twitter. Interestingly, on the 25 September, Dubai and India have both become the discussion centres in the world.

DISCUSSION

There are three major information dissemination patterns in Twitter, posting original tweets, using URL and Hashtag, retweeting and mentioning other people or parties (@other users). In the dataset of this chapter, over half of the tweets (i.e. 5926) include at least one URL. Compared with a random sample of tweets, the use of URL in VW tweets is very popular - only 22% of the random tweets have URL information. Java et al. (2007) state that sharing URLs information to report news is common in Twitter. In the VW emission scandal, the result of URL information sharing indicates that news and professional blogging are widely shared by customers via the uses of URLs in Tweets. The highly visible users (i.e. those that receive most retweets) are the press media and the environmental protection agencies. Additionally, among the #volkswagenscandal tweets, around 10% of them (over 800 tweets) have mentioned the Volkswagen group accounts (including @Volkswagen; @VW; @UKvolkswagen; @VWcanada). This indicates that the customers demonstrate a high demand to communicate with the company involved in this emission scandal. Nevertheless, although the involved companies (such as Volkswagen and Audi) have their twitter accounts, they are almost invisible in our dataset, which means that the companies received few retweets.

The findings from the tweets hashtag are consistent with the statement of Chae (2015) that tweets related to timely or 'breaking' issues are widely diffused by the use of hashtags. On average, there are two hashtags in a single tweet related to the VW scandal. The results show that the Twitter users who are interested in the VW emission scandal are more willing to diffuse the tweets by using the hashtags function. The heavy use of hashtags could also explain the high proportion of retweets. According to Suh et al. (2010), the use of hashtags has a strong relationship with

Figure 6. Geographic illustration of tweets: A. September 24, 2015, B. September 25, 2015, C. September 26, 2015

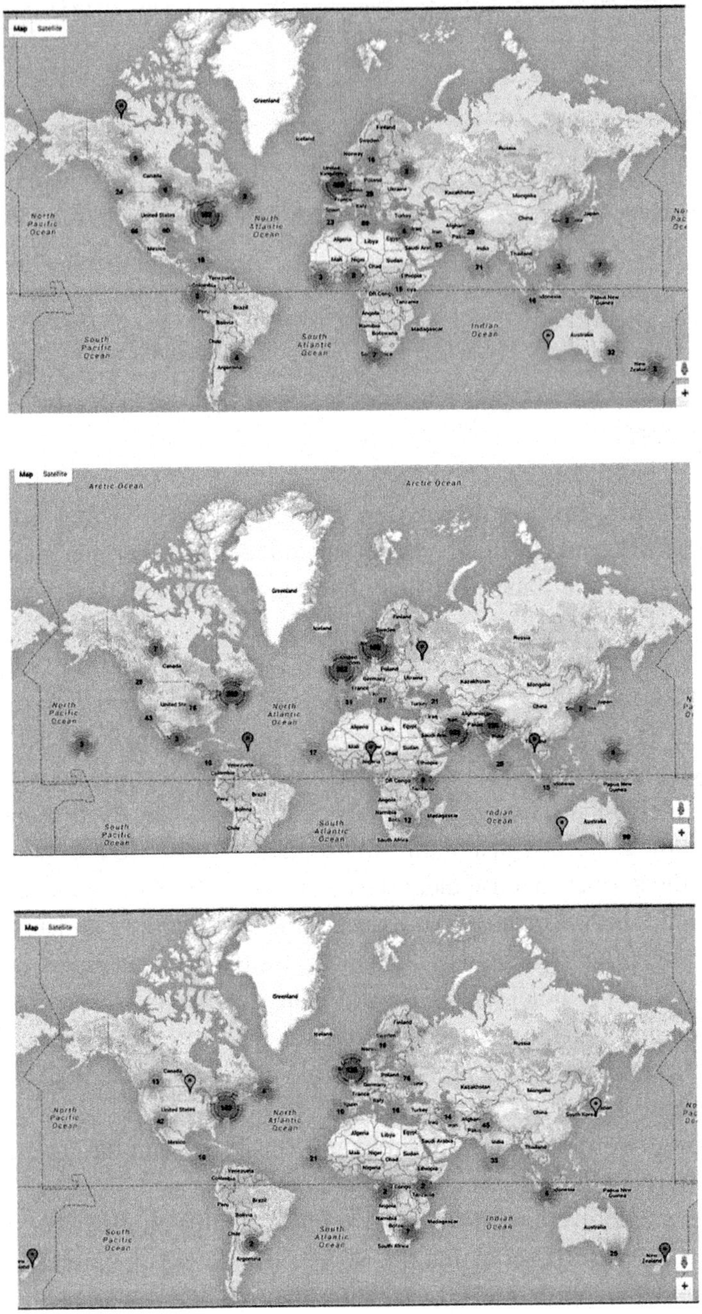

"retweetability". In the tweets of the VW scandal, over 40% of the tweets are retweets. Based on our further investigation, the tweet with highest retweet rate includes five hashtags in a single tweet. The main purpose of using a hashtag for Twitter users is to indicate the topic of the tweets and raise the interest of a wider audience (Chae, 2015). Among the topics of VW scandal tweets, users express concern about environmental issues such as; #climatechange and the influence of other automobile brands like #BMW and #AUDI. Also, a large proportion of users regarded the VW scandal as an extremely important topic as they are using #ICYMI[8].

Based on the data from the US Census Bureau, this chapter identifies the gender information of the tweets. Overall 2,000 tweets could be identified in terms of gender according to the usernames. Those tweets without gender information are due to two major reasons: language and public account. Because the username library is based on the data of English names, the username of other languages, such as Indian, Arabic, German and Chinese, etc., could not match the data from the gender library. Moreover, a large proportion of tweets were posted by public accounts, such as the press media and commercial accounts. Hence, this portion of the accounts could not be classified either. Although the rate of identification is relatively low, the absolute amount of identified tweets is still sizeable. Among the identified tweets, 658 and 1628 were posted by women and men respectively. This result implies that the topic of the emission scandal is more important to the men than the women. It seems contrary with previous research that women have higher environmental concern and stronger willingness to contribute (Hunter et al., 2004; L.C. et al., 2000). A possible implication of the gender difference is that practitioners can contribute a more effective strategy to communicate with the customers based on the gender information.

The topic of the VW emissions scandal has undoubtedly raised broad interest across the world. According to the geographic information within the tweets, we illustrated three global maps to indicate the popularity of the topic in different parts of the world. There is no doubt the US and UK are two key discussion centres, as these two countries were profoundly influenced by the scandal. Surprisingly, people of two Asian countries, the United Arab Emirates and India, also widely discussed the topic. The results could also explain why the gender information cannot be identified in some tweets, as a big proportion of them were posted in the Asian countries. The analysis shows that the emission scandal has already made a global impact, which is consistent with a brand of global reach.

The subjects of the VW tweets are diverse. Five groups of topics were identified by the clustering analysis. The analysis is based on the co-occurrence index of the elements within an individual group. One noticeable group concerns Air Pollution. Customers are more concerned with the consequences of air pollution, because of the emission scandal. According to Lave and Seskin (2013), air pollution has been a public problem with growing national and international interest. Moreover, the group showing supply chain concern has revealed that customers are also concerned with other companies in the VW Group, such as AUDI and Porsche. The clustering method could be a new approach for practitioners to identify different topic areas of customer importance, hence market segments and issues related to trading and business improvement strategy. It allows companies to segment marketing messages and communication strategies based on the customer reflections in the post-crisis period.

Additionally, understanding the sentiment of tweets could help the company to rebuild the consumer confidence and monitor market reaction. Opinions expressed by the consumers could be benchmarked against financial metrics (such as sales and stock prices) (Mostafa, 2013; Nguyen et al., 2015). In the VW emission scandal, the average sentiment of the tweets is negative (-0.21347). Nevertheless, the tweets of the emission scandal contain relatively low sentiment, as around 50% of them are zero. This can be explained by the tweets statistics that a considerable part of tweets are retweeted tweets of business news. The texts of these tweets are the title of the news. Exemplar tweets are "*RT @CNNMoney: Here's what you need to know about the #VolkswagenScandal*" and "*RT @avgerinosx: #VolkswagenScandal #Volkswagen (#BMW diesels also shown to be 11 TIMES over emissions limit)*". However, there are many tweets found to contain extremely negative sentiment toward the scandal, from the perspective of air pollution and trust (e.g. "how many have died because of #Volkswagen emission?? #fraud #corruption #VolkswagenScandal Lying bastards fuck their customers for money" and "VW lied on emission testing. Germany uses gas for evil once shame on U, use gas for evil twice...shame on U again actually #VolkswagenScandal").

In the integrated analytics, we combined the demographic and content analytics to investigate the important information regarding the gender differences and changes in customers' opinions. The word frequency and the sentiment analysis were broken down in a half-day manner to observe the changes in customers' sentiment during the outbreak of VW emission scandal. Except for the last day of the observation, the results show that users are more likely to post tweets in the afternoon. Also, the sentiment of the customers is also generally lower in the afternoon. At the very beginning of the scandal (i.e. the first day of the scandal), the sentiment score was the worst of the sample and thereafter improved. The findings from the time series analysis are consistent with the research of Franca et al. (2015), which indicates the difference of tweets usage in New York across 24 hours. A possible implication is that the company needs to prioritise and enhance the social media monitoring and communication in the afternoon time-period. Second, as shown in Figure 4 and Figure 5, more clustered groups were identified in the male users than female users. This indicates that the tweet topics of men are more diverse than that of women. Although the result is surprising initially, the frequency of tweets could help explain why. The identified male users are more than twice the number of female users. Moreover, the sentiment of men was worse than that of women. The result of the gender sentiment analysis might be contrary to previous studies which argue that women are more concerned with environmental issues (such as Stern et al., 1993). The tweets statistics of both gender groups could also confirm our argument; compared with the female users, male users are more likely to mention VW in their tweets, to express directly their opinions to the company. Women therefore can be seen to express their opinions more indirectly in our findings.

CONCLUSION

The VW emission scandal has revealed a significant challenge in managing the supply chain network. Moreover, with increased vulnerability of the global environment, topics related to environmental sustainability are of interest globally. The corporate fraud scandal is extremely important to customers, with the recent UK horsemeat scandal acting as a good example (Tse et al., 2016). Therefore, it is crucial for practitioners to learn the lessons of the VW emissions scandal through scrutinising public attitudes, particularly in businesses with global brands where the risk to the business can be perceived to be greater. 8,274 #volkswagenscandal tweets were analysed by a comprehensive tweets analysis framework. Using the demographic analytics, the user information and relative tweeting behaviour could be quickly generalised. Based on the username, our analysis identified the gender information from part of tweets and showed that male users of Twitter showed more interest than female users of Twitter in this scandal.

The frequent use of hashtags in tweets should also draw the attention of practitioners. Regarding the content analytics, this chapter adopts a mixed text mining method, including clustering analysis and sentiment analysis. Based on the MDS clustering approach, five clustered groups were identified. According to the identified groups, this chapter suggests that practitioners should explore new potential customer segments of importance. Also, the sentiment analysis indicates the general sentiment of customers in the VW emission scandal is negative. The integrated analytics indicate the gender difference and sentiment changes along the outbreak of emission scandal.

Certainly, this chapter is not without limitations. The gender data library is restricted to English names. Therefore, future research could extend the database of gender to identify more information, such as including more names from other languages. The duration of data collection is relatively short, as this chapter only focuses on the related tweets in the ten days after the scandal happened. A more longitudinal approach may provide further insights. Also, because this chapter collects the tweets by using only one search term (i.e. #volkswagenscandal), more related search terms could be used in the future research to get a more comprehensive sample. In spite of these few limitations, this chapter offers practitioners and policy makers useful insights.

REFERENCES

Agnihotri, R., Kothandaraman, P., Kashyap, R., & Singh, R. (2012). Bringing "Social" Into Sales: The Impact of Salespeople'S Social Media Use on Service Behaviors and Value Creation. *Journal of Personal Selling & Sales Management*, *32*(3), 333–348. doi:10.2753/PSS0885-3134320304

ALEXA. (2015). *The top 500 sites on the web.* Alexa. Available: http://www.alexa.com/topsites

Bach, D. (2015). *Seven Reasons Volkswagen Is Worse than Enron.* Yale Insights. Available: http://insights.som.yale.edu/insights/seven-reasons-volkswagen-worse-enron

Bennett, S. (2013). *Twitter Was The Fastest-Growing Social Network In 2013, Says Study [STATS].* SocialTimes. Available: http://www.adweek.com/socialtimes/social-networks-growth-2012/476560?red=at

Bertot, J. C., Jaeger, P. T., & Grimes, J. M. (2010). Using ICTs to create a culture of transparency: E-government and social media as openness and anti-corruption tools for societies. *Government Information Quarterly*, *27*(3), 264–271. doi:10.1016/j.giq.2010.03.001

Blackshaw, P., & Nazzaro, M. (2004). *Consumer-Generated Media (CGM) 101: Word-of-mouth in the age of the Web- fortified consumer.* Available: http://www.nielsenbuzzmetrics.com/whitepapers

Bollen, J., Mao, H. N., & Zeng, X. J. (2011). Twitter mood predicts the stock market. *Journal of Computational Science*, *2*(1), 1–8. doi:10.1016/j.jocs.2010.12.007

Bruns, A., & Stieglitz, S. (2013). Towards more systematic Twitter analysis: Metrics for tweeting activities. *International Journal of Social Research Methodology*, *16*(2), 91–108. doi:10.1080/13645579.2012.756095

Burger, J. D., Henderson, J., Kim, G., & Zarrella, G. (2011). Discriminant gender on Twitter.*Conference on Empirical Methods in Natural Language Processing*. Association for Computational Linguistics.

Ceron, A., Luigi, C., Iacus, S. M., & Porro, G. (2014). Every tweet counts? How sentiment analysis of social media can improve our knowledge of citizens' political preferences with an application to Italy and France. *New Media & Society*, *16*(2), 340–358. doi:10.1177/1461444813480466

Chae, B. (2015). Insights from hashtag #supplychain and Twitter Analytics: Considering Twitter and Twitter data for supply chain practice and research. *International Journal of Production Economics*, *165*, 247–259. doi:10.1016/j.ijpe.2014.12.037

De Vries, L., Gensler, S., & Leeflang, P. S. H. (2012). Popularity of Brand Posts on Brand Fan Pages: An Investigation of the Effects of Social Media Marketing. *Journal of Interactive Marketing*, *26*(2), 83–91. doi:10.1016/j.intmar.2012.01.003

Delen, D., Fast, A., Hill, T., Elder, J., Miner, G., & Nisbet, B. (2012). *Practical Text Mining and Statisitical Analysis for Non-structured Text Data Applications*. Elsevier.

Duan, W. J., Gu, G., & Whinston, A. B. (2008). Do online reviews matter? - An empirical investigation of panel data. *Decision Support Systems*, *45*(4), 1007–1016. doi:10.1016/j.dss.2008.04.001

ECOONSULTANCY. (2010). *Value of social media report (sample version)*. Author.

Elkington, J. (1994). Towards the Sustainable Corporation - Win-Win-Win Business Strategies for Sustainable Development. *California Management Review*, *36*(2), 90–100. doi:10.2307/41165746

Ellison, N. B. (2007). Social network site: Definition, history, and scholarship. *Journal of Computer-Mediated Communication*, *13*(1), 210–230. doi:10.1111/j.1083-6101.2007.00393.x

Feldman, R. (2013). Techniques and Applications for Sentiment Analysis. *Communications of the ACM*, *56*(4), 82–89. doi:10.1145/2436256.2436274

Feldman, R., & Sanger, J. (2007). *The text mining handbook advanced approaches in analyzing unstructured data*. Cambridge, UK: Cambridge University Press.

Ghiassi, M., Skinner, J., & Zimbra, D. (2013). Twitter brand sentiment analysis: A hybrid system using n-gram analysis and dynamic artificial neural network. *Expert Systems with Applications*, *40*(16), 6266–6282. doi:10.1016/j.eswa.2013.05.057

Hajli, M. N. (2014). A study of the impact of social media on consumers. *International Journal of Market Research*, *56*(3), 387–404. doi:10.2501/IJMR-2014-025

Hartman, N. (2015). *VW needs massive marketing campaign to regain consumer trust and survive.* MIT Sloan Management. Available: http://mitsloanexperts.mit.edu/tag/vw-scandal/

Hoffman, D. L., & Fodor, M. (2010). Can You Measure the ROI of Your Social Media Marketing? *Sloan Management Review*, *52*, 41.

Hotten, R. (2015). *Volkswagen: The scandal explained - BBC News.* BBCNews. Available: http://www.bbc.co.uk/news/business-34324772

Hunter, L. M., Hatch, A., & Johnson, A. (2004). Cross-national gender variation in environmental behaviors. *Social Science Quarterly*, *85*(3), 677–694. doi:10.1111/j.0038-4941.2004.00239.x

Jansen, B. J., Sobel, K., & Cook, G. (2011). Classifying ecommerce information sharing behaviour by youths on social networking sites. *Journal of Information Science*, *37*(2), 120–136. doi:10.1177/0165551510396975

Jansen, B. J., Zhang, M. M., Sobel, K., & Chowdury, A. (2009). Twitter Power: Tweets as Electronic Word of Mouth. *Journal of the American Society for Information Science and Technology*, *60*(11), 2169–2188. doi:10.1002/asi.21149

Java, A., Song, X., Finin, T., & Tseng, B. (2007). Why we twitter: understanding microblogging usage and communities. *9th WebKDD and 1st SNAKDD 2007 Workshop on Web Mining and Social Network Analysis*.

Jin, S. A. A., & Phua, J. (2014). Following Celebrities' Tweets About Brands: The Impact of Twitter-Based Electronic Word-of-Mouth on Consumers' Source Credibility Perception, Buying Intention, and Social Identification With Celebrities. *Journal of Advertising*, *43*(2), 181–195. doi:10.1080/00913367.2013.827606

Jin, Y., Liu, B. F., & Austing, L. L. (2014). Examining the role of social media in effective crisis management: The effects of crisis origin, information form, and source on publics' crisis responses. *Communication Research*, *41*(1), 74–94. doi:10.1177/0093650211423918

Kaplan, A. M., & Haenlein, M. (2010). Users of the world, unite! The challenges and opportunities of Social Media. *Business Horizons*, *53*(1), 59–68. doi:10.1016/j.bushor.2009.09.003

Kontopoulos, E., Berberidis, C., Dergiades, T., & Bassiliades, N. (2013). Ontology-based sentiment analysis of twitter posts. *Expert Systems with Applications*, *40*(10), 4065–4074. doi:10.1016/j.eswa.2013.01.001

Lave, L. B., & Seskin, E. P. (2013). *Air Pollution and Human Health*. Taylor & Francis.

Liau, B. Y., & Tan, P. P. (2014). Gaining customer knowledge in low cost airlines through text mining. *Industrial Management & Data Systems, 114*(9), 1344–1359. doi:10.1108/IMDS-07-2014-0225

Loader, B. D., & Mercea, D. (2011). Networking democracy? Social media innovations and participatory politics introduction. *Information Communication and Society, 14*, 757–769. doi:10.1080/1369118X.2011.592648

Malita, L. 2011. Social media time management tools and tips.*World Conference on Information Technology (Wcit-2010)*. doi:10.1016/j.procs.2010.12.123

Mcafee, A. P. (2006). Enterprise 2.0: The dawn of emergent collaboration. *Sloan Management Review, 47*, 21.

Michaelidou, N., Siamagka, N. T., & Christodoulides, G. (2011). Usage, barriers and measurement of social media marketing: An exploratory investigation of small and medium B2B brands. *Industrial Marketing Management, 40*(7), 1153–1159. doi:10.1016/j.indmarman.2011.09.009

Mostafa, M. M. (2013). More than words: Social networks' text mining for consumer brand sentiments. *Expert Systems with Applications, 40*(10), 4241–4251. doi:10.1016/j.eswa.2013.01.019

Ngai, E. W. T., Moon, K. L. K., Lam, S. S., Chin, E. S. K., & Tao, S. S. C. (2015). Social media models, technologies, and applications An academic review and case study. *Industrial Management & Data Systems, 115*(5), 769–802. doi:10.1108/IMDS-03-2015-0075

Nguyen, T. H., Shirai, K., & Velcin, J. (2015). Sentiment analysis on social media for stock movement prediction. *Expert Systems with Applications, 42*(24), 9603–9611. doi:10.1016/j.eswa.2015.07.052

O'Leary, D. E. (2011). The use of social media in the supply chain: Survey and extensions. *Intelligent Systems in Accounting, Finance & Management, 18*(2-3), 121–144. doi:10.1002/isaf.327

Paltoglou, G., & Thelwall, M. (2012). Twitter, MySpace, Digg: Unsupervised Sentiment Analysis in Social Media. *ACM Transactions on Intelligent Systems and Technology, 3*(4), 66. doi:10.1145/2337542.2337551

Pentina, I., Zhang, L., & Basmanova, O. (2013). Antecedents and consequences of trust in a social media brand: A cross-cultural study of Twitter. *Computers in Human Behavior*, *29*(4), 1546–1555. doi:10.1016/j.chb.2013.01.045

Piller, F. T., Vossen, A. & Ihl, C. (2012). From social media to social product development: the impact of social media on co-creation of innovation. *Die Unternehmung*, 65.

Rucker, P., & Gardner, T. (2015). *Porsche, more Audi models pulled into VW emissions scandal.* Available: http://www.reuters.com/article/us-volkswagen-usa-epa-idUSKCN0SR22L20151102

Saarinen, M. (2015). *VW emissions scandal: everything you need to know*. Available: http://www.autoexpress.co.uk/volkswagen/92893/vw-emissions-scandal-recalls-compensation-is-your-car-affected-latest-news

Shirky, C. (2011). The Political Power of Social Media Technology, the Public Sphere, and Political Change. *Foreign Affairs*, *90*, 28.

Stern, P. C., Dietz, T., & Kalof, L. (1993). Value orientations, gender, and environmental concern. *Environment and Behavior*, *25*(5), 322–348. doi:10.1177/0013916593255002

Suh, B., Hong, L., Pirolli, P., & Chi, E. H. (2010). Want to be retweeted? Large scale analytics on factors impacting retweet in Twitter network. In *Proceeding of the 2010 IEEE Second International Conference on Social Computing*. IEEE Computer Society. doi:10.1109/SocialCom.2010.33

Szekely, F. (2015). *Sustainable leadership means engaging honestly with your stakeholders: VW failed the test.* International Institute for Management Development. Available: http://www.imd.org/news/VW-scandal.cfm?mrk_cmpg_source=SM_TW_FI&utm_source=Twitter&utm_medium=Social&utm_campaign=SM_TW_FI

Tess, P. A. (2013). The role of social media in higher education classes (real and virtual) – A literature review. *Computers in Human Behavior*, *29*(5), A60–A68. doi:10.1016/j.chb.2012.12.032

Tsai, W. H. S., & Men, L. R. (2013). Motivations and antecedents of consumer engagement with brand pages on social networking sites. *Journal of Interactive Advertising*, *13*(2), 76–87. doi:10.1080/15252019.2013.826549

Tse, Y. K., Tan, K. H. & Zhang, M. H. (2014). *Exploring Quality Risk in the Food Supply Chain: Strategic Insights from Horsmeat Scandals*. Charter Institute of Logistics and Transport.

Tse, Y. K., Zhang, M., Doherty, B., Chappell, P. J., & Garnett, P. (2016). Insight from the horsemeat scandal: Exploring the consumers' opinion of tweets toward Tesco. *Industrial Management & Data Systems*, *116*(6), 1178–1200. doi:10.1108/IMDS-10-2015-0417

Twitter. (2013). *Twitter Developer Documentation*. Author.

Twitter. (n.d.). *About*. Retrieved from; https://about.twitter.com/company

Veil, S. R., Buehner, T., & Palenchar, M. J. (2011). A Work-In-Process Literature Review: Incorporating Social Media in Risk and Crisis Communication. *Journal of Contingencies and Crisis Management*, *19*(2), 110–122. doi:10.1111/j.1468-5973.2011.00639.x

Waller, K., Droge, E., & Puschmann, C. (2011). Citation Analysis in Twitter: Approaches for Defining and Measuring Information Flows within Tweets during Scientific Conference. *1st Workshop on Making Sense of Microposts*.

Winston, A. (2015). *What VW Didn't Understand About Trust*. Harvard Business Review. Available: https://hbr.org/2015/09/what-vw-didnt-understand-about-trust?utm_source=Socialflow&utm_medium=Tweet&utm_campaign=Socialflow

Wong, K. F., Xia, Y., Xu, R., Wu, M., & Li, W. (2008). Pattern-based opinion mining for stock market trend prediction. *International Journal of Computer Processing of Languages*, *21*, 347-361.

Zelezny, L. C., Chua, P.-P., & Aldrich, C. (2000). Elaborating on gender differences in environmentalism. *The Journal of Social Issues*, *56*(3), 443–457. doi:10.1111/0022-4537.00177

Zhang, W. H., Xu, H., & Wan, W. (2012). Weakness Finder: Find product weakness from Chinese reviews by using aspects based sentiment analysis. *Expert Systems with Applications*, *39*(11), 10283–10291. doi:10.1016/j.eswa.2012.02.166

Zhang, X., Fuehres, H., & Gloor, P. A. (2011). Predicting Stock Market Indicators Through Twitter "I hope it is not as bad as I fear".*2nd Collaborative Innovation Networks Conference (Coins2010)*.

ENDNOTES

1 The engines emitted nitrogen oxide pollutants up to 40 time above what is allowed in the US (Hotten, 2015).

2 Including geographic information, username, user's profile etc.

3 Note that the number of retweets received are the tweets already in the dataset.

4 Library – "gender-from-name" - https://github.com/Bemmu/gender-from-name.

5 Frequency of words.

6 A / (A+B+C), where A represents cases where both item occur, and B and C represent cases where one item is found but not the other. In this coefficient equal weight is given to matches and non matches.

7 Number in bracket represents the word count frequency of the words.

8 Initialism of "in case you missed it".

Chapter 11
Swift Guanxi Data Analysis and Its Application to E-Commerce Retail Strategies Improvement

Ewelina Lacka
Strathclyde University, UK

ABSTRACT

The Internet has changed the face and the pace of retail offering an opportunity to sell products online. This has led to the fast growth of e-commerce sites in which retailers envision a source of competitive advantage. Before they are able to benefit from e-commerce however, they have to understand the range of factors, which impact consumers' e-commerce acceptance. Even more, to ensure sustainability of online product sale, retailers have to go a step further and understand not only consumers' intentions to purchase online but also factors driving product re-purchase. To date, a number of factors driving consumers' e-commerce purchase and re-purchase have been examined. Most recently, the concept of swift guanxi has been studied. This study extends this stream of research by analysing social media data being a result of swift guanxi in order to help retailers in their online strategies improvement.

DOI: 10.4018/978-1-5225-0956-1.ch011

INTRODUCTION

Originally designed for data exchange, the Internet became a point of interest for retailers and consumers alike. This is because the Internet offers an indispensable opportunity to sell and purchase products online through e-commerce. E-commerce has since rapidly developed into a major retail platform (Sprano & Zakak, 2000). This fast development is linked to the advantages consumers might derive from e-commerce sites. The most important benefit appears to be effective and efficient satisfaction of consumer needs (Miyazaki & Frenandez, 2006). Despite advantages deriving from online shopping sites to consumers, it appears that not all consumers accept e-commerce and use it as their main shopping channel. In search of the factors stimulating consumers' e-commerce acceptance a number of research projects have been executed. At first, researchers focused on the examination of factors driving initial acceptance and e-commerce sites use. Due to the growing importance of consumer retention, researchers also looked at consumers' re-purchase intentions as only consumers regularly purchasing from e-commerce sites can ensure those sites' sustainability.

The aforementioned research streams highlight the importance of trust, which appears to be crucial for successful online transactions. The creation of online trust however appears to be a major challenge for e-retailers due to buyer-seller physical and temporal separation online. Recent research by Ou et al. (2014) however indicates that trust can be facilitated by the so-called 'swift- guanxi'. Swift guanxi is a form of Chinese oriented concept of 'guanxi' and it is defined as a close and pervasive interpersonal buyer-seller relationship online. Ou et al. (2014) claims that swift guanxi can address the above-mentioned limitation of online retailing as it increases perception of buyer-seller interaction and presence online. This is because swift guanxi allows for buyer-seller personalized communication via computer-mediated communication technologies. This in turn, enables the seller to address consumers' risk perception regarding online transaction and hence establish trust. This current study aims to closely examine and analyze the result of the buyer-seller interaction and specifically the exchange of information online (i.e. swift guanxi data), in order to identify the key consumers' concerns while making purchase online. Consequently, this study aims to analyze swift guanxi data in order to guide retailers in their e-commerce strategies improvement. By addressing consumers' concerns sellers can gain consumers' trust and hence ensure the sustainability of their e-commerce strategies.

The remainder of this chapter is organized as follows. First the literature relating to e-commerce acceptance is reviewed in the next section. Specifically, a range of intention-based models used to assess consumers' attitudes towards e-commerce, their intention to use online shopping sites and the actual use of those sites is discussed. Next, the importance of assessing not only the intentions to purchase but also products re-purchase intentions is stressed and the most recent research on consumers' online re-purchase behavior is also reviewed. This is subsequently linked to the discussion of swift guanxi, which is defined as swiftly formed buyer-seller relationships based on interaction and exchange of information online. The outcome of the online interactions and information exchange is argued to be a valuable data source, which this study aims to analyze. In the following section, the research methodology is discussed. Specifically, this study builds on an approach to social media data analysis proposed by Chan et al. (2015a). Data sourced from the result of buyer-seller interactions of online fashion retailer is extracted from Twitter and subsequently analyzed. The results of the analysis are presented and discussed in the penultimate section. The study finishes with a conclusion and recommendations section drawing on the analysis conducted.

E-Commerce Literature Review

Researchers have employed a range of models in order to identify the factors stimulating consumers' e-commerce acceptance. The employed models mainly originate from Theory of Reasoned Action (TRA) developed by Fishbein and Ajzen (1975). TRA is one of the first, and the most influential theory used to evaluate direct motives driving consumers' acceptance of technologies, such as e-commerce sites. As demonstrated by TRA, consumer behavior (e.g. e-commerce site use) can be predicted by intentions. Consumers' intentions, in turn are determined by attitudes towards a given behavior. This attitudes-intention-actual behavior paradigm initiated a series of the so-called intention-based models, which have been extensively applied by researchers, who focus on the assessment of consumers' e-commerce acceptance and use. This is because those models focus on behavior (e.g. e-commerce use) rather than on consumers' attitudes towards product or service offered on e-commerce sites (Hansen et al, 2004). In other words, intention-based models specifically focus on reasons driving consumers' e-commerce site acceptance and use, rather than characteristics of products being sold on those sites.

TRA exclusively focuses on two attitudes that supposedly determine consumers' intention to use and subsequent usage of e-commerce site. Those are; consumers' favorable or unfavorable feelings about the behavior, which Fishbain and Ajzen (1975) term attitudes towards behavior, and subjective norms (the perceived opinions of other people about the particular behavior). Later, Ajzen (1991) extended the original TRA by adding perceived behavioral control (the perception of the availability or lack of the necessary resources needed to exhibit the behaviour in question). This extension of the TRA resulted in the Theory of Planned Behaviour (TPB), which researchers examined when evaluating the direct motives driving consumers' e-commerce acceptance and use (e.g. Pavlou, 2002; Pavlou & Chai, 2002; George, 2004).

Introduced by Davis (1989), the Technology Acceptance Model (TAM) is yet another extension of Fishbein and Ajzen's (1975) TRA. Davis (1989), however, instead of adding attitudes to the TRA, replaced them with perceived usefulness (the belief that using a particular technology will enhance the consumers' exhibition of the behaviour in question) and perceived ease of use (the belief that using a particular technology will be free of effort). TAM, similar to TPB, has been extensively applied by researchers investigating consumers' e-commerce acceptance and use. Those researchers have confirmed the high explanatory power of the model (e.g. Gefen & Straub, 2000; Gefen et al., 2003).

In spite of the good explanatory power of both TAM and TPB, neither model has been acknowledged as being superior. As a result researchers continue to introduce and test new theories and models in order to provide better insight into the direct factors stimulating consumers' e-commerce acceptance and use. To this end, researchers have adopted other models based on an attitudes-intentions-actual behaviour paradigm. For example, researchers have employed the Motivational Model by Davis et al. (1992) in order to assess the impact of intrinsic motivation on e-commerce acceptance (e.g. Ha & Stoel, 2009; Luo et al., 2011). Furthermore, in this research stream we can also observe researchers not only adopting existing frameworks but also combining and deconstructing them. For example, Taylor and Todd (1995) deconstructed variables of TPB. Even more, in order to reveal factors stimulating consumers' e-commerce acceptance and use researchers have developed extensions to the existing theories and frameworks. For example, Venkatesh and Davis (2000) have extended TAM to TAM2 and later Venkatesh and Bala (2008) developed yet another TAM extension, which they termed TAM3. Most recently in the efforts to assess consumers intentions and technology use Venkatesh et al. (2003) introduced the Unified Theory of Acceptance and Use of Technology (UTAUT), which they claim explains 70% of the total variance in behavioural intentions and about 50% of usage. UTAUT has also been extended; in 2012 Venkatesh and colleagues introduced UTAUT2. Both UTAUT and UTAUT2 have been employed into the investigation of consumers' intentions to accept and use e-commerce sites.

All of those above-mentioned models have been successfully employed in the investigation of consumers' intention to use e-commerce sites and those sites usage. Nevertheless, there still seems to be a lack of agreement on the factors that truly stimulate consumers' e-commerce acceptance and use. This is because while some researchers recognized the key role of one model or a factor, others failed to identify its impact on e-commerce acceptance and use (see Gefen & Straub, 2000). This lack of agreement on which factors drive consumers' intentions to accept and use e-commerce sites has encouraged researchers to search for other reasons or factors which might play an important role in consumers' e-commerce acceptance. Among a range of factors studied (including demographic factors, economic factors etc.) trust have received significant research attention and in fact many researchers view trust as the 'preliminary condition to consumers' e-commerce acceptance' (Corbatt et al., 2003). In order to develop trust researchers proposed a number of trust-building techniques aimed at encouraging consumers to purchase as well as re-purchase from e-commerce sites (see Ranganathan & Ganapathy, 2002; Constantinides, 2002). This is because research has revealed that trust does not only impact consumers initial intentions to use e-commerce sites but it also encourages continuous use and product re-purchase (Wen et al, 2011; Lee et al, 2011).

Consequently, building on the consumers' e-commerce acceptance and use research stream, researchers attention has shifted to consumers' re-purchase intention and continuous use of e-commerce sites (see Chiu et al, 2009). This was due to the realization that attracting new consumers without retaining existing ones is unprofitable and unsustainable for online retailers (Zhang et al, 2011). However, research reports (ibid) that despite significant effort to retain consumers less than one percent of consumers decide to re-purchase products from e-commerce retailers. Consumers' reluctance to re-purchase products online results in low consumer retentions rates, which researchers claim, is directly related to a lack of trust in e-commerce intangible environment (Wen et al, 2011; Lee et al, 2011).

The literature acknowledges that trust plays an important role in an online environment, which due to its intangible nature, suffers from a number of limitations. For example, e-commerce sites are unable to effect a face-to-face interaction between the consumer and the seller, which ultimately results in both parties' social and temporal separation (Ba & Pavlou, 2002). This buyer-seller separation makes it difficult to form relationships, which are preconditions for trust (Lin & Lekhawipat, 2014). Researchers recognize therefore that due to the intangible nature of the e-commerce marketplace and hence buyer-seller social separation, it is impossible, or at least very difficult, to establish relationships and subsequent trust. This results in consumers struggling to accept e-commerce and continuously use it. It can be concluded therefore, that temporal and social separation of buyers and sellers has a profound impact on e-commerce retail and may result in its failure. However, a more recent study by Ou et al. (2014) seems to challenge this assumption. Ou et al. (2014) claim that in the online environment buyers and sellers are able to establish close and pervasive interpersonal relationships, which they refer to as a swift form of 'guanxi'.

To date researchers have executed numerous studies investigating guanxi; each provides a different definition of the concept. Chen and Chen (2004) for example, define guanxi as an informal, particularistic and personal connection between two individuals. Similarly, Gu et al. (2008) refers to guanxi as social connections or networks, which they state, are used to exchange favours. Lee at al. (2001) agrees with Gu et al. (2008) stating that guanxi can be used to exchange favours between two parties. They however refer to guanxi as 'particularized and personalized relationships' rather than simply connections or networks between individuals. Those relationships are naturally established in an offline environment. Nevertheless, Ou et al. (2014) believe that those connections, networks or relationships between two parties can be formed not only offline but also a swift form can be developed online. They claim that those online relationships are temporal and are created when a buyer aims to complete a transaction (i.e. purchase product online). Such a temporal social connection between online buyer and seller is termed 'swift guanxi'. Specifically, Ou et al. (2014) define swift guanxi as a buyer's perception of swiftly formed, informal, interpersonal relationships with an online seller. Ou et al. (2014) therefore contest previous research by arguing that buyer-seller relationships online can be established in a form of swift guanxi, which can facilitate trust and hence it plays an important role in consumers' e-commerce acceptance and its continuous use.

According to Ou et al. (2014), swift guanxi has three dimensions; mutual understanding, reciprocal favours and relationship harmony. Mutual understanding refers to 'buyers' and sellers' appreciation of each other's needs' that, they claim, can be achieved by effective communication. For example, a buyer and a seller can discuss and reach an agreement on pricing or delivery options that satisfy both parties. The second dimension of swift guanxi, reciprocal favours refers to 'positive beliefs from buyer's and sellers' interactions', which according to Ou et al. (2014) are 'magical openings to effective transactions'. In practice reciprocal favours refer to discounts offered to a buyer or small gifts, which may aid the conclusion of a transaction. Finally, the relationship harmony dimension of swift guanxi refers to mutual respect and conflict avoidance, which may reduce the perception of e-commerce sites' disadvantages (e.g. intangible nature of online environment, social and temporal buyer-seller separation etc.). Relationship harmony can be achieved when a seller shows interest in satisfying consumers' needs and solving problems encountered. For example, the seller can help solve delivery problems or show interest in consumer product satisfaction by offering after sale support. This, according to Ou et al. (2014), can be done via online conversation and effective communication at the time of e-commerce transaction. As such, Ou et al. (2014) echo previous research which argue that high quality buyer-seller communication is a key success factor for online transactions (Liu and Arnett, 2000)

Based on the above-stated dimensions of swift guanxi it appears that communication is the key to successful relationship formation online, i.e. guanxi. Ou et al. (2014) argue that by integrating computer-mediated communication tools, such as social media tools (e.g. instant messengers, message boxes and feedback systems) it is possible to facilitate repeated transactions with the seller by building swiftly formed relationships online. This was also supported by Kaplan and Haenlein (2009), who state that social media tools can be used to facilitate interpersonal connections between buyer and seller online. This is because via social media tools sellers can improve perception of interaction and presence (Fang et al., 2014). Specifically, via social media, buyers can communicate and interact with sellers in order to acquire the information needed to make purchase decision. Furthermore, via social media, sellers can enhance their presence, which refers to 'perception of intimacy or being close to the other person' (Lowry et al., 2009). This is a key component of guanxi (Ou et al., 2014). It can therefore be concluded that social media tools such as instant messengers, message boxes and feedback systems are necessary in order to facilitate buyer-seller relationships online and trust. These are important in consumers' e-commerce product purchase and re-purchase decisions.

Currently, a number of e-commerce retailers use social media tools to communicate and interact with consumers. For example Chinese online shopping mall – TaoBao.com introduced *Ali Wang Wang*, which is used to facilitate buyer-seller communication online and hence it helps to establish swift guanxi. Despite swift guanxi being a Chinese oriented concept, it can be observed that many western retailers also utilize computer-mediated communication tools in order to increase perception of sellers' interactivity and presence. For example, British online fashion retailer Asos.com uses social media sites such as Twitter in order to effectively communicate with its online consumers. It can be argued therefore that western e-retailers also use computer-mediated communication tools to build temporal relationship with consumers. Chan et al. (2015a) notes that such buyer-seller interaction via computer-mediated communication technologies (e.g. social media sites) leads to the generation of potentially valuable data known as online data, social media data or big data.

Social media sites are defined as 'web-based services that allow individuals to:

1. Construct a public or semi-public profile within a bounded system,
2. Articulate a list of other users with whom they share a connection, and
3. View and traverse their list of connections and those made by others within the system.

The nature and nomenclature of these connections may vary from site to site' (Ellison, 2007). Furthermore, Chan et al. (2015a) states that social media refers to the applications that allow users to exchange their views online. Those applications built on Web 2.0 technologies allow their users, both sellers and consumers, effective communication online (Kaplan & Haenlein, 2010). Both *Ali Wang Wang* utilized by TaoBao.com as well as Twitter used by Asos.com are examples of such applications. As already stated, communication via social media sites results in online content, also known as social media data (Akar & Topcu 2011). Chan et al. (2015a) argue that such content is a valuable source of data as it contains information and knowledge that are key to businesses operations. Furthermore, Ngai et al. (2009) argue that this information and knowledge extracted from social media data can be particularly useful in creating or adjusting business strategies. Chan et al. (2015a) and Chan et al. (2015b) confirmed this hypothesis by analyzing social media data in the context of new product development. This study aims to build on this research stream and demonstrate how companies can make effective use of the social media data resulting from the deployment of swift guanxi communication in their e-commerce strategies improvement. Therefore, for the purpose of this study we make a clear distinction between swift quanxi data and social media data. This is because as far as all swift guanxi data can be considered to be social media data, not all social media data can be classified as swift guanxi data. This is because, swift guanxi data refers to data arising from personalized buyer-seller communication online, while social media data is a much broader dataset and it includes not only buyer-seller online exchanges but also consumer-to-consumer interactions online. Consequently, this study aims to extend swift guanxi research while examining swift guanxi data in order to improve e-commerce strategies.

RESEARCH METHODOLOGY

This study builds on the approach to social media analysis proposed by Chan et al. (2015a). The approach by Chan et al. (2015a) was selected to drive data analysis, as to the best of our knowledge theirs is the only study that focuses on content of social media data rather than social media metrics. As such the approach allows for conversion of social media qualitative content into quantifiable factors. Furthermore, it also allows for the retrieval of relationships between individual factors, all of which results in the extraction of 'true value of social media data'. Consequently, by applying Chan et al.'s (2015a) approach the true value of swift guanxi data can be assessed. This value can directly inform retailers in their e-commerce strategy improvement.

Social media data based on the communications between a fashion retailer- Asos.com, and its consumers has been extracted by the means of NCapture, a plug-in for Nvivo 10. Twitter posts which were addressed to '@Asos_HeretoHelp' has been extracted for this study's analysis. This ensured that data used in this study refers to swift guanxi data, rather than any other buyer-seller communication via Twitter.

As it is with social media data, swift guanxi data is massive in terms of size and volume. Therefore, it is infeasible to analyze the entire database. Hence researchers (e.g. Chew et al., 2010) randomly select a sample of the larger dataset for detailed analysis. This current study adopts the same approach. Specifically, out of entire swift guanxi database over 4500 tweets were downloaded among which 1000 were randomly selected for the analysis. As indicated by Chan et al. (2015) the content analysis was carried out employing conceptual analysis and follow-up relational analysis, which allows for assessment of statistical cluster analysis. The conceptual analysis involves quantifying the occurrence of concepts in the dataset. This can be done on the basis of previously extracted concepts/codes from the literature according to which the data is coded. Alternatively, the so-called 'open coding' can be employed when researchers generate codes/concepts according to their occurrence in the dataset. In the case of this study open coding strategy was employed, as swift guanxi data seems to be explicit in nature. This is because swift guanxi communication refers to e-commerce transactions and factors that may affect it.

Next, following Chan et al. (2015) the relational analysis was conducted in order to assess relationships between individual concepts/codes. In order to examine those relationships statistically cluster analysis was carried out along with Pearson correlation analysis. The results of data analysis and discussion are presented next.

Data Analysis and Discussion

Following the random selection of swift guanxi data of 1000 tweets, 865 tweets were coded, while 135 tweets were excluded. This is because those tweets did not contain any 'useful' information concerning e-commerce transaction. Those tweets included graphical content or 'thank you' or 'ok' answer to seller lines of communication. The open coding analysis of the remaining tweets however revealed a number of concepts/codes, which directly concern e-commerce transaction. The full list of codes/concepts is presented in Table 1.

As can be seen from Table 1, delivery issues were the most common problems consumers discussed with online retailer in the selected sample. Among all codes/concepts coded, delivery was mentioned over 150 times, which equals almost a fifth (18%) of all the tweets coded. While discussing delivery issues with the seller, consumers mainly express their concerns with late deliveries or problems encountered with the 'next day delivery' option (see Twitter users 1–4)

- Twitter user 1; *'my order 179841529 is realllllly late. 3 days late'*
- Twitter user 2: *'Pay next day delivery and my parcel isn't here'*
- Twitter user 3: *Please am I still expecting the delivery on an order I made since 11/11/2015. Order number 177268584'*
- Twitter user 4: *'@Asos_HeretoHelp hey I've ordered some shoes and they've not turned up though it says they've been delivered? eek'* "

Table 1. Codes/concepts

Name	Frequency
Wrong items dispatched	18
Third party	18
Stock items	26
Returns	61
Refund	35
Price	4
Payment	8
Order dispatch info	36
Order change	6
Order placement	83
Missing order	8
Lost parcel	6
Item quality	23
Exchange	15
Discount	76
Damaged order	12
Delivery tracking	23
Delivery details change	29
Delivery	156
Consumer support	125
Cancel order	32
Account problem	11

Another issue discussed during swift guanxi buyer-seller interaction on social media site is related to consumer support. Out of 865 codes, 125 codes/concepts (14.4%) referred to 'consumer support'. Specifically, consumers referring to consumer support demanded more effective and efficient communication with sales support officers. Hence, they asked for direct phone numbers, e-mail addresses or other effective and efficient means of communication with the consumer support team (see Twitter users 5–7).

- Twitter user 5: '*I have DM you and still awaiting a reply?*'
- Twitter user 6: '*there not just a email or phone contact I could use*"
- Twitter user 7: '*@ASOS_HeretoHelp I'm desperately trying to find a phone number to contact you. Where will I find this?*'

The third issue consumers discussed with sellers via social media tools is related to 'order placement'. Specifically, problems encountered with order placement has been mentioned 83 times by consumers, which refers to nearly 10% of all tweets analyzed (see Twitter users 8–10).

- Twitter user 8: *'@ASOS_HeretoHelp for some reason my order from about 24 hous ago is still processing. This is the first time this has happened. Any reason?'*
- Twitter user 9: *'@ASOS_HeretoHelp hi there I placed an order this morning and still haven't had any conformation email'*
- Twitter user 10: *''@ASOS_HeretoHelp I've has an order with status 'order processing' for 3 days. Will this be confirmed?'*

Those three main factors discussed during the open coding of swift guanxi data are directly related to other issues, which have been revealed during relational analysis and Pearson correlation coefficient test (see Table 2).

Table 2. Pearson correlation coefficient

Concept/ Code	Concept/ Code	Pearson Correlation Coefficient
Cancel order	Order placement	0.832886
Order placement	Order dispatch info	0.826157
Account problem	Consumer support	0.821343
Delivery tracking	Delivery	0.813056
Third party	Delivery	0.812869
Returns	Refund	0.810093
Delivery tracking	Order placement	0.798729
Order placement	Delivery	0.797582
Returns	Consumer support	0.796511
Discount	Delivery	0.794848
Discount	Consumer support	0.787825
Delivery	Consumer support	0.77367
Cancel order	Refund	0.771583
Item quality	Demerged order	0.771184
Delivery details change	Delivery	0.764973
Item quality	Consumer support	0.762296

continued on following page

Table 2. Continued

Concept/ Code	Concept/ Code	Pearson Correlation Coefficient
Missing order	Consumer support	0.761294
Refund	Consumer support	0.749715
Account problem	Item quality	0.749498
Third party	Consumer support	0.743775
Returns	Delivery	0.741634
Account problem	Discount	0.741507
Account problem	Returns	0.741428
Order placement	Discount	0.739513
Delivery tracking	Cancel order	0.738651
Order placement	Refund	0.738482
Stock items	Consumer support	0.737926
Delivery tracking	Consumer support	0.735891
Order placement	Consumer support	0.733974
Lost parcel	Delivery	0.731961
Cancel order	Delivery	0.73172
Third party	Discount	0.727
Returns	Order placement	0.726116
Missing order	Delivery	0.724076
Returns	Discount	0.723475
Damaged order	Stock items	0.72103
Cancel order	Payment	0.716992
Order placement	Payment	0.716975
Item quality	Stock items	0.71217
Returns	Wrong items dispatched	0.712073
Cancel order	Consumer support	0.711201
Cancel order	Order dispatch info	0.711005
Delivery tracking	Discount	0.709939
Lost parcel	Third party	0.709386
Payment	Consumer support	0.708819
Delivery tracking	Returns	0.708652
Cancel order	Discount	0.708591
Delivery details change	Order placement	0.708328
Delivery tracking	Lost parcel	0.707389

continued on following page

Table 2. Continued

Concept/ Code	Concept/ Code	Pearson Correlation Coefficient
Delivery tracking	Third party	0.70689
Exchange	Returns	0.706635
Discount	Payment	0.704612
Missing order	Returns	0.70284
Damaged order	Consumer support	0.701063

As observed in Table 2, order placement is highly correlated with problems related to order cancellation as well as with the possibility to obtain product dispatch information online. Specifically, the correlation coefficients of order placement with order cancellation and order dispatch information are 0.832 and 0.826 respectively. Furthermore, order placement issues are highly correlated with problems related to delivery; delivery tracking issues as well as product delivery problems. According to Pearson correlation coefficient test results order placement is also highly correlated with delivery tracking, with a correlation coefficient of 0.798, while order placement and problems related to delivery have a correlation coefficient of 0.787. Furthermore, it can be observed that delivery issues are not only correlated with problems related to order placement but also online delivery tracking problems and issues concerning delivery by a third party. Pearson correlation coefficient test revealed that delivery is highly correlated with both delivery tracking and third party, with highly coefficient values of 0.813 and 0.812 respectively. Finally, according to relational analysis the third most commonly coded factor, consumer support, is also highly correlated with the following factors: discount (correlation coefficient of 0.787), delivery (correlation coefficient of 0.773), account problems (correlation coefficient of 0.821) and returns (correlation coefficient of 0.796). The correlations between individual factors are visually presented in Figure 1.

CONCLUSION

E-commerce is regarded as the fastest growing marketplace globally. In order to ensure continuous growth of e-commerce, retailers selling products online have to encourage consumers to purchase and also become return customers online. This is because previous research has recognised that only retaining consumers can ensure sustainable growth of e-business and hence the ultimate success of e-commerce

Figure 1. Dendogram of the cluster analysis

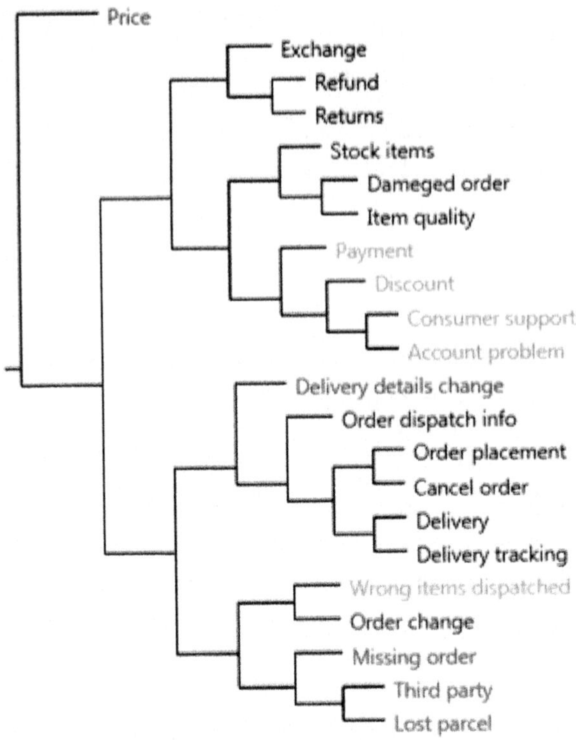

strategies. However, achieving this is challenging due to the intangible nature of the e-commerce environment. The intangibility of the online market place results in retailers finding it difficult to establish relationships with consumers, build trust and hence motivate consumers to purchase and re-purchase online. Ou et al. (2014) however challenges this assumption. They argue that in the online enviornment buyers and sellers form a swift form of relationship which is termed swift guanxi. According to Ou et al. (2014) swift guanxi can be faciliated by computer-mediated communication tools such as social media sites, which increase seller interractivity and presence online and also allows for effective and efficient online communication. This study extends this stream of research by analysing the results of this communication online in order to identify the factors that are of concern to consumers when shopping online. Addressing such factors can result in e-commerce strategies improvement.

Specifically, data arising from buyer-seller online communication was extracted from the Twitter account of online fashion retailer, Asos.com. The data was analysed by adopting the approach suggested by Chan et al. (2015a). Specifically, swift guanxi data was analysed following the principles of content analysis and relational analysis. The results show a clear pattern of codes/concepts, which can be used by retailers in their e-commerce strategies improvement.

The analysis of 865 randomly selected tweets suggests that consumers contact sellers while encountering problems related to delivery and order placement as well as when requesting contact information of consumer support teams. Retailers therefore should improve those three aspects in order to ensure that those problems are minimalised. Further analysis show that those three main concepts are highly correlated with other issues such as problems related to order cancellation, return and refund. Consumers are also experiencing problems with accessing products dispatch and shipping information, various account problems and deliveries by third party companies. It is recommended therefore that in the first instance companies should look into problems related to consumer experience with product delivery and order placement as well as issues related to access to consumer support teams. Once these are resolved, it is suggested that retailers closely monitor other factors highlighted by the content analysis and its relationship to the earlier stated three main issues. Significantly improvements in the identified areas could lead to retailers gaining consumer trust once consumers develop the view that their 'voices' are integral to the e-commerce strategies infrastructure.

REFERENCES

Ajzen, I. (1991). The Theory of Planned Behaviour. *Organizational Behavior and Human Decision Processes, 50*(2), 179–211. doi:10.1016/0749-5978(91)90020-T

Akar, E., & Topçu, B. (2011). An examination of the factors influencing consumers' attitudes toward social media marketing. *Journal of Internet Commerce, 10*(1), 35–67. doi:10.1080/15332861.2011.558456

Ba, S., & Pavlou, P. (2002). Evidence of the effect of trust building technology in electronic markets; price premium and buyer behavior. *Management Information Systems Quarterly, 26*(3), 243–268. doi:10.2307/4132332

Burgoon, J., Bonito, B., Bengtsson, C., Cederberg, M., Lundeberg, M., & Allspach, L. (2000). Interactivity in human- computer interaction; a case study of credibility, understanding and influence. *Computers in Human Behavior, 16*(6), 553–574. doi:10.1016/S0747-5632(00)00029-7

Fishbein, M., & Ajzen, I. (1975). *Belief, attitude, intention, and behaviour: an introduction to theory and research*. Reading, MA: Addison-Wesley.

Chan, H., Lacka, E., Yee, R., & Lim, M. (2015). The role of social media data in operations and production management. *International Journal of Production Research*.

Chen, X., & Chen, C. (2004). On the interactions of the Chinese quanix; a process model of guanix development. *Asia Pacific Journal of Management*, *21*(3), 305–324. doi:10.1023/B:APJM.0000036465.19102.d5

Chew, C., Eysenbach, G., & Sampson, M. (2010). Pandemics in the age of Twitter: Content analysis of Tweets during the 2009 H1N1 outbreak. *PLoS ONE*, *5*(11), 1–13. doi:10.1371/journal.pone.0014118 PMID:21124761

Chiu, C., Chang, H., Cheng, Y., & Fang, H. (2009). Determinants of consumer repurchase intention in online shopping. *Online Information Review*, *33*(4), 761–784. doi:10.1108/14684520910985710

Constantinides, E. (2002). Influencing the online consumer's behaviour; the Web experience. *Internet Research*, *14*(2), 11–126.

Corbatt, B., Thanasankit, T., & Yi, H. (2003). *Trust and e-commerce; a study of consumer perceptions* (Vol. 2). Electronic Research and Applications.

Davis, F. (1989). Perceived Usefulness, Perceived Ease of Use, and User Acceptance of Information Technology. *Management Information Systems Quarterly*, *13*(3), 319–339. doi:10.2307/249008

Davis, F., Bagozzi, R., & Warshaw, P. (1992). Extrinsic and Intrinsic motivation to use computers in the workplace. *The Journal of Applied Psychology*, *22*(14), 1111–1132.

Ellison, N. (2007). Social network sites: Definition, history, and scholarship. *Journal of Computer-Mediated Communication*, *13*(1), 210–230. doi:10.1111/j.1083-6101.2007.00393.x

Fang, Y., Qureshi, H., Sun, P., McCole, E., Ramsey, E., & Lim, K. (2014). Trust, satisfaction, and online repurchase intentions: The modeling role of perceived effectiveness of e-commerce institutional mechanisms. *Management Information Systems Quarterly*, *38*(2), 407–427.

Gefen, D., Karahanna, E., & Straub, D. (2003). Trust and TAM in online shopping; an integrated model. *Management Information Systems Quarterly*, *27*(1), 51–90.

Gefen, D., & Straub, D. (2000). A relative importance of perceived ease of use in IS adoption; a study of e-commerce adoption. *Journal of the Association for Information Systems*, *1*, 1–28.

George, J. (2004). Theory of Planned Behaviour and Internet purchasing. *Internet Research, 14*(3), 198–212. doi:10.1108/10662240410542634

Gu, F., Hung, K., & Tse, D. (2008). When does guanix matter? Issues of capitualization and its dark sides. *Journal of Marketing, 72*(4), 12–28. doi:10.1509/jmkg.72.4.12

Ha, S., & Stoel, L. (2009). Consumer e- shopping acceptance: Antecedents in technology acceptance model. *Journal of Business Research, 62*(5), 565–571. doi:10.1016/j.jbusres.2008.06.016

Hansen, T., Jensen, J., & Solgaard, H. (2004). Predicting online grocery buying intention; a comparison of the theory of reasoned action and theory of planned behaviour. *International Journal of Information Management, 24*(6), 539–550. doi:10.1016/j.ijinfomgt.2004.08.004

Kaplan, A., & Haenlein, M. (2009). Users of the word, unite! The challenges and opportunities of social media. *Business Horizons, 53*(1), 59–68. doi:10.1016/j.bushor.2009.09.003

Liu, C., & Arnett, K. (2000). Exploring the factors associated with web site success in the context of electronic commerce. *Information & Management, 38*(1), 23–33. doi:10.1016/S0378-7206(00)00049-5

Lee, C., & Eze, N. (2011). Analyzing key determinants of online repurchase intentions. *Asia Pacific Journal of Marketing and Logistics, 23*(2), 200–221. doi:10.1108/13555851111120498

Lee, D., Pae, J., & Wong, Y. (2001). A model of close business relationships in China (guanix). *European Journal of Marketing, 35*(1/2), 51–69. doi:10.1108/03090560110363346

Lin, C., & Lekhawipat, W. (2014). Factors affecting online repurchase intentions. *Industrial Management & Data Systems, 114*(4), 597–611. doi:10.1108/IMDS-10-2013-0432

Lowry, P., Romano, C., Jenkins, J., & Guthrie, R. (2009). The CMC interactivity model; How interactivity enhances communication quality and process satisfaction in lean-media groups. *Journal of Management Information Systems, 26*(1), 155–196. doi:10.2753/MIS0742-1222260107

Luo, M., Chea, S., & Chen, J. (2011). Web-based information service adoption: A comparison of the motivational model and the uses and gratifications theory. *Decision Support Systems, 51*(1), 21–30. doi:10.1016/j.dss.2010.11.015

Miyazaki, A., & Fernandez, A. (2006). Consumer perceptions of privacy and security risks for online shopping. *The Journal of Consumer Affairs*, *35*(1), 27.

Ou, C., Pavlou, P., & Davison, R. (2014). Swift Guanix in online marketplace; the role of computer-mediated communication technologies. *Management Information Systems Quarterly*, *38*(1), 209–230.

Pavlou, P. (2002). *What drives electronic commerce? A theory of planned behaviour perspective*. Academy of Management Proceedings.

Pavlou, P., & Chai, L. (2002). What drives electronic commerce across cultures? A cross- cultural empirical investigation of the theory of planned behavior. *Journal of Electronic Commerce*, *3*(4), 240–253.

Ranganathan, C., & Ganapathy, S. (2002). Key dimensions of business-to- consumer web site. *Information & Management*, *39*(6), 457–465. doi:10.1016/S0378-7206(01)00112-4

Sprano, E., & Zakak, A. (2000). E-commerce capable; competitive advantage for consumeries in work economy. *Competitiveness Review:An International Business Journal Incorporating Journal of Global Competitiveness*, *10*(2), 114–131. doi:10.1108/eb046404

Taylor, S., & Todd, P. (1995). Assessing IT usage: The role of prior experience. *Management Information Systems Quarterly*, *19*(2), 561–570. doi:10.2307/249633

Venkatesh, V., & Bala, H. (2008). Technology Acceptance Model 3 and a research agenda on interventions. *Decision Sciences*, *39*(2), 273–315. doi:10.1111/j.1540-5915.2008.00192.x

Venkatesh, V., & Davis, F. (2000). A theoretical extension of the technology acceptance model: Four longitudinal field studies. *Management Science*, *46*(2), 186–204. doi:10.1287/mnsc.46.2.186.11926

Venkatesh, V., Morris, M., Davis, G., & Davis, F. (2003). User Acceptance of Information Technology: Toward a Unified View. *Management Information Systems Quarterly*, *27*(3), 425–478.

Venkatesh, V., Thong, J., & Xu, X. (2012). Consumer Acceptance and Usage of Information Technology. *Extending the Unified Theory of Acceptance and Use of Technology MIS Quarterly VoL.*, *36*(1), 157–178.

Wen, C., Prybutok, P., & Xu, C. (2011). An integrated model for consumer online purchase intention. *Journal of Computer Information Systems, 14*.

Zhang, Y., Fang, K., Wei, E., Ramsey, P., McCole, P., & Chen, H. (2011). Repurchase intention in B2C e-commerce- A relationship quality perspective. *Information & Management*, *48*(6), 192–200. doi:10.1016/j.im.2011.05.003

Chapter 12
Applying Big Data with Fuzzy DEMATEL to Discover the Critical Factors for Employee Engagement in Developing Sustainability for the Hospitality Industry under Uncertainty

Kuo-Jui Wu
Dalian University of Technology, China

Ming-Lang Tseng
Lunghwa University of Science and Technology, Taiwan

Li Cui
Dalian University of Technology, China

Jiayao Hu
The University of Nottingham, UK

Pham Minh Huy
Lunghwa University of Science and Technology, Taiwan

ABSTRACT

The hospitality industry is one of the fastest-growing industries in the world. The growth of this industry has been accompanied by issues of sustainability development. Employees expect firms to have the ability to address their negative impacts

DOI: 10.4018/978-1-5225-0956-1.ch012

on the environment and society. However, firms are generally unable to reach such expectations due to an inability to acquire feedback from employees, which leads to employee dissatisfaction. In addition, there has been a lack in the theoretical linkage between employee engagement and sustainability development. Thus, this study determines the critical factors of employee engagement based on big data (using social media and quantitative and qualitative data) and integrates such data by using decision-making tests and laboratory evaluation methods to identify these interrelationships. The findings reveal that sustainability development can be enhanced through aggressive employee engagement, which also can generate a positive influence on economic performance. A detailed discussion is also presented.

INTRODUCTION

The hospitality industry is one of the top service industries, and it provides the highest annual employment (15%) (Martínez et al., 2013). The hospitality industry generates employment and economic growth for local communities. However, to satisfy its expanding growth needs, the industry has had several negative impacts on the environment and society, including environmental degradation, unsatisfied customers, unstable and seasonal employment, and non-compliance with fundamental labor standards (Agarwal, 2002). Therefore, firms in the hospitality industry should take more responsibility with regard to social and environmental issues and minimize their negative impacts on sustainable development (Martínez et al., 2013). Social media has become an essential channel for employees to spread information about firm performance and sustainability development (Wu et al., 2016). Therefore, firms are expected to take more responsibility concerning such feedback and make the appropriate reflections to prevent negative impacts (O'Shaughnessy et al., 2007; Park & Ghauri, 2015). If firms ignore employee feedback, they may encounter problems with job satisfaction and employee engagement, which will result in lower productivity and decreased service quality (Bhattacharya et al., 2008).

In the literature, employee engagement refers to a situation in which employees feel satisfied in their work: if employees are satisfied, they will invest more effort and become more loyal to a firm (Schaufeli et al., 2002). Two triggers can lead to effective employee engagement: job satisfaction and job commitment (Schneider et al., 2005; Shuck & Wollard, 2009). These triggers occur only when employees consider their firm to be a worthwhile place to work and are proud of it (Alfalla-Luque et al., 2012). Once firms use such triggers, employees would voluntarily give greater effort and would prefer to cooperate in performing their job automatically, thus increasing the probability that the firm will attain better economic performance (Richman, 2006; Jung et al., 2010; Kuo, 2013). Similarly, the engagement of employees is a great motivation for firms to become concerned with the environment and social initiatives (O'Shaughnessy et al., 2007). Park and Ghauri (2015) indicated that employees are the primary actors who actively encourage firms to take action in environmental protections and social issues in the development of sustainability. Hence, employee engagement is a critical element for firms to improve sustainability (Richman, 2006; Karatepe, 2013; Thompson & Mathys, 2013).

Some studies have indicated that efforts by firms to develop sustainability helps raise job satisfaction and encourage employee engagement (Turker, 2009; Kim et al., 2010; Rego et al., 2010; Lee et al., 2012). Several studies have suggested that the practices of firms in protecting the environment increase employee awareness and make their work meaningful, which can also boost employee engagement (Rodrigo & Arenas, 2008; Ellemers et al., 2011). However, Farooq et al. (2014) argued that employees differ in their level of response to different types of initiatives. Although environmental initiatives are important to achieve sustainability for firms, employees pay attention to the economic benefits and social initiatives that can improve their welfare, rather than focus on environmental issues (Farooq et al., 2013; Farooq et al., 2014). Accordingly, Ferreira and de Oliveira (2014) emphasized that employees barely respond when firms engage in social initiatives that do not directly reflect their interests. Given that there is a gap in the literature with regard to the relationship between sustainability and employees, a study is needed to provide a theoretical basis to strengthen our understanding of the satisfaction and engagement of employees. Hence, two questions are proposed to clarify the gap in this area of research:

1. What are the driving and dependent powers of sustainability and employee engagement?
2. What are the cause and effect criteria of sustainability and employee engagement?

The proposed measures play a significant role in discovering the impacts of sustainability on employee engagement. However, the measures contain qualitative information and linguistic descriptions from social media and experts. Social media information and human judgements contain subjective opinions and preferences. Firms often suffer due to difficulties in analyzing such information in the decision making process. Thus, this study adopts big data (which refers to social media and quantitative and qualitative data) to acquire comprehensive results, and it proposes a fuzzy logic evaluation to overcome the limitations of statement-based data (Chang et al., 1998; Chen & Chiou, 1999; Tseng, 2010). At the same time, the interrelationship among the proposed aspects and criteria can be classified by decision-making tests and laboratory evaluations (DEMATEL). The fuzzy DEMATEL is an assessment tool that considers fuzziness and addresses uncertain conditions; it then maps the interrelationships into visual causal diagrams (Wu et al., 2015). The results of this study reveal that aggressive employee engagement enables hospitality firms to strengthen their performance in sustainability development. In particular, the performance of social initiatives is found to have a more significant influence on this process than environmental initiatives. The detailed discussion is organized as follows. Section 2 presents the proposed theories and measures. Section 3 provides a detailed illustration of the methodology, which contains big data, fuzzy set theory and the DEMATEL method. Section 4 presents the industrial background and empirical results. The theoretical and managerial implications are stated in Section 5. Conclusions and the research limitations of this study are addressed in the last section.

LITERATURE REVIEW

This section provides the background of employee engagement. The linkage between engagement and S is also addressed in this section. In addition, the proposed method and measures are discussed in the following subsection to illustrate the linkage between employee engagement and Sustainability

Employee Engagement

Kahn (1990) initially proposed the concept of employee engagement as personal engagement in work. Employee engagement describes how employees can experience a sense of connection and disconnection in their roles at work. Schaufeli et al. (2002) defined engagement as "a positive, fulfilling, work related state of mind that is characterized by vigor, dedication, and absorption." Vigor means that energy stays at a higher level due to mental resilience. Engaged employees are willing to invest their efforts in their work, can face difficulties, and can maintain enthusiasm. Dedication refers to a consciousness of meaning, passion, encouragement, satisfaction, and challenge. Further, absorption means to be fully concentrated in one's work; employees who experience absorption may have difficulty separating themselves from their work.

Employees are considered to be a firm's most valuable asset and cannot be duplicated or easily imitated by competitors. Thus, employee engagement is a critical element in the development of competitive advantage (Baumruk, 2004; Anitha, 2014). Previous studies have highlighted the importance of engagement to enhance employee motivation, job performance, productivity, commitment, service quality, and information retention (Xanthopoulou et al., 2008; Christian et al., 2011). Shuck and Wollard (2009) indicated that firms attempt to establish EE to ensure targeted outcomes with higher productivity and economic performance. Therefore, some studies have confirmed the benefits of engagement in the improvement of a firm's economic performance and business enhancement sustainability (Jung et al., 2010;

Richman, 2006; Maas & Reniers, 2014). Gallup (2002) illustrated that in addition to engaged employees, there are two other types of employees: "not engaged" employees and "actively disengaged" employees. Not-engaged employees focus on tasks without much action and effort, whereas actively disengaged employees have a negative impact on other employees; such employees do not perform their major tasks individually and have a negative influence on the motivation of other employees. To reduce these negative impacts, firms should diagnose the factors that enhance job satisfaction and increase engagement.

In the recent literature, increased attention has been given to the investigation of employee engagement from a management perspective rather than a psychological perspective (Karatepe, 2013; Karatepe & Demir, 2014; Sambrook et al., 2014; Lee & Ok, 2015). Previous studies have concentrated on the investigation of a psychological perspective to understand the structure of engagement; however, discussions on how to facilitate practices and manage relative issues have been lacking (Leiter & Maslach, 2010). Furthermore, these studies have provided insufficient managerial implications for firms; this limitation has generated gaps between theories and employee engagement (Sambrook et al., 2014; Maas & Reniers, 2014; Pérez & Bosque, 2014). Jones (2007) revealed that employee engagement may be enhanced by conducting environmental and social studies of firms. Other studies have shown that the effects of social and environmental initiatives on employees should be investigated (Farooq et al., 2014). Empirical studies are needed to support the concept of sustainability, which raises employee satisfaction and engagement (Gond & Igalens, 2011).

Employee Engagement and Sustainability

Laurence (2011) presented sustainability as a safe and efficient way to triple the bottom line (society, environment, and economy) simultaneously. Sustainability can reach these three aspects simultaneously, given the systematic linkage within the socio-economic environment, and the three aspects are addressed individually but ultimately integrated (Wang & Lin, 2007). Several studies have been conducted and have provided significant support in applying the triple bottom line to reach sustainability (Jamali, 2006; Markley & Davis, 2007; Carter & Rogers, 2008). Moreover, the triple bottom line is widely considered a framework within which to assess the performance of sustainability (Foran et al., 2005; Hubbard, 2009; Wang & Lin, 2007).

Hutchins and Sutherland (2008) indicated that sustainability requires firms to reduce the negative impacts of social and environmental systems while appropriately managing human resources as well as maximizing economic performance. Sustainability depends not only on the efforts that are made by management but also requires employee engagement (Cramer, 2005). Employee engagement can improve management efficiency and effectiveness. In addition, ethical and fair treatment are the essential requirements for employees to advance sustainability, and employees may resist the implementation of sustainability-related programs if they feel that such programs are unethical or unfair (Gopalakrishnan et al., 2012). Accordingly, employees play an important role in firms' development of sustainability (Thompson & Mathys, 2013).

However, sustainability can also encourage employee engagement. Several studies have offered evidence to support that environment and social initiatives can promote employee engagement, job satisfaction, business ethics, productivity, and economic performance (Brammer et al., 2007; Turker, 2009; Stites & Michael, 2011). However, Kim et al. (2010) argued that the performance of environment and society are effective in maintaining a positive relationship with employees. Employees will only appreciate and be satisfied with their work when firms perform well with their environmental and social initiatives; these initiatives relate directly to employees (Rodrigo & Arenas, 2008; Kim et al., 2010; Ellemers et al., 2011; Ferreira & de Oliveira, 2014). In summary, the environmental and social initiatives for the development of sustainability can enhance job satisfaction and engagement (Brammer et al., 2007; Turker, 2009; Stites & Michael, 2011).

Proposed Method and Measures

Most of the previous studies have adopted a qualitative approach and applied survey and basic statistical methods to demonstrate issues of employee engagement (Karatepe, 2013; Karatepe & Demir, 2014; Lee & Ok, 2015). To explore the drivers of employee engagement, Lee and Ok (2005) adopted hierarchical multiple regression analysis. Karatepe (2013) utilized structural equation modeling to recognize the effective relationship between employee engagement and job performance. Sambrook et al. (2014) proposed an autoethnographic approach to consider the insider and outsider phenomenon within employee engagement. However, few studies have focused on the interrelationship among employee engagement and sustainability factors under conditions of uncertainty. Hence, this study proposes a hybrid method that integrates fuzzy set theory and a DEMATEL method to overcome the gap. Fuzzy set theory addresses uncertain and subjective conditions and converts qualitative opinions into quantitative measures (Tseng et al., 2015). A DEMATEL approach enables the categorization of the factors into cause and effect groups and provides a visual analysis to facilitate decision-making.

Although the existing literature has proposed several aspects and criteria for employee engagement and sustainability, no studies have considered the interrelationship among these proposed aspects and criteria (Chi & Gursoy, 2009; Lozano & Huisingh, 2011; Lee et al., 2012; Karatepe, 2013; Matthews et al., 2014; Farooq et al.,

Table 1. Proposed aspects and criteria

Aspects	Criteria		References
Environmental initiatives (AS1)	C1	Reducing material consumption	Farooq et al. (2014); Matthews et al. (2014)
	C2	Decreasing water and energy utilization	
	C3	Contributing to environmental improvements	
Social initiatives (AS2)	C4	Establishing policies for balanced employee lives	Lozano and Huisingh (2011); Farooq et al. (2014)
	C5	Making fair judgments on behalf of employees	
	C6	Providing fair wages, welfare and working condition with legal working hours	
	C7	Offering career training and development	
	C8	Joining charitable activities	
	C9	Striving for corporate social responsibility	
Economic performance (AS3)	C10	Generating profitability from firm operations	Chi and Gursoy (2009)
	C11	Acquiring market presence and a good reputation	
	C12	Adding values for shareholders	
Employee engagement (AS4)	C13	Employees are willing to invest efforts in their work	Lee et al. (2012); Karatepe (2013)
	C14	Employees' pride in the firm	
	C15	Employees have enthusiasm for their work	
	C16	Employees are satisfied with their work and able to maintain satisfaction	
	C17	Firm demonstrates concern for employee commitment	

2014). To explore the critical factors of employee engagement in the development of sustainability, this study proposes four aspects to develop a framework and explore the critical factors for firms under conditions of uncertainty. These four aspects are environmental initiatives (AS1), social initiatives (AS2), economic performance (AS3), and employee engagement (AS4), as shown in Table 1.

Environmental initiatives refer to firm activities that prevent or improve negative impacts on the natural environment, such as 3R, adopting environmentally friendly products, hazardous waste management, and pollution control (Grimmer & Bingham, 2013). Given the exhaustion of natural resources, the public has become highly concerned with environmental initiatives (Sauvante, 2001). Increasing firm performance in terms of these initiatives can improve not only a firm's public reputation but also employee commitment (Turker, 2009; Ellemers et al., 2011; Christensen et al., 2013). Valentine and Fleischman (2008) demonstrated that the effects of environmental performance have a positive relationship with job satisfaction, and they showed that employees prefer to work in environmentally friendly firms. Furthermore, several studies have confirmed this positive relationship and stated that this relationship can reduce turnover intention and enhance employee engagement (Riordan et al., 1997; Collier & Esteban, 2007; Men, 2012).

Social initiatives represent the relationship among firms, employees, customers, legal systems, communities, educational programs, and governmental institutions (Dwyer, 2005). From the viewpoint of employee engagement, social initiatives are used to ensure employee welfare to support employees through good working conditions, vocation opportunities, organizational justice, family-friendly policies, and employee training and development (Turker, 2009). Once employees receive such rewards and benefits from firms, the employees' feedback will be reflected in their engagement and positive job outcomes (Cropanzano & Mitchell, 2005; Saks, 2006; Karatepe, 2011). In addition, social initiatives have several benefits, such as increasing employee loyalty, business ethics, and reputation (Henderson, 2007; Freeman et al., 2010). Thus, the purpose of social initiatives is to enhance job satisfaction and employee engagement (Kim et al., 2010).

Sustainability is measured by economic performance. Nevertheless, economic performance can be affected by many factors. Employee engagement is one of the important factors that can enhance economic performance and affect job performance, productivity, commitment, service quality, and maintenance (Xanthopoulou et al., 2008; Christian et al., 2011). Moreover, environmental and social initiatives have a positive influence on firm economic performance (Barnett & Salomon, 2006; Nicolau, 2008). If firms can generate profits, they also possess the ability to add value for shareholders and achieve the interests of other stakeholders (Nicolau, 2008). Thus, economic performance in developing sustainability should be assessed by evaluating market presence, profitability, and value adding.

Schaufeli et al. (2002) found that the features of employee engagement are vigor, dedication, and absorption. Employee engagement can be identified by the enthusiasm of employees and their willingness to invest effort in their work (Salanova et al., 2005). Several studies have indicated that a high level of employee engagement significantly decreases turnover intentions (Maslach et al., 2001; Saks, 2006). Thus, the results of employee engagement allow firms to enhance job satisfaction, commitment, and organizational citizenship behavior and reduce the intention to quit.

METHODOLOGY

This section illustrates the concepts of big data, fuzzy set theory and the DEMATEL approach and provides the proposed procedures for practitioners to demonstrate how the theories work. The empirical results are discussed in the next section.

Big Data

Social Media

This study refers to big data that are obtained from social media and quantitative and qualitative data. To gather social media data from websites, the Nvivo 10 software was adopted to capture the significant fragment terms and frequencies from several websites. These terms were used to identify the existence and frequency of the attributes through content analysis (Chan et al., 2015). However, the frequencies present a gray relational grade that needs to transfer into comparable weights in the computation, which is called entropy weight (Delgado & Romero, 2016; Wu et al., 2016).

Entropy weights are used to identify the impacts of social media in this study. Assuming there are x fragment terms and the accumulated frequencies are defined as $e_a, a = 1, 2, 3, \cdots x$. The value of e_a has to be normalized by the following equation:

$$\bar{e}_a = \frac{e_a}{\sum_{i=1}^{x} e_a} \quad (1)$$

Adopting normalized value $\bar{e}_a$ generates the entropy value E_a:

$$E_a = -(\ln x)^{-1} \times \sum_{i=1}^{n} \bar{e}_a \ln \bar{e}_a \quad (2)$$

Subsequently, computing the degree of divergence from the intrinsic information gives

$$E'a = 1 - E_a \quad (3)$$

Thus, the entropy weight $\tilde{E}a$ can be acquired through the following equation:

$$\tilde{E}a = \frac{E'a}{\sum_{i=1}^{x} E'a} \quad (4)$$

Quantitative Data

This study obtains data from firm financial statements that relate to the employee expenses over the past five years, such as the number of recruitments, welfare expenses, and insurance. Although these quantitative data are stated in the figures, they still lack the uniform units to make a comparison (Lin et al., 2014; Wu et al., 2016). Thus, these data must be transformed into comparable values using the following equations.

$$x_{ij} = \frac{x_{ij}^{b} - \min x_{ij}^{b}}{\max x_{ij}^{b} - \min x_{ij}^{b}}, x_{ij}^{b} \in [0,1], i = 1,2,\ldots \alpha, j = 1,2,\ldots \beta, b = 1,2,\ldots k \tag{5}$$

where $\min x_{ij}^{b} = \min\left(x_{11}^{1}, x_{12}^{1}, \cdots x_{ij}^{k}\right)$ and $\max x_{ij}^{b} = \max\left(x_{11}^{1}, x_{12}^{1}, \cdots x_{ij}^{k}\right)$

Aggregating the related expenses for n^{th} terms from all firms' gives

$$x_{ij}^{n} = \frac{\sum_{j=1}^{\beta} x_{ij}}{j \times n} \tag{6}$$

Fuzzy Set Theory

Expert judgments have been considered extensively in attempts to solve the problem of decision-making. However, such judgments give rise to vague, imprecise, and qualitative information. To consider these features, fuzzy set theory is adopted to overcome the uncertainty and convert qualitative information into quantitative evaluations. Additionally, fuzzy logic is required in the conversion process because each number can indicate a partial truth and present numerical correspondence within the range between 0 and 1. Thus, this study proposes triangular fuzzy numbers (TFNs) as the numerical correspondence to convert expert linguistic terms, as shown in Table 2.

At the beginning of the conversion process, a universe of discourse $D = \{a, b, \ldots, n\}$ exists. Subsequently, using a fuzzy set λ denotes a pair of D as $\{(a, f_\lambda(a)), (b, f_\lambda(b)), \cdots, (n, f_\lambda(n))\}$. Thus, $f_\lambda(D)$ is a membership function of λ, which belongs to the range of 0 to 1. Conversely, $f_\lambda(a)$ expresses the degree of membership a within the fuzzy set λ. Several essential definitions and notations

Table 2. Corresponding TFNs

Scale	Linguistic Terms	TFNs	Triangular Fuzzy Membership Functions
1	No influence	(0, 0.1, 0.3)	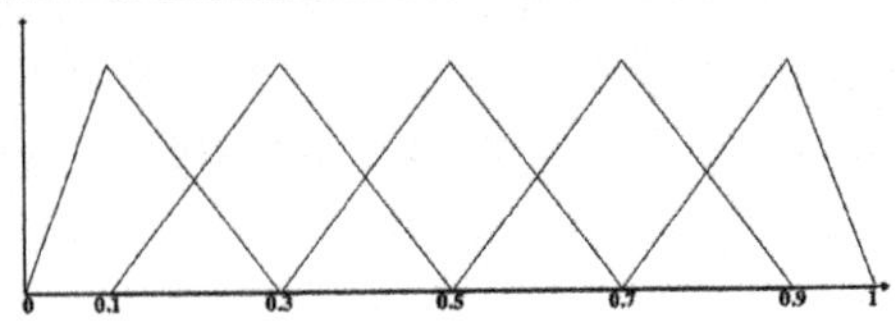
2	Very low influence	(0.1, 0.3, 0.5)	
3	Low influence	(0.3, 0.5, 0.7)	
4	High influence	(0.5, 0.7, 0.9)	
5	Very high influence	(0.7, 0.9, 1.0)	

of fuzzy set theory were proposed by Chen (1996), Cheng and Lin (2002), Tseng (2010) and Wu et al. (2015):

Definition 1: Fuzzy set λ is defined as λ^i or λ^f based on the D if it is an infinite or a finite set:

$$\lambda^i = \frac{\int_D f_\lambda(d_i)}{d}, d \in D \text{, then D is an infinite set}$$

$$\lambda^f = \frac{\sum_i f_\lambda(d_i)}{(d_i)}, d_i \in D \text{, then D is a finite set}$$

Definition 2: When a fuzzy set λ is a normal universe of discourse D, and the membership function $f_\lambda(D)$ must meet $\max f_\lambda(D) = 1$.

Definition 3: A TFN can be expressed as a triplet (l, m, r); the membership function of the fuzzy number λ is expressed as follows:

$$f_\lambda(D) = \begin{cases} 0, D \prec l \\ \dfrac{(D-l)}{(m-l)}, l \le x \le m \\ \dfrac{(r-D)}{(r-m)}, m \le x \le r \\ 0, D \succ r \end{cases}$$

Given that expert judgments are stated as linguistic terms and categorized into TFNs, a defuzzification method is needed to make all fuzzy data measurable. Defuzzification selects a specific crisp element and converts the TFNs into crisp values. This study adopts a fuzzy max-min method to make conversions and to determine the left and right values, as proposed by Opricovic and Tzeng (2003). Accordingly, the computation of a total score is acquired from the weighted average, which can be obtained from the membership function.

Assuming there are q experts to make judgments, these judgments can be rewritten as TFN $j_{\alpha\beta} = \left(\dot{j}^{lq}_{\alpha\beta}, \dot{j}^{mq}_{\alpha\beta}, \dot{j}^{rq}_{\alpha\beta}\right)$. TFN represents the degree that criterion α influences criterion β under q^{th} expert's judgment. Once the judgments are finished by all q experts, normalization can be conducted through max-min method:

$$\begin{cases} \forall \dot{j}^{lq}_{\alpha\beta} = \dfrac{\left(\dot{j}^{lq}_{\alpha\beta} - \min \dot{j}^{lq}_{\alpha\beta}\right)}{\Delta^{\max}_{\min}} \\ \forall \dot{j}^{mq}_{\alpha\beta} = \dfrac{\left(\dot{j}^{mq}_{\alpha\beta} - \min \dot{j}^{lq}_{\alpha\beta}\right)}{\Delta^{\max}_{\min}} \\ \forall \dot{j}^{rq}_{\alpha\beta} = \dfrac{\left(\dot{j}^{rq}_{\alpha\beta} - \min \dot{j}^{lq}_{\alpha\beta}\right)}{\Delta^{\max}_{\min}} \end{cases} \tag{7}$$

where $\Delta^{\max}_{\min} = \max \dot{j}^{rq}_{\alpha\beta} - \min \dot{j}^{lq}_{\alpha\beta}$

The normalized left (l) and right (r) values are gathered:

$$\begin{cases} \forall l^{q}_{\alpha\beta} = \dfrac{\forall \dot{j}^{mq}_{\alpha\beta}}{\left(1 + \forall \dot{j}^{mq}_{\alpha\beta} - \forall \dot{j}^{lq}_{\alpha\beta}\right)} \\ \forall r^{q}_{\alpha\beta} = \dfrac{\forall \dot{j}^{rq}_{\alpha\beta}}{\left(1 + \forall \dot{j}^{rq}_{\alpha\beta} - \forall \dot{j}^{mq}_{\alpha\beta}\right)} \end{cases} \tag{8}$$

The total normalized crisp values $\forall^{q}_{\alpha\beta}$ are calculated:

$$\forall^{q}_{\alpha\beta} = \frac{\left[\forall l^{q}_{\alpha\beta} \times \left(1 - \forall l^{q}_{\alpha\beta}\right) + \left(\forall r^{q}_{\alpha\beta}\right)^{2}\right]}{\left(1 - \forall l^{q}_{\alpha\beta} + \forall r^{q}_{\alpha\beta}\right)} \tag{9}$$

The total crisp values are obtained:

$$\theta^{q}_{\alpha\beta} = \min j^{lq}_{\alpha\beta} + \forall^{q}_{\alpha\beta} \times \Delta^{\max}_{\min} \tag{10}$$

Finally, the crisp values are aggregated:

$$\theta^{q}_{\alpha\beta} = \frac{\left(\sum_{1}^{q} \theta^{q}_{\alpha\beta}\right)}{q} \tag{11}$$

DEMATEL

The DEMATEL method has been extensively applied for problem solving in complicated systems and has received much attention from researchers and practitioners in multi-criteria decision-making (Patil & Kant, 2014; Wu et al., 2015). The DEMATEL method can categorize factors into cause and effect groups and map these factors in diagrams to provide a visual analysis for decision makers. Previous studies have experienced difficulties in considering the interrelationship among factors. The DEMATEL method not only overcomes this difficulty but also reduces the complexity of searching for critical factors through quadrant division.

Before applying the DEMATEL method, the first priority is to arrange all of the crisp values from fuzzy set theory in a pairwise comparison, which can denote the comparison as a direct relation matrix $T^{d}_{n \times n} = \left[\theta^{q}_{\alpha\beta}\right]_{n \times n}$. This step is conducted to normalize the direct relation matrix. The following equations are used to obtain the normalized matrix $T_{n \times n}$:

$$T_{n \times n} = \Delta \times T^{d}_{n \times n}, \Delta = \frac{1}{\max\limits_{1 \le a \le n} \sum_{\beta=1}^{n} \theta_{\alpha\beta}} \tag{12}$$

Subsequently, identity matrix I is used to attain the total relation matrix $\overline{T}_{n \times n}$:

$$\overline{T}_{n \times n} = T'_{n \times n} \times \left(I - T_{n \times n}\right)^{-1} \tag{13}$$

Vectors D and R can be obtained by summing the rows and columns in the total relation matrix. The vectors can be computed using the following equations:

$$\begin{cases} \bar{T}_{n\times n} = \left[\bar{\theta}_{\alpha\beta}\right]_{n\times n}, \alpha, \beta = 1, 2, \cdots n \\ D = \left[\sum_{\alpha=1}^{n} \bar{\theta}_{\alpha\beta}\right]_{n\times 1} = \left[\bar{\theta}_{\alpha}\right]_{n\times 1} \\ R = \left[\sum_{\beta=1}^{n} \bar{\theta}_{\alpha\beta}\right]_{1\times n} = \left[\bar{\theta}_{\beta}\right]_{1\times n} \end{cases} \tag{14}$$

$(D+R)$ and $(D-R)$ are utilized to represent the horizontal and vertical axes in the driving-dependence power diagram. When the criterion satisfies $(D-R) > 0$, this criterion can be considered a driving factor. Contrarily, if the criterion falls into $(D-R) < 0$, then the criterion is considered a dependence factor. The horizontal axis $(D+R)$ presents the importance of the criterion. A higher value of $(D+R)$ means that the criterion has greater importance than other criteria. In addition, the diagram can be divided into four quadrants to determine the driving factors. The criteria that are located in quadrant I have high influence and can affect other criteria. Quadrant II presents the voluntary factors that have high influence but low importance. Quadrant III indicates the criteria with low influence and importance. Quadrant IV is called the core problem. The criteria that are located in this quadrant are important but suffer the difficulty of improving by themselves. Significant improvements could only be achieved through other criteria with higher influence.

Proposed Analytical Procedures

1. Collecting relevant information – relevant information must be collected from social media and an expert group, and academic researchers should be included in the expert group to purify the fragment terms from literature reviews to enhance the study's validity. To ensure reliability and consistency in the evaluation process, the experts were required to have a strong working knowledge and working experience related to sustainability development and employee engagement for at least ten years.
2. Transferring the data into comparable units – the frequencies need to adopt Eqs. (1)-(4) to transfer into entropy weight, then quantitative data are required to apply Eqs. (5) and (6) to unify the units. In addition, the experts' response is stated in linguistic terms, which should utilize Eqs. (7)-(11) to normalize into crisp values.
3. Applying the DEMATEL method – this step uses Eqs. (12) and (13) to attain the total relation matrix to generate a cause and effect diagram.

4. Aggregating entropy weights and normalized quantitative data – once the total relation matrix is obtained, all of the transferred data need to be aggregated into a total relation matrix. Consequently, the vectors D and R must be obtained through Eq. (14).
5. Generating the cause and effect diagram – mapping aspects and criteria that are based on the coordinates $\left[\left(D+R\right),\left(D-R\right)\right]$, which can provide decision makers with a visual analysis.

EMPIRICAL RESULTS

This section presents the case information to provide an overview in the Vietnam hospitality industry. The driving and dependence power for aspects and a cause and effect diagram for criteria are presented in the following subsections.

Industrial Background

The hospitality industry is undergoing expansion and diversification, and it has become one of the largest and fastest-growing economic sectors in the world (UNWTO Tourism Highlights, 2013). In Vietnam, this industry is considered to support an important strategy in socio-economic development because it can provide working opportunities, attract foreign investments, and accelerate development in rural areas. Accordingly, the hospitality industry not only provides a venue for customers to relieve stresses but also plays an important role in directly or indirectly affecting the Vietnamese society and economy. However, the industry has encountered difficulty in maintaining well-qualified employees, a lower turnover rate, and engaged workers in the development of sustainability, which implies that there are limitations for industry growth. These features indicate that the Vietnam National Administration of Tourism needs to establish regulations to ensure the rights of employees and require firms to follow these regulations in developing their human resources management.

The purpose of this study is to explore the critical factors of employee engagement to assist firms in the development of sustainability. The research process for this study involved uncertainty. There are interrelationships among the proposed aspects and criteria that have not been considered in previous studies. Thus, a fuzzy DEMATEL method was adopted in the present study to overcome uncertainty and to reflect the interrelationships in the analysis. Surveys were translated into Vietnamese and sent by e-mail to 21 experts, including professors, CEOs, VPs, senior managers, and engineers who have more than ten years of relevant working experience in the hospitality industry. The responses from the experts are stated in the linguistic scale. The responses were converted into TFNs as shown in Table 1. The detailed case analysis and results are discussed in the following sections with significant insights to guide Vietnam hospitality firms in addressing employee engagement and the development of sustainability.

CASE ANALYSIS

This section provides a detailed description of the process of data analysis and the results. The driving and dependence power for aspects and a cause-and-effect diagram are shown in the following subsections.

Driving and Dependence Power for Aspects

1. Table 3 presents the sample of the experts' responses. The sample was stated on a linguistic scale, which needed to be converted into the corresponding TFNs. These TFNs needed to be normalized first by adopting Eq. (7) to (10). The results of the normalization are shown in Table 4.
2. Eq. (11) is utilized to aggregate all of the experts' crisp values and transfer them to the DEMATEL direct relation matrix (Table 5). This direct relation matrix must be normalized through Eq. (12). Subsequently, applying Eq. (13) obtains the total relation matrix, as shown in Table 6.
3. The total relation matrix is associated with Eq. (14) to acquire the driving and dependence power $\left(D+R\right)$ and $\left(D-R\right)$, as shown in Table 7. These aspects are arranged into a diagram of driving and dependence power. AS3 is the only aspect with the lowest driving power, which represents that the aspect is affected by AS1, AS2, and AS4.
4. Figure 1 shows that the highest driving power is AS2, and the highest dependence power is AS4. Therefore, AS2 drives the effects with AS1 and AS3 and then interacts with AS4. AS4 interacts with AS2 and AS1. AS1 has the lowest dependence power, which is affected by AS2 and AS4.

Table 3. Sample of expert responses and corresponding TFNs

	Responses				Corresponding TFNs			
	AS1	AS2	AS3	AS4	AS1	AS2	AS3	AS4
AS1	1	1	1	1	(0.0,0.1,0.3)	(0.0,0.1,0.3)	(0.0,0.1,0.3)	(0.0,0.1,0.3)
AS2	3	2	3	2	(0.3,0.5,0.7)	(0.1,0.3,0.5)	(0.3,0.5,0.7)	(0.1,0.3,0.5)
AS3	3	2	3	2	(0.3,0.5,0.7)	(0.1,0.3,0.5)	(0.3,0.5,0.7)	(0.1,0.3,0.5)
AS4	3	3	3	2	(0.3,0.5,0.7)	(0.3,0.5,0.7)	(0.3,0.5,0.7)	(0.1,0.3,0.5)

Table 4. Normalization of expert responses

	AS1	$(\forall l^1_{AS1\beta}, \forall r^1_{AS1\beta})$	$\forall^1_{AS1\beta}$	$\theta^1_{AS1\beta}$	AS2	$(\forall l^1_{AS2\beta}, \forall r^1_{AS2\beta})$	$\forall^1_{AS2\beta}$	$\theta^1_{AS2\beta}$
AS1	(0.000,0.000,0.000)	(0.000,0.000)	0.000	0.000	(0.000,0.000,0.000)	(0.000,0.000)	0.000	0.000
AS2	(0.429,0.571,0.571)	(0.500,0.571)	0.538	0.377	(0.143,0.286,0.286)	(0.250,0.286)	0.260	0.182
AS3	(0.429,0.571,0.571)	(0.500,0.571)	0.538	0.377	(0.143,0.286,0.286)	(0.250,0.286)	0.260	0.182
AS4	(0.429,0.571,0.571)	(0.500,0.571)	0.538	0.377	(0.429,0.571,0.571)	(0.500,0.571)	0.538	0.377
	AS3	$(\forall l^1_{AS3\beta}, \forall r^1_{AS3\beta})$	$\forall^1_{AS3\beta}$	$\theta^1_{AS3\beta}$	AS4	$(\forall l^1_{AS4\beta}, \forall r^1_{AS4\beta})$	$\forall^1_{AS4\beta}$	$\theta^1_{AS4\beta}$
AS1	(0.000,0.000,0.000)	(0.000,0.000)	0.000	0.000	(0.000,0.000,0.000)	(0.000,0.000)	0.000	0.000
AS2	(0.429,0.571,0.571)	(0.500,0.571)	0.538	0.377	(0.200,0.400,0.400)	(0.333,0.400)	0.358	0.179
AS3	(0.429,0.571,0.571)	(0.500,0.571)	0.538	0.377	(0.200,0.400,0.400)	(0.333,0.400)	0.358	0.179
AS4	(0.429,0.571,0.571)	(0.500,0.571)	0.538	0.377	(0.200,0.400,0.400)	(0.333,0.400)	0.358	0.179

Table 5. Direct relation matrix of aspects

	AS1	AS2	AS3	AS4
AS1	0.000	1.117	1.315	1.516
AS2	1.114	0.000	1.708	2.109
AS3	1.114	0.922	0.000	1.122
AS4	1.309	1.510	1.909	0.000

Table 6. Total relation matrix of aspects

	AS1	AS2	AS3	AS4
AS1	0.995	1.181	1.506	1.461
AS2	1.376	1.194	1.813	1.774
AS3	1.014	0.988	1.080	1.208
AS4	1.343	1.368	1.760	1.398

Table 7. Driving and dependence power for aspects

	D	R	Dependence Power (D+R)	Driving Power (D-R)
AS1	5.142	4.728	9.871	0.414
AS2	6.158	4.730	10.888	1.428
AS3	4.290	6.160	10.449	(1.870)
AS4	5.869	5.840	11.710	0.029

Cause and Effect Diagram for Criteria

1. The analysis of the criteria follows almost the same procedure as that of the aspects. However, there is a major difference in considering the social media and quantitative data by applying Eqs. (1) to (4) into the total relation matrix. The entropy weights of social media and the transformations of the quantitative data are listed separately in the Table 8.
2. The experts' responses need to be normalized and transferred from the TFNs into crisp values. Then, the crisp values must be arranged into the DEMATEL direct relation matrix, as shown in Table 9.

Figure 1. Diagram of driving and dependence power

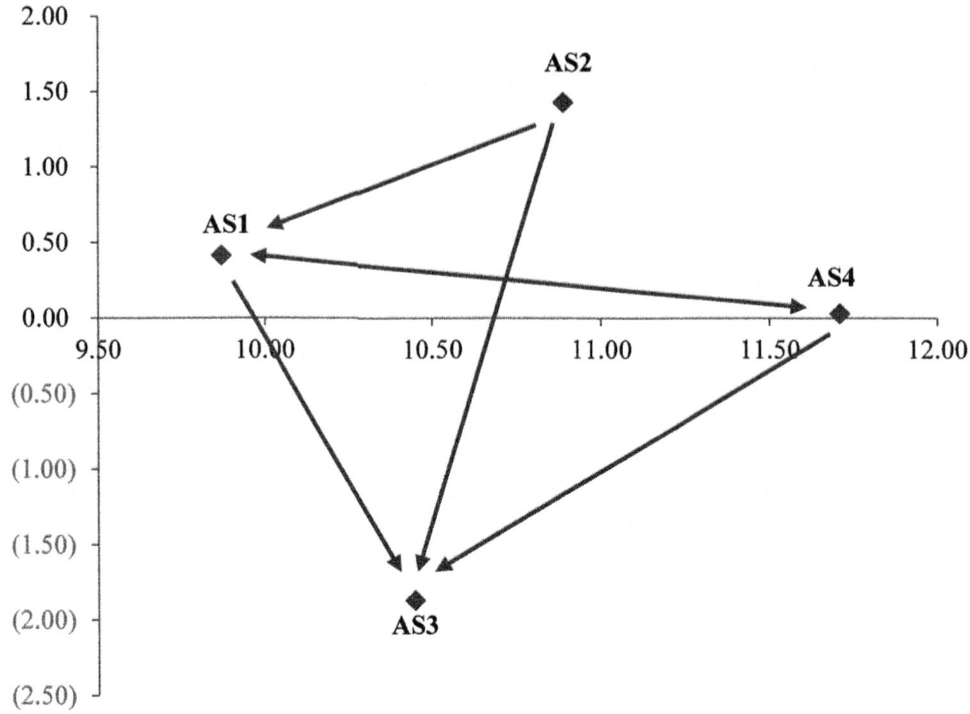

3. Table 10 presents the normalized results from the direct relation matrix and integrates them with the social media and quantitative data, which is referred to as the total integrated relation matrix. Once the total integrated relation matrix is obtained, the cause and effect group can be identified through $(D-R)>0$. Table 11 presents C2 to C7 and C13 are categorized in the cause group; C1, C8 to C12 and C14 to C17 are the effect group. C4 has the highest influence and is the most important criterion; C9 has the least importance among the criteria.
4. Figure 2 shows that C4 has the most important influence on the other criteria; the subsequent order is C7, C6, C2 and C3. The comparison of the experts' responses given in Figure 3 demonstrates that these criteria are the critical factors of employee engagement. Although the social media and quantitative data are integrated into the experts' responses, it still reflects the same result as experts' judgement. In addition, Figure 3 provides a visual analysis from an expert's viewpoint.

Table 8. Entropy weight and quantitative data transformation

	Social Media					Quantitative Data
	Frequency	Ratio	Normalize	Entropy	Entropy Weight	Transformation
C1	2475	0.0287	0.0367	0.9633	0.0602	0.0728
C2	9915	0.1148	0.0896	0.9104	0.0569	0.1860
C3	7642	0.0885	0.0774	0.9226	0.0576	0.1654
C4	6604	0.0765	0.0709	0.9291	0.0580	0.4483
C5	1434	0.0166	0.0245	0.9755	0.0609	0.1430
C6	6967	0.0807	0.0732	0.9268	0.0579	0.2804
C7	8570	0.0992	0.0827	0.9173	0.0573	0.3263
C8	2531	0.0293	0.0373	0.9627	0.0601	0.0777
C9	2464	0.0285	0.0366	0.9634	0.0602	0.0235
C10	8408	0.0974	0.0818	0.9182	0.0574	0.0038
C11	4588	0.0531	0.0562	0.9438	0.0590	0.0800
C12	5427	0.0628	0.0627	0.9373	0.0586	0.0551
C13	2402	0.0278	0.0359	0.9641	0.0602	0.1809
C14	8635	0.1000	0.0830	0.9170	0.0573	0.0015
C15	3803	0.0440	0.0496	0.9504	0.0594	0.0549
C16	4497	0.0521	0.0555	0.9445	0.0590	0.0067
C17	2826	0.0327	0.0404	0.9596	0.0600	0.0229

IMPLICATIONS

This section presents the theoretical and managerial implications for developing sustainability and employee engagement. Several direct influences and interactions are addressed in the following section.

Theoretical Implications

Several studies have demonstrated that environmental initiatives can generate benefits to encourage employee engagement (Brammer et al., 2007; Ellemers et al., 2011; Stites & Michael, 2011). This study not only confirmed the direct impacts between environmental initiatives and employee engagement but also determined the interactions. For example, if firms can decrease their water and energy utilization and contribute to environmental improvement, then they can increase their firm image and ethical reputation. When firms obtain a good public reputation, employees are

Table 9. Direct relation matrix for criteria

	C1	C2	C3	C4	C5	C6	C7	C8	C9	C10	C11	C12	C13	C14	C15	C16	C17
C1	0.000	0.394	0.394	0.367	0.385	0.384	0.394	0.394	0.403	0.394	0.394	0.394	0.404	0.409	0.413	0.412	0.411
C2	0.424	0.000	0.424	0.397	0.424	0.424	0.424	0.424	0.424	0.424	0.424	0.424	0.433	0.439	0.433	0.442	0.440
C3	0.439	0.439	0.000	0.421	0.439	0.439	0.439	0.439	0.449	0.439	0.439	0.439	0.448	0.454	0.449	0.448	0.449
C4	0.458	0.458	0.458	0.000	0.458	0.468	0.458	0.458	0.450	0.458	0.458	0.458	0.468	0.473	0.449	0.475	0.467
C5	0.421	0.440	0.421	0.375	0.000	0.422	0.421	0.422	0.421	0.233	0.421	0.421	0.431	0.428	0.450	0.431	0.447
C6	0.460	0.469	0.459	0.414	0.460	0.000	0.460	0.459	0.459	0.459	0.460	0.459	0.513	0.436	0.460	0.495	0.495
C7	0.430	0.430	0.430	0.405	0.430	0.439	0.000	0.420	0.430	0.496	0.430	0.430	0.464	0.436	0.420	0.466	0.431
C8	0.423	0.423	0.458	0.358	0.413	0.413	0.423	0.000	0.423	0.367	0.423	0.432	0.475	0.400	0.423	0.476	0.450
C9	0.404	0.394	0.420	0.348	0.423	0.404	0.394	0.375	0.000	0.394	0.384	0.394	0.493	0.371	0.394	0.448	0.413
C10	0.438	0.438	0.464	0.421	0.205	0.456	0.271	0.438	0.438	0.000	0.429	0.430	0.195	0.203	0.148	0.490	0.465
C11	0.357	0.442	0.357	0.415	0.432	0.432	0.432	0.432	0.432	0.440	0.000	0.413	0.450	0.391	0.195	0.357	0.451
C12	0.357	0.367	0.392	0.331	0.357	0.375	0.357	0.357	0.357	0.383	0.357	0.000	0.366	0.156	0.319	0.411	0.384
C13	0.205	0.480	0.270	0.263	0.451	0.451	0.214	0.461	0.451	0.496	0.477	0.451	0.000	0.437	0.451	0.176	0.461
C14	0.214	0.401	0.408	0.365	0.401	0.401	0.392	0.392	0.420	0.409	0.575	0.392	0.428	0.000	0.374	0.382	0.539
C15	0.310	0.433	0.450	0.406	0.424	0.433	0.433	0.414	0.433	0.442	0.424	0.433	0.442	0.429	0.000	0.252	0.469
C16	0.280	0.412	0.401	0.356	0.393	0.364	0.383	0.393	0.383	0.383	0.383	0.383	0.382	0.363	0.355	0.000	0.409
C17	0.214	0.271	0.412	0.385	0.402	0.421	0.412	0.421	0.412	0.498	0.412	0.412	0.412	0.399	0.404	0.430	0.000

Table 10. Total integrated relation matrix for criteria

	C1	C2	C3	C4	C5	C6	C7	C8	C9	C10	C11	C12	C13	C14	C15	C16	C17
C1	0.0015	0.0019	0.0019	0.0018	0.0019	0.0019	0.0018	0.0019	0.0020	0.0019	0.0020	0.0020	0.0020	0.0018	0.0018	0.0019	0.0021
C2	0.0045	0.0044	0.0050	0.0046	0.0049	0.0050	0.0048	0.0050	0.0051	0.0050	0.0051	0.0051	0.0051	0.0047	0.0047	0.0050	0.0053
C3	0.0042	0.0047	0.0041	0.0043	0.0046	0.0047	0.0044	0.0047	0.0047	0.0047	0.0048	0.0047	0.0047	0.0044	0.0043	0.0046	0.0050
C4	0.0118	0.0133	0.0131	0.0106	0.0129	0.0134	0.0126	0.0133	0.0134	0.0133	0.0136	0.0134	0.0135	0.0125	0.0123	0.0132	0.0141
C5	0.0036	0.0040	0.0040	0.0036	0.0035	0.0040	0.0038	0.0040	0.0041	0.0038	0.0041	0.0041	0.0041	0.0038	0.0038	0.0040	0.0043
C6	0.0074	0.0083	0.0082	0.0075	0.0081	0.0074	0.0079	0.0083	0.0084	0.0083	0.0085	0.0084	0.0085	0.0078	0.0077	0.0083	0.0089
C7	0.0080	0.0090	0.0089	0.0082	0.0088	0.0091	0.0076	0.0090	0.0091	0.0092	0.0093	0.0091	0.0092	0.0085	0.0084	0.0090	0.0096
C8	0.0020	0.0022	0.0022	0.0020	0.0021	0.0022	0.0021	0.0020	0.0022	0.0022	0.0023	0.0022	0.0023	0.0021	0.0020	0.0022	0.0023
C9	0.0006	0.0006	0.0006	0.0006	0.0006	0.0006	0.0006	0.0006	0.0006	0.0006	0.0006	0.0006	0.0007	0.0006	0.0006	0.0006	0.0007
C10	0.0001	0.0001	0.0001	0.0001	0.0001	0.0001	0.0001	0.0001	0.0001	0.0001	0.0001	0.0001	0.0001	0.0001	0.0001	0.0001	0.0001
C11	0.0019	0.0021	0.0021	0.0019	0.0021	0.0021	0.0020	0.0021	0.0022	0.0021	0.0019	0.0021	0.0022	0.0020	0.0018	0.0021	0.0023
C12	0.0011	0.0013	0.0013	0.0012	0.0012	0.0013	0.0012	0.0013	0.0013	0.0013	0.0013	0.0011	0.0013	0.0011	0.0012	0.0013	0.0014
C13	0.0039	0.0048	0.0045	0.0041	0.0047	0.0048	0.0042	0.0048	0.0048	0.0049	0.0049	0.0048	0.0042	0.0045	0.0044	0.0044	0.0051
C14	0.0000	0.0000	0.0000	0.0000	0.0000	0.0000	0.0000	0.0000	0.0000	0.0000	0.0000	0.0000	0.0000	0.0000	0.0000	0.0000	0.0000
C15	0.0013	0.0015	0.0015	0.0014	0.0015	0.0015	0.0014	0.0015	0.0015	0.0015	0.0015	0.0015	0.0015	0.0014	0.0012	0.0014	0.0016
C16	0.0001	0.0002	0.0002	0.0002	0.0002	0.0002	0.0002	0.0002	0.0002	0.0002	0.0002	0.0002	0.0002	0.0002	0.0002	0.0001	0.0002
C17	0.0005	0.0006	0.0006	0.0006	0.0006	0.0006	0.0006	0.0006	0.0006	0.0006	0.0006	0.0006	0.0006	0.0006	0.0006	0.0006	0.0006

Table 11. Cause and effect group for criteria

Criteria	D	R	Effect (D + R)	Cause (D - R)
C1	0.0321	0.0525	0.0846	(0.0204)
C2	0.0832	0.0591	0.1423	0.0240
C3	0.0775	0.0583	0.1359	0.0192
C4	0.2203	0.0526	0.2729	0.1677
C5	0.0666	0.0577	0.1244	0.0089
C6	0.1380	0.0591	0.1971	0.0790
C7	0.1502	0.0554	0.2056	0.0948
C8	0.0365	0.0595	0.0960	(0.0230)
C9	0.0105	0.0603	0.0709	(0.0498)
C10	0.0015	0.0600	0.0615	(0.0585)
C11	0.0351	0.0609	0.0960	(0.0258)
C12	0.0211	0.0601	0.0812	(0.0390)
C13	0.0780	0.0602	0.1382	0.0178
C14	0.0006	0.0560	0.0566	(0.0553)
C15	0.0250	0.0551	0.0801	(0.0301)
C16	0.0028	0.0588	0.0616	(0.0561)
C17	0.0101	0.0635	0.0736	(0.0535)

not only willing to invest more effort and find high satisfaction in their work but also feel proud of their firms. Consequently, the effective implementation of environmental initiatives will result in increased employee engagement (Turker, 2009; Christensen et al., 2013).

Social initiatives have a direct influence on environmental initiatives and economic performance and interact with employee engagement. Social initiatives require firms to offer career training and development; provide fair wages, welfare, and decent working conditions with legal working hours, contribute to charitable activities, and establish policies for balance employees' lives. Job commitment and performance are improved when employees receive adequate compensation and rewards (Cropanzano & Mitchell, 2005; Karatepe, 2011). Furthermore, people prefer to work for firms that maintain corporate social responsibility (Valentine & Fleischman, 2008). Hence, economic performance can be improved by carrying out social initiatives to promote employee engagement; when employee engagement is improved, firms can reduce training costs and increase productivity (Riordan et al., 1997; Jung et al., 2010; Maas & Reniers, 2014).

Figure 2. Cause and effect diagram for criteria

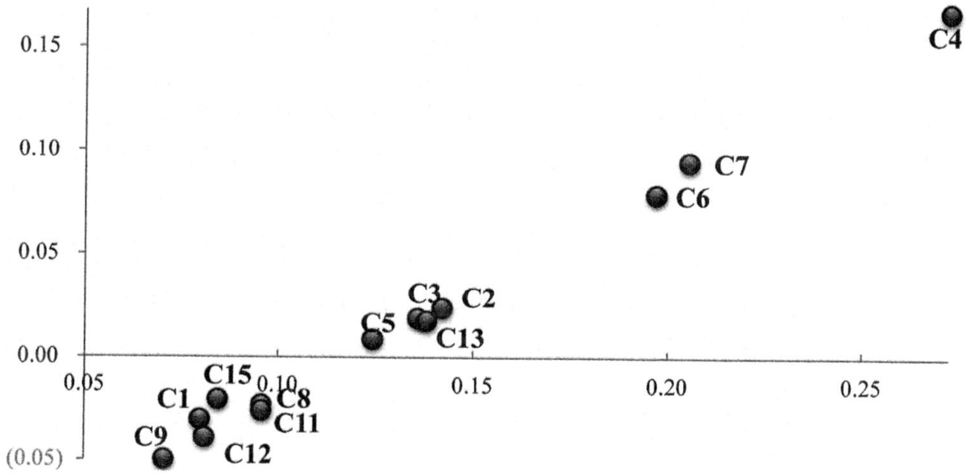

Figure 3. Cause and effect diagram from experts' respondent

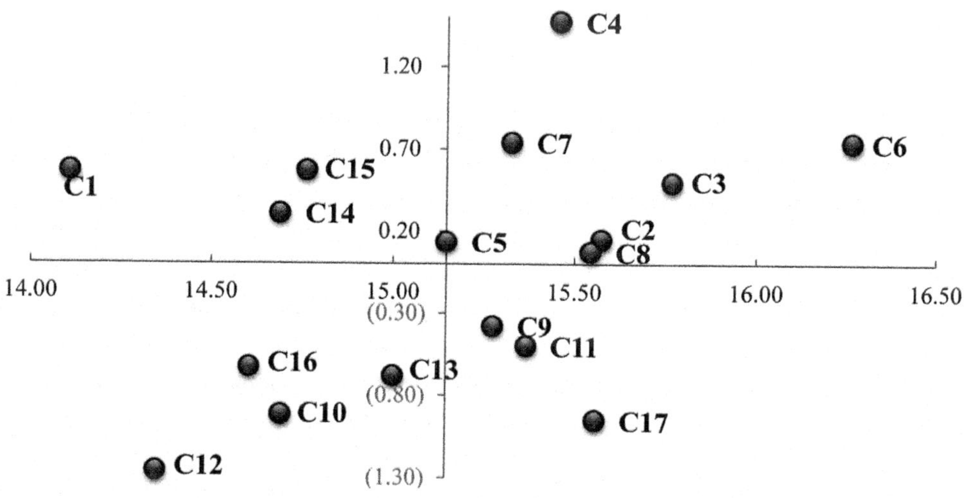

Employee engagement interacts with both environmental and social initiatives, which can directly affect economic performance. Firms are concerned with the commitment of employees, which is the critical problem in employee engagement. If firms can develop employee engagement, customer loyalty will be improved, which will positively affects the firms' economic performance. Several studies have confirmed that when firms succeed in establishing employee engagement, they can reduce employee turnover rate, save on the costs of recruiting and training new workers and removing opportunities for disruptions to business operations (Richman, 2006; Kuo, 2013; Maas & Reniers, 2014).

This study reveals that economic performance is influenced by social initiatives, environmental initiatives, and employee engagement in the development of sustainability. This study also confirms the role of employee engagement in assisting firms to improve their economic performance (Richman, 2006; Maas & Reniers, 2014). In addition, the evidence supports that firms can promote employee engagement by considering sustainability development (Turker, 2009; Kim et al., 2010; Rego et al., 2010; Lee et al., 2012). However, the results of this study have a different viewpoint than that of Farooq et al. (2014), who proposed that environmental protection has no significant influence on employee engagement.

Managerial Implications

Employees have the right to manage their time and energy between work and other activities. This is an important rule that helps employees maintain job productivity and satisfaction. Therefore, establishing policies to balance employees' lives (C4) has the highest influence among the other factors. The working life of employees resembles a rubber band: employees cannot be too engaged with work, or they will experience fatigue. In the hospitality industry, employees are susceptible to stress, which can result in decreased productivity, job dissatisfaction, burnout, and service misbehavior (Lee & Ok, 2015). If firms have policies that can encourage employees to take leave for several days, such a policy will play an important role in balancing employees' lives. To ensure the quality of service in the hospitality industry, relevant government departments should consult with several benchmarking firms to establish policies, such as flexibility in work schedules, frequent breaks, and adequate absence or vacation policies.

Offering career training and development (C7) is an essential criterion to guarantee employee engagement (Kaliprasad, 2006). Most employees expect that their career can also provide guidelines for their lives. The provision of opportunities for employees to learn different skills is a good way to improve firm flexibility. Employees may combine their new skills into their current work to assist firms in decreasing costs or enhancing production efficiency. The hospitality industry focuses on service. Firms can offer diverse training courses and help employees develop skills that add value for customers. Thus, firms must offer career training and development to expand the awareness of employees in developing sustainability; the firms can then aggressively engage and reward employees in relevant activities that will enhance firm reputation.

Providing fair wages, welfare, and decent working conditions with legal working hours (C6) is of the highest importance and influence on social initiatives. From the viewpoint of employees, this criterion is the primary consideration for working in a firm. Hence, employees need to ensure their own welfare (Turker, 2009). However, a fair wage is the most critical issue for firms to consider because several negative impacts can be generated due to unfair payment and workloads (Kaliprasad, 2006). When wages and welfare do not reflect the efforts of employees, firms will suffer difficulties in motivating their employees. Without motivation, costs may increase because of inefficient productivity, poor quality, and increased lead time, among other issues. Accordingly, firms in the hospitality industry must carry out initiatives, including bonuses or profit-sharing plans, health care benefits, retirement, paid holidays, and reasonable sick leave policies, to increase employee satisfaction. Economic performance can be improved through this small social initiative practice.

Decreasing water and energy utilization (C2) can improve employee engagement. Employees have a higher preference and are favorable to working for a firm with an ethical reputation (Valentine & Fleischman, 2008). If firms can contribute to their employees' social well-being, they may enhance the employees' level of engagement (Men, 2012). In some firms, to encourage employees to save water and energy, firms can create competitions within different departments. When the monthly bill is lower than the previous one, the firms can give rewards to the top three departments to encourage them to save energy continuously. During this competition, firms not only save costs in water and energy utilization but also engage employees by offering rewards to promote their efforts.

Contributing to environmental improvement (C3) is one of the most important criteria in environmental initiatives. Although the hospitality industry produces significant economic gains and contributes to GDP growth in Vietnam, the industry also has significant negative impacts on the environment, such as increased energy consumption, water utilization, and waste generation (Agarwal, 2002). Thus, employees expect firms to take responsibility for these negative impacts (Park & Ghauri, 2015). Some travel agencies have proposed to offer "green tourism" to satisfy the expectations of employees and the public. Travelers are required to stay in local hostels instead of famous hotels. This type of tour focuses on concern for the welfare of local inhabitants and tries to minimize the environmental impacts. The features of green tourism include staying longer in one place to reduce CO_2 emissions and visiting natural environments or cultural sites rather than urban areas. Accommodation has an effect on the environment; for instance, local inhabitants can develop infrastructures for accommodation.

The empirical results reveal that employee engagement has an effect on environmental and social initiatives. These initiatives are confirmed by the five most influential criteria: policies to balancing employees' lives (C4), establishing and offering career training and development (C7), providing fair wages, welfare and working conditions with legal working hours (C6), decreasing water and energy utilization (C2) and contributing to environmental improvements (C3). Hence, if firms want to enhance the level of engagement of their employees, they should adopt the above critical factors in the development of sustainability to improve their public reputation. Once their employees recognize that the firm for which they work has a good reputation, they will be more willing to invest greater effort into their work. Subsequently, a significant improvement in economic performance can be obtained when employees feel proud of their firm.

CONCLUSION

With the rapid growth of the hospitality industry, the competition within the industry has intensified. This intensity has forced firms to develop sustainability to satisfy public expectations and increase employee loyalty. To obtain an overview of the public's awareness of these issues, social media provides a good channel to monitor the public spread of information. In addition, quantitative data from the financial reports of focal firms play an important role in the identification of the degree of employee engagement within the industry. However, these firms suffer from the difficulties of integrating big data into the decision making process, and they recognize the specific gap between sustainability development and employee engagement. Thus, this study applies big data using a fuzzy DEMATEL approach to explore the critical factors of employee engagement to enhance firms' sustainability development.

This study makes three contributions. First, it offers guidelines for firms in the hospitality industry to simultaneously develop sustainability and consider employee engagement. Firms can concentrate their resources into the top five influential criteria to improve economic performance and engagement. Second, the proposed big data approach is integrated with a fuzzy DEMATEL method, which not only assists firms in their consideration of public awareness of the decision making process but also categorizes the criteria into cause-and-effect groups to reduce complexity in decision-making. In addition, this study considers the interrelationships among aspects and criteria, which have lacked discussion in previous studies. Third, several unexplored interactions are found in this study, which provides evidence and significant insights to fill the theoretical gaps in the literature.

The empirical findings reveal that economic performance is directly influenced by environmental initiatives, social initiatives, and employee engagement. Additionally, employee engagement has an effect on environmental and social initiatives. Furthermore, the relationship between environmental and social initiatives has a direct influence on social and environmental initiatives. Therefore, firms that invest effort in the development of sustainability can foster employee engagement. In particular, environmental and social initiatives can facilitate engagement and increase job satisfaction. Additionally, the findings confirm that economic performance can be enhanced by employee engagement because employees are satisfied with their role within a firm and commit to performing their job with higher productivity and quality.

There are several limitations in this study. The proposed aspects and criteria may not offer a comprehensive assessment of the hospitality industry. Future studies should include the aspects and criteria that are required to present a holistic assessment of the industry. Furthermore, this study focuses only on the Vietnamese hospitality industry. Future studies should adopt the same framework to investigate the industry in different countries and make extensive comparisons. Future studies should also apply the same idea in diverse industries to explore the guidelines in different industry contexts. The proposed big data were only gathered from Facebook, and future studies should obtain information from other social media channels. Other methods should be applied in future studies to enhance reliability and to overcome research gaps.

REFERENCES

Agarwal, S. (2002). Restructuring seaside tourism. *Annals of Tourism Research*, *29*(1), 25–55. doi:10.1016/S0160-7383(01)00002-0

Alfalla-Luque, R., Marin-Garcia, J. A., & Medina-Lopez, C. (2012). Is worker commitment necessary for achieving competitive advantage and customer satisfaction when companies use HRM and TQM practices? *Universia Business Review*, *36*, 64–89.

Anitha, J. (2014). Determinants of employee engagement and their impact on employee performance. *International Journal of Productivity and Performance Management*, *63*(3), 308–323. doi:10.1108/IJPPM-01-2013-0008

Barnett, M. L., & Salomon, R. M. (2006). Beyond dichotomy: The curvilinear relationship between social responsibility and financial performance. *Strategic Management Journal*, *27*(11), 1101–1122. doi:10.1002/smj.557

Baumruk, R. (2004). The missing link: The role of employee engagement in business success. *Workspan*, *47*(11), 48–52.

Bhattacharya, C. B., Sen, S., & Korschun, D. (2008). Using corporate social responsibility to win the war for talent. *MIT Sloan Review*, *49*(2), 37–44.

Brammer, S., Millington, A., & Rayton, B. (2007). The contribution of corporate social responsibility to organizational commitment. *International Journal of Human Resource Management*, *18*(10), 1701–1719. doi:10.1080/09585190701570866

Carter, C., & Rogers, D. (2008). A framework of sustainable supply chain management: Moving toward new theory. *International Journal of Physical Distribution & Logistics Management*, *38*(5), 360–387. doi:10.1108/09600030810882816

Chan, H.K., Wang, X., Lacka, E., Zhang, M., 2015. A mixed-method approach to extracting the value of social media data. *Prod. Oper. Manag.*, *25*(3), 568-583.

Chang, Y., Yeh, C., & Cheng, J. (1998). Decision support for bus operations under uncertainty: A fuzzy expert system approach. *Omega*, *26*(3), 367–380. doi:10.1016/S0305-0483(97)00074-1

Chen, L., & Chiou, T. (1999). A fuzzy credit-rating approach for commercial loans: A Taiwan case. *Omega*, *27*(4), 407–419. doi:10.1016/S0305-0483(98)00051-6

Chen, S. (1996). Forecasting enrollments based on fuzzy time series. *Fuzzy Sets and Systems*, *81*(3), 311–319. doi:10.1016/0165-0114(95)00220-0

Cheng, C., & Lin, Y. (2002). Evaluating the best main battle tank using fuzzy decision theory with linguistic criteria evaluation. *European Journal of Operational Research*, *142*(1), 174–186. doi:10.1016/S0377-2217(01)00280-6

Chi, C., & Gursoy, D. (2009). Employee satisfaction, customer satisfaction, and financial performance: An empirical examination. *International Journal of Hospitality Management*, *28*(2), 245–253. doi:10.1016/j.ijhm.2008.08.003

Christensen, L. T., Morsing, M., & Thyssen, O. (2013). CSR as aspirational talk. *Organization*, *20*(3), 372–393. doi:10.1177/1350508413478310

Christian, M. S., Garza, A. S., & Slaughter, J. E. (2011). Work engagement: A quantitative review and test of its relations with and contextual performance. *Personnel Psychology*, *64*(1), 89–136. doi:10.1111/j.1744-6570.2010.01203.x

Collier, J., & Esteban, R. (2007). Corporate social responsibility and employee commitment. *Business Ethics (Oxford, England)*, *16*(1), 19–33. doi:10.1111/j.1467-8608.2006.00466.x

Cramer, J. (2005). Experiences with structuring corporate social responsibility in Dutch industry. *Journal of Cleaner Production*, *13*(6), 583–592. doi:10.1016/j.jclepro.2003.12.008

Cropanzano, R., & Mitchell, M. (2005). Social Exchange Theory: An Interdisciplinary Review. *Journal of Management, 31*(6), 874–900. doi:10.1177/0149206305279602

Delgado, A., Romero, I. (2016). Environmental conflict analysis using an integrated grey clustering and entropy-weight method: A case study of a mining project in Peru. *Environ. Model. Softw., 77*, 108-121.

Dwyer, L. (2005). Relevance of triple bottom line reporting to achievement of sustainable tourism: A scoping study. *Tourism Review International, 9*(1), 79–938. doi:10.3727/154427205774791726

Ellemers, N., Kingma, L., Van den Burgt, J., & Barreto, M. (2011). Corporate Social Responsibility as a source of organizational morality, employee commitment and satisfaction. *Journal of Organizational Moral Psychology, 1*(2), 97–124.

Farooq, M., Farooq, O., & Jasimuddin, S. (2014). Employees response to corporate social responsibility: Exploring the role of employees' collectivist orientation. *European Management Journal, 32*(6), 916–927. doi:10.1016/j.emj.2014.03.002

Farooq, O., Payaud, M., Merunka, D., & Valette-Florence, P. (2013). The impact of corporate social responsibility on organizational commitment: Exploring multiple mediation mechanisms. *Journal of Business Ethics, 125*(4), 563–580. doi:10.1007/s10551-013-1928-3

Ferreira, P., & de Oliveira, E. R. (2014). Does corporate social responsibility impact on employee engagement? *Journal of Workplace Learning, 26*(3/4), 232–247. doi:10.1108/JWL-09-2013-0070

Fontela, E., & Gabus, A. (1976). *The DEMATEL observer, DEMATEL 1976 report.* Geneva, Switzerland: Battelle Geneva Research Center.

Foran, B., Lenzen, M., Dey, C., & Bilek, M. (2005). Integrating sustainable chain management with triple bottom line accounting. *Ecological Economics, 52*(2), 143–157. doi:10.1016/j.ecolecon.2004.06.024

Freeman, R. (2010). *Strategic management.* Cambridge, UK: Cambridge University Press. doi:10.1017/CBO9781139192675

Gabus, A., & Fontela, E. (1973). *Perceptions of the world problematique: Communication procedure, communicating with those bearing collective responsibility, DEMATEL report no. 1.* Geneva, Switzerland: Battelle Geneva Research Centre.

Gallup. (2002, April 15). The high cost of disengaged employees. *Gallup Business Journal.* Retrieved from http://businessjournal.gallup.com/content/247/the-high-cost-of-disengaged-employees.aspx

Gond, J. P., Igalens, J., Swaen, V., & El Akremi, A. (2011). The human resources contribution to responsible leadership: An exploration of the CSR-HR Interface. *Journal of Business Ethics*, *98*(1), 115–132. doi:10.1007/s10551-011-1028-1

Googins, B., Mirvis, P., & Rochlin, S. (2007). *Beyond "good company"*. New York: Palgrave Macmillan. doi:10.1057/9780230609983

Gopalakrishnan, K., Yusuf, Y., Musa, A., Abubakar, T., & Ambursa, H. (2012). Sustainable supply chain management: A case study of British Aerospace (BAe) Systems. *International Journal of Production Economics*, *140*(1), 193–203. doi:10.1016/j.ijpe.2012.01.003

Grimmer, M., & Bingham, T. (2013). Company environmental performance and consumer purchase intentions. *Journal of Business Research*, *66*(10), 1945–1953. doi:10.1016/j.jbusres.2013.02.017

Henderson, J. (2007). Corporate social responsibility and tourism: Hotel companies in Phuket, Thailand, after the Indian Ocean tsunami. *International Journal of Hospitality Management*, *26*(1), 228–239. doi:10.1016/j.ijhm.2006.02.001

Herrera, F., Herrera-Viedma, E., & Martínez, L. (2000). A fusion approach for managing multi-granularity linguistic term sets in decision making. *Fuzzy Sets and Systems*, *114*(1), 43–58. doi:10.1016/S0165-0114(98)00093-1

Hubbard, G. (2009). Measuring organizational performance: Beyond the triple bottom line. *Business Strategy and the Environment*, *18*(3), 177–191. doi:10.1002/bse.564

Hutchins, M., & Sutherland, J. (2008). An exploration of measures of social sustainability and their application to supply chain decisions. *Journal of Cleaner Production*, *16*(15), 1688–1698. doi:10.1016/j.jclepro.2008.06.001

Jamali, D. (2006). Insights into triple bottom line integration from a learning organization perspective. *Business Process Management Journal*, *12*(6), 809–821. doi:10.1108/14637150610710945

Jones, T. (2007, May 15). The business value of virtue: Corporate social responsibility and employee engagement. *Talent Management Magazine*.

Jung, H., Namkung, Y., & Yoon, H. (2010). The effects of employees' business ethical value on person–organization fit and turnover intent in the foodservice industry. *International Journal of Hospitality Management*, *29*(3), 538–546. doi:10.1016/j.ijhm.2009.08.005

Kahn, W. (1990). Psychological conditions of personal engagement and disengagement at work. *Academy of Management Journal*, *33*(4), 692–724. doi:10.2307/256287

Kaliprasad, M. (2006). The human factor I: Attracting, retaining, and motivating capable people. *Coastal Engineering*, *48*(6), 20–26.

Karatepe, O. (2011). Procedural justice, work engagement, and job outcomes: Evidence from Nigeria. *Journal of Hospitality Marketing & Management*, *20*(8), 855–878. doi:10.1080/19368623.2011.577688

Karatepe, O. (2013). High-performance work practices and hotel employee performance: The mediation of work engagement. *International Journal of Hospitality Management*, *32*, 132–140. doi:10.1016/j.ijhm.2012.05.003

Karatepe, O., & Demir, E. (2014). Linking core self-evaluations and work engagement to work-family facilitation. *International Journal of Contemporary Hospitality Management*, *26*(2), 307–323. doi:10.1108/IJCHM-01-2013-0008

Kim, H., Lee, M., Lee, H., & Kim, N. (2010). Corporate social responsibility and employee-company identification. *Journal of Business Ethics*, *95*(4), 557–569. doi:10.1007/s10551-010-0440-2

Kuo, Y. (2013). Organizational commitment in an intense competition environment. *Industrial Management & Data Systems*, *113*(1), 39–56. doi:10.1108/02635571311289656

Laurence, D. (2011). Establishing a sustainable mining operation: An overview. *Journal of Cleaner Production*, *19*(2-3), 278–284. doi:10.1016/j.jclepro.2010.08.019

Lee, J., & Ok, C. (2015). Drivers of work engagement: An examination of core self-evaluations and psychological climate among hotel employees. *International Journal of Hospitality Management*, *44*, 84–98. doi:10.1016/j.ijhm.2014.10.008

Lee, Y., Kim, Y., Lee, K., & Li, D. (2012). The impact of CSR on relationship quality and relationship outcomes: A perspective of service employees. *International Journal of Hospitality Management*, *31*(3), 745–756. doi:10.1016/j.ijhm.2011.09.011

Lin, Y. H., Chen, C. C., Tsai, C. F., & Tseng, M. L. (2014). Balanced scorecard performance evaluation in a closed-loop hierarchical model under uncertainty. *Applied Soft Computing*, *24*, 1022–1032. doi:10.1016/j.asoc.2014.08.029

Lozano, R., & Huisingh, D. (2011). Inter-linking issues and dimensions in sustainability reporting. *Journal of Cleaner Production*, *19*(2-3), 99–107. doi:10.1016/j.jclepro.2010.01.004

Maas, S., & Reniers, G. (2014). Development of a CSR model for practice: Connecting five inherent areas of sustainable business. *Journal of Cleaner Production*, *64*, 104–114. doi:10.1016/j.jclepro.2013.07.039

Markley, M., & Davis, L. (2007). Exploring future competitive advantage through sustainable supply chains. *International Journal of Physical Distribution & Logistics Management*, *37*(9), 763–774. doi:10.1108/09600030710840859

Martínez, P., Pérez, A., & Rodríguez del Bosque, I. (2013). Measuring Corporate Social Responsibility in tourism: Development and validation of an efficient measurement scale in the hospitality industry. *Journal of Travel & Tourism Marketing*, *30*(4), 365–385. doi:10.1080/10548408.2013.784154

Maslach, C., Schaufelli, W. B., & Leiter, M. P. (2001). Job burnout. *Annual Review of Psychology*, *52*(1), 397–422. doi:10.1146/annurev.psych.52.1.397 PMID:11148311

Matthews, E., Sattler, M., & Friedland, C. (2014). A critical analysis of hazard resilience measures within sustainability assessment frameworks. *Environmental Impact Assessment Review*, *49*, 59–69. doi:10.1016/j.eiar.2014.05.003

Men, L. (2012). CEO credibility, perceived organizational reputation, and employee engagement. *Public Relations Review*, *38*(1), 171–173. doi:10.1016/j.pubrev.2011.12.011

Nicolau, J. (2008). Corporate social responsibility: Worth-creating activities. *Annals of Tourism Research*, *35*(4), 990–1006. doi:10.1016/j.annals.2008.09.003

O'Shaughnessy, K., Gedajlovic, E., & Reinmoeller, P. (2007). The influence of firm, industry and network on the corporate social performance of Japanese firms. *Asia Pacific Journal of Management*, *24*(3), 283–303. doi:10.1007/s10490-007-9043-6

Opricovic, S., & Tzeng, G. H. (2003). Defuzzification within a multi-criteria decision model. *International Journal of Uncertainty, Fuzziness and Knowledge-based Systems*, *11*(5), 635–652. doi:10.1142/S0218488503002387

Park, B., & Ghauri, P. (2015). Determinants influencing CSR practices in small and medium sized MNE subsidiaries: A stakeholder perspective. *Journal of World Business*, *50*(1), 192–204. doi:10.1016/j.jwb.2014.04.007

Patil, S., & Kant, R. (2014). A hybrid approach based on fuzzy DEMATEL and FMCDM to predict success of knowledge management adoption in supply chain. *Applied Soft Computing*, *18*, 126–135. doi:10.1016/j.asoc.2014.01.027

Pérez, A., & Rodríguez del Bosque, I. (2014). Sustainable development and stakeholder relations management: Exploring sustainability reporting in the hospitality industry from a SD-SRM approach. *International Journal of Hospitality Management*, *42*, 174–187. doi:10.1016/j.ijhm.2014.07.003

Rego, A., Leal, S., Cunha, M., Faria, J., & Pinho, C. (2009). How the perceptions of five dimensions of corporate citizenship and their inter-inconsistencies predict affective commitment? *Journal of Business Ethics*, *94*(1), 107–127. doi:10.1007/s10551-009-0252-4

Richman, A. (2006). Everyone wants an engaged workforce how can you create it? *Workspan*, *49*, 36–39.

Riordan, C. M., Gatewood, R. D., & Bill, J. B. (1997). Corporate image: Employee reactions and implications for managing corporate social performance. *Journal of Business Ethics*, *16*(4), 401–412. doi:10.1023/A:1017989205184

Rodrigo, P., & Arenas, D. (2007). Do Employees care about csr programs? A typology of employees according to their attitudes. *Journal of Business Ethics*, *83*(2), 265–283. doi:10.1007/s10551-007-9618-7

Saks, A. (2006). Antecedents and consequences of employee engagement. *Journal of Managerial Psychology*, *21*(7), 600–619. doi:10.1108/02683940610690169

Salanova, M., Agut, S., & Peiró, J. (2005). Linking organizational resources and work engagement to employee performance and customer loyalty: The mediation of service climate. *The Journal of Applied Psychology*, *90*(6), 1217–1227. doi:10.1037/0021-9010.90.6.1217 PMID:16316275

Sambrook, S. A., Jones, N., & Doloriert, C. (2014). Employee engagement and autoethnography: Being and studying self. *Journal of Workplace Learning*, *26*(3/4), 172–187. doi:10.1108/JWL-09-2013-0072

Sauvante, M. (2001). The triple bottom line: A boardroom guide. *Directors Monthly*, *25*(11), 1–6.

Schaufeli, W. B., Salanova, M., González-Romá, V., & Bakker, A. B. (2002). The measurement of engagement and burnout: A two sample confirmatory factor analytic approach. *Journal of Happiness Studies*, *3*(1), 71–92. doi:10.1023/A:1015630930326

Schneider, B., Ehrhart, M., Mayer, D., Saltz, J., & Niles-Jolly, K. (2005). Understanding organization-customer links in service settings. *Academy of Management Journal*, *48*(6), 1017–1032. doi:10.5465/AMJ.2005.19573107

Shuck, B., & Wollard, K. (2009). Employee Engagement and HRD: A Seminal review of the foundations. *Human Resource Development Review*, *9*(1), 89–110. doi:10.1177/1534484309353560

Slatten, T., & Mehmetoglu, M. (2011). Antecedents and effects of engaged frontline employees. *Managing Service Quality: An International Journal*, *21*(1), 88–107. doi:10.1108/09604521111100261

Stites, J., & Michael, J. (2011). Organizational commitment in manufacturing employees: Relationships with corporate social performance. *Business & Society*, *50*(1), 50–70. doi:10.1177/0007650310394311

Thompson, K., & Mathys, N. (2013). It's time to add the employee dimension to the balanced scorecard. *Organizational Dynamics*, *42*(2), 135–144. doi:10.1016/j.orgdyn.2013.03.007

Tseng, M. (2010). Using linguistic preferences and grey relational analysis to evaluate the environmental knowledge management capacity. *Expert Systems with Applications*, *37*(1), 70–81. doi:10.1016/j.eswa.2009.05.020

Tseng, M., Lin, Y., Lim, M., & Teehankee, B. (2015). Using a hybrid method to evaluate service innovation in the hotel industry. *Applied Soft Computing*, *28*, 411–421. doi:10.1016/j.asoc.2014.11.048

Tseng, M. L. (2010). Implementation and performance evaluation using the fuzzy network balanced scorecard. *Computers & Education*, *55*(1), 188–201. doi:10.1016/j.compedu.2010.01.004

Turker, D. (2009). How corporate social responsibility influences organizational commitment. *Journal of Business Ethics*, *89*(2), 189–204. doi:10.1007/s10551-008-9993-8

Valentine, S., & Fleischman, G. (2008). Professional ethical standards, corporate social responsibility, and the perceived role of ethics and social responsibility. *Journal of Business Ethics*, *82*(3), 657–666. doi:10.1007/s10551-007-9584-0

Wang, L., & Lin, L. (2007). A methodological framework for the triple bottom line accounting and management of industry enterprises. *International Journal of Production Research*, *45*(5), 1063–1088. doi:10.1080/00207540600635136

Wang, R., & Chuu, S. (2004). Group decision-making using a fuzzy linguistic approach for evaluating the flexibility in a manufacturing system. *European Journal of Operational Research*, *154*(3), 563–572. doi:10.1016/S0377-2217(02)00729-4

Williams, S., & Adams, C. (2013). Moral accounting? Employee disclosures from a stakeholder accountability perspective. *Accounting, Auditing & Accountability Journal*, *26*(3), 449–495. doi:10.1108/09513571311311892

Wu, K. J., Liao, C. J., Tseng, M. L., & Chiu, A. S. (2015). Exploring decisive factors in green supply chain practices under uncertainty. *International Journal of Production Economics*, *159*, 147–157. doi:10.1016/j.ijpe.2014.09.030

Wu, K. J., Liao, C. J., Tseng, M. L., Ming, K. L., Hu, J., & Tan, K. (2016). (article in press). Toward sustainability: Using big data to explore the decisive attributes of supply chain risks and uncertainties. *Journal of Cleaner Production*.

Wu, W. (2008). Choosing knowledge management strategies by using a combined ANP and DEMATEL approach. *Expert Systems with Applications*, *35*(3), 828–835. doi:10.1016/j.eswa.2007.07.025

Xanthopoulou, D., Bakker, A., Demerouti, E., & Schaufeli, W. (2009). Work engagement and financial returns: A diary study on the role of job and personal resources. *Journal of Occupational and Organizational Psychology*, *82*(1), 183–200. doi:10.1348/096317908X285633

Compilation of References

Aburto, L., & Weber, R. (2007). Improved supply chain management based on hybrid demand forecasts. *Applied Soft Computing*, *7*(7), 136–144. doi:10.1016/j.asoc.2005.06.001

Afuah, A., & Tucci, C. L. (2012). Crowdsourcing as a solution to distant search. *Academy of Management Review*, *37*(3), 355–375. doi:10.5465/amr.2010.0146

Agarwal, R., Gao, G., DesRoches, C., & Jha, A. K. (2010). Research commentary—the digital transformation of healthcare: Current status and the road ahead. *Information Systems Research*, *21*(4), 796–809. doi:10.1287/isre.1100.0327

Agarwal, S. (2002). Restructuring seaside tourism. *Annals of Tourism Research*, *29*(1), 25–55. doi:10.1016/S0160-7383(01)00002-0

Agnihotri, R., Kothandaraman, P., Kashyap, R., & Singh, R. (2012). Bringing "Social" Into Sales: The Impact of Salespeople'S Social Media Use on Service Behaviors and Value Creation. *Journal of Personal Selling & Sales Management*, *32*(3), 333–348. doi:10.2753/PSS0885-3134320304

Ajzen, I. (1991). The Theory of Planned Behaviour. *Organizational Behavior and Human Decision Processes*, *50*(2), 179–211. doi:10.1016/0749-5978(91)90020-T

Akar, E., & Topçu, B. (2011). An examination of the factors influencing consumers' attitudes toward social media marketing. *Journal of Internet Commerce*, *10*(1), 35–67. doi:10.1080/15332861.2011.558456

Akkermans, H., Bogerd, P., & Vos, B. (1999). Virtuous and vicious cycles on the road towards international supply chain management. *International Journal of Operations & Production Management*, *19*(5/6), 565–581. doi:10.1108/01443579910260883

Akkiraju, R., Farrell, J., Miller, J., Nagarajan, M., Schmidt, M., Sheth, A., & Verma, K. (2005). *Web Service Semantics - WSDL-S, A joint UGA-IBM Technical Note, version 1.0*. Retrieved from http://lsdis.cs.uga.edu/projects/METEOR-S/WSDL-S

Al-Anbuky, A., Bataineh, S., & Al-Aqtash, S. (1995). Power demand prediction using fuzzy logic (Vol. 3). Elsevier.

ALEXA. (2015). *The top 500 sites on the web*. Alexa. Available: http://www.alexa.com/topsites

Alfalla-Luque, R., Marin-Garcia, J. A., & Medina-Lopez, C. (2012). Is worker commitment necessary for achieving competitive advantage and customer satisfaction when companies use HRM and TQM practices? *Universia Business Review*, *36*, 64–89.

Ali, Ö. G., Sayın, S., Woensel, T., & Fransoo, J. (2009). SKU demand forecasting in the presence of promotions. *Expert Systems with Applications*, *36*(10), 12340–12348. doi:10.1016/j.eswa.2009.04.052

Alonso, O., Rose, D. E., & Stewart, B. (2008, November). Crowdsourcing for relevance evaluation. In *ACM SigIR Forum* (Vol. 42, No. 2, pp. 9-15). ACM. doi:10.1145/1480506.1480508

Aman, S., Frincu, M., Chelmis, C., Noor, M., Simmhan, Y., & Prasanna, V. K. (2015). *Prediction Models for Dynamic Demand Response*. Paper presented at the 2015 IEEE International Conference on Smart Grid Communications (SmartGridComm): Data Management, Grid Analytics, and Dynamic Pricing.

Anderson, J., & Rainie, L. (2012). *The future of big data, pew research*. Retrieved November 14, 2015, from http://www.pewinternet.org/2012/07/20/the-future-of-big-data/

Anitha, J. (2014). Determinants of employee engagement and their impact on employee performance. *International Journal of Productivity and Performance Management*, *63*(3), 308–323. doi:10.1108/IJPPM-01-2013-0008

Anthony, R. N. (1965). *Planning and Control Systems: A Framework for Analysis*. Boston: Harvard University.

Antoniou, G., & Harmelen, F. V. (2008). *A Semantic Web Primer*. Cambridge, MA: The MIT Press.

Armstrong, A. W., Cheeney, S., Wu, J., Harskamp, C. T., & Schupp, C. W. (2012). Harnessing the Power of Crowds. *American Journal of Clinical Dermatology*, *13*(6), 405–416. doi:10.2165/11634040-000000000-00000 PMID:23039257

Attar, K. S. (2016). *Proposed Methodology of Intelligent System Using Support Vector Regression for Demand Forecasting*. Academic Press.

Autry, C. W., Grawe, S. J., Daugherty, P. J., & Richey, R. G. (2010). The Effects of Technological Turbulence and Breadth on Supply Chain Technology Acceptance and Adoption. *Journal of Operations Management*, *28*(6), 522–536. doi:10.1016/j.jom.2010.03.001

Aviv, Y. (2001). The effect of collaborative forecasting on supply chain performance. *Management Science*, *47*(10), 1326–1343. doi:10.1287/mnsc.47.10.1326.10260

Aviv, Y. (2007). On the benefits of collaborative forecasting partnerships between retailers and manufacturers. *Management Science*, *53*(5), 777–794. doi:10.1287/mnsc.1060.0654

Baader, F., & Nutt, W. (2003). Basic Description Logics, The description logic handbook. Cambridge University Press.

Bach, D. (2015). *Seven Reasons Volkswagen Is Worse than Enron*. Yale Insights. Available: http://insights.som.yale.edu/insights/seven-reasons-volkswagen-worse-enron

Bain. (2013). *Big data: The organization challenge*. Retrieved November 7, 2015, from www.bain.com

Barnett, M. L., & Salomon, R. M. (2006). Beyond dichotomy: The curvilinear relationship between social responsibility and financial performance. *Strategic Management Journal*, *27*(11), 1101–1122. doi:10.1002/smj.557

Barney, J. B. (1991). Firm resources and sustained competitive advantage. *Journal of Management*, *17*(1), 99–120. doi:10.1177/014920639101700108

Barratt, M. A., & Oke, A. (2007). Antecedents of Supply Chain Visibility: A Resource-based Theory Perspective. *Journal of Operations Management*, *25*(6), 1217–1233. doi:10.1016/j.jom.2007.01.003

Barratt, M., & Oliveira, A. (2001). Exploring the experiences of collaborative planning initiatives. *International Journal of Physical Distribution & Logistics Management*, *31*(4), 266–289. doi:10.1108/09600030110394932

Ba, S., & Pavlou, P. (2002). Evidence of the effect of trust building technology in electronic markets; price premium and buyer behavior. *Management Information Systems Quarterly*, *26*(3), 243–268. doi:10.2307/4132332

Baumruk, R. (2004). The missing link: The role of employee engagement in business success. *Workspan*, *47*(11), 48–52.

Beamon, B. M. (1999). Measuring supply chain performance. *International Journal of Operations & Production Management*, *19*(3/4), 275–292. doi:10.1108/01443579910249714

Behrend, T. S., Sharek, D. J., Meade, A. W., & Wiebe, E. N. (2011). The viability of crowdsourcing for survey research. *Behavior Research Methods*, *43*(3), 800–813. doi:10.3758/s13428-011-0081-0 PMID:21437749

Bekkers, R., & Bodas Freitas, I. (2008). Analysing knowledge transfer channels between universities and industry: To what degree do sectors also matter? *Research Policy*, *37*(10), 1837–1853. doi:10.1016/j.respol.2008.07.007

Bennett, S. (2013). *Twitter Was The Fastest-Growing Social Network In 2013, Says Study [STATS]*. SocialTimes. Available: http://www.adweek.com/socialtimes/social-networks-growth-2012/476560?red=at

Bergmann, R., & Schaaf, M. (2003). Structural Case-Based Reasoning and Ontology-Based Knowledge Management: A Perfect Match? *Journal of Universal Computer Science, UCS*, *9*(7), 608–626.

Berners-Lee, T., Hendler, J., & Lassila, O. (2001). The Semantic Web. *Scientific American*, *284*(May), 34–43. doi:10.1038/scientificamerican0501-34 PMID:11323639

Bertot, J. C., Jaeger, P. T., & Grimes, J. M. (2010). Using ICTs to create a culture of transparency: E-government and social media as openness and anti-corruption tools for societies. *Government Information Quarterly*, *27*(3), 264–271. doi:10.1016/j.giq.2010.03.001

Beynon-Davies, P. (2016). Instituting facts: Data structures and institutional order. *Information and Organization*, *26*(1-2), 28–44. doi:10.1016/j.infoandorg.2016.04.001

Bhattacharya, C. B., Sen, S., & Korschun, D. (2008). Using corporate social responsibility to win the war for talent. *MIT Sloan Review*, *49*(2), 37–44.

Bianchini, D., Antonellis, V. A., Melchiori, M., & Salvi, D. (2006). Semantic Enriched Service Discovery. In *International Conference in Data Engineering Workshop*.

Blackshaw, P., & Nazzaro, M. (2004). *Consumer-Generated Media (CGM) 101: Word-of-mouth in the age of the Web-fortified consumer.* Available: http://www.nielsenbuzzmetrics.com/whitepapers

Bloodgood, J. (2013). Crowdsourcing: Useful for problem solving, but what about value capture? *Academy of Management Review*, *38*(3), 455–457. doi:10.5465/amr.2012.0318

Bodenheimer, T. (2005). High and rising health care costs. Part 1: Seeking an explanation. *Annals of Internal Medicine*, *142*(10), 847–854. doi:10.7326/0003-4819-142-10-200505170-00010 PMID:15897535

Bollen, J., Mao, H. N., & Zeng, X. J. (2011). Twitter mood predicts the stock market. *Journal of Computational Science*, *2*(1), 1–8. doi:10.1016/j.jocs.2010.12.007

Bourland, K. E., Powell, S. G., & Pyke, D. F. (1996). Exploiting timely demand information to reduce inventories. *European Journal of Operational Research*, *92*(2), 239–253. doi:10.1016/0377-2217(95)00136-0

Bousonville, T., Ebert, C. & Rath, J. (2015). *A comparison of reward systems for truck drivers based on telematics data and driving behavior assessments.* Technical reports on Logistics of the Saarland Business School.

Brabham, D. C. (2008). Crowdsourcing as a model for problem solving an introduction and cases. *Convergence (London)*, *14*(1), 75–90. doi:10.1177/1354856507084420

Brammer, S., Millington, A., & Rayton, B. (2007). The contribution of corporate social responsibility to organizational commitment. *International Journal of Human Resource Management*, *18*(10), 1701–1719. doi:10.1080/09585190701570866

Bruns, A., & Stieglitz, S. (2013). Towards more systematic Twitter analysis: Metrics for tweeting activities. *International Journal of Social Research Methodology*, *16*(2), 91–108. doi:10.1080/13645579.2012.756095

Burger, J. D., Henderson, J., Kim, G., & Zarrella, G. (2011). Discriminant gender on Twitter. *Conference on Empirical Methods in Natural Language Processing*. Association for Computational Linguistics.

Burgoon, J., Bonito, B., Bengtsson, C., Cederberg, M., Lundeberg, M., & Allspach, L. (2000). Interactivity in human- computer interaction; a case study of credibility, understanding and influence. *Computers in Human Behavior*, *16*(6), 553–574. doi:10.1016/S0747-5632(00)00029-7

Byrne, P. J., & Heavey, C. (2006). The impact of information sharing and forecasting in capacitated industrial supply chains: A case study. *International Journal of Production Economics*, *103*(1), 420–437. doi:10.1016/j.ijpe.2005.10.007

Cachon, G. P., & Fisher, M. (1997). Campbell soups continuous product replenishment program: Evaluation and enhanced decision rules. *Production and Operations Management*, *6*, 266–275. doi:10.1111/j.1937-5956.1997.tb00430.x

Cachon, G. P., & Fisher, M. (2000). Supply chain inventory management and the value of shared information. *Management Science*, *46*(8), 1032–1048. doi:10.1287/mnsc.46.8.1032.12029

Cai, M. Zhang, W. Y., Zhang, K. & Li, S. T. (2010). SWMRD: A Semantic Web-based manufacturing resource discovery system for cross-enterprise collaboration. *International Journal of Production Research, 48*(120), 3445-3460.

Calvillo, C. F., Sánchez-Miralles, A., & Villar, J. (2016). Energy managementandplanninginsmart-cities. *Renewable and Sustainable Energy Reviews.*, *55*, 273–287.

Camdereli, A. Z., & Swaminathan, J. M. (2010). Misplaced inventory and radio-frequency identification (RFID) technology: Information and coordination. *Production and Operations Management*, *19*(1), 1–18. doi:10.1111/j.1937-5956.2009.01057.x

Carbonneau, R., Laframboise, K., & Vahidov, R. (2008). Application of machine learning techniques for supply chain demand forecasting. *European Journal of Operational Research*, *184*(3), 1140–1154. doi:10.1016/j.ejor.2006.12.004

Cardoso, J. (2006). Discovering Semantic Web Services with and without a Common Ontology Commitment. In *IEEE Service Computing Workshop*, (pp. 183-190). IEEE.

Cardoso, J., & Sheth, A. (2003). Semantic e-Workflow Composition. *Journal of Intelligent Information Systems*, *21*(3), 191–225. doi:10.1023/A:1025542915514

Carter, C., & Rogers, D. (2008). A framework of sustainable supply chain management: Moving toward new theory. *International Journal of Physical Distribution & Logistics Management*, *38*(5), 360–387. doi:10.1108/09600030810882816

Cassidy, W. (2014). *Tech savvy truckers search big data for drivers.* Retrieved November 4, 2015, from http://www.joc.com/trucking-logistics/labor/tech-savvy-truckers-search-big-data-drivers_20140523.html

Ceron, A., Luigi, C., Iacus, S. M., & Porro, G. (2014). Every tweet counts? How sentiment analysis of social media can improve our knowledge of citizens' political preferences with an application to Italy and France. *New Media & Society*, *16*(2), 340–358. doi:10.1177/1461444813480466

Chae, B. (2015). Insights from hashtag #supplychain and Twitter Analytics: Considering Twitter and Twitter data for supply chain practice and research. *International Journal of Production Economics, 165*, 247–259. doi:10.1016/j.ijpe.2014.12.037

Chan, H.K., Wang, X., Lacka, E., Zhang, M., 2015. A mixed-method approach to extracting the value of social media data. *Prod. Oper. Manag., 25*(3), 568-583.

Chang, T., Fu, H., Lee, W., Lin, Y., & Hsueh, H. (2007). A study of an augmented CPFR model for the 3C retail industry. *Supply chain management. International Journal (Toronto, Ont.), 12*, 200–209.

Chang, Y., Yeh, C., & Cheng, J. (1998). Decision support for bus operations under uncertainty: A fuzzy expert system approach. *Omega, 26*(3), 367–380. doi:10.1016/S0305-0483(97)00074-1

Chan, H., Lacka, E., Yee, R., & Lim, M. (2015). The role of social media data in operations and production management. *International Journal of Production Research.*

Chao, L. (2015). *Riding on that truck: Big data on economy.* Retrieved November 6, 2015, from http://www.wsj.com/articles/riding-on-that-truck-big-data-on-the-economy-1430954699

Charalabidis, Y. N., Loukis, E., Androutsopoulou, A., Karkaletsis, V., & Triantafillou, A. (2014). Passive crowdsourcing in government using social media. *Transforming Government: People. Process and Policy, 8*(2), 283–308.

Chen, F. (1998). Echelon reorder points, installation re-order points, and the value of centralized demand information. *Management Science, 44*(12), 221–234. doi:10.1287/mnsc.44.12.S221

Chen, F., Drezner, Z., Ryan, J. K., & Simchi-Levi, D. (2000). Quantifying the Bullwhip effect in a simple supply chain: The impact of forecasting, lead times and information. *Management Science, 46*(3), 436–443. doi:10.1287/mnsc.46.3.436.12069

Cheng, C., & Lin, Y. (2002). Evaluating the best main battle tank using fuzzy decision theory with linguistic criteria evaluation. *European Journal of Operational Research, 142*(1), 174–186. doi:10.1016/S0377-2217(01)00280-6

Chen, I. J., & Paulraj, A. (2004). Towards a theory of supply chain management: The constructs and measurements. *Journal of Operations Management, 22*(2), 119–150. doi:10.1016/j.jom.2003.12.007

Chen, L., & Chiou, T. (1999). A fuzzy credit-rating approach for commercial loans: A Taiwan case. *Omega, 27*(4), 407–419. doi:10.1016/S0305-0483(98)00051-6

Chen, L., Olhanger, J., & Tang, O. (2014). Manufacturing facility location and sustainability: A literature review and research agenda. *International Journal of Production Economics, 149*, 154–163. doi:10.1016/j.ijpe.2013.05.013

Chen, S. (1996). Forecasting enrollments based on fuzzy time series. *Fuzzy Sets and Systems, 81*(3), 311–319. doi:10.1016/0165-0114(95)00220-0

Chen, X., & Chen, C. (2004). On the interactions of the Chinese quanix; a process model of guanix development. *Asia Pacific Journal of Management, 21*(3), 305–324. doi:10.1023/B:APJM.0000036465.19102.d5

Chew, C., Eysenbach, G., & Sampson, M. (2010). Pandemics in the age of Twitter: Content analysis of Tweets during the 2009 H1N1 outbreak. *PLoS ONE, 5*(11), 1–13. doi:10.1371/journal.pone.0014118 PMID:21124761

Chi, C., & Gursoy, D. (2009). Employee satisfaction, customer satisfaction, and financial performance: An empirical examination. *International Journal of Hospitality Management, 28*(2), 245–253. doi:10.1016/j.ijhm.2008.08.003

Chiu, C. M., Liang, T. P., & Turban, E. (2014). What can crowdsourcing do for decision support? *Decision Support Systems, 65*, 40–49. doi:10.1016/j.dss.2014.05.010

Chiu, C., Chang, H., Cheng, Y., & Fang, H. (2009). Determinants of consumer repurchase intention in online shopping. *Online Information Review, 33*(4), 761–784. doi:10.1108/14684520910985710

Christensen, L. T., Morsing, M., & Thyssen, O. (2013). CSR as aspirational talk. *Organization, 20*(3), 372–393. doi:10.1177/1350508413478310

Christian, M. S., Garza, A. S., & Slaughter, J. E. (2011). Work engagement: A quantitative review and test of its relations with and contextual performance. *Personnel Psychology, 64*(1), 89–136. doi:10.1111/j.1744-6570.2010.01203.x

Cleff, E. (2007). Privacy issues in mobile advertising. *International Review of Law Computers and Technology, 21*(3), 225-236.

Cohen, M. A., Cull, C., Lee, H. L., & Willen, D. (2000). Saturn's supply-Chain Innovation: High Value in After-Sales Service. *Sloan Management Review, 41*(4), 93–101.

Collier, J., & Esteban, R. (2007). Corporate social responsibility and employee commitment. *Business Ethics (Oxford, England), 16*(1), 19–33. doi:10.1111/j.1467-8608.2006.00466.x

Constantinides, E. (2002). Influencing the online consumer's behaviour; the Web experience. *Internet Research, 14*(2), 11–126.

Copacino, W., & Anderson, D. (2003). Connecting with the Bottom Line: A Global Study of Supply Chain Leadership and its Contribution to the High Performance Business. *Accenture, 1.*

Corbatt, B., Thanasankit, T., & Yi, H. (2003). *Trust and e-commerce; a study of consumer perceptions* (Vol. 2). Electronic Research and Applications.

Crainic, T., Gendreau, M., & Potvin, J. (2009). Intelligent freight transportation systems: Assessment and the contribution of operations research. *Transportation Research Part C, Emerging Technologies, 17*(6), 541–557. doi:10.1016/j.trc.2008.07.002

Cramer, J. (2005). Experiences with structuring corporate social responsibility in Dutch industry. *Journal of Cleaner Production, 13*(6), 583–592. doi:10.1016/j.jclepro.2003.12.008

Cropanzano, R., & Mitchell, M. (2005). Social Exchange Theory: An Interdisciplinary Review. *Journal of Management*, *31*(6), 874–900. doi:10.1177/0149206305279602

Crumbly, J., & Carter, L. (2015). The impact of information technology on product recalls: Exploring the role of the six "Ts" of supply chain management. *Production Planning and Control*, *26*(12), 958–968. doi:10.1080/09537287.2015.1009521

Cunha, B., & Silva, M. (2007). A genetic algorithm for the problem of configuring a hub-and-spoke network for a LTL trucking company in Brazil. *European Journal of Operational Research*, *179*(3), 747–758. doi:10.1016/j.ejor.2005.03.057

D'alisa, S., Miscio, G., Baudo, S., Simone, A., Tesio, L., & Mauro, A. (2006). Depression is the main determinant of quality of life in multiple sclerosis: A classification-regression (CART) study. *Disability and Rehabilitation, 28*(5).

Da Xu, L., He, W., & Li, S. (2014). Internet of Things in industries: A survey. *Industrial Informatics. IEEE Transactions on*, *10*(4), 2233–2243.

Danese, P. (2007). Designing CPFR collaborations: Insights from seven case studies. *International Journal of Operations & Production Management*, *27*(2), 181–204. doi:10.1108/01443570710720612

Danese, P., & Kalchschmidt, M. (2011). The role of the forecasting process in improving forecast accuracy and operational performance. *International Journal of Production Economics*, *131*(1), 204–214. doi:10.1016/j.ijpe.2010.09.006

Davis, F. (1989). Perceived Usefulness, Perceived Ease of Use, and User Acceptance of Information Technology. *Management Information Systems Quarterly*, *13*(3), 319–339. doi:10.2307/249008

Davis, F., Bagozzi, R., & Warshaw, P. (1992). Extrinsic and Intrinsic motivation to use computers in the workplace. *The Journal of Applied Psychology*, *22*(14), 1111–1132.

De Roos, D. (2013). *Big data in practice: requirements, Plan.* Infrastruct. Retrieved from: http://www.thinkconference.ca/wp-content/uploads/2013/04/Dirk-deRoos-Big-Data-In-Practice_2013-April-25.pdf

De Vries, L., Gensler, S., & Leeflang, P. S. H. (2012). Popularity of Brand Posts on Brand Fan Pages: An Investigation of the Effects of Social Media Marketing. *Journal of Interactive Marketing*, *26*(2), 83–91. doi:10.1016/j.intmar.2012.01.003

Delen, D., Fast, A., Hill, T., Elder, J., Miner, G., & Nisbet, B. (2012). *Practical Text Mining and Statisitical Analysis for Non-structured Text Data Applications*. Elsevier.

Delgado, A., Romero, I. (2016). Environmental conflict analysis using an integrated grey clustering and entropy-weight method: A case study of a mining project in Peru. *Environ. Model. Softw., 77*, 108-121.

Domingue, J., Cabral, L., Galizia, S., Tanasescu, V., Gugliotta, A., Norton, B., & Pedrinaci, C. (2008). IRS-III: A Broker-based Approach to Semantic Web Service. *Journal of Web Semantics*, *6*(2), 109–132. doi:10.1016/j.websem.2008.01.001

Dornier, P. P., Ernst, R., Fender, M., & Kouvelis, P. (1998). *Global Operations and Logistics: Text and Cases*. Academic Press.

Duan, W. J., Gu, G., & Whinston, A. B. (2008). Do online reviews matter? - An empirical investigation of panel data. *Decision Support Systems*, *45*(4), 1007–1016. doi:10.1016/j.dss.2008.04.001

Dumbill, E., Liddy, E., Stanton, J., Mueller, K., & Farnham, S. (2013). *Educating the Next Generation of Data Scientists*. Academic Press.

Dwyer, L. (2005). Relevance of triple bottom line reporting to achievement of sustainable tourism: A scoping study. *Tourism Review International*, *9*(1), 79–938. doi:10.3727/154427205774791726

Eastin, M. S., Brinson, N. H., Doorey, A., & Wilcox, G. (2016). Living in a big data world: Predicting mobile commerce activity through privacy concerns. *Computers in Human Behavior*, *58*, 214–220. doi:10.1016/j.chb.2015.12.050

ECOONSULTANCY. (2010). *Value of social media report (sample version)*. Author.

Einav, L., & Levin, J. (2014). Economics in the age of big data. *Science*, *346*(6210), 1243089. doi:10.1126/science.1243089 PMID:25378629

Eisenhardt, K. M. (1989). Building theories from case study research. *Academy of Management Review*, *14*(4), 532–550.

Elkington, J. (1994). Towards the Sustainable Corporation - Win-Win-Win Business Strategies for Sustainable Development. *California Management Review*, *36*(2), 90–100. doi:10.2307/41165746

Ellemers, N., Kingma, L., Van den Burgt, J., & Barreto, M. (2011). Corporate Social Responsibility as a source of organizational morality, employee commitment and satisfaction. *Journal of Organizational Moral Psychology*, *1*(2), 97–124.

Ellison, N. B. (2007). Social network site: Definition, history, and scholarship. *Journal of Computer-Mediated Communication*, *13*(1), 210–230. doi:10.1111/j.1083-6101.2007.00393.x

Encarnação, J. L., & Fellner, D. W. (2015). Computer graphics "Made in Germany" Darmstadt, the leading "Computer Graphics and Visual Computing Hub" in Europe: The way from 1975 to 2014. *Computers & Graphics*, *53*, 13–27.

Estellés-Arolas, E., & González-Ladrón-de-Guevara, F. (2012). Towards an integrated crowdsourcing definition. *Journal of Information Science*, *38*(2), 189–200. doi:10.1177/0165551512437638

Europe, E. C. R. (2002). European CPFR Insights. ECR European facilitated by Accenture, Brussels.

Exton, T., & Labib, A. (2002). Spare parts decision analysis–The missing link in CMMSs (Part II). *Journal of Maintenance & Asset Management*, *17*(1), 14–21.

Faiz, R., & Edirisinghe, E. A. (2009). Decision making for predictive maintenance in asset information management. *Interdisciplinary Journal of Information, Knowledge, and Management, 4*, 23–36.

Fang, Y., Qureshi, H., Sun, P., McCole, E., Ramsey, E., & Lim, K. (2014). Trust, satisfaction, and online repurchase intentions: The modeling role of perceived effectiveness of e-commerce institutional mechanisms. *Management Information Systems Quarterly, 38*(2), 407–427.

Farooq, M., Farooq, O., & Jasimuddin, S. (2014). Employees response to corporate social responsibility: Exploring the role of employees' collectivist orientation. *European Management Journal, 32*(6), 916–927. doi:10.1016/j.emj.2014.03.002

Farooq, O., Payaud, M., Merunka, D., & Valette-Florence, P. (2013). The impact of corporate social responsibility on organizational commitment: Exploring multiple mediation mechanisms. *Journal of Business Ethics, 125*(4), 563–580. doi:10.1007/s10551-013-1928-3

Federal Motor Carriers Safety Administration (FMCSA). (2015). *Motor Carriers Safety Administration.* Retrieved November 11, 2015, from https://www.fmcsa.dot.gov/registration/commercial-drivers-license/compliance

Feldman, R. (2013). Techniques and Applications for Sentiment Analysis. *Communications of the ACM, 56*(4), 82–89. doi:10.1145/2436256.2436274

Feldman, R., & Sanger, J. (2007). *The text mining handbook advanced approaches in analyzing unstructured data.* Cambridge, UK: Cambridge University Press.

Fensel, D., & Bussler, C. (2002). The Web Service Modeling Framework WSMF. *Electronic Commerce Research and Applications, 1*(2), 113–137. doi:10.1016/S1567-4223(02)00015-7

Ferreira, P., & de Oliveira, E. R. (2014). Does corporate social responsibility impact on employee engagement? *Journal of Workplace Learning, 26*(3/4), 232–247. doi:10.1108/JWL-09-2013-0070

Ferrer, M., Santa, R., Hyland, P. W., & Bretherton, P. (2010). Relational factors that explain supply chain relationships. *Asia Pacific Journal of Marketing and Logistics, 22*(3), 419–440. doi:10.1108/13555851011062304

Fishbein, M., & Ajzen, I. (1975). *Belief, attitude, intention, and behaviour: an introduction to theory and research.* Reading, MA: Addison-Wesley.

Fisher, M. L. (1997). What is the right supply chain for your product? *Harvard Business Review, 75*(2), 105–116.

Fisher, M. L., Hammond, J. H., Obermeyer, W. R., & Raman, A. (1994, May-June). Making supply meet demand in an uncertain world. *Harvard Business Review*, 83–93.

Fliedner, G. (2003). CPFR: An emerging supply chain tool. *Industrial Management + Data Systems, 103*(1/2), 14-21.

Fontela, E., & Gabus, A. (1976). *The DEMATEL observer, DEMATEL 1976 report*. Geneva, Switzerland: Battelle Geneva Research Center.

Foran, B., Lenzen, M., Dey, C., & Bilek, M. (2005). Integrating sustainable chain management with triple bottom line accounting. *Ecological Economics*, *52*(2), 143–157. doi:10.1016/j.ecolecon.2004.06.024

Forme, F. G. L., Genoulaz, V. B., & Campagne, J. P. (2007). A framework to analyse collaborative performance. *Computers in Industry*, *58*(7), 687–697. doi:10.1016/j.compind.2007.05.007

Fosso Wamba, S., Akter, S., Edwards, A., Chopin, G., & Gnanzou, D. (2015). How 'big data' can make big impact: Findings from a systematic review and a longitudinal case study. *International Journal of Production Economics*, *165*, 234–246. doi:10.1016/j.ijpe.2014.12.031

Fosso Wamba, S., Gunasekaran, A., Bhattacharya, M., & Dubey, R. (2016). *Determinants of RFID adoption intention by SMEs: an empirical investigation*. Production Planning & Control, Published Online.

Fosso Wamba, S., & Ngai, E. W. T. (2015). Importance of issues related to RFID-enabled healthcare transformation projects: Results from a Delphi study. *Production Planning and Control*, *26*(1), 19–33. doi:10.1080/09537287.2013.840015

Franzoni, C., & Sauermann, H. (2014). Crowd science: The organization of scientific research in open collaborative projects. *Research Policy*, *43*(1), 1–20. doi:10.1016/j.respol.2013.07.005

Freeman, R. (2010). *Strategic management*. Cambridge, UK: Cambridge University Press. doi:10.1017/CBO9781139192675

Fu, C., Ye, L., Liu, Y., Yu, R., Iung, B., Cheng, Y., & Zeng, Y. (2004). Predictive maintenance in intelligent-control-maintenance-management system for hydroelectric generating unit. *Energy Conversion. IEEE Transactions on*, *19*(1), 179–186.

Fugate, B., Sahin, F., & Mentzer, J. T. (2006). Supply Chain Management Coordination Mechanisms. *Journal of Business Logistics*, *27*(2), 129–161. doi:10.1002/j.2158-1592.2006.tb00220.x

Gabus, A., & Fontela, E. (1973). *Perceptions of the world problematique: Communication procedure, communicating with those bearing collective responsibility, DEMATEL report no. 1*. Geneva, Switzerland: Battelle Geneva Research Centre.

Gallup. (2002, April 15). The high cost of disengaged employees. *Gallup Business Journal*. Retrieved from http://businessjournal.gallup.com/content/247/the-high-cost-of-disengaged-employees.aspx

Ganeshan, R., & Harrison, T. P. (1995). *An introduction to supply chain management*. Supply Chain Management, Version 1. Available from http://silmaril.smeal.psu.edu/misc/supply_chain_intro.html

Gao, H., Barbier, G., & Goolsby, R. (2011). Harnessing the crowdsourcing power of social media for disaster relief. *IEEE Intelligent Systems*, *26*(3), 10–14. doi:10.1109/MIS.2011.52

Garcia, M. C., Sanz-Bobi, M. A., & del Pico, J. (2006). SIMAP: Intelligent System for Predictive Maintenance: Application to the health condition monitoring of a windturbine gearbox. *Computers in Industry*, *57*(6), 552–568. doi:10.1016/j.compind.2006.02.011

Gavirneni, S., Kapuscinski, R., & Tayur, S. (1999). Value of information in capacitated supply chains. *Management Science*, *45*(1), 16–24. doi:10.1287/mnsc.45.1.16

Gefen, D., Karahanna, E., & Straub, D. (2003). Trust and TAM in online shopping; an integrated model. *Management Information Systems Quarterly*, *27*(1), 51–90.

Gefen, D., & Straub, D. (2000). A relative importance of perceived ease of use in IS adoption; a study of e-commerce adoption. *Journal of the Association for Information Systems*, *1*, 1–28.

George, J. (2004). Theory of Planned Behaviour and Internet purchasing. *Internet Research*, *14*(3), 198–212. doi:10.1108/10662240410542634

Ghiassi, M., Skinner, J., & Zimbra, D. (2013). Twitter brand sentiment analysis: A hybrid system using n-gram analysis and dynamic artificial neural network. *Expert Systems with Applications*, *40*(16), 6266–6282. doi:10.1016/j.eswa.2013.05.057

Giunchiglia, F., Shvaiko, P., & Yatskevich, M. (2004). S-Match: an algorithm and an implementation of semantic matching. In Proceedings of 1st European Semantic Web Symposium (ESWS) (LNCS), (*vol. 3053*, pp. 61-75). Springer. doi:10.1007/978-3-540-25956-5_5

Golob, T., & Regan, A. (2001). Trucking industry adoption of information technology: A multivariate discrete choice model. *Transportation Research*, *10*(Part C), 205–228.

Gond, J. P., Igalens, J., Swaen, V., & El Akremi, A. (2011). The human resources contribution to responsible leadership: An exploration of the CSR-HR Interface. *Journal of Business Ethics*, *98*(1), 115–132. doi:10.1007/s10551-011-1028-1

Googins, B., Mirvis, P., & Rochlin, S. (2007). *Beyond "good company"*. New York: Palgrave Macmillan. doi:10.1057/9780230609983

Gopalakrishnan, K., Yusuf, Y., Musa, A., Abubakar, T., & Ambursa, H. (2012). Sustainable supply chain management: A case study of British Aerospace (BAe) Systems. *International Journal of Production Economics*, *140*(1), 193–203. doi:10.1016/j.ijpe.2012.01.003

Grant, R. M. (1991). The Resource-Based Theory of Competitive Advantage: Implications for Strategy Formulation. *California Management Review*, *33*(3), 114–135. doi:10.2307/41166664

Graves, S.C. (1999). A single-item inventory model for a non-stationary demand process. *Manufacturing and Service operations Management, 1*(2), 50-61.

Gregory, S. (1999). Logistics, strategy and structure: A conceptual framework. *International Journal of Physical Distribution & Logistics Management*, *29*(Iss: 4), 224–239. doi:10.1108/09600039910273948

Grimmer, M., & Bingham, T. (2013). Company environmental performance and consumer purchase intentions. *Journal of Business Research*, *66*(10), 1945–1953. doi:10.1016/j.jbusres.2013.02.017

Grimm, S., Monk, B., & Preist, C. (2006). Matching Semantic Service Descriptions with Local Closed-World Reasoning. In *European Semantic Web Conference*, (pp. 575-589). doi:10.1007/11762256_42

Gruber, T. R. (1993). *A Translation Approach to Portable Ontology Specifications*. Technical Report KSL 92-71. Stanford University, Computer Science Department, Knowledge Systems Laboratory.

Guarino, N., & Giaretta, P. (1995). *Ontologies and Knowledge Base: Towards a Terminological Classification Toward Very Large Knowledge Base: Knowledge Building and Knowledge Sharing*. Amsterdam: IOS Press.

Gu, F., Hung, K., & Tse, D. (2008). When does guanix matter? Issues of capitualization and its dark sides. *Journal of Marketing*, *72*(4), 12–28. doi:10.1509/jmkg.72.4.12

Gunasekaran, A., Irani, Z., Choy, K.-L., Filippi, L., & Papadopoulos, T. (2015). Performance Measures and Metrics in Outsourcing Decisions: A Review for Research and Applications. *International Journal of Production Economics*, *161*, 153–166. doi:10.1016/j.ijpe.2014.12.021

Gunasekaran, A., & Kobu, B. (2007). Performance measures and metrics in logistics and supply chain management: A review of recent literature (1995–2004) for research and applications. *International Journal of Production Research*, *45*(12), 2819–2840. doi:10.1080/00207540600806513

Gunasekaran, A., & Ngai, E. W. T. (2004). Information systems in supply chain integration and management. *European Journal of Operational Research*, *159*(2), 269–295. doi:10.1016/j.ejor.2003.08.016

Gunasekaran, A., Ngai, E. W. T., & McGaughey, R. E. (2006). Information technology and systems justification: A review for research and applications. *European Journal of Operational Research*, *173*(3), 957–983. doi:10.1016/j.ejor.2005.06.002

Gunasekaran, A., Patel, C., & McGaughey, R. (2004). A framework for supply chain management performance measurement. *International Journal of Production Economics*, *87*(3), 333–347. doi:10.1016/j.ijpe.2003.08.003

Gunasekaran, A., Patel, C., & Tirtiroglu, E. (2001). Performance measure and metrics in a supply chain environment. *International Journal of Operations & Production Management*, *21*(1/2), 71–87. doi:10.1108/01443570110358468

Hajli, M. N. (2014). A study of the impact of social media on consumers. *International Journal of Market Research*, *56*(3), 387–404. doi:10.2501/IJMR-2014-025

Hall, R. E. (2000). The vision of a smart city. In *Proceedings of the 2nd international life extension technology workshop*.

Hansen, T., Jensen, J., & Solgaard, H. (2004). Predicting online grocery buying intention; a comparison of the theory of reasoned action and theory of planned behaviour. *International Journal of Information Management*, *24*(6), 539–550. doi:10.1016/j.ijinfomgt.2004.08.004

Hartman, N. (2015). *VW needs massive marketing campaign to regain consumer trust and survive.* MIT Sloan Management. Available: http://mitsloanexperts.mit.edu/tag/vw-scandal/

Ha, S., & Stoel, L. (2009). Consumer e- shopping acceptance: Antecedents in technology acceptance model. *Journal of Business Research*, *62*(5), 565–571. doi:10.1016/j.jbusres.2008.06.016

Heese, S. (2007). Inventory record inaccuracy, double marginalisation and RFID adoption. *Production and Operations Management*, *16*(5), 542–553. doi:10.1111/j.1937-5956.2007.tb00279.x

Henderson, J. (2007). Corporate social responsibility and tourism: Hotel companies in Phuket, Thailand, after the Indian Ocean tsunami. *International Journal of Hospitality Management*, *26*(1), 228–239. doi:10.1016/j.ijhm.2006.02.001

Herrera, F., Herrera-Viedma, E., & Martínez, L. (2000). A fusion approach for managing multigranularity linguistic term sets in decision making. *Fuzzy Sets and Systems*, *114*(1), 43–58. doi:10.1016/S0165-0114(98)00093-1

Herrick, D. M., Gorman, L., & Goodman, J. C. (2010). *Health Information Technology: Benefits and Problems*. Dallas, TX: National Center for Policy Analysis.

Hertz, S., & Alfredsson, M. (2003). Strategic development of third party logistics providers. *Industrial Marketing Management*, *32*(2), 139–149. doi:10.1016/S0019-8501(02)00228-6

Hoffman, D. L., & Fodor, M. (2010). Can You Measure the ROI of Your Social Media Marketing? *Sloan Management Review*, *52*, 41.

Holweg, M., Disney, S., Holmström, J., & Småros, J. (2005). Supply Chain Collaboration: Making Sense of the Strategy Continuum. *European Management Journal*, *23*(2), 170–181. doi:10.1016/j.emj.2005.02.008

Hotten, R. (2015). *Volkswagen: The scandal explained - BBC News*. BBCNews. Available: http://www.bbc.co.uk/news/business-34324772

Houston, J. B., Hawthorne, J., Perreault, M. F., Park, E. H., Goldstein Hode, M., Halliwell, M. R., & Griffith, S. A. et al. (2015). Social media and disasters: A functional framework for social media use in disaster planning, response, and research. *Disasters*, *39*(1), 1–22. doi:10.1111/disa.12092 PMID:25243593

Howe, J. (2006). The rise of crowdsourcing. *Wired Magazine, 14*(6), 1-4.

Howe, J. (2008). *Crowdsourcing: How the power of the crowd is driving the future of business.* Random House.

Hubbard, G. (2009). Measuring organizational performance: Beyond the triple bottom line. *Business Strategy and the Environment*, *18*(3), 177–191. doi:10.1002/bse.564

Hunter, L. M., Hatch, A., & Johnson, A. (2004). Cross-national gender variation in environmental behaviors. *Social Science Quarterly, 85*(3), 677–694. doi:10.1111/j.0038-4941.2004.00239.x

Hutchins, M., & Sutherland, J. (2008). An exploration of measures of social sustainability and their application to supply chain decisions. *Journal of Cleaner Production, 16*(15), 1688–1698. doi:10.1016/j.jclepro.2008.06.001

Irani, Z., & Love, P. E. (2002). Developing a frame of reference for ex ante IT/IS investment evaluation. *European Journal of Information Systems, 11*(1), 74–82. doi:10.1057/palgrave.ejis.3000411

Ireland, R. K., & Crum, C. (2005). *Supply chain collaboration: How to implement CPFR and other best collaborative practices. J.* Ross Publishing Inc.

Jamali, D. (2006). Insights into triple bottom line integration from a learning organization perspective. *Business Process Management Journal, 12*(6), 809–821. doi:10.1108/14637150610710945

Jansen, B. J., Sobel, K., & Cook, G. (2011). Classifying ecommerce information sharing behaviour by youths on social networking sites. *Journal of Information Science, 37*(2), 120–136. doi:10.1177/0165551510396975

Jansen, B. J., Zhang, M. M., Sobel, K., & Chowdury, A. (2009). Twitter Power: Tweets as Electronic Word of Mouth. *Journal of the American Society for Information Science and Technology, 60*(11), 2169–2188. doi:10.1002/asi.21149

Jardine, A. K., & Tsang, A. H. (2013). *Maintenance, replacement, and reliability: theory and applications.* CRC Press.

Jarrah, A. (2009). *Large-Scale, Less-than-Truckload Service Network.* Informs.

Java, A., Song, X., Finin, T., & Tseng, B. (2007). Why we twitter: understanding microblogging usage and communities. *9th WebKDD and 1st SNAKDD 2007 Workshop on Web Mining and Social Network Analysis.*

Jia, C., Wang, H., & Wei, L. (2016). Research on Visualization of Multi-Dimensional Real-Time Traffic Data Stream Based on Cloud Computing. *Procedia Engineering, 137*, 709–718. doi:10.1016/j.proeng.2016.01.308

Jian, A., Xiaolin, G., Jianwei, Y., Yu, S., & Xin, H. (2015, April). Mobile Crowd Sensing for Internet of Things: A Credible Crowdsourcing Model in Mobile-Sense Service. In *Multimedia Big Data (BigMM), 2015 IEEE International Conference on* (pp. 92-99). IEEE. doi:10.1109/BigMM.2015.62

Jiang, J. J., & Conrath, D. W. (1997). Semantic Similarity Based on Corpus Statistics and Lexical Taxonomy. In *Proceedings of International Conference Research on Computational Linguistics.*

Jinag, W., Vaidya, J., Balaporia, Z., Clifton, C., & Banich, B. (2005). Knowledge Discovery from Transportation Network Data. In *IEEE Computer Society Proceedings of the 21st International Conference on Data Engineering*. Tokyo, Japan: IEEE.

Jin, S. A. A., & Phua, J. (2014). Following Celebrities' Tweets About Brands: The Impact of Twitter-Based Electronic Word-of-Mouth on Consumers' Source Credibility Perception, Buying Intention, and Social Identification With Celebrities. *Journal of Advertising*, *43*(2), 181–195. doi:10.1080/00913367.2013.827606

Jin, Y., Liu, B. F., & Austing, L. L. (2014). Examining the role of social media in effective crisis management: The effects of crisis origin, information form, and source on publics' crisis responses. *Communication Research*, *41*(1), 74–94. doi:10.1177/0093650211423918

Johnson. (2014). *How crowdsourcing is Helping Connect Internet of Things*. Retrieved from http://asmarterplanet.com/blog/2014/11/aeris-internet-of-things.html

Johnston, R., & Clark, G. (2001). *Service Operations Management*. Harlow, UK: Prentice-Hall.

Jones, T. (2007, May 15). The business value of virtue: Corporate social responsibility and employee engagement. *Talent Management Magazine*.

Jugga, J. (2008). Strategic positioning of logistics service providers. *International Journal of Logistics: Research and Applications*, *11*(6), 443–455. doi:10.1080/13675560802373472

Jung, H., Namkung, Y., & Yoon, H. (2010). The effects of employees' business ethical value on person–organization fit and turnover intent in the foodservice industry. *International Journal of Hospitality Management*, *29*(3), 538–546. doi:10.1016/j.ijhm.2009.08.005

Kahn, W. (1990). Psychological conditions of personal engagement and disengagement at work. *Academy of Management Journal*, *33*(4), 692–724. doi:10.2307/256287

Kaiser, K. A., & Gebraeel, N. Z. (2009). Predictive maintenance management using sensor-based degradation models. *Systems, Man and Cybernetics, Part A: Systems and Humans. IEEE Transactions on*, *39*(4), 840–849.

Kalakota, R., & Whiston, A. (1997). *Electronic commerce: A manager's guide*. Reading, MA: Addison Wesley.

Kaliprasad, M. (2006). The human factor I: Attracting, retaining, and motivating capable people. *Coastal Engineering*, *48*(6), 20–26.

Kaplan, A. M., & Haenlein, M. (2010). Users of the world, unite! The challenges and opportunities of Social Media. *Business Horizons*, *53*(1), 59–68. doi:10.1016/j.bushor.2009.09.003

Karatepe, O. (2011). Procedural justice, work engagement, and job outcomes: Evidence from Nigeria. *Journal of Hospitality Marketing & Management*, *20*(8), 855–878. doi:10.1080/19368623.2011.577688

Karatepe, O. (2013). High-performance work practices and hotel employee performance: The mediation of work engagement. *International Journal of Hospitality Management*, *32*, 132–140. doi:10.1016/j.ijhm.2012.05.003

Karatepe, O., & Demir, E. (2014). Linking core self-evaluations and work engagement to work-family facilitation. *International Journal of Contemporary Hospitality Management*, *26*(2), 307–323. doi:10.1108/IJCHM-01-2013-0008

Kaufer, F., & Klusch, M. (2006). WSMO-MX: A Logic Programming Based Hybrid Service Matchmaker. In *European Conference on Web Services*, (pp. 161-170). doi:10.1109/ECOWS.2006.39

Kawasaki, A., Berman, M. L., & Guan, W. (2013). The growing role of web-based geospatial technology in disaster response and support. *Disasters*, *37*(2), 201–221. doi:10.1111/j.1467-7717.2012.01302.x PMID:23278379

Keeney, R. L. (1994). *Creativity in decision making with value-focused thinking*. Sloan Management Review.

Ker, J. I., Wang, Y., Hajli, M. N., Song, J., & Ker, C. W. (2014). Deploying lean in healthcare: Evaluating information technology effectiveness in US hospital pharmacies. *International Journal of Information Management*, *34*(4), 556–560. doi:10.1016/j.ijinfomgt.2014.03.003

Ketokivi, M., & Choi, T. (2014). Renaissance of case research as a scientific method. *Journal of Operations Management*, *32*(5), 232–240. doi:10.1016/j.jom.2014.03.004

Ketzenberg, M. (2009). The value of information in a capacitated closed loop supply chain. *European Journal of Operational Research*, *198*(2), 491–503. doi:10.1016/j.ejor.2008.09.028

Khoury, M. J., & Ioannidis, J. P. A. (2014). Big data meets public health. *Science*, *346*(6213), 1054–1055. doi:10.1126/science.aaa2709 PMID:25430753

Kiefer, C., & Bernstein, A. (2008). The Creation and Evaluation of iSPARQL Strategies for Matchmaking. In *European Semantic Web Conference*, (pp. 463-477). doi:10.1007/978-3-540-68234-9_35

Kim, H., Lee, M., Lee, H., & Kim, N. (2010). Corporate social responsibility and employee-company identification. *Journal of Business Ethics*, *95*(4), 557–569. doi:10.1007/s10551-010-0440-2

Klusch, M., Fries, B., & Sycara, K. (2008). OWLS-MX: A Hybrid Semantic Web Service Matchmaker for OWL-S Services. *Journal of Web Semantics*.

Klutke, G.-A., Kiessler, P. C., & Wortman, M. (2003). A critical look at the bathtub curve. *IEEE Transactions on Reliability*, *52*(1), 125–129. doi:10.1109/TR.2002.804492

Kontopoulos, E., Berberidis, C., Dergiades, T., & Bassiliades, N. (2013). Ontology-based sentiment analysis of twitter posts. *Expert Systems with Applications*, *40*(10), 4065–4074. doi:10.1016/j.eswa.2013.01.001

Kotler, P. (2000). *Marketing Management*. Upper Saddle River, NJ: Prentice-Hall.

Kounelis, I., Baldini, G., Neisse, R., Steri, G., Tallacchini, M., & Guimaraes Pereira, A. (2014). Building Trust in the Human? Internet of Things Relationship. *Technology and Society Magazine, IEEE*, *33*(4), 73–80. doi:10.1109/MTS.2014.2364020

Kulp, S. C., Lee, H. L., & Ofek, E. (2004). Manufacturer Benefits from Information Integration with Retail Customers. *Management Science*, *50*(4), 431–444. doi:10.1287/mnsc.1030.0182

Kuo, Y. (2013). Organizational commitment in an intense competition environment. *Industrial Management & Data Systems*, *113*(1), 39–56. doi:10.1108/02635571311289656

Lai, F., Li, D., Wang, Q., & Zhao, X. (2004). The Information Technology Capability Of Third Party Logistics Providers: A resource based view and empirical evidence from China. *Journal of Supply Chain Management*, *44*(3), 22–38. doi:10.1111/j.1745-493X.2008.00064.x

Lajmi, S., Ghedira, C., & Ghedira, K. (2006). How to apply CBR method in web service composition. *Second International Conference on Signal-Image Technology and Internet Based Systems* (SITI'2006). Hammamet, Tunisia: Springer Verlag.

Lajmi, S., Ghedira, C., Ghedira, K., & Benslimane, D. (2006b). Web_CBR: How to compose web service via case based reasoning. *IEEE International Symposium on Service-Oriented Applications, Integration and Collaboration held with the IEEE International Conference on eBusiness Engineering (ICEBE 2006)*. Shanghai, China: IEEE.

Laliwala, Z., Khosla, R., Majumdar, P., & Chaudhary, S. (2006). Semantic and Rule Based Event-Driven Dynamic Web Service Composition for Automation of Business Processes. In *Proceedings of the IEEE Service Computing Workshop* (SCW06). IEEE.

Lambert, D. M., & Cooper, M. C. (2000). Issues in Supply Chain Management. *Industrial Marketing Management*, *29*(1), 65–83. doi:10.1016/S0019-8501(99)00113-3

Laosirihongthong, T., Adebanjo, D., & Choon Tan, K. (2013). Green supply chain management practices and performance. *Industrial Management & Data Systems*, *113*(8), 1088–1109. doi:10.1108/IMDS-04-2013-0164

Larsen, T. S., Thenoe, C., & Andresen, C. (2003). Supply chain collaboration: Theoretical perspectives and empirical evidence. *International Journal of Physical Distribution & Logistics Management*, *33*(6), 531–549. doi:10.1108/09600030310492788

Larson, P. D. (1998). Carrier reduction: Impact of logistics performance and interaction with EDI. *Transportation Journal*, *38*, 40–47.

Laurence, D. (2011). Establishing a sustainable mining operation: An overview. *Journal of Cleaner Production*, *19*(2-3), 278–284. doi:10.1016/j.jclepro.2010.08.019

Lave, L. B., & Seskin, E. P. (2013). *Air Pollution and Human Health*. Taylor & Francis.

Ledyard, J. O., Olson, M., Porter, D., Swanson, J. A., & Torma, D. P. (2002). The first use of a combined value auction for transportation services. *Transportation Journal*, *32*(5), 4–12.

Lee, C., & Eze, N. (2011). Analyzing key determinants of online repurchase intentions. *Asia Pacific Journal of Marketing and Logistics*, *23*(2), 200–221. doi:10.1108/13555851111120498

Lee, D., Pae, J., & Wong, Y. (2001). A model of close business relationships in China (guanix). *European Journal of Marketing*, *35*(1/2), 51–69. doi:10.1108/03090560110363346

Lee, H. L. (2002). Aligning Supply Chain Strategies with Product Uncertainties. *California Management Review*, *44*(3), 105–119. doi:10.2307/41166135

Lee, H. L., Padmanabhan, V., & Whang, S. (1997). The Bullwhip Effect in Supply Chains. *Sloan Management Review*, *38*(3), 93–102.

Lee, H. L., So, K. C., & Tang, C. S. (2000). The value of information sharing in a two-level supply chain. *Management Science*, *46*(5), 626–643. doi:10.1287/mnsc.46.5.626.12047

Lee, H., & Özer, Ö. (2007). Unlocking the Value of RFID. *Production and Operations Management*, *16*(1), 40–64. doi:10.1111/j.1937-5956.2007.tb00165.x

Lee, I., & Lee, B. C. (2010). An investment evaluation of supply chain RFID technologies: A normative modelling approach. *International Journal of Production Economics*, *125*(2), 313–323. doi:10.1016/j.ijpe.2010.02.006

Lee, J., Ardakani, H. D., Yang, S., & Bagheri, B. (2015). Industrial big data analytics and cyber-physical systems for future maintenance & service innovation. *Procedia CIRP*, *38*, 3–7. doi:10.1016/j.procir.2015.08.026

Lee, J., Kao, H.-A., & Yang, S. (2014). Service innovation and smart analytics for industry 4.0 and big data environment. *Procedia CIRP*, *16*, 3–8. doi:10.1016/j.procir.2014.02.001

Lee, J., & Ok, C. (2015). Drivers of work engagement: An examination of core self-evaluations and psychological climate among hotel employees. *International Journal of Hospitality Management*, *44*, 84–98. doi:10.1016/j.ijhm.2014.10.008

Lee, Y., Kim, Y., Lee, K., & Li, D. (2012). The impact of CSR on relationship quality and relationship outcomes: A perspective of service employees. *International Journal of Hospitality Management*, *31*(3), 745–756. doi:10.1016/j.ijhm.2011.09.011

Levi, R., Pal, M., Roundy, R. O., & Shmoys, D. B. (2007). Approximation algorithms for stochastic inventory control models. Mathematics of Operation Research, 32.

Li, L., Bagheri, S., Goote, H., Hasan, A., & Hazard, G. (2013). *Risk adjustment of patient expenditures: A big data analytics approach.* Paper presented at the Big Data, 2013 IEEE International Conference on. doi:10.1109/BigData.2013.6691790

Li, S. H. (2002). *An Integrated Model for Supply Chain Management Practice, Performance and Competitive Advantage*. (PhD Dissertation). University of Toledo, Toledo, OH.

Liang, T., & Konsynski, B. R. (1993). Modeling by analogy: Use of analogical reasoning in model management systems. *Decision Support Systems*, *9*(1), 113–125. doi:10.1016/0167-9236(93)90026-Y

Liau, B. Y., & Tan, P. P. (2014). Gaining customer knowledge in low cost airlines through text mining. *Industrial Management & Data Systems, 114*(9), 1344–1359. doi:10.1108/IMDS-07-2014-0225

Li, G., Yan, H., Wang, S., & Xia, Y. (2005). Comparative analysis on value of information sharing in supply chains. *Supply Chain Management. International Journal (Toronto, Ont.), 10*(1), 34–46.

Li, J., Sikora, R., Shaw, M. J., & Woo Tan, G. A. (2006). Strategic analysis of inter-organizational information sharing. *Decision Support Systems, 42*(1), 251–266. doi:10.1016/j.dss.2004.12.003

Li, L., & Horrocks, I. (2003). A Software Framework for Matchmaking Based on Semantic Web Technology. In *International Conference in World Wide Web,* (pp. 331-339). doi:10.1145/775152.775199

Li, M., Yu, B., Rana, O. F., & Wang, Z. (2008). Grid Service Discovery with Rough Sets. *IEEE Transactions on Knowledge and Data Engineering, 20*(6), 851–862. doi:10.1109/TKDE.2007.190744

Lin, C. Y., & Ho, Y. H. (2009). RFID technology adoption and supply chain performance: An empirical study in China's logistics industry. *Supply Chain Management: An International Journal, 14*(5), 369–378. doi:10.1108/13598540910980288

Lin, C., & Lekhawipat, W. (2014). Factors affecting online repurchase intentions. *Industrial Management & Data Systems, 114*(4), 597–611. doi:10.1108/IMDS-10-2013-0432

Lin, Y. H., Chen, C. C., Tsai, C. F., & Tseng, M. L. (2014). Balanced scorecard performance evaluation in a closed-loop hierarchical model under uncertainty. *Applied Soft Computing, 24,* 1022–1032. doi:10.1016/j.asoc.2014.08.029

Liu, C., & Arnett, K. (2000). Exploring the factors associated with web site success in the context of electronic commerce. *Information & Management, 38*(1), 23–33. doi:10.1016/S0378-7206(00)00049-5

Liu, J., Li, J., Li, W., & Wu, J. (2016). Rethinking big data: A review on the data quality and usage issues. *Journal of Photogrammetry and Remote Sensing, 115,* 134–142. doi:10.1016/j.isprsjprs.2015.11.006

Li, X., & Wang, Q. (2007). Coordination mechanisms of supply chain systems. *European Journal of Operational Research, 179*(1), 1–16. doi:10.1016/j.ejor.2006.06.023

Loader, B. D., & Mercea, D. (2011). Networking democracy? Social media innovations and participatory politics introduction. *Information Communication and Society, 14,* 757–769. doi: 10.1080/1369118X.2011.592648

Logistic Management Report. (2011). *LTL Special Report: Rising out of the doldrums.* Retrieved November 9, 2015, from http://www.logisticsmgmt.com/article/ltl_special_report_rising_out_of_the_doldrums/special_reports

Lohr, S. (2012). *The age of big data*. Retrieved November 4, 2015, from http://www.nytimes.com/2012/02/12/sunday-review/big-datas-impact-in-the-world.html?_r=1&scp=1&sq=Big%20Data&st=cse

Lowry, P., Romano, C., Jenkins, J., & Guthrie, R. (2009). The CMC interactivity model; How interactivity enhances communication quality and process satisfaction in lean-media groups. *Journal of Management Information Systems*, *26*(1), 155–196. doi:10.2753/MIS0742-1222260107

Lozano, R., & Huisingh, D. (2011). Inter-linking issues and dimensions in sustainability reporting. *Journal of Cleaner Production*, *19*(2-3), 99–107. doi:10.1016/j.jclepro.2010.01.004

Luo, M., Chea, S., & Chen, J. (2011). Web-based information service adoption: A comparison of the motivational model and the uses and gratifications theory. *Decision Support Systems*, *51*(1), 21–30. doi:10.1016/j.dss.2010.11.015

Lüttgens, D., Pollok, P., Antons, D., & Piller, F. (2014). Wisdom of the crowd and capabilities of a few: Internal success factors of crowdsourcing for innovation. *Journal of Business Economics*, *84*(3), 339–374. doi:10.1007/s11573-014-0723-7

Maas, S., & Reniers, G. (2014). Development of a CSR model for practice: Connecting five inherent areas of sustainable business. *Journal of Cleaner Production*, *64*, 104–114. doi:10.1016/j.jclepro.2013.07.039

Malita, L. 2011. Social media time management tools and tips.*World Conference on Information Technology (Wcit-2010)*. doi:10.1016/j.procs.2010.12.123

Markley, M., & Davis, L. (2007). Exploring future competitive advantage through sustainable supply chains. *International Journal of Physical Distribution & Logistics Management*, *37*(9), 763–774. doi:10.1108/09600030710840859

Martin, D., Burstein, M., Mcdermott, D., Mcilraith, S., Paolucci, M., Sycara, K., & Srinivasan, N. et al. (2007). Bringing Semantics to Web Services with OWL-S. *World Wide Web (Bussum)*, *10*(3), 243–277. doi:10.1007/s11280-007-0033-x

Martin, D., Paolucci, M., McIlraith, S., Burstein, M., McDermott, D., McGunness, D., & Sycara, K. et al. (2004). Bringing Semantics to Web Services: The OWL-S Approach. *Proceeding of First International Workshop Semantic Web Services and Web Process Composition.*

Martínez, P., Pérez, A., & Rodríguez del Bosque, I. (2013). Measuring Corporate Social Responsibility in tourism: Development and validation of an efficient measurement scale in the hospitality industry. *Journal of Travel & Tourism Marketing*, *30*(4), 365–385. doi:10.1080/10548408.2013.784154

Maslach, C., Schaufelli, W. B., & Leiter, M. P. (2001). Job burnout. *Annual Review of Psychology*, *52*(1), 397–422. doi:10.1146/annurev.psych.52.1.397 PMID:11148311

Matchette, J., & Seikel, A. (2004). How to win friends and influence supply chain partners. *Logistics Today*, *45*(12), 40–42.

Matos, S., & Hall, J. (2007). Integrating sustainable development in the supply chain: The case of life cycle assessment in oil and gas and agricultural biotechnology. *Journal of Operations Management, 25*(6), 1083–1102. doi:10.1016/j.jom.2007.01.013

Matskin, M., Maigre, R., & Tyugu, E. (2007). Computational logical semantics for business process language. In *Proceedings of second international conference on Internet and Web applications and services* (ICIW 2007). IEEE Computer Society.

Matthews, E., Sattler, M., & Friedland, C. (2014). A critical analysis of hazard resilience measures within sustainability assessment frameworks. *Environmental Impact Assessment Review, 49*, 59–69. doi:10.1016/j.eiar.2014.05.003

Mcafee, A. P. (2006). Enterprise 2.0: The dawn of emergent collaboration. *Sloan Management Review, 47*, 21.

McCarthy, T. M., & Golicic, S. L. (2002). Implementing collaborative forecasting to improve supply chain performance. *International Journal of Physical Distribution & Logistics Management, 32*(6), 431–454. doi:10.1108/09600030210437960

McIlraith, S., & Martin, D. (2003). Bringing Semantics to Web Services. *IEEE Intelligent Systems, 18*(1), 90–93. doi:10.1109/MIS.2003.1179199

McIvor, R., Humphreys, P., & McCurry, L. (2003). Electronic commerce: Supporting collaboration in the supply chain? *Journal of Materials Processing Technology, 139*(1-3), 147–152. doi:10.1016/S0924-0136(03)00196-1

McKinsey Report. (2011). *Big data: The next frontier for innovation, competition, and productivity*. Retrieved November 5, 2015, from http://www.mckinsey.com/insights/business_technology/big_data_the_next_frontier_for_innovation

Men, L. (2012). CEO credibility, perceived organizational reputation, and employee engagement. *Public Relations Review, 38*(1), 171–173. doi:10.1016/j.pubrev.2011.12.011

Mentzer, J. T., DeWitt, W., Keebler, J. S., Min, S., Nix, N. W., Smith, C. D., & Zacharia, Z. G. (2001). *Defining supply chain management*. Academic Press.

Michaelidou, N., Siamagka, N. T., & Christodoulides, G. (2011). Usage, barriers and measurement of social media marketing: An exploratory investigation of small and medium B2B brands. *Industrial Marketing Management, 40*(7), 1153–1159. doi:10.1016/j.indmarman.2011.09.009

Middleton, S. E., Middleton, L., & Modafferi, S. (2014). Real-time crisis mapping of natural disasters using social media. *IEEE Intelligent Systems, 29*(2), 9–17. doi:10.1109/MIS.2013.126

Miles, M. B., & Huberman, A. M. (1994). *Qualitative data analysis: An expanded sourcebook*. Thousand Oaks, CA: Sage Publications.

Miragliotta, G., Perego, A., & Tumino, A. (2009). A quantitative model for the introduction of RFId in the fast moving consumer goods supply chain: Are there any profits? *International Journal of Operations & Production Management, 29*(10), 1049–1082. doi:10.1108/01443570910993483

Miyazaki, A., & Fernandez, A. (2006). Consumer perceptions of privacy and security risks for online shopping. *The Journal of Consumer Affairs*, *35*(1), 27.

Mostafa, M. M. (2013). More than words: Social networks' text mining for consumer brand sentiments. *Expert Systems with Applications*, *40*(10), 4241–4251. doi:10.1016/j.eswa.2013.01.019

Msiza, I. S., Nelwamondo, F. V., & Marwala, T. (2008). Water Demand Prediction using Artificial Neural Networks and Support Vector Regression. *Journal of Computers, 3*(11).

Muhtaroglu, F., Demir, S., Obali, M., & Girgin, C. (2013). *Business model canvas perspective on big data applications.* Paper presented at the Big Data, 2013 IEEE International Conference on. doi:10.1109/BigData.2013.6691684

Nakano, M. (2009). Collaborative forecasting and planning in supply chains. *International Journal of Physical Distribution & Logistics Management*, *39*(2), 84–105. doi:10.1108/09600030910942377

Narvaez, R. W. M. (2012). *Crowdsourcing for disaster preparedness: Realities and opportunities.* (Master's thesis). Graduate Institute of International and Development Studies, Geneva, Switzerland.

Neisse, R., Steri, G., Fovino, I. N., & Baldini, G. (2015). SecKit: A Model-based Security Toolkit for the Internet of Things. *Computers & Security*, *54*, 60–76. doi:10.1016/j.cose.2015.06.002

Ngai, E. W. T., Moon, K. L. K., Lam, S. S., Chin, E. S. K., & Tao, S. S. C. (2015). Social media models, technologies, and applications An academic review and case study. *Industrial Management & Data Systems*, *115*(5), 769–802. doi:10.1108/IMDS-03-2015-0075

Ngai, E. W. T., Moon, K., Riggins, F., & Yi, C. (2008). RFID research: An academic literature review (1995-2005) and future research directions. *International Journal of Production Economics*, *112*(2), 510–520. doi:10.1016/j.ijpe.2007.05.004

Nguyen, T. H., Shirai, K., & Velcin, J. (2015). Sentiment analysis on social media for stock movement prediction. *Expert Systems with Applications*, *42*(24), 9603–9611. doi:10.1016/j.eswa.2015.07.052

Nicolau, J. (2008). Corporate social responsibility: Worth-creating activities. *Annals of Tourism Research*, *35*(4), 990–1006. doi:10.1016/j.annals.2008.09.003

Nyaga, G. N., Whipple, J. M., & Lynch, D. F. (2010). Examining supply chain relationships: Do buyer and supplier perspectives on collaborative relationships differ? *Journal of Operations Management*, *28*(2), 101–114. doi:10.1016/j.jom.2009.07.005

O'Leary, D. E. (2011). The use of social media in the supply chain: Survey and extensions. *Intelligent Systems in Accounting, Finance & Management*, *18*(2-3), 121–144. doi:10.1002/isaf.327

O'Shaughnessy, K., Gedajlovic, E., & Reinmoeller, P. (2007). The influence of firm, industry and network on the corporate social performance of Japanese firms. *Asia Pacific Journal of Management*, *24*(3), 283–303. doi:10.1007/s10490-007-9043-6

OASIS. (2004). *Introduction to UDDI: Important Features and Functional Concepts*. Organization for the Advancement of Structured Information Standards.

OMG. (2009). *Business Process Model and Notation*. Retrieved from http://www.omg.org/spec/BPMN/1.2/(2009)

Opricovic, S., & Tzeng, G. H. (2003). Defuzzification within a multi-criteria decision model. *International Journal of Uncertainty, Fuzziness and Knowledge-based Systems*, *11*(5), 635–652. doi:10.1142/S0218488503002387

Osman, T., Thakker, D., & Al-Dabass, D. (2006a). Semantic-Driven Matching of Web services using Case-Based Reasoning. In *Fourth IEEE International Conference on Web Services* (ICWS 2006). IEEE.

Osman, T., Thakker, D., & Al-Dabass, D. (2006b). S-CBR: Semantic Case Based Reasoner for Web services discovery and matchmaking. In *20th European Conference on Modeling and Simulation (ECMS2006)*.

Ou, C., Pavlou, P., & Davison, R. (2014). Swift Guanix in online marketplace; the role of computer-mediated communication technologies. *Management Information Systems Quarterly*, *38*(1), 209–230.

Pagell, M., & Wu, Z. (2009). Building a more complete theory of sustainable supply chain management using case studies of 10 exemplars. *Journal of Supply Chain Management, 45*(2), 37-56.

Pagell, M. (2004). Understanding the factors that enable and inhibit the integration of operations, purchasing and logistics. *Journal of Operations Management*, *22*(5), 459–487. doi:10.1016/j.jom.2004.05.008

Pal, K., & Karakostas, B. (2014). A Multi Agent-based Service Framework for supply Chain Management. *Procedia Computer Science*, *32*, 53–60.

Pal, K., & Palmer, O. (2000). A decision-support systems for business acquisition. *Decision Support Systems*, *27*(4), 411–429. doi:10.1016/S0167-9236(99)00083-4

Paltoglou, G., & Thelwall, M. (2012). Twitter, MySpace, Digg: Unsupervised Sentiment Analysis in Social Media. *ACM Transactions on Intelligent Systems and Technology*, *3*(4), 66. doi:10.1145/2337542.2337551

Papazoglou, M. (2012). *Web Services and SOA: Principles and Technology*. Pearson.

Park, B., & Ghauri, P. (2015). Determinants influencing CSR practices in small and medium sized MNE subsidiaries: A stakeholder perspective. *Journal of World Business*, *50*(1), 192–204. doi:10.1016/j.jwb.2014.04.007

Pathak, J., Koul, N., Caragea, D., & Honavar, V. G. (2005). A Framework for Semantic Web Services Discovery. In *ACM International Workshop on Web Information and Data Management*, (pp. 45-50). doi:10.1145/1097047.1097057

Patil, A., Oundhaka, S., Sheth, A., & Verma, K. (2004). METEOR-S Web service Annotation Framework. In *Proceedings of the Thirteenth International World Wide Web Conference*, (pp. 553-562).

Patil, S., & Kant, R. (2014). A hybrid approach based on fuzzy DEMATEL and FMCDM to predict success of knowledge management adoption in supply chain. *Applied Soft Computing*, *18*, 126–135. doi:10.1016/j.asoc.2014.01.027

Paulraj, A., Lado, A. A., & Chen, I. J. (2008). Inter-organizational communication as a relational competency: Antecedents and performance outcomes in collaborative buyer-supplier relationships. *Journal of Operations Management*, *26*(1), 45–64. doi:10.1016/j.jom.2007.04.001

Pavlou, P. (2002). *What drives electronic commerce? A theory of planned behaviour perspective*. Academy of Management Proceedings.

Pavlou, P., & Chai, L. (2002). What drives electronic commerce across cultures? A cross- cultural empirical investigation of the theory of planned behavior. *Journal of Electronic Commerce*, *3*(4), 240–253.

Pentina, I., Zhang, L., & Basmanova, O. (2013). Antecedents and consequences of trust in a social media brand: A cross-cultural study of Twitter. *Computers in Human Behavior*, *29*(4), 1546–1555. doi:10.1016/j.chb.2013.01.045

Pérez, A., & Rodríguez del Bosque, I. (2014). Sustainable development and stakeholder relations management: Exploring sustainability reporting in the hospitality industry from a SD-SRM approach. *International Journal of Hospitality Management*, *42*, 174–187. doi:10.1016/j.ijhm.2014.07.003

Pero, M., & Rossi, T. (2014). RFID technology for increasing visibility in ETO supply chains: A case study. *Production Planning and Control*, *25*(11), 892–901. doi:10.1080/09537287.2013.774257

Peteraf, M. A. (1993). The Cornerstones of Competitive Advantage: A Resource-Based View. *Strategic Management Journal*, *14*(3), 179–191. doi:10.1002/smj.4250140303

Pfahl, L., & Moxham, C. (2014). Achieving sustained competitive advantage by integrating ECR, RFID and visibility in retail supply chains: A conceptual framework. *Production Planning and Control*, *25*(7), 548–571. doi:10.1080/09537287.2012.729100

Piller, F. T., Vossen, A. & Ihl, C. (2012). From social media to social product development: the impact of social media on co-creation of innovation. *Die Unternehmung*, 65.

Powell, B., & Koskosidis, A. (1992). Shipment routing algorithms with tree constraints. *Transportation Science*, *26*(3), 230–245. doi:10.1287/trsc.26.3.230

Powell, B., & Sheffi, Y. (1989). Design and implementation of an interactive optimization system for network design in the motor carrier industry. *Operations Research*, *37*(1), 12–29. doi:10.1287/opre.37.1.12

Powell, W. (2001). *A local improvement heuristic for the design of less-than-truckload motor carrier networks*. Princeton University.

Press, G. (2013). *A very short history of data science*. Academic Press.

Quetti, C., Pigni, F., & Clerici, A. (2012). Factors Affecting RFid Adoption in a Vertical Supply Chain: The Case of the Silk Industry in Italy. *Production Planning and Control*, *23*(4), 315–331. doi:10.1080/09537287.2011.627661

Radhakrishnan, P., Prasad, V. M., & Gopalan, M. R. (2009). *Genetic Algorithm Based Inventory Optimization Analysis in Supply Chain Management*. Academic Press.

Raghunathan, S. (1999). Interorganizational collaborative forecasting and replenishment systems and supply chain implications. *Decision Sciences*, *30*(4), 1053–1071. doi:10.1111/j.1540-5915.1999.tb00918.x

Raghunathan, S. (2001). Information sharing in a supply chain: A note on its value when demand is non-stationary. *Management Science*, *47*(4), 605–610. doi:10.1287/mnsc.47.4.605.9833

Ramanathan, U. (2012). Supply chain collaboration for improved forecast accuracy of promotional sales. *International Journal of Operations & Production Management*, *32*(6), 676–695. doi:10.1108/01443571211230925

Ramanathan, U., Gunasekaran, A., & Subramanian, N. (2011). Supply chain collaboration performance metrics: A conceptual framework. *Benchmarking: An International Journal*, *18*(6), 856–872. doi:10.1108/14635771111180734

Ramanathan, U., & Muyldermans, L. (2010). Identifying demand factors for promotional planning and forecasting: A case of a soft drink company in the UK. *International Journal of Production Economics*, *128*(2), 538–545. doi:10.1016/j.ijpe.2010.07.007

Ranganathan, C., & Ganapathy, S. (2002). Key dimensions of business-to- consumer web site. *Information & Management*, *39*(6), 457–465. doi:10.1016/S0378-7206(01)00112-4

Reategui, E. B., & Campbell, J. A. (1995). A Classification System for Credit Card Transactions, In *Advances in Case-Based Reasoning:Second European Workshop* (EWCBR-94). Springer. doi:10.1007/3-540-60364-6_43

Rego, A., Leal, S., Cunha, M., Faria, J., & Pinho, C. (2009). How the perceptions of five dimensions of corporate citizenship and their inter-inconsistencies predict affective commitment? *Journal of Business Ethics*, *94*(1), 107–127. doi:10.1007/s10551-009-0252-4

Reyes, P. M., Li, S., & Visich, J. K. (2012). Accessing antecedents and outcomes of RFID implementation in health care. *International Journal of Production Economics*, *136*(1), 137–150. doi:10.1016/j.ijpe.2011.09.024

Richman, A. (2006). Everyone wants an engaged workforce how can you create it? *Workspan*, *49*, 36–39.

Riggins, F. J., & Fosso Wamba, S. (2015). *Research Directions on the Adoption, Usage and Impact of the Internet of Things through the Use of Big Data Analytics*. The 48 Hawaii International Conferences on System Sciences (HICSS), Kauai, HI.

Riordan, C. M., Gatewood, R. D., & Bill, J. B. (1997). Corporate image: Employee reactions and implications for managing corporate social performance. *Journal of Business Ethics*, *16*(4), 401–412. doi:10.1023/A:1017989205184

Rodrigo, P., & Arenas, D. (2007). Do Employees care about csr programs? A typology of employees according to their attitudes. *Journal of Business Ethics*, *83*(2), 265–283. doi:10.1007/s10551-007-9618-7

Rogstadius, J., Vukovic, M., Teixeira, C. A., Kostakos, V., Karapanos, E., & Laredo, J. A. (2013). CrisisTracker: Crowdsourced social media curation for disaster awareness. *IBM Journal of Research and Development*, *57*(5), 4–1. doi:10.1147/JRD.2013.2260692

Roman, D., Keller, U., Lausen, H., de Bruijn, J., Lara, R., Stollberg, M., & Fensel, D. et al. (2005). Web service modeling ontology. *Applied Ontology*, *1*(1), 77–106.

Roman, D., Kopecky, J., Vitvar, T., Domingue, J., & Fensel, D. (2015). WSMO-Lite and hRESTS: Lightweight semantic annotations for Web services and RESTful APIs. *Web Semantics: Science, Services, and Agents on the World Wide Web*, *31*, 39–58. doi:10.1016/j.websem.2014.11.006

Ross, D. F. (1998). *Competing Through Supply Chain Management*. Academic Press.

Rowley, J., & Slack, F. (2004). Conducting a literature. *Management Research News*, *27*(6), 31–39. doi:10.1108/01409170410784185

Roy, J. (2001). Recent Trends in Logistics and the need for real-time Decision Tools in the Trucking Industry.*Proceedings of the 34th Hawaii International Conference on System Sciences*.

Rucker, P., & Gardner, T. (2015). *Porsche, more Audi models pulled into VW emissions scandal*. Available: http://www.reuters.com/article/us-volkswagen-usa-epa-idUSKCN0SR22L20151102

Ryu, S.-J., Tsukishima, T., & Onari, H. (2009). A study on evaluation of demand information sharing methods in supply chain. *International Journal of Production Economics*, *120*(1), 162–175. doi:10.1016/j.ijpe.2008.07.030

Saarinen, M. (2015). *VW emissions scandal: everything you need to know*. Available: http://www.autoexpress.co.uk/volkswagen/92893/vw-emissions-scandal-recalls-compensation-is-your-car-affected-latest-news

Saks, A. (2006). Antecedents and consequences of employee engagement. *Journal of Managerial Psychology*, *21*(7), 600–619. doi:10.1108/02683940610690169

Salanova, M., Agut, S., & Peiró, J. (2005). Linking organizational resources and work engagement to employee performance and customer loyalty: The mediation of service climate. *The Journal of Applied Psychology*, *90*(6), 1217–1227. doi:10.1037/0021-9010.90.6.1217 PMID:16316275

Sambrook, S. A., Jones, N., & Doloriert, C. (2014). Employee engagement and autoethnography: Being and studying self. *Journal of Workplace Learning*, *26*(3/4), 172–187. doi:10.1108/JWL-09-2013-0072

Sanders, N. R. (2014). *Big Data Driven Supply Chain Management: A Framework for Implementing Analytics and Turning Information into Intelligence*. Academic Press.

Sanders, N. R., & Premus, R. (2005). Modelling the relationship between firm IT capability collaboration and performance. *Journal of Business Logistics*, *26*(1), 1–23. doi:10.1002/j.2158-1592.2005.tb00192.x

Santos, R., Orozco, J., Ochoa, S. F., & Meseguer, R. (2013). The Internet of things to support urban incident responses. In Ubiquitous Computing and Ambient Intelligence. Context-Awareness and Context-Driven Interaction (pp. 286-293). Springer International Publishing. doi:10.1007/978-3-319-03176-7_37

Sarac, A., Absi, N., & Dauzere-Peres, S. (2010). A literature review on the impact of RFID technologies on supply chain management. *International Journal of Production Economics*, *128*(1), 77–95. doi:10.1016/j.ijpe.2010.07.039

Sari, K. (2008). On the benefits of CPFR and VMI: A comparative simulation study. *International Journal of Production Economics*, *113*(2), 575–586. doi:10.1016/j.ijpe.2007.10.021

Sauvante, M. (2001). The triple bottom line: A boardroom guide. *Directors Monthly*, *25*(11), 1–6.

Schaufeli, W. B., Salanova, M., González-Romá, V., & Bakker, A. B. (2002). The measurement of engagement and burnout: A two sample confirmatory factor analytic approach. *Journal of Happiness Studies*, *3*(1), 71–92. doi:10.1023/A:1015630930326

Schneider, B., Ehrhart, M., Mayer, D., Saltz, J., & Niles-Jolly, K. (2005). Understanding organization-customer links in service settings. *Academy of Management Journal*, *48*(6), 1017–1032. doi:10.5465/AMJ.2005.19573107

Seifert, D. (2003). *Collaborative Planning Forecasting and Replenishment: How to create a supply chain advantage*. Saranac Lake, NY: AMACOM.

Sharma, R., Mithas, S., & Kankanhalli, A. (2014). Transforming decision-making processes: A research agenda for understanding the impact of business analytics on organisations. *European Journal of Information Systems*, *23*(4), 433–441. doi:10.1057/ejis.2014.17

Shingo, S. (1988). *Non-Stock Production*. Cambridge, MA: Productivity Press.

Shirky, C. (2011). The Political Power of Social Media Technology, the Public Sphere, and Political Change. *Foreign Affairs*, *90*, 28.

Shuck, B., & Wollard, K. (2009). Employee Engagement and HRD: A Seminal review of the foundations. *Human Resource Development Review*, *9*(1), 89–110. doi:10.1177/1534484309353560

Siegel, D., Waldman, D., & Link, A. (2003). Assessing the impact of organizational practices on the relative productivity of university technology transfer offices: An exploratory study. *Research Policy*, *32*(1), 27–48. doi:10.1016/S0048-7333(01)00196-2

Sievers, J. A. (2015). Embracing Crowdsourcing A Strategy for State and Local Governments Approaching "Whole Community" Emergency Planning. *State & Local Government Review*, *47*(1), 57–67. doi:10.1177/0160323X15575184

Sikorska, J., Hodkiewicz, M., & Ma, L. (2011). Prognostic modelling options for remaining useful life estimation by industry. *Mechanical Systems and Signal Processing*, *25*(5), 1803–1836. doi:10.1016/j.ymssp.2010.11.018

Simchi-Levi, D., & Zhao, Y. (2005). Safety Stock Positioning in Supply Chains with Stochastic Lead Times. *Manufacturing & Service Operations Management*, *7*(4), 295–318. doi:10.1287/msom.1050.0087

Skoutas, D., Simitsis, A., & Sellis, T. (2007). A Ranking Mechanism for Semantic Web Service Discovery. In *IEEE Congress on Services*, (pp. 41-48).

Slatten, T., & Mehmetoglu, M. (2011). Antecedents and effects of engaged frontline employees. *Managing Service Quality: An International Journal*, *21*(1), 88–107. doi:10.1108/09604521111100261

Smaros, J. (2007). Forecasting collaboration in the European grocery sector: Observations from a case study. *Journal of Operations Management*, *25*(3), 702–716. doi:10.1016/j.jom.2006.06.005

Smart, A., Bunduchi, R., & Gerst, M. (2010). The costs of adoption of RFID technologies in supply networks. *International Journal of Operations & Production Management*, *30*(4), 423–447. doi:10.1108/01443571011029994

Sprano, E., & Zakak, A. (2000). E-commerce capable; competitive advantage for consumeries in work economy. *Competitiveness Review:An International Business Journal Incorporating Journal of Global Competitiveness*, *10*(2), 114–131. doi:10.1108/eb046404

Srinivasan, D. (2008). Energy demand prediction using GMDH networks. Elsevier.

Steckel, J. H., Gupta, S., & Banerji, A. (2004). Supply chain decision making: Will shorter cycle times and shared point of sale information necessarily help? *Management Science*, *50*(4), 458–464. doi:10.1287/mnsc.1030.0169

Stern, P. C., Dietz, T., & Kalof, L. (1993). Value orientations, gender, and environmental concern. *Environment and Behavior*, *25*(5), 322–348. doi:10.1177/0013916593255002

Stites, J., & Michael, J. (2011). Organizational commitment in manufacturing employees: Relationships with corporate social performance. *Business & Society*, *50*(1), 50–70. doi:10.1177/0007650310394311

Studer, R., Benjamins, V. R., & Fensel, D. (1998). Knowledge engineering: Principles and methods. *Data & Knowledge Engineering*, *25*(1-2), 161–197. doi:10.1016/S0169-023X(97)00056-6

Suh, B., Hong, L., Pirolli, P., & Chi, E. H. (2010). Want to be retweeted? Large scale analytics on factors impacting retweet in Twitter network. In *Proceeding of the 2010 IEEE Second International Conference on Social Computing*. IEEE Computer Society. doi:10.1109/SocialCom.2010.33

Sycara, K. P., Paolucci, M., Ankolekar, A., & Srinivasan, N. (2003). Automated Discovery, Interaction and Computation of Semanticmweb Services. *Journal of Web Semantics*, *1*(1), 27–46. doi:10.1016/j.websem.2003.07.002

Sycara, K., Widoff, S., Klusch, M., & Lu, J. (2002). LARKS: Dynamic Matching Among Heterogeneous Software Agents in Cyberspace. *Autonomous Agents and Multi-Agent Systems*, *5*(2), 173–203. doi:10.1023/A:1014897210525

Szakonyi, M. (2014). Big data to rescue. *The Journal of Commerce*, 64-65.

Szekely, F. (2015). *Sustainable leadership means engaging honestly with your stakeholders: VW failed the test*. International Institute for Management Development. Available: http://www.imd.org/news/VW-scandal.cfm?mrk_cmpg_source=SM_TW_FI&utm_source=Twitter&utm_medium=Social&utm_campaign=SM_TW_FI

Tarrell, A., Tahmasbi, N., Kocsis, D., Tripathi, A., Pedersen, J., Xiong, J., & de Vreede, G. J. et al. (2013). Crowdsourcing: A snapshot of published research.*Proceedings of the Nineteenth Americas Conference on Information Systems*.

Taylor, D. (1997). *Global Cases in Logistics and Supply Chain Management*. International Thompson Business Press.

Taylor, S., & Todd, P. (1995). Assessing IT usage: The role of prior experience. *Management Information Systems Quarterly*, *19*(2), 561–570. doi:10.2307/249633

Tess, P. A. (2013). The role of social media in higher education classes (real and virtual) – A literature review. *Computers in Human Behavior*, *29*(5), A60–A68. doi:10.1016/j.chb.2012.12.032

Thompson, K., & Mathys, N. (2013). It's time to add the employee dimension to the balanced scorecard. *Organizational Dynamics*, *42*(2), 135–144. doi:10.1016/j.orgdyn.2013.03.007

Tierney, T. F. (2014). Crowdsourcing Disaster Response: Mobilizing Social Media for Urban Resilience. *The European Business Review*. Retrieved from http://www.europeanbusinessreview.com/?p=4911

Toktay, L. B., Wein, L. M., & Zenios, S. A. (2000). Inventory management of remanufacturable products. *Management Science*, *46*(11), 1412–1426. doi:10.1287/mnsc.46.11.1412.12082

Tsai, W. H. S., & Men, L. R. (2013). Motivations and antecedents of consumer engagement with brand pages on social networking sites. *Journal of Interactive Advertising*, *13*(2), 76–87. doi:10.1080/15252019.2013.826549

Tse, Y. K., Tan, K. H. & Zhang, M. H. (2014). *Exploring Quality Risk in the Food Supply Chain: Strategic Insights from Horsmeat Scandals*. Charter Institute of Logistics and Transport.

Tseng, M. (2010). Using linguistic preferences and grey relational analysis to evaluate the environmental knowledge management capacity. *Expert Systems with Applications*, *37*(1), 70–81. doi:10.1016/j.eswa.2009.05.020

Tseng, M. L. (2010). Implementation and performance evaluation using the fuzzy network balanced scorecard. *Computers & Education*, *55*(1), 188–201. doi:10.1016/j.compedu.2010.01.004

Tseng, M., Lin, Y., Lim, M., & Teehankee, B. (2015). Using a hybrid method to evaluate service innovation in the hotel industry. *Applied Soft Computing*, *28*, 411–421. doi:10.1016/j.asoc.2014.11.048

Tse, Y. K., Zhang, M., Doherty, B., Chappell, P. J., & Garnett, P. (2016). Insight from the horsemeat scandal: Exploring the consumers' opinion of tweets toward Tesco. *Industrial Management & Data Systems*, *116*(6), 1178–1200. doi:10.1108/IMDS-10-2015-0417

Tsitchizris, D. C., & Lochovsky, F. H. (1982). *Data models.* Prentice-Hall.

Turker, D. (2009). How corporate social responsibility influences organizational commitment. *Journal of Business Ethics*, *89*(2), 189–204. doi:10.1007/s10551-008-9993-8

Twitter. (2013). *Twitter Developer Documentation.* Author.

Twitter. (n.d.). *About.* Retrieved from; https://about.twitter.com/company

Valentine, S., & Fleischman, G. (2008). Professional ethical standards, corporate social responsibility, and the perceived role of ethics and social responsibility. *Journal of Business Ethics*, *82*(3), 657–666. doi:10.1007/s10551-007-9584-0

Varelas, G., Voutsakis, E., Raftopoulou, P., Petrakis, E. G. M., & Milios, E. (2005). Semantic Similarity methods in WordNet and their application to information retrieval on the Web. *Proceedings of the 7th annual ACM international workshop on web information and data management.* Bremen, Germany: ACM. doi:10.1145/1097047.1097051

Veil, S. R., Buehner, T., & Palenchar, M. J. (2011). A Work-In-Process Literature Review: Incorporating Social Media in Risk and Crisis Communication. *Journal of Contingencies and Crisis Management*, *19*(2), 110–122. doi:10.1111/j.1468-5973.2011.00639.x

Venkatesh, V., & Bala, H. (2008). Technology Acceptance Model 3 and a research agenda on interventions. *Decision Sciences*, *39*(2), 273–315. doi:10.1111/j.1540-5915.2008.00192.x

Venkatesh, V., & Davis, F. (2000). A theoretical extension of the technology acceptance model: Four longitudinal field studies. *Management Science*, *46*(2), 186–204. doi:10.1287/mnsc.46.2.186.11926

Venkatesh, V., Morris, M., Davis, G., & Davis, F. (2003). User Acceptance of Information Technology: Toward a Unified View. *Management Information Systems Quarterly*, *27*(3), 425–478.

Venkatesh, V., Thong, J., & Xu, X. (2012). Consumer Acceptance and Usage of Information Technology. *Extending the Unified Theory of Acceptance and Use of Technology MIS Quarterly VoL.*, *36*(1), 157–178.

Verma, K., Sivashanmugam, K., Sheth, A., Patil, A., Oundhakar, S., & Miller, J. (2005). METEOR-S WSDI: A Scalable P2P Infrastructure of Registries for Semantic Publication and Discovery of Web Services. *Information Technology Management*, *6*(1), 17–39. doi:10.1007/s10799-004-7773-4

VICS. (2002). *CPFR guidelines Voluntary Inter-industry Commerce Standards.* Available at: www.cpfr.org

Visich, J. K., Li, S., Khumawala, B. M., & Reyes, P. M. (2009). Empirical evidence of RFID impacts on supply chain performance. *International Journal of Operations & Production Management*, *29*(12), 1290–1315. doi:10.1108/01443570911006009

Voss, C., Tsikriktsis, N., & Frohlich, M. (2002). Case research in Operations Management. *International Journal of Operations & Production Management*, *22*(2), 195–219. doi:10.1108/01443570210414329

Vrijhoef, R., & Koskela, L. (1999). Role of supply chain management in construction. *Proceedings of the Seventh Annual Conference of the International Group for Lean Construction.*

Vukovic, M., & Bartolini, C. (2010). Towards a research agenda for enterprise crowdsourcing. In *Leveraging applications of formal methods, verification, and validation* (pp. 425–434). Springer Berlin Heidelberg. doi:10.1007/978-3-642-16558-0_36

Waller, K., Droge, E., & Puschmann, C. (2011). Citation Analysis in Twitter. Approaches for Defining and Measuring Information Flows within Tweets during Scientific Conference. *1st Workshop on Making Sense of Microposts.*

Waller, M. A., & Fawcett, S. E. (2013). *Data science, predictive analytics, and big data: A revolution that will transform supply chain design and management.* Academic Press.

Waller, J., & Fawcett, B. (2013). Data science, predictive analytics, and big data: A revolution that will transform supply chain design and management. *Journal of Business Logistics*, *34*(2), 77–84. doi:10.1111/jbl.12010

Wang, G., Gunasekaran, A., Ngai, E. W. T., & Papadopoulos, T. (2016). Big data analytics in logistics and supply chain management: Certain investigations for research and applications. *International Journal of Production Economics*, *176*, 98–110. doi:10.1016/j.ijpe.2016.03.014

Wang, L., & Cao, J. (2007). Web Services Semantic Searching enhanced by Case Based Reasoning. *18th International Workshop on Database and Expert Systems Applications.*

Wang, L., & Lin, L. (2007). A methodological framework for the triple bottom line accounting and management of industry enterprises. *International Journal of Production Research*, *45*(5), 1063–1088. doi:10.1080/00207540600635136

Wang, P., Jin, Z., Liu, L., & Cai, G. (2008). Building Toward Capability Specifications of Web Services Based on an Environment Ontology. *IEEE Transactions on Knowledge and Data Engineering*, *20*(4), 547–561. doi:10.1109/TKDE.2007.190719

Wang, R., & Chuu, S. (2004). Group decision-making using a fuzzy linguistic approach for evaluating the flexibility in a manufacturing system. *European Journal of Operational Research, 154*(3), 563–572. doi:10.1016/S0377-2217(02)00729-4

Wang, Y., Kung, L. A., & Byrd, T. A. (2015). Big data analytics: Understanding its capabilities and potential benefits for healthcare organizations. *Technological Forecasting and Social Change*. doi:10.1016/j.techfore.2015.12.019

Watson, I. (1997). *Applying Case-Based Reasoning: Techniques for Enterprise Systems*. Morgan Kaufman.

Wen, C., Prybutok, P., & Xu, C. (2011). An integrated model for consumer online purchase intention. *Journal of Computer Information Systems, 14*.

Whitaker, J., Mithas, S., & Krishman, M. S. (2007). A Field of RFID deployment and return expectations. *Production and Operations Management, 16*(5), 599–612. doi:10.1111/j.1937-5956.2007.tb00283.x

Wielki, J. (2013). *Implementation of the big data concept in organizations-possibilities, impediments and challenges*. Paper presented at the Computer Science and Information Systems (FedCSIS), 2013 Federated Conference on.

Wikipedia. (2016a). *Data mining*. Retrieved from https://en.wikipedia.org/wiki/Data_mining

Wikipedia. (2016b). *Smart planet*. Retrieved from https://en.wikipedia.org/wiki/SmartPlanet

Williams, S., & Adams, C. (2013). Moral accounting? Employee disclosures from a stakeholder accountability perspective. *Accounting, Auditing & Accountability Journal, 26*(3), 449–495. doi:10.1108/09513571311311892

Winston, A. (2015). *What VW Didn't Understand About Trust*. Harvard Business Review. Available: https://hbr.org/2015/09/what-vw-didnt-understand-about-trust?utm_source=Socialflow&utm_medium=Tweet&utm_campaign=Socialflow

Wong, K. F., Xia, Y., Xu, R., Wu, M., & Li, W. (2008). Pattern-based opinion mining for stock market trend prediction. *International Journal of Computer Processing of Languages, 21*, 347-361.

Wooldridge, M., & Jennings, N. (1995). Intelligent Agents: Theory and Practice. *The Knowledge Engineering Review, 10*(2), 115–152. doi:10.1017/S0269888900008122

WSDL-S. (2005). Retrieved from: http://www.w3.org/Submission/WSDL-S/

Wu, K. J., Liao, C. J., Tseng, M. L., & Chiu, A. S. (2015). Exploring decisive factors in green supply chain practices under uncertainty. *International Journal of Production Economics, 159*, 147–157. doi:10.1016/j.ijpe.2014.09.030

Wu, K. J., Liao, C. J., Tseng, M. L., Ming, K. L., Hu, J., & Tan, K. (2016). (article in press). Toward sustainability: Using big data to explore the decisive attributes of supply chain risks and uncertainties. *Journal of Cleaner Production*.

Wu, S.-j., Gebraeel, N., Lawley, M. A., & Yih, Y. (2007). A neural network integrated decision support system for condition-based optimal predictive maintenance policy. *Systems, Man and Cybernetics, Part A: Systems and Humans. IEEE Transactions on, 37*(2), 226–236.

Wu, W. (2008). Choosing knowledge management strategies by using a combined ANP and DEMATEL approach. *Expert Systems with Applications, 35*(3), 828–835. doi:10.1016/j.eswa.2007.07.025

Wu, Z., & Choi, T. Y. (2005). Supplier–supplier relationships in the buyer–supplier triad: Building theories from eight case studies. *Journal of Operations Management, 24*(1), 27–52. doi:10.1016/j.jom.2005.02.001

Wyld, D. C. (2005). *RFID: The Right Frequency for Government*. Washington, DC: IBM Center for the Business of Government.

Xanthopoulou, D., Bakker, A., Demerouti, E., & Schaufeli, W. (2009). Work engagement and financial returns: A diary study on the role of job and personal resources. *Journal of Occupational and Organizational Psychology, 82*(1), 183–200. doi:10.1348/096317908X285633

Xin, N. Y., & Ling, L. Y. (2013). *How we could realize big data value*. Paper presented at the Instrumentation and Measurement, Sensor Network and Automation (IMSNA), 2013 2nd International Symposium on.

Yang, L., Yang, S. H., & Plotnick, L. (2013). How the internet of things technology enhances emergency response operations. *Technological Forecasting and Social Change, 80*(9), 1854–1867. doi:10.1016/j.techfore.2012.07.011

Yee-Loong Chong, A., Liu, M. J., Luo, J., & Keng-Boon, O. (2015). Predicting RFID adoption in healthcare supply chain from the perspectives of users. *International Journal of Production Economics, 159*(0), 66–75. doi:10.1016/j.ijpe.2014.09.034

Yin, R. (1994). *Case study research: Design and methods. CA*. Thousand Oaks, CA: Sage Publications.

Yin, R. K. (1994). *Case study research Design and Methods Applied Social Research Methods Series* (2nd ed.; Vol. 5). London: Sage Publications.

Zelbst, P. J., Green, K. W., Sower, V. E., & Reyes, P. M. (2012). Impact of RFID on manufacturing effectiveness and efficiency. *International Journal of Operations & Production Management, 32*(3-4), 329–350. doi:10.1108/01443571211212600

Zelezny, L. C., Chua, P.-P., & Aldrich, C. (2000). Elaborating on gender differences in environmentalism. *The Journal of Social Issues, 56*(3), 443–457. doi:10.1111/0022-4537.00177

Zhang, Y. (2010). *Advances in LTL Load Plan design*. (Doctorate Thesis). Georgia Institute of Technology.

Zhang, W. H., Xu, H., & Wan, W. (2012). Weakness Finder: Find product weakness from Chinese reviews by using aspects based sentiment analysis. *Expert Systems with Applications, 39*(11), 10283–10291. doi:10.1016/j.eswa.2012.02.166

Zhang, W. Y., Cai, M., Qiu, J., & Yin, J. W. (2009). Managing distributed manufacturing knowledge through multi-perspective modelling for Semantic Web applications. *International Journal of Production Research*, *47*(23), 6525–6542. doi:10.1080/00207540802311114

Zhang, X., Fuehres, H., & Gloor, P. A. (2011). Predicting Stock Market Indicators Through Twitter "I hope it is not as bad as I fear". *2nd Collaborative Innovation Networks Conference (Coins2010)*.

Zhang, Y., Fang, K., Wei, E., Ramsey, P., McCole, P., & Chen, H. (2011). Repurchase intention in B2C e-commerce- A relationship quality perspective. *Information & Management*, *48*(6), 192–200. doi:10.1016/j.im.2011.05.003

Zhao, X., Xie, J., & Leung, J. (2002). The impact of forecasting model selection on the value of information sharing in a supply chain. *International Journal of Production Economics*, *142*, 321–344.

Zhong, R. Y., Huang, G. Q., Lan, S., Dai, Q. Y., Chen, X., & Zhang, T. (2015). A big data approach for logistics trajectory discovery from RFID-enabled production data. *International Journal of Production Economics*, *165*, 260–272. doi:10.1016/j.ijpe.2015.02.014

About the Contributors

Nachiappan (Nachi) Subramanian is a Reader in Operations and Logistics Management at University of Sussex. Nachi is a Senior Fellow of Higher Education Academy, UK and Charted member of Institute of Logistics and Transport. Previously, Nachi worked at University of Nottingham Ningbo, China for five years and at Thiagarajar College of Engineering, Madurai, India for twelve years. Nachi has 17 years of academic experience and 2 years of industrial experience. He has post-doctoral research experience at University of Nottingham, United Kingdom, RMIT University Melbourne, Australia and Indian Institute of Science Bangalore, India. He has received several research fellowship awards including BOYSCAST fellowship, Career award and Young Scientist fellowship award from Indian government agencies as well as Australian Endeavour Research Fellowship Award.His research works centres on novel research topics in logistics and supply chain management such as sustainability, risk and innovation and these topics are within our University priority research areas. Nachi is the principal investigator for two major research projects under the sustainable business model development theme of Innovation team project at UNNC. Nachi has published over 65 refereed research papers in leading operations and supply chain management journals. He also serves as a reviewer to many leading journals and has organised internationals conferences.

* * *

Mahmood Ali is an Assistant Professor in Supply Chain Management. He received his PhD from University of Greenwich, UK. Before undertaking his PhD, he has worked in major corporate in USA for several years. His research interest includes Supply chain management, Enterprise Systems, Logistics, Decision Support systems, User resistance and Information Technology.

Maria Balta is a Lecturer in Strategy within Brunel Business School. Her current interests include, inter alia, technology strategy, the strategic positioning of social enterprises and small firms. Her research has appeared in journals such as Organization and Work, Employment, and Society.

Li Cui is a lecturer in Dalain University of Technology, Panjin campus. Her research area focuses on the green supply chain management, environment and risk management. Currently, she tries to integrate these ideas into agriculture industry in Panjin City.

Bob Doherty is professor of marketing at The York Management School, University of York. Bob specialises in research on the marketing aspects of fair trade and social enterprises. Bob is currently principal investigator on a large research programme centred on food resilience called IKnowFood, funded by the Global Food Security Fund. Bob is also a member of of the organising committees for both the International Social Innovation Research Conference (ISIRC) and the International Fair Trade Symposium. For the past five years he has been editor of the Social Enterprise Journal and is also editorial board member of the Corporate Responsibility and Environmental Management Journal. Supply chain issues have been, and remain, a consistent factor addressed by Bob's work.

Rameshwar Dubey is full time faculty and research mentor at Symbiosis Institute of Operations Management (a constituent of a Symbiosis International University, Nashik). He promotes research based teaching using refereed articles published in reputable journals in class room. He actively conducts research methodology workshop for young researchers and PhD scholars. Prof. Rameshwar Dubey has published over 25 articles in Scopus/SCI/SSCI indexed journals which includes IJPR, Optimization, IJCIM, IJLSM, IJSOM, IJPM, IJPQM, Benchmarking and over 15 articles which are in acceptance stage in reputable journal that includes IJPE, AOR, Omega, IJSTL and some other reputable journals. At present he is also an editor-in-chief of Journal of Supply Chain Management Systems and Associate Editor of Global Journal of Flexible Systems Management. Beside regular editorial responsibility, he is also an editorial member of International Journal of Innovation Science. In recent days he is actively involved in handling special issues of over 6 journals which are published by Inderscience and Springer. His area of research interest includes manufacturing strategy, sustainable supply chain network design, soft TQM, sustainable Six-Sigma, sustainable development and humanitarian logistics and supply chains.

Angappa Gunasekaran is a professor and dean at the Charlton College of Business, University of Massachusetts, Dartmouth. Gunasekaran has held academic positions in UK, Australia, Finland, India and Canada. He has over 250 articles published in peer-reviewed journals. He has presented about 50 papers and published 50 articles in conferences and given a number of invited talks in many countries. He is on the Editorial Board of several journals. He has organised several international workshops and conferences in the emerging areas of operations management and information systems. He is currently interested in researching logistics and supply chain management. Gunasekaran has been the founding Director of Business Innovation Research Center (BIRC) since 2006.

Jiayao Hu is a PhD candidate in the Nottingham University Business School at The University of Nottingham. His doctoral research focuses on supply chain quality management and sustainable supply chain management.

Pham Minh Huy is a MBA student in Lunghwa University of Science & Technology, Taiwan.

Tom Keefe received his MSc from the University of York in Mathematics and Computer Science in 2015. He currently works in the field of cybersecurity.

Vikas Kumar is an Associate Professor of Enterprise Operations Management at Bristol Business School, University of the West of England, UK. He holds a PhD degree in Management Studies from Exeter University, UK and a Bachelor's degree in Engineering from Ranchi University, India. He has published more than 100 articles in leading international journals and conferences. He is currently acting as a reviewer for more than 10 international journals and also sits on the editorial board of more than six international journals. He is an active member of British Academy of management (BAM), Production and Operations Management Society (POMS) and European Operations Management Association (EurOMA). His current research interests include general operations management and operations research, supply chain management, process modelling, service operations, and open innovation.

Ewelina Lacka is a Lecturer in Marketing at Strathclyde Business School, Strathclyde University. She holds a PhD from the Norwich Business School, University of East Anglia. Ewelina's core research interests provide insights into consumers' attitudes towards e-commerce, social media and the user generated content. She published in journals such as Industrial Marketing Management, Production and Operations Management and International Journal of Production Research. She is the Editor of a book published by Springer in 2014; 'E-commerce platform acceptance; suppliers, retailers and consumers'.

C. K. M. Lee is currently an assistant professor in the Department of Industrial and Systems Engineering, The Hong Kong Polytechnic University, Hong Kong. She obtained her PhD and B. Eng degree from The Hong Kong Polytechnic University. She was awarded Bronze Award of 16th China National Invention Exhibition Award in 2006 and Outstanding Professional Service and Innovation Award, The Hong Kong Polytechnic University in 2006. Dr Lee has authored or co-authored more than 100 journal and conferences papers. Her current research areas include logistics information management, industry 4.0 and big data analysis.

John Loonam is a Lecturer in Management at Dublin City University Business School. He holds a Bachelor of Arts in European Studies and a Masters of Business Studies from the University of Limerick. He received his PhD in Business Studies from Trinity College, Dublin. He teaches in the fields of Management and Strategic Management at Postgraduate level. His research focuses on the role of Management Teams when leading large-scale Change initiatives. John is currently researching in the areas of Enterprise Systems and Enterprise Social Systems, Digital Strategies, and Big Data.

Susan R. Moore's professional background is in the local government sector in the UK, predominantly as an agent of change. She has worked in a variety of management and executive roles, one of which saw her manage the introduction of PCs within a public service organisation from a customer service perspective, overseeing the growth in hardware of over 5,000% in four years combined with both software and platform changes. Another role involved working closely with local policymakers, in their roles as decision makers and decision and policy scrutineers, on a variety of issues impacting not only locally, but regionally and nationally. Her journey combines this experience with a degree in sociology (from the University of Salford) and an MBA (from the University of Hull), and research interest in the ethnomethodology of social media, which has led to undertaking PhD study at the University of York, England.

Kam K. H. Ng received the B.Sci. degree in Logistics Engineering and Management from The Hong Kong Polytechnic University in 2015. He is currently an M.Phil. candidate in the Hong Kong Polytechnic University upon his completion on bachelor degree. His research activities aim at providing insights into swarm intelligence, logistics information management and airport operation management.

Kamalendu Pal is with the Department of Computer Science, School of Mathematics, Computer Science and Engineering, City, University of London. Kamalendu received his BSc (Hons) degree in Physics from Calcutta University, India, Postgraduate Diploma in Computer Science from Pune, India; MSc degree in Software Systems Technology from University of Sheffield, Postgraduate Diploma in Artificial Intelligence from Kingston University, MPhil degree in Computer Science from University College London, and MBA degree from University of

Hull, United Kingdom. He has published dozens of research papers in international journals and conferences. His research interests include knowledge-based systems, decision support systems, computer integrated design, software engineering, and service oriented computing. He is a member of the British Computer Society, the Institution of Engineering and Technology, and the IEEE Computer Society.

Thanos Papadopoulos is Professor of Management (Operations Management/ Information Systems) at Kent Business School. Previously, he held appointments as Senior Lecturer in Information Systems and MBA Director at Sussex School of Business, Management, and Economics, University of Sussex, Senior Lecturer in Information Systems at Hull University Business School, and Lecturer in Knowledge and Information Systems Management at Southampton Business School. His articles have been published in international journals such as the British Journal of Management, International Journal of Production Economics, Journal of the Operational Research Society, Journal of Strategic Information Systems, International Journal of Operations and Production Management.

Usha Ramanathan is a Reader in Supply Chain Management in Nottingham Trent University, UK. Her research interest includes supply chain collaboration, Collaborative Planning Forecasting and Replenishment (CPFR), value of information sharing and forecasting, Structural equation modelling, simulation, AHP and SERVQUAL. She has published in leading journals such as International Journal of Production Economics, Expert Systems with Applications and Omega: The International Journal of Management Science. Usha is interested in on-going research topics such as green supply chain, collaboration, maintaining customer loyalty and big data.

Kim Hua Tan is a Professor in Lean Operations and Supply Management. Prior to this, he was a researcher and teaching assistant at Centre for Strategy and Performance, University of Cambridge. Dr. Tan spent many years in industry, before joining academia in 1999. His current research interests are lean management, operations strategy, decision making, and supply chain risk management. Dr. Tan has published a book called 'Winning Decisions: Translating Business Strategy into Action Plans,' and numerous articles in academic journals such as Decision Sciences, International Journal of Operations and Production Management, International Journal of Production Economics, International Journal of Innovation Management, and others.

Ying Kei Tse (Mike) is a Lecturer in Operations Management at the University of York (The York Management School). Before taking up this post, He worked as a researcher at Nottingham University Business School and The Hong Kong Polytechnic University. His research crosses over different disciplines, including empirical research in risk management and supply chain management, data-mining of big social data, decision support in supply chain management, and development of OM educational simulation platform.

Ming-Lang Tseng used to work as Executive Vice President in an international medical consumable products manufacturing group in South Africa from 2002 to 2004 and, meanwhile, as a part-time lecturer in the University of Swaziland, Swaziland, South Africa. Also, he was experienced the vice president of an international construction group in Kenya and South Sudan in 2012- 2013. Presently, he is a Professor at department of business administration in Lunghwa University of Science&Technology, Taiwan. Currently, he is an EBM of ASOC, EBM of IMDS and EBM of other journals. He contributes as Vice President of International Society for Business Innovation&Technology Management (ISBITM). He has been published in TQM&BE, EMAS, ASOC, ESWA, JCLP, C&E,C&IE,PPC etc. His total publication is 92 Journal articles (Scopus H-index=20).

Arvind Upadhyay is a Senior Lecturer in Logistics and Supply Chain Management. He has MSc degree from Heriot-Watt University, Edinburgh, UK and PhD from University of Bergamo, Italy. He was a visiting scholar to Cambridge Judge Business School and King's College of the University of Cambridge and Cranfield School of Management in UK. His varied research work is published in book chapters, case studies, academic journals and presented in International conferences. He is on the editorial and review committee board of various journals and also member of Chartered Institute of Purchasing and Supply (CIPS), British Academy of Management (BAM), Production and Operations Management Society (POMS) and European Operations Management Association (EurOMA).

Kuo-Jui Wu received his PhD degree in the industrial management at Taiwan University of Science and Technology. Currently, he is a lecturer in the school of business at Dalian university of technology, Panjin Campus. In addition, Dr. Wu is striving to explore the critical factors for assisting firms in developing the sustainability under uncertainty. Sustainable development and assessment, decision making, eco-innovation and business management are his research interests.

Shuojiang Xu is a PhD candidate in Computer Science. Prior to this, he was a student and got first class bachelor degree at the University of Nottingham, Ningbo, China. His current research interests are supply chain management, inventory management, data mining and decision making.

Minhao Zhang is a PhD candidate in The York Management School at the University of York. He holds a master's degree in Management with Business Finance also from University of York. His doctoral research focuses on managerial risk perception, supply chain risk management, quality management and the social media analytics. He has published in Supply Chain Management: An International Journal and Industrial Management and Data System.

Index

G

H

I

L

M

O

P

R

S

T

U

V

W

CPSIA information can be obtained
at www.ICGtesting.com
Printed in the USA
BVOW10*1156110717
488299BV00002B/9/P

9 781522 509561